LENIN: A POLITICAL LIFE

Volume 3
The Iron Ring

ROBERT SERVICE

MACMILLAN

First published 1995 by
MACMILLAN PRESS LTD
Houndmills, Basingstoke, Hampshire RG21 2XS
and London
Companies and representatives
throughout the world

ISBN 0–333–29392–4

A catalogue record for this book is available
from the British Library.

10 9 8 7 6 5 4 3 2 1
04 03 02 01 00 99 98 97 96 95

Copy-edited and typeset by Povey–Edmondson
Okehampton and Rochdale, England

Printed and bound in Great Britain by
Antony Rowe Ltd
Chippenham, Wiltshire

To Emma, Owain, Hugo and Francesca

Contents

List of Plates

(Assistance with the choice of pictures of Lenin was given by Francesca Service.)

Introduction

This is the last volume of a trilogy on the political life of Vladimir Ilich Lenin. The chapters resume the account in March 1918 with the treaty of Brest-Litovsk, laying it down at Lenin's death in January 1924. The Soviet republic had issued a summons to foreign far-left socialists to raise up the working classes of Europe and North America against their governments. The global capitalist order was challenged, and in 1919 the Communist International was formed. The Bolshevik party and the Red Army won the Civil War – or rather civil wars – that broke out across the former Russian Empire; and they survived to see the lifting of the Allied economic blockade and the ending of foreign military intervention. In 1921, as armed conflict drew to a close, the state's intensive control of the economy was somewhat relaxed and a New Economic Policy was ordained so that industrial, agricultural and commercial activity might recover. Treaties were signed with several major powers. In these extraordinary circumstances a public commitment had been made which had no precedent. Dominated by a single party and a single ideology, the government proclaimed that a social order was to be constructed to eradicate all oppression and exploitation. Lenin held the pre-eminent position in his country's politics. His dynamic career was compressed into a short period; for the illness that killed him had already been debilitating him over the three previous years. Yet who can deny that his ideas and behaviour demand scrutiny? He belongs to a handful of figures who made the twentieth century.

His importance is attested by the interest in him shown in subsequent decades, an interest that increased in the mid-1980s when Mikhail Gorbachev introduced reforms to the USSR. Amongst other things, Gorbachev tried to renovate Marxism-Leninism and to identify his own project for change with the precepts of the October Revolution; and for this reason there was an accelerated accumulation of literature about the founder of the Soviet state.

Under Gorbachev, fresh material was supplied by archival journals. A selection was printed of official minutes and correspondence as well as memoirs by Lenin's associates. It was difficult to keep abreast of everything because, in a break with custom, items of significance appeared in quite obscure organs. Yet the expansion in our knowledge about Lenin came to an even greater extent through the easing of access to Soviet archives. Even foreigners were allowed to inspect an increasing proportion of their holdings. Lenin, however, had always been a sacred figure in the USSR's mythology; and it was only after August 1991 that I was authorised to use the collections in the Central Party Archive, presently known as the Russian Centre for the Conservation and Study of Documents of Contemporary History. Much new information is consequently included here from unpublished party and governmental sources. After years of painstakingly drawing conclusions from Moscow-sponsored documentary publications and from memoirs and other materials printed in the West, it was a thrill to examine original documents. Not everything that might enter an account of Lenin has yet been found or made available; but I have gathered most of what was needed for the general task at hand.

Meanwhile a debate on Lenin has been taking place in Russia. When instigating research and discussion on the founder of the Soviet state, Gorbachev hoped to maintain public reverence for his memory. He controlled the choice of publishable documents, and assumed that the refashioning of Lenin's historical image would stay within his gift and that Soviet citizens would be convinced by the propaganda of professional party historians.

This strategy of manipulation rapidly fell apart. In 1987 he appointed a team of communist scholars to compose a single party-history textbook, but met resistance from the professional historians; it was agreed that a book of 'sketches' would be produced instead. This ambition, too, was unfulfilled despite the sanctions of party discipline. Historians intended to clear their names of political servility by writing works transparently free from the Kremlin's interference. The agenda of debate was anyway beginning to be set by novelists or press commentators who were antagonistic to the October Revolution. Inhibitions on commentary about Lenin were eroded as detailed descriptions were given of Lenin's support for ruthless mass terror within months of seizing power. From Stalin the critical focus was turned upon Lenin. Conferences were held in Moscow. Scholars from abroad were invited to attend, and academic exchanges were fostered between research institutes in Russia and Britain as well as other countries. Publications in Moscow by Western scholars about Lenin became almost conventional. It was a bracing experience. The 'Lenin Question' was being asked with a vivacity which demonstrated that the knot which tied politics to history in Russia was tightly-pulled.

Often the answers proposed by Russian scholars only replicated contributions long since made in Western historical writings. This was natural since the number of broad potential interpretations is not infinite. Hostility to Lenin became the fashion as a conventional portraiture of Lenin the Demon replaced the postcards, posters and drapery of the Red Saint Vladimir of Simbirsk. His non-detractors were few; the field was dominated by commentators, including several who had held posts at the party's disposal, offering damning opinions. Attention was drawn to Bolshevik finances in 1917 (were they sustained by German gold?); to the killing of the Imperial family (did Lenin order it directly?); to Lenin's illness (was it syphilis?).

In the West such sensationalism has been rare in recent scholarship, but many historians have provided a similarly negative basic interpretation. But also there have been admirers, not all of whom have been communists. In addition, many scholars have refrained from both total approval and total contempt. For Lenin is still kaleidoscopically controversial. Some accounts depict him primarily as a far-sighted statesman, others as a narrow-minded party leader. Disagreement persists, too, about his ideology. Against the notion that he was a megalomaniac without lasting, sincere beliefs is pitted the notion that he adhered to a credo of constant tenets; and, between these poles, several writers have asserted that he really had beliefs but changed them to greater or lesser extent at various times. In this regard, one proposition is that his strategical thinking changed radically in 1914 at the outbreak of the Great War; another is that a transformation occurred with the New Economic Policy in 1921. At the level of practical measures, by contrast, there has been wider consensus: Lenin has been seen as a highly flexible politician who could switch his line from day to day. About his impact there has been much agreement. All have concurred that his was the crucial personal influence upon events, and to this end it is thought that his steady determination and sharp intelligence won the day for him in every debate he considered important. Equally it is accepted that the régime he founded was in many ways without parallel in world history. Nowadays few even among his apologists gainsay that this was accomplished by means of immense carnage. Altercations have been concentrated on two main questions: first, whether his violent activities were self-induced or resulted from situations beyond his capacity to predict and regulate; second, whether his legacy predetermined the Terror of the 1930s under Stalin.

This volume take a position about each of these matters, and it is sensible to mark out the ground in advance. The contours of interpretation in the previous two volumes stay in place. Much that I propose was demonstrable on the basis of materials available before 1985. Even so, it is good to be able to write less tentatively than once was necessary. A sharpening of Lenin's image has become possible; and dusty corners, too, can have light introduced to them.

On violence, he was an enthusiastic state-terrorist and recurrently overruled party comrades who objected to his propensity. In 1917 he probably had not expected to use the Cheka as widely as he did, and he reduced its deployment in 1921–1922. Nevertheless he refused to discard the instrumentalities of terror even under the New Economic Policy. If he consistently professed legal nihilism, he was also an advocate of the possibilities of imminent socialist revolution across Europe. Only defeat in the Soviet-Polish campaign of 1920 gave him pause; his projects for Hungary, Czechia, Slovakia and Germany in 1919 indicate a readiness to throw the Red Army westwards. Nevertheless, after the Brest-Litovsk treaty in March 1918, he also followed a dual track in foreign policy. He despaired that the Soviet régime could reconstruct its economy alone, and the need to invite the collaboration of foreign concessionaires was a constant theme of his industrial pronouncements from 1918. Similarly, he was worried by the backwardness of Russian agriculture. He introduced the New Economic Policy in 1921 not only to pacify the peasantry but also to thrust agriculture in the direction of large-scale production and state control. It is true that on 'national' policy he proposed a gentler treatment than most of his colleagues; but he nonetheless remained a centraliser in relation to the other Soviet republics. For in all his policies he was a militant state interventionist. He had started his October Revolution with a conditional faith in 'the masses'; but pretty soon he was turning his guns on striking workers, peasant rebels and sailor mutineers – and his behind-the-scenes memoranda show a ruthlessness towards the régime's critics regardless of social class.

On military policy he had little original to say, and indeed he acknowledged that he was not an expert. He turns out to have been as polite and charming as has traditionally been suggested. There was no 'side' to him. He was also strong-willed, confident and argumentative. But this is not an exhaustive list of his traits. Lenin was highly volatile; his famous emotional self-restraint was not always evident. His wish to be at the centre of things, moreover, had an obsessional character, leading him sometimes to act in a derisible way. His demand in mid-

1922 for the Central Committee to be cut down, in his absence through illness, to three persons was a noteworthy example. His degenerative medical condition exaberbated the choleric disposition. On his sickbed, his anger sometimes went beyond rational bounds.

And yet Lenin, while wanting and enjoying power, did not seek it for its own sake; he was a Marxist believer and a man of ideas. His thought was not as exploratory as before 1917: the conditions of the October Revolution, Civil War and the New Economic Policy gave him scant time for reflection. Lenin's claim that Bolshevism alone stood in the authentic ideological line of succession to Marx and Engels lacks cogency. He himself in any case drew ideas from Russian agrarian socialist traditions as well as from Marxism. His ideas, furthermore, were not unchanging. As practical difficulties mounted after 1917, his resort to authoritarianism and arbitrariness was reinforced. Such a tendency had always been obvious in him. Before the October Revolution, Lenin developed some libertarian ideas; but these were always undermined by his greater enthusiasm for central state authority, class bias and anti-legalism; and, although he encountered unanticipated situations when at last he wielded power, his previous statements had not been entirely frank. The dictatorship was always going to be dictatorial, even more dictatorial than he had indicated in public. All this notwithstanding, Lenin truly thought that a better world should and would be built, a world without oppression and exploitation, a world without even a state; and it was his judgement, woeful as it was, that the Dictatorship of the Proletariat would act as midwife to the birth of such a world.

As he lay dying, he did not change his mind about these inclinations. He continued to lean in favour of dictatorship, terror, a one-party and one-ideology state, massive state economic ownership, a class-biased social system and legal nihilism. There were great changes in his policies; there were even shifts in the general strategy of Bolshevism: the Brest-Litovsk treaty and the New Economic Policy were the feats of a political acrobat. But an underlying rigidity was equally observable. Lenin was one person. He was true to himself and his career; his death-bed reconsiderations touched secondary aspects of his Revolution, not the primary ones.

These secondary aspects nonetheless had large significance. Not the easiest to resolve was the so-called 'national question', and Lenin and Stalin conflicted over this in 1922. Sickness and isolation made the struggle arduous on Lenin's side. No one else could have taken on Stalin in such circumstances. Much has rightly been written about the uncompromising features of Lenin's behaviour; but what also requires examination is his skilful handling of his colleagues. He had no rival in moving delicately among Politburo members. For instance, nobody could emulate his ability to induce associates to take on jobs that would inevitably get them into trouble. Lev Trotski in the Red Army and Lev Kamenev in the drafting commissions for the New Economic Policy did a lot of Lenin's dirty work for him. For Lenin was a foxy politician. Indubitably he was far from perfect, and could be ungovernably prickly. The well-known spat with Stalin in 1922 led him to demand his sacking from the General Secretaryship; but this was not the first time he had called for demotions: an unremarked example was the dispute with Mikhail Tomski in 1921. Yet he was less prickly and more widely admired than Trotski, Stalin, Kamenev and Zinoviev; and he perpetually impressed colleagues with his intellectual breadth and depth.

Consequently, if I corrected a large prejudgement in compiling this trilogy, it was the feeling that Lenin's influence at political conjunctures such as the decisions to seize power in October 1917, to sign the Brest-Litovsk treaty in 1918, to establish a Communist International in 1919 and to initiate the New Economic Policy in 1921 had been exaggerated. The chapters describe his deep imprint upon events. The course of his country's history would have been different had Lenin not lived.

Yet the subtlety whereby he achieved his ends within his party should not be underestimated. Yes, he often led from the front and lambasted those who would not follow him. But there were also occasions when he kept his own counsel. Having inaugurated the New Economic Policy, he rationed his public defences of it. He could also wheel and deal with the best (and the worst) of them, settling for half a deal when the full deal was too great a gamble or involved too many adverse consequences. Lenin the manoeuvrer and fudger has been neglected because attention has been given to 1917–1918 at the expense of the subsequent years. The party's objections to the New Economic Policy were bitter, and he had to be astute in dealing with them. Lenin guided his fellow Bolsheviks in conditions wherein any sustained controversy might destabilise the régime. His indomitability, further-more, had a crucial effect on his reputation in the country. There is much impressionistic evidence that, outside the party, the antagonism to him personally diminished considerably with the New Economic Policy. After his bloody career there was no likelihood of universal acclaim; but he had built on the popularity acquired by measures such as the Decree on Land in the October Revolution and, at his death, there was heartfelt mourning for him.

At this point the historical recidivist in me re-asserts himself. Although Lenin was a gigantic figure, there was a ceiling to his eminence. The mechanisms of public administration and consultation were shaky in the period after 1917. Newspapers were the most direct means of information, and these also had practical limitations: Lenin could have an impact only where a structure of command and communication already existed; and even where this was in place there still could be intermissions. Lenin influenced but could not unchallengeably direct his party. The difficulties he faced on agrarian and national questions are picked out in the following chapters. He did not win every political debate, and sometimes became victorious only after several attempts.

His tenacity as a political leader was linked to a lifelong confidence in his ideas. I want to emphasise, as in the previous two volumes, that Lenin had no no fixed and clear-cut creed; but his thought exhibits a recurrent interplay of inclinations – and these inclinations became more definite in reaction to the pressures of power and survival. The ideological consistency buoyed his self-assurance. And yet it could also spill over into recklessness. His was the responsibility for the invasion of Poland in mid-1920; he badgered his doubting colleagues into the military disaster. His subsequent failure to take soundings among second-échelon Bolshevik leaders produced a débâcle about agrarian policy at the Eighth Congress of Soviets in December 1920; and inattention to the foreign communist movement led to the fiasco of the insurrection in Berlin in the March Action of 1921. In addition, Lenin's demand for the execution of the Socialist-Revolutionary leaders in 1922 was not only morally ghastly; it was also imprudent. The great tactician and strategist was capable of astonishing errors in tactics and strategy. He was also a great state-builder, but not one who could run the governmental offices with complete efficiency. He failed to delegate authority properly. Whereas he could run a meeting with punctilio, he scorned functional demarcation and legal inhibition; and he loved to establish new bureaucratic organs whenever a new problem arose. His sense of duty and order was allied to a faith in Revolution. He cultivated his roots in rebellion, and the necessity to react flexibly in a changing situation was axiomatic for him.

And so the behaviour, policies and attitudes of Lenin and Stalin were not so very far apart. Lenin exploited Stalin so long as he thought him useful. Until late summer 1922 Stalin was Lenin's closest confederate in the central party leadership and had occupied this position for some months. Lenin had himself to blame. Stalin was not his errand boy; he was one of the handful of major Bolshevik leaders. Lenin's miscalculation had been that he could continue to control him even when his own health was deteriorating.

He went to his death knowing that he had made a mistake; but other episodes of his political life are less densely treated in the literature on Lenin. Certain remaining gaps are filled in the pages that follow. Moscow-based publications since 1985 allow consideration of the closed-session discussions at the Eighth Party Congress in March 1919; a selection of Central Committee and Politburo minutes; the dispute between Lenin and Stalin in 1922-1923. From the archives this volume adduces the debate in the commission on the first Russian Soviet Constitution in 1918; unpublished sections of minutes of the Ninth Party Conference; the records of the People's Commissariat of Nationality Affairs; the minutes of the Central Committee and Politburo (as well as Sovnarkom) which were not included in the official documentary collections even after 1985. But possibly the most remarkable gap is constituted by the minutes of the Tenth Party Conference in May 1921, a Conference where Lenin received a battering in the party. So bruising was the experience that all but a very few Soviet historians were barred from citing the minutes through to the 1990s. It hardly needs to be added that much still needs to be investigated. Lenin was at the centre of most major decisions on politics, economics and society after the October Revolution. Scarcely any aspect of central party and governmental authority was unaffected by him. In Russia and elsewhere, we are at the beginning of the enterprise to prise fully open the window on this period.

And Lenin will continue to exercise his fascination. As the poet Mayakovski put it: 'Lenin lived, Lenin lives, Lenin will live!' He had a point. Lenin is one of those personae attracting a polemic about Russia's past and future. Questions of national potential, pride and destiny are pulled into a field of enquiry about Ivan the Terrible, Peter the Great, Vladimir Lenin, Iosif Stalin and Mikhail Gorbachev. For Russians, these rulers embodied the complexities of their age as well as something more durable about Russia. Lenin (and Stalin and Gorbachev) is also deemed by Russian citizens and the rest of the world to embody issues about the establishment of socialism. His career appears, too, to pose general questions about authoritarian administration, state economic intervention, governmental terror, ideological repression and individual political influence.

Although this volume is intended as a balanced, multifaceted account, nobody can write detachedly about Lenin. His intolerance and repressiveness continue to appal me; and yet there were other sides to him which make the telling of the story of his political life an invigorating task. Lenin was not a Stalin. He was engaged in a pioneering endeavour to lead a state committed to socialism. He had genuine convictions about the attainability of a society without exploitation and oppression. He had intellectual, organisational and political talents as well as deficiencies, and had them on a grand scale. He had in many ways an appealing temperament; friends and relatives found him boundlessly attractive. He was an exceptional man even if there can be no excuse for his actions and, in essence, his ideas. Relativism is not appropriate to the final judgement. Certainly we must recapitulate his environment, influences, motivations and understandings; but, when all is said and done, the Russia of his day was part of a wider culture. Lenin had greater access to it than most Russians. He made his choices, and they were among the sternest and most pernicious in his society. In his day, too, it was pointed out to him that his objectives involved a method of rule counter-productive to their realisation. Lenin was a man of his time, but his time did not narrowly predetermine his thought.

What remains to be considered is the impact made by the kind of state and society he bequeathed to the world. It took a unique combination of factors to produce the world's first communist régime: Marxism; Russian intellectual traditions; the country's political, social and economic characteristics; and the Great War. It also took Lenin. Contingency was highly influential. But outside the USSR, once Lenin and his Bolsheviks had set the precedent, there were other combinations of factors which permitted the model to be copied. Peculiar circumstances yielded up a Lenin; thereafter it was not too difficult to re-produce Leninism abroad. Without Lenin, furthermore, Stalinism in the Soviet Union would have been impossible: institutions, practices and modes of thinking were initiated in the half-decade after the October Revolution which were applied on a murderously grander plane in the 1930s. With Lenin, if he had lived, several Stalinist horrors would have been avoided. But Leninism under Lenin would have remained a political prison and an economic cul-de-sac.

Controversy is inevitable, and has often been both useful and enjoyable. In this country the debates have on the whole been temperate (although in 1992 I debated with a group of Trotskyists who wished to replicate Lenin's Red Terror in London N19: is nothing

learnt from history?). The book has benefited from the secondary
literature on Lenin. References to it in ths volume are brief because the
dominant intention has been to look at Lenin through the primary
sources. When I began the research in 1978 there was no
comprehensive account of his political life based upon the fifth
edition of the collected works, whose publication had been completed
in 1965; and since 1985 there has been the abundance of further
archival revelations. Nevertheless, while offering new material and
fresh arguments in this volume, I must emphasise the irreplaceable
assistance derived from each account mentioned in the endnotes.
Equally helpful have been friends in the University of Keele and the
University of London. Since his retirement from Keele, Genia Lampert
has continued to advise on the trilogy's interpretative line. Particular
mention, too, must be made of our Post-Soviet Press Group in the
School of Slavonic and East European Studies. While following the
politics of Gorbachev and Yeltsin, the Group has not neglected history;
Geoffrey Hosking, Peter Duncan, John Klier, Judith Schapiro, John
Channon and Israel Getzler have frequently helped me to hunt down
the latest publications on Lenin. In the School's Library, Leslie Pitman
and Ursula Phillips have been unfailingly resourceful in obtaining such
publications. In addition, the late William Biagi, Michael Dalton,
Mary Gallagher, Rodney Walker and Edwin Gale have most kindly
given me the benefit of their medical expertise for the section of the
volume relating to Lenin's illness.

The chapters have been improved by the School's research exchange
with the Institute of Russian History of the Russian Academy of
Sciences in Moscow (and the British Council is to be thanked for its
financial support). Advice from Andrei Nikolaevich Sakharov,
Lyudmila Kolodnikova and Vladimir Buldakov has been of
inestimable assistance. Nor do I forget the archivists of the Russian
Centre for the Conservation and Study of Documents of Contemporary History and the State Archive of the Russian Federation. Not all
discussions with other historians in Moscow were equally productive.
Offence was sometimes taken at a foreign 'falsifier' who did not
worship at Lenin's shrine. Perhaps, however, the ritualism of obeisance
is a thing of the past even for his admirers in Russia. When in 1988 the
director of the Institute of Marxism-Leninism took umbrage at my
analysis, he denied that he regarded Lenin as an icon. Since then the
Lenin cult has all but vanished. His embalmed and truncated corpse
remains, however temporarily, in the Red Square mausoleum. For
what it is worth, I have never visited it despite the occasional

temptation: the building has a sociological interest, but stands for a cultural mystification that today's Russia ought to put aside.

Above all, I gladly acknowledge my debts to those who scrutinised the manuscript of the volume: to Francesco Benvenuti, Adele Biagi, Vladimir Buldakov, John Channon, Bob Davies, Israel Getzler, Geoffrey Hosking, Brian Pearce, László Péter and Arfon Rees. Their monitoring has improved the contents immeasurably not only in details but also in argument. I am deeply grateful for the generosity they showed with their time and expertise. The writing of the three volumes has involved a kind of psychological co-habitation with Lenin which Adele has shared. He has been a curious lodger, provoking baffling questions that we frequently tried to unravel together over supper. He has also taken up space: we could well have done with the space occupied by the bookcase containing the fifty five volumes of the fifth edition of his collected works. Now that he is about to quit the house, I recognise that this third volume is not the end of the debate on Lenin either in our home or elsewhere. I have held pretty close to the trilogy's perspective as disclosed in the first volume, and hope this is not a case of someone seeing only what he wants to see. But to put things like this is to look at the world differently from Lenin. Not for him the allowance that reasonable alternative world-views are possible. Not for him any provisionality in the interpretation of evidence. I have done him as much justice as he deserves, but no more than this – and it is more than his opponents received from him.

London RJS
Maundy Thursday 1994

1 Merciless Retreat

Lenin was a mercurial mixture as a political leader. He was an ideologist, a class warrior and a party boss. Contradictions and uncertainties as well as plainly-spoken simplicities were characteristic of him. No wonder his career eludes easy definition. And yet such a persona was not without its parallels. Muhammed, prophet of Islam, frequently took decisions seemingly based on considerations of prudence; and his ideas were not without their confusion. Yet a believer he was. His interests and understandings were transformed as he registered the impact of circumstances. Another example is Oliver Cromwell, who constantly surprised his followers by the shifts in his ideas but was a man of deep Christian belief. The elusiveness of a Muhammed, a Cromwell or a Lenin is among the factors which enable them to dominate political life around them.

Lenin, unlike Muhammed and Cromwell, made a virtue out of changeability. For him, a refusal to shift positions with the movement of history was self-defeating. Decking it out in Marxist vocabulary, he urged his followers to take a dialectical approach. Among his favourite sayings was that 'theory is grey but life is green'. He took it from Marx who had found it in Goethe. The changes made by the Bolsheviks in their policies after the October Revolution of 1917 were drastic. They had promised a popularly-elected government, but disbanded the Constituent Assembly in January 1918 when they got less than a quarter of the seats. They had promised the least repressive revolutionary régime in the annals of mankind. And yet the Cheka, their security police, became unprecedentedly violent and arbitrary. They had promised economic reconstruction. Yet both the collapse of industry and the disruption of trade between town and countryside continued. Food supplies were increasingly obtained by armed urban squads, and labour discipline in the factories was tightened. The Bolsheviks had also expected to rule a multinational state with the support of the non-Russian nationalities. Yet the Ukrainian and Georgian administrations easily mobilised forces in their own defence.

1

And Lenin and his comrades had promised peace across Europe. They had assumed that their October Revolution would be followed, within weeks if not days, by insurrections against the continental capitalist order. Instead they had signed the treaty of Brest-Litovsk in March 1918, disclaiming sovereignty over Ukraine and the entire Baltic region.

These set-backs would have overwhelmed most governments. Public opinion had been prepared by Bolshevik propaganda, insofar as such propaganda had any effect, for a revolutionary process unmarred by problems. The party survived the storms of disapproval through its early months in office only by the skin of its teeth. Opposition sprang up everywhere. Socialist-Revolutionary delegates to the dispersed Constituent Assembly gathered in Samara by the river Volga to plan their return to the capital. Mensheviks in central and northern Russia experienced a resurgence of popularity. Officers in their thousands from the demobilised Imperial Army were assembling in southern Russia and in mid-Siberia; their objective was the overthrow of Lenin's régime. After the treaty of Brest-Litovsk, moreover, Russia's allies Britain and France sent forces to the East. British regiments landed in Murmansk and Archangel, the French navy docked in Odessa. The Japanese put troops into the Russian Far East. Nor could it be discounted that the Germans might rip up the Brest-Litovsk treaty and invade what remained of Soviet Russia.

Sovnarkom, as Lenin's government was known, had survived for a number of reasons. His Decree on Land gave him credit with the peasants, and the Bolsheviks at least did well among the working class and garrison soldiers in the Constituent Assembly elections. The exhausting conditions of everyday life also worked in the Bolshevik party's favour. The energy of the régime's opponents was diminishing. Chaotic communications and transport were a further factor. The Cheka's campaign to root out opposition in the towns and cities under Soviet control was ruthless. Yet the Bolsheviks could not afford to be complacent. Lenin had not lost his faith in the inevitability of communism's global triumph; but he recognised the weaknesses of the party's position. Survival was not the same as success. Most peasants unsurprisingly objected to being compelled by local soviets to hand over grain for what they regarded as derisory compensation. A rising number of workers turned against the Bolsheviks. The October Revolution, which had been made in the name of the so-called masses, was losing its original social base. Every leading Bolshevik appreciated the acuteness of the régime's crisis. In the phrase of the day, they lived and worked while 'sitting on suitcases': they kept themselves ready, mentally and physically, for flight from the capital. None forgot the abruptness of the emperor Nikolai II's forced abdication in February 1917 or minister-president Aleksandr Kerenski's flight from the Winter Palace in October. Spring 1918 had left the outcome of the Bolshevik party's revolutionary project undetermined.

No Bolshevik leader was in greater danger than Lenin. In 1917 there had been calls in the conservative press for him to be hanged as a traitor to the nation. His actions since the October Revolution had identified him as the instigator of abuses and excesses. About his likely fate in the event of the Bolshevik party's overthrow there could be little doubt. The nastier posters of the period show him as an insidious, brooding figure with dark, penetrating eyes and a Star of David above his head. The defining of Bolshevism as a Jewish conspiracy against the Russian people began not in Germany but in Russia. Aside from such black propaganda, however, Lenin was undeniably more responsible than any fellow Bolshevik for the actions of his party. The timing and method of the seizure of power in October 1917 were largely his choice, and Sovnarkom's programme was mainly of his making. But Lenin had to live with the consequences and was in no mood to regret or apologise.

As the prospect of European revolution receded, so the obligation to provide a short-term plan of action for his party pressed itself upon him. Lenin's political friends were sorely in need of guidance. The Party of Left Socialist Revolutionaries, which was the junior partner in the Soviet government, rejected the treaty of Brest-Litovsk. Nor was his own Bolshevik party quiescent. Bukharin and his associates, known as the Left Communists, detested the treaty so much that they refused to serve in the newly-elected Central Committee. Lenin's proposals took the form of a lengthy pamphlet written in the second fortnight of 1918. Pamphleteering was his most congenial medium of communication with fellow Bolsheviks except for speeches to their Congresses. The calling of yet another Congress would have poisoned the wounds he sought to heal. No national radio service existed. Cinema facilities were not widely available. But Lenin was an experienced journalist and could write fast and, when he set his mind to it, forcefully. The result was *The Current Tasks of Soviet Power*. Lenin avoided reference to opponents in the Bolshevik party and mentioned the Left Socialist Revolutionaries only fleetingly.[1] He also largely overlooked international questions. The Brest-Litovsk treaty, that momentous treaty which had ended hostilities on the Eastern front in the Great War, was scarcely cited. In contrast with his recent writings, the pamphlet gave little consideration to either Germany or the Allies. No doubt diplomatic calculations were at work; but the main reason why he desisted from his usual violent castigation of the contending imperialist powers was his ambition to concentrate the thoughts of his party on a single basic theme: political and economic policies in the former Russian empire. The 'breathing-space' secured by the Brest-Litovsk treaty was to be used to consolidate the tasks of the October Revolution.

He was astonishingly casual about armed resistance to the Bolsheviks. The Cossack leader M.P. Bogaevski had just been captured and executed, and this event was adduced by Lenin as a sign that the phase of 'open civil war' had now passed. The country's peacetime reconstruction could now be inaugurated.[2] This was so egregious a misprognosis that the question arises whether he meant it seriously. Possibly his dismissal of the potential military threat was a mere device to fix Bolshevik eyes on the politics and the economy. But this is unlikely. Lenin seldom failed to bang the war-drum when alarmed about the future. A Red Army was already being formed, and he would surely not have failed to alert his readers to its importance if he had not believed what he said about Bogaevski. Residing in the Kremlin in Moscw and hearing about events elsewhere in Russia only intermittently, Lenin simply blundered.

Not that he ceased to anticipate civil war altogether. The pamphlet suggested that 'any great revolution, and especially a socialist one' was inconceivable without such a war. But he proceeded to describe civil war in terms of a conflict between the revolutionary administration and the perpetrators of 'crimes, hooliganism, bribery, speculation, abuses of all kinds'.[3] Not counter-revolutionary armies but 'petit-bourgeois anarchic elementalism' held a knife to the throat of the October Revolution.[4] The party's priority, according to Lenin, should be the introduction of strict account-keeping and control. 'Bribe-takers and scoundrels' should be shot. At present the Soviet power was 'more like blancmange than like iron'.[5] Showing that his zeal for mass political participation had not faded, he urged that workers be inducted into state administrative responsibilities. Meetings at factory gates should be encouraged. Lenin's basic aim was less to create an atmosphere of liberation than to get labourers, skilled and unskilled, to raise their level of discipline and productivity.[6] He was blunt: 'The Russian worker is a bad worker in comparison with the advanced nations.'[7] This led him to recommend the adoption of time-and-motion techniques of the American manager and writer F. W. Taylor. Before 1917 he had castigated Taylorism routinely as yet another bourgeois trick to extract more labour for less wages. In Lenin's estimation, the occurrence of the October Revolution made Taylor's techniques deployable without damage to the working class's interests.[8] He also insisted that 'bourgeois specialists' should be retained in state enterprises and should be rewarded above the rate for ordinary workers. Their expertise would be indispensable for the foreseeable future.[9] The party should also halt the campaign for nationalisations in industry and commerce. Instead the objective should be to reinforce the changes in the economy already made.[10]

Lenin admitted that all this constituted a 'compromise', even a 'retreat' from unbridled revolutionary optimism. But his skills as a propagandist were undiminished. He contrived to indicate that his proposals involved an advance from the methods of conquest to the methods of administration.[11] A competitive spirit should be fostered. Local political and economic organs should enter a contest with each other in pursuit of increased efficiency; and 'model communes' should receive material prizes for their achievements.[12]

Yet this was a single gentle remark in a pamphleteering tirade. His tone was aggressive, strident, threatening. The Lenin who in 1917 had publicly claimed that 'the transition to socialism' would be accomplishable without undue difficulty had vanished. Images of violence, retrenchment and self-sacrifice became recurrent. Dictatorship was lauded. His sole recommendation as to how workers were to be trained to assume tasks of responsibility in the state was to recruit them for service in revolutionary courts. Anyone caught breaking labour discipline in factory should be punished mercilessly. In other words, workers should repress workers without compunction. 'But our revolutionary courts and our popular courts,' lamented Lenin, 'are exceedingly, incredibly weak.'[13] What was required was the '*unconditional submission* of the masses *to the single will* of the leader of the labour process'. At this point his language started to become opaque. He obviously intended to state that officials, administrators and managers should be accorded dictatorial powers as individuals; but he put this in jargon, demanding 'the dictatorship of particular persons *for definite processes of work* at definite moments of *purely executive* functions'.[14] What he declared would not commend itself to all party comrades. But attack was preferable to defence for Lenin: 'We don't need hysterical outbursts. We need the measured step of the iron battalions of the proletariat.'

OPPOSITION AND SURVIVAL

The resistance was beginning to cause panic. It would be an exaggerated claim that, had Lenin cracked under the strain, the Bolsheviks would have gone under. Yet his resilience was crucial when his colleagues were blundering around: even Trotski and Dzierzynski made wholly avoidable mistakes.[15] The fervid atmosphere seemed to leave Lenin cool. Trotski was to record his admiration as follows: 'At the sharpest moments he seemed to become deaf and blind to everything lying beyond the boundaries of whatever interest consumed him.'[16] The capacity to close off his mind to distractions was accompanied by an ability to impart his confidence to the rest of the Bolshevik central leadership. According to Trotski, Lenin had the advantage of obviously 'believing in that which he said'.[17]

Even the Left Socialist-Revolutionaries, who wanted to see the treaty of Brest-Litovsk torn up, did not envisage Lenin's permanent removal from the chairmanship of Sovnarkom. Karl Radek, a Bolshevik opponent of the treaty, was approached by the Left Socialist-Revolutionary Pavel Proshyan at a meeting of the All-Russian Central Executive Committee of the Congress of Soviets with the question: 'Wouldn't it be simpler to arrest Lenin for a day, declare war on the Germans and then wholeheartedly elect comrade Lenin again as Sovnarkom chairman?'[18] The matter was not just personal (although a recognition of Lenin's exceptional qualities as a leader was involved). The Left Communists and Left Socialist-Revolutionaries also judged that any split with Lenin would cause a destructive narrowing of the political base of the October Revolution. Their revulsion against the treaty did not disappear. The Left Communists continued to battle for its abandonment in the lower party committees. The Urals Regional Committee and the Moscow Regional Committee, as well as the Taganrog Conference of Bolsheviks fleeing from Ukraine in the path of the German military occupation, were vehemently hostile to Brest-Litovsk and all it stood for.[19] The problem for them was that they could not get many ordinary rank-and-file Bolshevik party members to join armed units willing to take on the Germans.[20] Neither demobbed Russian peasants nor untrained Russian workers wanted to see military action. Moreover, Sverdlov and Lenin determined on an organisational decapitation of the Left Communists by means of the disbandment of the several regional committees. The Moscow Regional Committee was their first and most important victim.[21]

At the same time Lenin no more wanted to lose the Left Communists than they him. Having won the Brest-Litovsk debate at the Seventh Party Congress, he hoped to keep them working for the party. The Central Committee met on 31 March, and he and his supporters decided to make overtures to their 'opponents', or at least to the more 'businesslike' figures among them.[22] Lenin saw that the Bolsheviks were too few to be able to dispense with a faction's assistance; but the words of the decision reflect also his condescension to the Left Communists as being given to light-headed abstractions in their thinking. It was urgent only to have the more practical of them back in his administration.

He would not go down on his knees to invite them. Their opinions on foreign policy were matched, in his eyes, by an equally pernicious plan for domestic legislation. They demanded faster nationalisation in industry and commerce. They were centralisers to an even higher degree than Lenin. In agriculture they wanted a more rapid movement towards collective farming; and they argued that the Bolshevik party, having seized power from the Provisional Government in the name of the working class, should reject Lenin's call for 'state capitalism'. Nikolai Bukharin, Nikolai Osinski and V. M. Smirnov – the most prominent theorists of Left Communism – urged that the party should pursue the objective of 'proletarian' class interests. Bukharin had already produced a pamphlet entitled *The Programme of the Communists (Bolsheviks)*.[23] Despite being schematic and full of jargon, the writings of this left-wing Bolshevik troika appealed to many, perhaps even most, long-standing party activists. Lenin consequently had reason to fear Bukharin's return to the fold. Nevertheless there were also grounds for welcoming them. The Left Communists, while preaching on the need for the maximum of initiative 'from below', put an extreme emphasis on central state control. They were still more utopian and incoherent than Lenin;[24] but in practice, like him, they tended to support centralist force against locally-established collective endeavours whenever they had to make a choice.

This meant that their alliance with the Left Socialist-Revolutionaries over the Brest-Litovsk treaty could not last. Lenin saw this as he tackled the shortages of food supplies in Russian cities in April and May 1918. A. D. Tsyurupa as People's Commissar for Food Supplies requested plenipotentiary powers to requisition grain throughout the country, and Lenin agreed with him. On 8 May the matter came before Sovnarkom. Tsyurupa's draft decree bluntly threatened sanctions against anyone not complying with the law.[25] Here was a cause that bound the Left Communists and Lenin back together against the Left Socialist Revolutionaries. The requisitioning of grain by urban detachments appealed strongly to the Left Communists as being a long-overdue return to 'proletarian' priorities!

Lenin's enthusiasm was as strong as theirs; he even criticised Tsyurupa's wording as being weak and ambiguous. At Sovnarkom he demanded the insertion of a clause declaring the need 'to wage and carry through a merciless and terroristic defence and war against the peasant bourgeoisie and any other bourgeoisie keeping grain surpluses to themselves'.[26] Punishments should be specified. Lenin recommended a minimum of ten years' forced labour and permanent expulsion from the village commune in any case of hoarding.[27] Sovnarkom was unconvinced. On 9 May a further discussion took place and Lenin's amendment was rejected.[28] Yet there was essential agreement by 13 May that the People's Commissariat of Food Supplies should receive plenipotentiary authority to requisition grain.[29] No central governmental organ below Sovnarkom could overrule its decisions, and all local institutions were to render obedience. Lenin kept up the pressure. On 26 May he drafted further theses on the gathering of grain from the villages, even proposing to turn Trotski's People's Commissariat of Military Affairs into a 'Military and Food Supply Commissariat' which would devote nine tenths of its efforts to acquiring grain. If kulaks were to be punished for hoarding, so Trotski should order the decimation of any army unit found to have committed acts of plunder in the villages.[30] Lenin's blood was up. Neither he nor his party would brook opposition to the basic re-orientation of policy. Their will to resolve the problem of grain supplies by means of centrally-organised violence was unflinching.

The requisitioning campaign predictably infuriated the Left Socialist-Revolutionaries. But Bolsheviks of all persuasions hardly cared. If matters had come to a total break with the Left Socialist-Revolutionaries, so be it! Lenin and his opponents in his own party had found common cause once more, and were relieved that they could work together again. On 11 June there came the decree establishing committees of the village poor (or, in the Russian acronym, *kombedy*). This was an attempt to split off the poorest peasants from the rest of the peasantry, especially from the so-called kulaks. The committees of the village poor were enjoined to inform the armed urban detachments where the grain was being hoarded, and were promised a share of the grainstocks seized.[31]

Not only Lenin but also his colleagues were recklessly narrowing the political base of their régime. Their alienation of the Left Socialist-Revolutionary Party was accompanied by persecution of the Mensheviks and Socialist Revolutionaries. Bolsheviks were made anxious by the rise in working-class antipathy to themselves. Elections to soviets which put Mensheviks back in a majority were ruled invalid by Sovnarkom. But this did not eradicate the difficulty. The discontent was simply transferred to other arenas: anti-Bolshevik sentiment found expression in the growing popularity of the movement for an Assembly of Plenipotentiaries among Petrograd workers. Strikes broke out in northern Russia, and an improvised demonstration at Kolpino on 9 May was fired upon by troops loyal to the Bolsheviks. The incident caused revulsion in Petrograd. The Putilov Works, which in 1917 had prominently supported the Bolshevik political advance, came out in sympathy with the Kolpino demonstrators.[32] But Lenin was in no mood to yield. Repression was swift whenever and wherever the writ of Sovnarkom was infringed. Blaming the troubles on the Mensheviks and the Socialist Revolutionaries, he looked forward to confronting them on 9 May when he was scheduled to deliver a report to the Central Executive Committee of the Congress of Soviets. At the last moment his appearance had to be cancelled. In the previous twenty-four hours the Germans had pushed over the demarcation line established by the treaty of Brest-Litovsk. This might have signalled the treaty's total breakdown. Lenin was pre-occupied by the diplomatic and military crisis rather than rendered cowardly by the prospect of justifying his policies to the Central Executive Committee.[33] Sverdlov took his place, and was catcalled for his pains. Five days later, on 14 May, Lenin returned to the political fray and castigated the Mensheviks and Socialist Revolutionaries with ferocity. If they had expected to witness his humiliation, they were sadly disappointed.[34]

They also suffered repression at his hand. Worried lest they should use the Central Executive Committee as an instrument to mobilise support among discontented workers, he took the awesome step of expelling them from its membership on 14 June.[35] It was an event quite as historic as the dispersal of the Constituent Assembly in January 1918. The Mensheviks and Socialist Revolutionaries continued to participate fitfully in public affairs over the ensuing three years, but always on Bolshevik terms. Arrests were to become frequent. Yet another stride had been taken towards the establishment of a one-party state. That Lenin and the rest of the Bolshevik Central Committee should have rushed so fast to impose such a dictatorship is evidence of

their extraordinary confidence that, despite the terrific reverses
endured by them at home and abroad since October 1917, history
was on their side.

It testifies, too, to a reckless willingness to take a gamble. Never had
the military threat to Sovnarkom been greater. Lenin was extremely
dull about anticipating the scale and timing of outbreaks of civil war.[36]
A particularly acute threat was poised over Sovnarkom by the 15,000
Czech prisoners-of-war who, by agreement with Trotski, were being
shipped along the Transsiberian railway to Vladivostok. They were
armed, and their purpose was to join the Allies on the Western front in
the Great War. But Trotski and Sovnarkom were in two minds. They
were tempted by by the possibility of recruiting the Czechs into the Red
Army. The Latvian riflemen were being used to great advantage. Why
not also use the Czechoslovak Legion?[37] At any rate Trotski was
disinclined to treat these troops with much circumspection. He made
no effort to smooth relations between the Legion and the Bolshevik-led
soviets of the towns they passed through along the railway line. A
conflict broke out in Chelyabinsk in the Urals region on 17 May.
Instead of rushing to quieten things down, Trotski blustered and
threatened the Legion. By 23 May his subordinate S. I. Aralov was
ordering the disarming of all Czech troops in every town.[38] This was
attempted even though the Legion at the time was the strongest force in
the territory ruled by the soviets. Omsk fell to the enraged Czechs on 25
May. On the same day Trotski telegrammed from Moscow: 'All soviets
are hereby ordered immediately to disarm all Czech trains.' In his brisk
style, he added that any member of the Legion bearing a rifle should be
shot on the spot.[39]

Where Trotski lurched, Lenin followed. Despite the Legion's revolt,
it was on 26 May that Lenin proposed to Sovnarkom that Trotski's
Red Army should be diverted to the grain-requisitioning campaign.[40]
Trotski did not accept the scheme; but neither he nor Lenin retrieved
themselves sufficiently to make the necessary overtures to the Legion.
Some Czech troops had not yet reached even the Urals and were in
south eastern Russia. Detachments of them were resting at Penza, only
560 kilometres from Moscow. Lenin received an appeal for assistance
from the Penza Bolshevik leader Minkin. The replies that went back
from Moscow ordered the town and district soviets of Penza province
to dispatch military aid to the provincial capital.[41] Lenin and Trotski
were digging a hole for themselves, but refused to stop digging. After
skirmishings in Penza, the Czechs occupied the town on 29 May. Even
then Trotski was undaunted. On 4 June he announced a new slogan:

'Up with Civil War!' Four days later the Czech legion took Samara. The entire Volga region and most towns on the Transsiberian railway in the Urals and Siberia were under their control.[42]

EMERGENCY IN MOSCOW

The Czechoslovaks had had no intention of overthrowing Sovnarkom; but on arrival in Samara they were besought by the Socialist Revolutionaries, whose leaders had fled there after the dissolution of the Constituent Assembly, to fight on behalf of Komuch. This was the abbreviated title of the Committee of Members of the Constituent Assembly. Komuch asserted that it had the most legitimate claim to rule the country, and called for the overthrow of the Bolshevik party dictatorship. The Legion, exasperated by what they regarded as Sovnarkom's treachery, accepted the invitation. A half-day's train journey separated them from the Russian capital, the Kremlin and Lenin. By mid-June the danger could no longer be underestimated. Unless a Red Army could quickly and effectively be moved into action, the Bolshevik leadership would be caught in Moscow and overthrown. Nonetheless it still appeared to the Central Committee under Lenin that political retreat and reconciliation would endanger the régime to a greater extent than pursuit of the existing policies. Anti-socialist groupings were rounded up by the Cheka; and a conspiracy called the Union of the Motherland and Freedom was crushed. Lenin also refused to be intimidated by the resumption of assassinations as a tactic by the Socialist Revolutionaries. V. Volodarski was killed by them on 21 June 1918. Moscow became unsafe for the Bolshevik Central Committee even though the Czechoslovaks had not yet moved from the river Volga.

Such doubts as Lenin entertained he did not express. Martov was the world's greatest Lenin-watcher, and claimed to be able to detect a muffled uncertainty in his speeches in mid-1918. Supposedly Lenin was questioning whether the Brest-Litovsk treaty had really been worth signing. His arguments against Bukharin and the Left Communists, according to Martov, were essentially a means of persuading himself as much as the Left Communists: 'The nub of the matter here is not a struggle of citizen Lenin with some group standing to his left, but rather an inner struggle of the two souls which constitute contemporary Bolshevism.'[43]

Martov, for once in his life, underestimated Lenin's determination. Possibly the Bolshevik leader may have been wondering whether the benefits of the treaty were as great as he had originally supposed; but not for a moment did he deny that the signature of a separate peace with Germany and Austria-Hungary was a better option than any conceivable alternative. Thus he remained firmly committed to his foreign policy. This would necessarily involve an assault on the Left Socialist-Revolutionaries. But when? And who would initiate it? Lenin waited on events, and did not have to wait long. On 24 June the Central Committee of the Party of Left Socialist-Revolutionaries met secretly to approve the assassination of German diplomats in Moscow. They planned to provoke a reaction by the German armed forces which would shatter the Brest-Litovsk treaty. The Left Socialist-Revolutionary leaders hoped that this would lead to a rapprochement of their party and the Bolsheviks in the cause of revolutionary war.[44] The idea was as audacious as it was ill-considered, overlooking the utter unpreparedness of the Red Army to resist German armed forces. Intimations of the Left Socialist-Revolutionary conspiracy reached the ears of Felix Dzierzynski, Bolshevik chairman of the Cheka, on 28 June. But Dzierzynski seemingly lacked knowledge of the details. Certainly he took no preventive action, and even continued to work alongside Left Socialist-Revolutionaries in the Cheka.[45] Yet the two parties eyed each other like boxers edging around the ring before throwing the first punch; their dissent about Brest-Litovsk and about grain seizures was so fundamental that a violent contest was virtually inevitable. When the Fifth All-Russian Congress of Soviets opened on 4 July, they each arranged their own guards in the area inside and around the Kremlin. The tension between them was intense.[46]

The Congress quickly became an irrelevance. The items on the agenda were important: agrarian policy, the Brest-Litovsk treaty, the Constitution. Yet victory for the Bolsheviks was already guaranteed by their majority over the Left Socialist-Revolutionaries of voting places. In any case, the debates were put abruptly into the shade on 6 July by the assassination of German ambassador Count von Mirbach. Cheka functionary and Left Socialist-Revolutionary Yakov Blyumkin had entered the embassy premises accompanied by an associate. He had an official Cheka pass and was received respectfully when he asked for an interview with Mirbach. On Mirbach's appearance in the ante-room, Blyumkin had pulled out a gun and shot him.[47]

Blyumkin ran off from the melée and evaded capture; but reports of the assassination came to Dzierzynski and Lenin. Lenin had no hesitation. Despite being taken by surprise, he immediately resolved upon the complete suppression of the Party of Left Socialist-Revolutionaries. Blyumkin's murderous action gave the Bolsheviks a chance to behave as if reacting to an outrage rather than merely persecuting fellow socialists. His cynicism was remarkable. At this moment he had no sure information that the Left Socialist-Revolutionary Central Committee had instigated Blyumkin's action. Leonid Krasin recalled him smiling and saying: 'In short, we'll levy *an internal loan* from among our SR comrades . . . and thus we'll both be drawing attention to our innocence and be acquiring some capital.'[48] His meaning was about to become clear. Lenin had it in mind to arrest and execute a member of the Left Socialist-Revolutionary Central Committee. Blyumkin was too lowly a figure to offer to the German government in expiation of Mirbach's death. Legal procedures and basic personal fairness were not considerations for Sovnarkom's chairman.[49] He intended nothing less than judicial murder. Dispositions were made for the detention of Left Socialist-Revolutionary delegates to the Congress of Soviets in the Bolshoi Theatre. Dzierzynski, whose inaction had facilitated the assassination, was dispatched to Left Socialist-Revolutionary headquarters to make further arrests. Lenin was realistically contemptuous about the potential strength of the armed resistance to his forces. He opined that, for all the inefficiencies of the Bolsheviks, the Left Socialist-Revolutionaries were in a sorrier condition and were chattering instead of organising.[50]

Lenin acted speedily for two reasons. First, he wanted to catch the Left Socialist-Revolutionaries unawares. Second and even more urgently, he had to reassure the German authorities that his own party had had no part in the assassination. The sole advantage to Berlin in retaining the Bolsheviks in power was their adherence to Brest-Litovsk. Without this, Lenin would be useless to the Germans. It was therefore decided that a delegation of Yakov Sverdlov, Georgi Chicherin and Lenin should present their condolences at the embassy within hours of Mirbach's death. Sverdlov was head of state and Chicherin had been appointed People's Commissar for External Affairs. Their rank, it was hoped, would have a positive effect upon the contents of the official German report on the shocking event about to be cabled.[51]

Lenin carried out the mission with distaste. In March, when the Brest-Litovsk treaty was being signed, he had firmly refused to attend the ceremony: he wanted to limit his association with what he described as 'the obscene peace'. Still less did he desire to be seen, when the treaty retained its disrepute, to be going cap in hand to the Germans. But unlike Trotski and Dzierzynski, he could not plead that military duties precluded him from joining Sverdlov and Chicherin. Off they set in grim mood. Trotski was later to record the scene: 'In the sense of internal experiences this was probably one of the heaviest moments of his life.'[52] On arrival at the embassy, Lenin carried out the necessary formalities. Even so, a German official noted that the Soviet leader's comportment was very stiff, being marked by a 'cold politeness'.[53] Lenin was glad to leave the embassy a few minutes later. But his feeling of relief was quickly dissipated by news of further bungling. Dzierzynski again was the culprit. At the Left Socialist-Revolutionary headquarters he tried to arrest all those in the building. The Left Socialist-Revolutionaries perceived what fate lay in store for them. Until then they had neither revolted nor intended to break permanently with the Bolsheviks; their strategy of assassination displayed an infantile standard of calculation, but they had genuinely meant no harm to the Bolshevik party. To their horror they saw that the Bolsheviks aimed at their suppression. Dzierzynski and his companions were seized as hostages. With nothing left to lose, the Left Socialist-Revolutionaries resolved to take control of key points in the capital. An unplanned revolt against Bolshevik power began.[54]

Dzierzynski's ineptitude was such that rumours were to circulate that he secretly wanted the Left Socialist-Revolutionary terrorist campaign to succeed.[55] He had been a Left Communist, and he still detested the Brest-Litovsk treaty. Thus he purportedly turned a blind eye to Blyumkin's conspiracy. This is no more cogent than the story that Trotski deliberately provoked the Czechoslovak Legion to revolt. Dzierzynski affirmed in his own defence that Blyumkin had forged his signature on the Cheka pass-card used to gain access to the German embassy; and that the information about a possible attempt on the embassy was too vague to enable the Bolshevik Cheka leaders to prevent Mirbach's death.[56] Be that as it may, Dzierzynski surely did not act as if he was trying to aid the Left Socialist-Revolutionaries once the assassination had taken place. His armed detachment went to arrest and not to reinforce the Left Socialist-Revolutionaries. No nods or winks were made about Brest-Litovsk at the Left Socialist-Revolutionary headquarters. The episode was so botched that Dzierzynski, the feared head of the Cheka, found himself under arrest.

Lenin resumed practical control. Returning to the Kremlin, he summoned General I. I. Vacietis of the Latvian Riflemen. Vacietis's support was crucial in view of the military weakness of the Bolsheviks in Moscow; and the deployment of the Red Army to the Volga region cramped the possibilities of reinforcement from elsewhere. To Vacietis he posed the question: 'Comrade, will we last out till morning?' It is possible that this was a subtle attempt to strengthen the resolution of the Riflemen.[57] Yet he may also have begun to understand that the balance of forces, ill-trained as most of them were on both sides, might suddenly change to the disadvantage of the Bolsheviks. In the Great War he had scoffed at theories stressing the technical sophistication required in modern warfare.[58] He was learning his mistake by harsh experience, and drew the conclusion repeatedly stressed by the less naïve Lev Trotski: namely that even a small number of well-trained, well-led troops could prove more than a match for countless amateur soldiers such as the Red Guards and assorted people's militias.[59] Yet Trotski can hardly have been high in Lenin's esteem at the time. Trotski and Dzierzynski had between them nearly given away the October Revolution; and Lenin's tendency to rely on his own judgement must have been reinforced by the midsummer crisis. The preservation of 'Soviet power' depended entirely upon the loyalty and efficiency of a Latvian officer who was neither a Bolshevik nor a proven military officer.

Fortunately for Lenin, Vacietis completed his task splendidly. By the next day, 7 July, he had driven the rebels from their strongholds so that Lenin could announce to the rest of the country: 'The uprising of Left SRs in Moscow has been liquidated.'[60] Dzierzynski was liberated and further arrests of Left Socialist-Revolutionaries took place. V. A. Aleksandrovich, one of their Central Committee members, was executed by Dzierzynski in person on 8 July: the expiatory sacrifice demanded by *Realpolitik*.[61] An uprising of Left Socialist-Revolutionaries had also been started in Yaroslavl, a town to Moscow's north east, on 6 July, but was suppressed a fortnight later. The former coalition partners of the Bolsheviks went down to defeat; almost without noticing it, Lenin and the core of Bolshevik Central Committee members had passed over the threshold from a two-party revolutionary dictatorship into an outright dictatorship by one party. That this was accomplished with so little comment shows that the movement was congenial for them. They would rather fight alone and against the odds than rally a coalition by compromising their political and economic policies.

MANOEUVRE, RETREAT, WAIT

Lenin knew that the treaty of Brest-Litovsk depended entirely on the German government's intentions, and that these in turn were shaped by success or failure for German forces on the Western front. Belgium and northern France, not the Pripet marshes, held the answer to the enigma of the October Revolution. If Ludendorff rolled through into Paris, it would not be long before he moved smoothly into Moscow and Petrograd.

Lenin did not lie supine in the meantime. But he wanted to leave behind what he ridiculed as the politics of the 'revolutionary phrase'.[62] As he recognised, the October Revolution had survived because the extreme militarists in Germany had yet not opted to cross the limits set by the Brest-Litovsk treaty.[63] The Bolsheviks deferred to Berlin; their forces were pathetically incompetent to resist. Moscow's policy was merely to kow-tow to Kaiser Wilhelm. The sections of the treaty forbidding hostile propaganda could in practice be ignored, and the Soviet state would continue to hope for European socialist revolution. 'We know,' Lenin had reassured the Fourth Congress of Soviets in March 1918, 'that Liebknecht will be victorious one way or another; this is inevitable in the development of the workers' movement.'[64] But how this would happen was unpredictable. At a session of the All-Russian Central Executive Committee on 29 April he was brutally frank: 'Yes, the peace we have arrived at is unstable in the highest degree; the breathing space obtained by us can be broken off any day both from the West and from the East.'[65] But what did Lenin say to those who claimed that, since Brest-Litovsk, he had no independent policy?[66] Not a lot in public: he was constrained to avoid giving offence to the German government. But to the Central Committee he was more forthcoming. In mid-May he drafted theses urging that the priority of Soviet diplomacy should be 'to manoeuvre, to retreat, to wait'.[67] Playing one capitalist power against another was, Lenin urged, the sole option available in the circumstances. Imperialism could not yet be confronted directly.[68]

Exactly how the Germans might be manipulated against the Allies was not examined by him;[69] but he suggested that America's interest in obtaining raw materials from Russia might encourage president Woodrow Wilson to deter the inroads of the Japanese.[70] Nor did he describe how much further the Soviet state could 'retreat' before disappearing. This was sensible. Brest-Litovsk remained too divisive to permit him to state what bits of territory might be abandoned; and, for the same reason, Lenin did not want to define the temporal limits of 'waiting'. There was only one small point, tucked into a subsidiary clause, which was controversial. This was Lenin's proposal that the Soviet state should not absolutely repudiate 'military agreements with one of the imperialist coalitions against another'.[71] He would let the Red Army fight on the side of either the Central Powers or the Allies if the situation demanded. Quite a manoeuvrer he was willing to become. Fresh from compelling his party to accede to a separate peace treaty, he now contemplated joint campaigns with 'imperialism'!

What had produced this shift in a man who in 1917 had imperiously castigated the imperialist states is a matter of guesswork. That he had intended a permanent 'German orientation' in international relations is unlikely. His faith in the inevitability of continental revolution was genuine. Immediately he pursued a policy of appeasement. The Germans exploited Brest-Litovsk to concentrate forces in the West and even to transfer troops from the Russian front. Ludendorff bet that, once the Allies had been defeated, the Soviet government would be an easy victim. Lenin's political survival depended on Allied military success in the West at least until such time as the long-expected revolution should break out in Berlin.[72] Never had German might seemed so invincible. Ludendorff's Western offensive was initiated on 21 March 1918, and continued through spring. Nor were the Germans inactive in the East. On 7 March they signed a treaty with the Finnish government, threatening the interests of the Soviet republic.[73] In April they overthrew the Rada, which ruled Ukraine, and installed a client, Pavlo Skoropadsky as 'Hetman'.[74] In the same month they marched into Crimea in contravention of the Brest-Litovsk treaty.[75] The Red Army was not yet formed. Every political party in Russia regarded the Bolsheviks as traitors. Food supplies were dangerously low. Working-class and peasant discontent was rising. Lenin, the vociferous advocate of a separate peace with Germany, insisted on all diplomatic efforts complying with Berlin's demands.

Not even Lenin wished to give public display of such submissiveness. Patriotic emotion could not be offended. As his party's patriarch, he did not ignore the unease felt even by his sympathisers. Grigori Sokolnikov, who had opposed the Left Communists, jibbed at the appeasement demanded. Six out of fifteen Central Committee members had gathered on 10 May to discuss Lenin's 'Theses On The Current Political Situation'.[76] Sokolnikov argued that Germany's political coup in Kiev introduced new factors into diplomacy. Allegedly the action showed that an alliance had been formed between the Russian bourgeoisie and German imperialism. Sokolnikov had belonged to the Soviet delegation which had signed the treaty of Brest-Litovsk. Now he claimed that it was not worth the paper it was printed on. It appears to have staggered Sokolnikov, who until then had been Lenin's supporter, that the Germans had chosen and been able to rule Ukraine through local stooges. Sokolnikov however, was undeterred. War had supposedly become inevitable, and he urged a 'military agreement with the Anglo-French coalition with the object of military cooperation on certain conditions'.[77] The vote went four to one in favour of Lenin's policy of continued appeasement of Germany. Sokolnikov had no supporter. Stalin pointedly abstained; he had been shaken by the German occupation of Kharkov, and began to question his own earlier advocacy of a separate peace with Germany.[78] Sokolnikov had touched a sore spot. Lenin's high-risk strategy did not go unperceived as such. A fuller debate was necessary. Two major party leaders, Trotski and Zinoviev, had not been present. Lenin was especially keen to secure backing from Trotski, who had been on the left side in the Brest-Litovsk controversy. On 13 May the Central Committee met once more. By then a report was available from the Sovnarkom plenipotentiary in Berlin, Adolf Ioffe, who gave the reassurance that Germany did not intend to disavow the treaty.[79] Trotski and Zinoviev backed Lenin. Trotski was judged by Allied representatives in Moscow as a genuine promoter of an Allied foreign-policy orientation.[80] His support for Lenin disproved this. Probably he pretended otherwise in public so as to keep the Soviet government's options open. At any rate the result of the Central Committee's decision of 13 May was to publicise the stronger turn than ever to the German orientation. Contacts with Allied diplomats waned. The frostiness over the British landings in Arkhangelsk became downright icy.

It is true that Trotski as late as 24 May confided to British attaché Bruce Lockhart that Sovnarkom did not seek the departure of the British forces from Murmansk.[81] What shattered the possibility of this vestigial manoeuvring between the Germans and the British was the Czech Legion's revolt on 25 May 1918. Unequivocal appeasement of Germany became unavoidable. Lenin and the Bolsheviks were recognised in Berlin as godless and anti-monarchical. But Bolshevism was allowed to stay in power because it represented the sole Russian party which would adhere to the Brest-Litovsk treaty; and, unless the Red Army could reassure Berlin about its capacity to resist insurrection on Russian soil, the Bolshevik party would have been cast down by

Ludendorff. The situation's urgency was demonstrated by Lenin's willingness to remove Red units from the demarcation line separating them from the German-occupied zone even though there was no guarantee that the Germans would not take military advantage. The Czechoslovak Legion had to be suppressed at all costs.[82] Extreme care was exercised in relation to Germany. On 10 June, Lenin rebuked the Bolsheviks in Kuban for mounting an attack on German troops in Taganrog, and similar instructions were issued two days later to Red Army and Bolshevik party personnel on the Southern front: no military engagement with the Germans was permissible.[83] Then came the assassination of Count Mirbach on 6 July. Rapid proof that Sovnarkom was uninvolved had to be offered. On 7 July, S. P. Natsarenus in Petrozavodsk was ordered to destroy the railway linking Petrograd and Murmansk after the British landings in the north in late June. Anyone collaborating with 'the Anglo-French imperialists' should be shot.[84] Lenin not only wanted to exhibit enthusiasm for Brest-Litovsk; he also increasingly wished to enlist the Germans in defence of Soviet-held territory against further landings by the Allies. The dispatch of a British expedition to Arkhangelsk was imminent. Lenin, who had refused to rule out the possibility of a 'military agreement' with the Germans in mid-May, got Chicherin to indicate to the new German ambassador, K. Helfferich, that Sovnarkom would not object to a German-Finnish action in Karelia. The conversation between Chicherin and Helfferich occurred on 1 August. By then the German offensive on the Western front was collapsing: a massive victory for the French had occurred at Villers-Cotteret on 18 July. Ludendorff sank into despair. This information was as yet unavailable to Lenin. The Western front was too far away. Yet Lenin anyway considered he had little choice. 'Soviet power' was so helpless that, as the Czechoslovaks had shown, even a moderately efficient small corps could threaten it severely. Consequently Lenin was even willing on 13 August to risk inviting the Germans, through Chicherin, to bomb Arkhangelsk on Sovnarkom's behalf.[85]

In a memorandum to V. V. Vorovski, Lenin asserted that 'we would be idiots not to make use' of the confluence of Soviet and German governmental interests.[86] It took until 17 August for *Pravda* to announce that the German military menace to Sovnarkom itself had drastically diminished. The British break-through at Amiens on the Western front made this unmistakably clear. The Germans and Russians had initialled a supplementary treaty to the Brest-Litovsk arrangements on 10 August, and this was formally signed on 27

August. The German terms remained severe, including a huge indemnity to be paid to Berlin. Russia obtained in return only a German promise to refrain from giving assistance to her enemies.[87] But the supplementary treaty was already a dead letter. Germany had failed in her ultimate intensive effort to crush the British and French in the West. A new era in the Soviet republic's relations with the governments and peoples of the rest of the world was heralded. The two treaties with the Germans had not really brought about a 'breathing-space' for the development of socialism at home. Chaos, immiseration and civil war made any such development impossible. Lenin had misled himself. But Brest-Litovsk had at least ensured the sheer survival of the Bolsheviks in power. It was an achievement of Lenin's gamble in international relations.

THE WRITING OF A CONSTITUTION

Lenin scoffed at constitutionalism in politics. Before the October Revolution he had repeatedly scorned fixed laws, demarcations, customs. In November 1917 he declared: 'The living creativity of the masses is the basic factor in our new public order'; and he added: 'Socialism is not created by commands from above.'[88] And yet clarity about the state's institutional principles was recognised as being overdue. The Third Congress of Soviets in January 1918 had also called for the drafting of a Constitution; but nothing followed quickly. The Brest-Litovsk dispute pre-occupied the minds of both the Bolsheviks and the Left SRs. Not until 30 March did the Bolshevik Central Committee approve a proposal for the All-Russian Central Executive Committee of the Congress of Soviets to set up a drafting commission.[89] Sverdlov chaired the first discussions on 5 April, with representatives in attendance from the Bolsheviks, Left Socialist-Revolutionaries and SR-Maximalists as well as from particular People's Commissariats. Sverdlov was commission chairman, and Stalin was included as the Bolshevik official expert on the question of the nationalities.[90] Notable by his absence was Lenin. Not only did he refrain from joining the commission, but he also made no comment on constitutional matters in ensuing months. It was a sign of the low immediate priority he assigned to the task.

The federal basis of the forthcoming Constitution had been established, on Lenin's recommendation, at the Third Congress of

Soviets in January 1918.[91] On this he insisted. Having previously been a vehement anti-federalist, he had come to sense that the non-Russian regions of the old Russian Empire would be difficult to re-incorporate in a multinational state unless administrative units based on the national principle were introduced.[92] He left it to Stalin to give a response to *Pravda*'s enquiry about federalism as the commission began work. Stalin firstly emphasised that the details of the federal structure could not be formulated until the various non-Russian regions were to join the Russian Federation.[93] Sovnarkom at present ruled only Russia – and not all Russia at that. He also claimed that the existing federal states abroad, the USA and Switzerland, were more centralist than federal in reality and that their administrative units were founded more on territorial convenience than national aspirations. The Russian federation, he maintained, would be different.[94]

Thus Stalin did not forbear to stress that federation was not designed to be a permanent phenomenon. He asserted that it was to be regarded as merely a transitional stage towards 'an equally voluntary and fraternal union of the labouring masses of all the nations and races of Russia'. Stalin ultimately wanted a fully unitary state.[95] This was not all. Talking of the potential members of the 'Russian Federal Republic' he mentioned not only Siberia, Turkestan, Crimea and Ukraine but even Finland and Poland as well.[96] The contrast with Lenin was impressive. Lenin, no less than Stalin, accepted federalism only under strong duress. But he ceased publicly to announce that he would overturn it at the earliest available opportunity. Nor did Lenin raise the possibility about the re-incorporation of Poland and Finland just months after Sovnarkom had vouchsafed their independence.[97] In Poland's case this had made no practical difference while German armies remained in occupation. Even so, Stalin was tossing aside the argument that Russians would be politically unwelcome in those parts of the Russian Empire unless the Bolshevik party went out of its way to disclaim territorial acquisitiveness. The plan to win support for socialism elsewhere in Europe by pointing to Sovnarkom's anti-imperialist commitment was also being undermined.[98] Yet Lenin was so unexercised by the constitutional question that he did nothing until Sverdlov's commission reported back to the Central Committee.[99]

Stalin was in any case closer to Lenin's viewpoint than were other commission members. Bolsheviks such as M. N. Pokrovski and Y. M. Steklov angrily opposed the insertion of 'the national principle' into the Constitution, and their hostility was shared by Left Socialist-Revolutionary M. A. Reisner.[100] Sverdlov had to intervene on Stalin's side to insist that the government had already laid down 'national self-determination' as an unalterable basis of policy. Stalin returned to the commission on 12 April to defend himself. This time the accusation was slightly different. Previously he had been criticised for making concessions to nationalism; now his proposal was said to offer insincere promises. The Left Socialist-Revolutionary went further: 'Comrade Stalin has got so accustomed to such a situation that he has perfectly assimilated even the jargon of imperialism. "They demand and we give" And of course, according to Stalin, we don't bother to give if they don't make any demands of us.'[101]

Rivalry continued about the draft Constitution to be taken as the basis for further deliberation. The three main proposals came from Sverdlov, Stalin and Reisner. Stalin won more support than Sverdlov,[102] and there followed a contest between Stalin and Reisner. The two of them argued their cases on 19 April. Reisner teased him for advocating exactly the 'anarchic' ideas espoused by Lenin in *The State and Revolution*. This booklet, which had recently been published but had been written in mid-1917, envisaged a revolutionary order with much greater scope for popular initiative than Lenin was willing to tolerate by 1918. Reisner's sarcasm got under Stalin's skin. All he could say in reply was: 'Mention has been made here of comrade Lenin. I would permit myself to remark that Lenin, so far as I know – and I know very well –, has said that this project is worthless.'[103] Some Bolshevik members remained unhappy with his performance. The need for any reference to national issues rankled so much that Pokrovski, a Bolshevik, preferred Reisner's draft. But Stalin got his way.[104] The majority of the participants, some more enthusiastically than others, gave approval to his draft. Almost certainly they judged that any failure to support him would not be the end of the matter. Lenin and Stalin in 1917 had taken pains to get the slogan of national self-determination accepted in the Bolshevik party, and were convinced that its deployment would help the Bolsheviks in the Civil War. Neither was a man lightly to be trifled with.

Stalin subsequently left the commission to Sverdlov for the Constitution's elaboration. Lenin began to take an interest from a distance. His main ambition for the Constitution was for it to rouse workers and peasants to support the Bolsheviks. Unfortunately the draft was flat and unrhetorical. Sverdlov was no stylist, and the various amendments made since the departure of Stalin, who was a crude but effective writer, had not led to improvements. Lenin seized control, persuading his colleagues on the Central Committee to include an entirely new preamble. Even then he refused to write it. Instead he substituted a text already accepted at the Third Congress of Soviets, namely 'The Declaration of Rights of the Labouring and Exploited People' submitted by Lenin to the Constituent Assembly in January 1918.[105]

Sverdlov, understandably miffed, behaved like a disciplined Bolshevik and induced the commission to comply on 17 June.[106] The Bolshevik Central Committee, looking at the result nine days later, was unimpressed. Lenin even threatened to remove the Constitution from the agenda of the forthcoming Congress of Soviets.[107] Sverdlov, who had many other duties to fulfil at the same time, felt unappreciated by his party leader.[108] The commission redoubled its labours; detailed consideration of the definition of Soviet state institutions took place at a commission meeting held on the same day.[109] Its final draft was perused by the Central Committee, in the presence of Lenin and Trotski, on 3 July.[110] The stitching together of the commission's clauses and the 'The Declaration of Rights of the Labouring and Exploited People' had been done in a rough and ready fashion. Terminological inconsistencies were plentiful. But no one worried any longer. A last effort at polishing the style, but not the contents, was entrusted to Yuri Steklov; and it was Steklov, a leading ex-Menshevik writer and editor, who was instructed to present the draft Constitution to the Fifth Congress of Soviets on 10 July 1918.[111] By then the Left Socialist-Revolutionary revolt had been suppressed. Nevertheless the Bolshevik Central Committee did not introduce further amendments after being released from the need to conciliate the party's coalition partners. Nor did it fret over Steklov's lowly status as rapporteur on the Constitution. Lenin did not even bother to speak at the Congress of Soviets session.[112]

The Constitution of the Russian Socialist Federal Soviet Republic came into effect on publication in *Izvestiya*.[113] The objective was defined as a 'free union of free nations as a federation of Soviet national republics'. Yet direct reference to the federal structure occurred only in the Constitution's title and the preamble, and essentially the clauses described not a federal but a unitary state. Already there was more flim-flam than substance in the Bolshevik party's commitment to creating a federation. Nothing in this was surprising to those few citizens who had read the articles of Lenin and Stalin carefully. But the Bolshevik party leadership cynically hoped to attract the support of non-Russian peoples by showing off federalism as a slogan.

The dominant theme was class struggle. Article nine ran as follows: 'The basic task of the Constitution of the Russian Socialist Federal Soviet Republic, as adapted to the current transitional period, consists in the establishment of the dictatorship of the urban and rural proletariat and poorest peasantry in the form of the mighty All-Russian Soviet power with the aims of the complete suppression of the bourgeoisie, the elimination of the exploitation of man by man and the introduction of socialism, under which there will be neither a division into classes nor state power.'[114] Here was yet another sign that Lenin approached the commission's draft without his customary attentiveness. Lenin had argued at length in his recently-published *State and Revolution* that socialism would be an entirely distinct phase of history between capitalism and communism. Marx, he claimed, had argued exactly this.[115] It was Lenin who made this inference for the first time, and it is by no means proven that he had correctly understood the standpoint of Marx; but it quickly became a tenet of Bolshevism. Yet Lenin did not intend to agitate himself and his comrades over a question of Marxism which since 1917 had been dear to him. Possibly Sverdlov, like most party members, had neither the time nor the inclination at such a moment to indulge in theoretical speculation. Monolithism of ideology did not yet exist.

The Constitution itself unambiguously supported the interests of the 'labouring people' against those of the employers. Universal suffrage was derided; and the principle was proclaimed: 'He that does not work, neither shall he eat.'[116] The disenfranchisement of the middle and upper classes was phrased as follows: 'In the general interest of the working class the RSFSR deprives individuals or particular groups of any privileges which may be used by them to the detriment of the socialist revolution.'[117] This was clarified in the definition of those who were allowed to vote. Among those excluded were private employers, private investors, private businessmen, monks, priests, former policemen, criminals and registered imbeciles.[118] The same section implicitly cleared the ground for the Bolsheviks to outlaw any political parties, organisations or newspapers.

The rights of those retaining the franchise were ostensibly comprehensive. Freedoms of thought, organisation, religion and assembly were emphasised, and the Constitution promised to realise them by putting the necessary resources at the disposal of the 'masses'.[119] But these masses were not to be treated equally. The clauses on the franchise gave a disproportionate number of places in central and local representative institutions to the towns. Thus workers and other urban employees were favoured in voting capacity at the expense of peasants.[120] But the distinction was more formal than real. The Constitution was not only propagandistic; it was also vague. For example, the demarcation between the Congress of Soviets and its All-Russian Central Executive Committee remained obscure; and, although Sovnarkom was endowed only with authority to issue decrees, no explanation was given as to how they would differ from legislation passed by the All-Russian Central Executive Committee.[121] As a legal document, the Constitution was dangerously skimpy. No one could have been more deeply aware of this than the man who had graduated with a first-class honours degree in law as an external student at St Petersburg University in 1891. Vladimir Lenin would only bother with constitutional trifles when his current political purposes were threatened. As things turned out, this did not occur until the 'Georgian Affair' in 1922, when Lenin disputed Stalin's policy towards the non-Russian nations of the Soviet multinational state.[122]

TO KAZAN!

The national question had been debated hard in the commission on the Constitution, but was scarcely mentioned in the finally-published version. In similar fashion it was important but secret in the discussions on security in midsummer 1918. Trotski, Dzierzynski and Lenin confronted a near-disastrous military situation. They perceived the vital necessity to retain Latvian sympathies so long as the size and competence of the Workers' and Peasants' Red Army remained small. The Bolshevik leaders had also seen the uses of the prisoners-of-war taken by Russian armies in 1914–1917, especially those from the lands of the Hapsburg monarchy (and the Constitution itself had been formulated so as to grant citizenship to all foreigners working in Russia or fighting in the Red Army).[123] Hungarians, Czechs, Slovaks, Ruthenes and even Germans and Poles were looked upon as potential enlisters.[124] The problems of recruitment are readily comprehensible. The decree of 22 January 1918 establishing the Red Army was expected to result in the enlistment of hundreds of thousands of Russians. But few Russians were willing to fight. By late March, when Trotski was People's Commissar of Military Affairs, only around 10,000 Red troops were under arms.[125] Peasants wanted to stay with their recently-acquired land, and had heard from demobilised soldiers about the awful conditions on the Eastern front. Workers supplied slightly greater enthusiasm. Moscow and Petrograd gave most volunteers; but there were difficulties elsewhere, even in major industrial centres such as Ekaterinburg, in convincing the working class that the Civil War affected their interests and required their participation.[126] Trotski's efforts were intensified when the Czechoslovak Legion, on entering into Samara, put itself at the disposal of the Komuch government of Socialist Revolutionaries aiming to overthrow the Bolsheviks in Moscow. His initial military expert was General M. D. Bonch-Bruevich (who, despite his anti-socialist convictions, was brother to Lenin's personal assistant Vladimir Bonch-Bruevich). They agreed that officers from the Imperial armed forces would be essential to the technical functioning of the Red Army. Trotski also insisted, in line with practice in the existing Red units, on the exercise of rigorous political control. Hostages were taken from serving officers' families, to be shot in cases of desertion or betrayal. A system was also introduced whereby serving officers were accompanied by commissars whose task was to ensure the loyalty of commanders and spread communist ideas among the troops.[127]

Down to the Volga sped the hastily-mobilised contingents of the Red Army. The commander-in-chief was I. I. Vacietis, replacing M. A. Muraviev (who was a Left Socialist Revolutionary and had tried to defect to the side of Komuch). Kazan fell to Komuch's forces on 7 August. So swift was the attack that they moved on to Sviyazhsk. If successful, they would have cut off contingents of the Red Army moving upon Kazan. Trotski showed courage and tenacity; his train lay within range of enemy fire until the battle was won. Sviyazhsk was held and the Reds marched upon Kazan. Lenin stayed in Moscow in August. The central administration of the Red war effort was still chaotic, and he sent telegrams to the government's military and food-supplies officials to the north around Arkhangelsk and to the south around Astrakhan.[128] But the crucial region was the Volga. The following note was dispatched to Trotski from Lenin: 'I'm sure that the suppression of the Czechs and White Guards, as well as the bloodsucking kulaks who support them, will be a model of mercilessness.'[129] Such 'encouragement' gave way to irritated demands by 10 September: 'I'm astonished and worried by the delay of the operation against Kazan, especially if my information is correct that you have a complete opportunity to annihilate the enemy by artillery. In my view, there should be no sparing of the city or any further postponement since what is required is merciless destruction as soon as Kazan is definitely within an iron ring.'[130]

If Lenin harboured a suspicion that Trotski might wage war in too sensitive a spirit, he had misjudged him. On 29 August 1918 Trotski had held a field court martial of troops and their officers who had retreated against orders under fire. He re-introduced the Roman punishment of decimation, and refused to exempt a certain Panteleev, political commissar and Bolshevik party activist, from execution. This provoked outrage in the Bolshevik party. Not only did Trotski employ Imperial officers but he also handed over party members to the firing squad. The fear lest he might eventually set himself up as the Napoleon Bonaparte of the October Revolution struck roots. Trotski, whose associate A. P. Rozengolts headed the court martial, was unrepentant and sought Lenin's support on 23 October. In the opinion of the People's Commissar of Military Affairs, all deserters regardless of party affiliation should suffer the same fate.[131]

On 10 September 1918 the Red Army entered Kazan and drove out the Komuch forces. To the south a further operation was already under way. Its commander was Mikhail Tukhachevski. He was one of thousands of both junior commissioned and non-commissioned officers from the Imperial Army given rapid promotion by Trotski, and on 12 September he repaid this trust by taking the Volga town of Simbirsk. This was Lenin's birthplace. But the chairman of Sovnarkom was unsentimental about the fact. He was anyway out of touch with Trotski's whereabouts (and had to telegram 'to Kazan or Sviyazhsk'). After curtly 'welcoming the capture of Simbirsk', he adjured: 'In my opinion, maximum forces must be concentrated for the accelerated cleansing of Siberia. Don't spare any cash in the form of rewards. Telegraph whether Kazan's treasures, and how many of them, have been saved.' Lenin had approved a scheme to expropriate ecclesiastical and historic valuables; but, since such a step might have caused popular indignation, the telegram was marked 'highly secret'.[132] This was as well for other reasons. Lenin failed to understand the geographical limitations of the Red victory. Talk of reconquering Siberia was vastly premature. First the Komuch authorities had to be overthrown in Samara. Only on 7 October could this be accomplished, nearly a month later. The Socialist Revolutionaries decamped eastwards. Komuch was no more.

Lenin was not the sole Bolshevik to exult, and *Pravda* editorials were understandably keen to emphasise the successes in battle. The Czechoslovak Legion was demoralised. The Volga peasantry had proved reluctant to enlist in Komuch's defence; and potential recruits were anyway fewer by far than in Moscow and Petrograd. Yet the central party leaders, both in the Kremlin and by the Volga, had little knowledge about other Russian forces being formed to attack the Reds. Admiral Kolchak and Generals Denikin and Yudenich were assembling armies in the peripheral regions of the old empire. The Civil War was at last about to explode in all fury. Admiral A. V. Kolchak was based in the Siberian city of Omsk, and was building advantageous links with the British government. In his turn he was able to attract the remnants of the Czechoslovak Legion. His confidence was growing. Undoubtedly he would have laughed to read Lenin's carefree command for an immediate cleansing of Siberia. General A. I. Denikin, after the death of Lavr Kornilov in action in April 1918, had taken over the armed units of anti-Bolshevism in southern Russia. Denikin was looking to the local Cossacks for joint military operations. As yet he had few contacts with either Kolchak or the Allies; but his threat to Sovnarkom would soon become as acute as Kolchak's. General N. N. Yudenich led the smallest of the so-called White armies. But he was organising on Estonian territory and menaced the security of Petrograd. From three sides of the compass there was a threat to the existence of the Bolshevik party and the Soviet government. Yet Lenin referred to none of them in his telegrams in 1918. Having blundered by assuming that the arrest of Cossack leader M. P. Bogaevski in February would signal the Civil War's end, he believed Trotski's success at Kazan and Samara was definitive. He failed to anticipate that resistance to Sovnarkom could become much more serious if conducted by the counterrevolutionary elements of the Imperial officer corps. He had read Karl von Clausewitz the military theorist and drawn the stupidest conclusion that, in modern times, the waging of war would get steadily easier. He was about to learn the error of his ways.

2 Closing the Circle

ASSASSINATION ATTEMPT

Rulers of any state usually try to regulate how much is known about them by their society. Their general custom before the twentieth century was to emphasise their majesty and difference from those whom they governed; but few of them failed to identify themselves somehow with their subjects. Some presented themselves as the embodiment of the virtues of their class, nation or empire. They explained their purposes as involving a public good which goes beyond mere personal self-aggrandisement. Practically every monarch of France, England or Spain in history engaged in all these enterprises.

Yet a chasm was kept between rulers and ruled: the mystique of authority had to be preserved or else the existing social order might be dissolved. Only in small, primitive societies was it possible to maintain greater familiarity. The Bolsheviks were therefore the first to challenge this tradition in a modern society. Theirs was purportedly a workers' state. The interests of the working class were meant to take precedence over any other consideration. Lenin, Trotski, Zinoviev, Kamenev, Sverdlov: the entire leading cadre of the party took it as their duty to go frequently among the workers and impress them with their commitment to ideals which would soon become the predominant political reality. In fact the Bolshevik central leadership lived in conditions which, if they were modest by the standards of the tsars, were yet far removed from the still increasing poverty of Russian factory workers. Nor did any Central Committee member or People's Commissar intend to accede to popular aspirations when these included a demand that the one-party dictatorship should be brought to an end. But social intercourse with workers at their place of work was accorded a priority. In Petrograd this had involved a short walk from the government's offices to the nearest factories. The Kremlin in Moscow was some kilometres from industrial suburbs, but both Lenin and his comrades continued to intercalate speeches to mass meetings in their schedules of official activity.

So it was on 30 August 1918 that Lenin had arranged to give a fifteen minutes' address in two separate places. The first was to be the Corn Exchange in the Basmanny suburb in Moscow. He was expected to

speak there in the afternoon and again at the Mikhelson Armaments
Factory at around 6.00 p.m. He dressed normally: his black three-
piece suit, a black lightweight knee-length overcoat. He was picked up
from the Kremlin ground by his regular chauffeur S.K. Gil. And he
had prepared an aggressive set of remarks. At the Corn Exchange he
was on good form, telling his audience: 'Let every worker and peasant
who has vacillated on the question of power take a look at the Volga,
at Siberia, at Ukraine, and then the answer will come back by itself,
clear and definite!'.[1]

Then on to Mikhelson's. In the factory yard, in the bright early
evening, he gave a similar speech asking his audience to compare
foreign capitalist countries with the nascent socialism of Russia.[2] Even
in the USA, he cried, ordinary working people were reduced to 'feudal
slavery': 'Where the 'democrats' rule is the place that you'll find
genuine, unvarnished robbery!'[3] Russian workers ought by then to
know better than the working classes abroad. Talk about a democratic
republic or a Constituent Assembly should be treated as what it really
was: a fairy-tale! There could be no compromise. Civic rights ought to
be denied to 'the fraudsters, the parasites who are squeezing the blood
out of the labouring people'.[4] Lenin was now well into a rhythm. He
needed no microphone. The crowd that had been gathering strained to
hear him as others came along from off the street. Lenin's chauffeur
Stepan Gil had parked the official car not far from the improvised
platform. Lenin barked out the words, fist raised in the air and eyes
sparkling in front of the jostling listeners. This was not an audience to
regale with Marxist refinements. The October Revolution was in
danger. The workers had to appreciate the jeopardy facing the régime –
their régime, as Lenin claimed it to be: 'We must hurl everything on to
the Czechoslovak front so as to crush and shatter this entire gang
which disguises itself with slogans of freedom and equality and shoots
workers and peasants in their hundreds and thousands. There is only
one way out for us: victory or death!'[5]

These words in an instant acquired a sinister meaning. It was around
8.00 p.m. that Lenin pressed his way through the crowd, waving good-
bye, towards the car. Gil started the engine. Yet before the car could
start, three shots were heard. By-standers scattered, shouting: 'They've
killed him, they've killed him!'[6] Lenin had fallen to the ground. He had
been hit twice on the left side of his body. One bullet lodged in his neck,
the other in the lower part of his shoulder. Bleeding profusely, he was
bundled into the vehicle by Gil and others. The car sped away from the
scene of the shooting to the Kremlin. Doctors were summoned; the

Central Committee was alerted. Sverdlov took control of the governmental apparatus and waited to hear how badly hurt Lenin was. It was already clear that, if he lived, he would have survived by the last-minute reflex of jerking his head away from the perceived threat. Otherwise one of those two bullets would have done for him.[7]

Back at the factory there was pandemonium. The Cheka had had its men present at both the Corn Exchange and the Mikhelson Factory, and Bolshevik party officials like N. Y. Ivanov had also been there to greet Lenin when he arrived to speak.[8] The gun, a Browning pistol numbered 150489, was picked up from the floor; but the would-be assassin had not been apprehended in the act. Such was the panic that, even though the shots had been fired at a range of a few metres, no one had tried to prevent the crowd's dispersal. Minutes later, the mistake was recognised and a frantic search was begun in the vicinity. This yielded an immediate result. A certain Fanya Kaplan had been seen coming to the factory gates as Lenin was finishing his speech, and she was detained.[9] Gil later claimed to recognise her as the assailant. But there were doubts whether he had really been in a position to see things clearly or even whether his testimony was consistent in all its versions.[10] No one else had much claim to be taken seriously as an eyewitness. The only other person who may have seen the assailant was Lenin himself; yet he was convalescing during Kaplan's interrogation and had no influence on its course.[11] He had in fact been remarkably self-possessed while all around them lost their heads: 'Comrades, be quiet! It's not serious! Stay orderly!'[12] Kaplan herself had not been much more forthcoming. When stopped in the factory yard, she blurted out: 'It wasn't me who did it!'[13]

This was eventually taken to be a suspicious statement; but it was in itself hardly an unusual thing to say: everyone in the yard knew by then what had happened to Lenin. She never confessed to having fired the shots. Spirited away into the custody of the Cheka, she entirely refused to co-operate with the authorities; and, in contrast with what might have happened to her a few months later, no physical pressure was applied to elicit further information.

By then Yakov Sverdlov had been told what had happened. He took charge of the situation as Lenin's trusted governmental and party colleague, announcing at 10.40 p.m. that the attempted assassination was the work of the Party of Socialist Revolutionaries.[14] Sverdlov was hasty in two respects. Among his colleagues there were several who thought that he displayed an undue enthusiasm about imposing personal control. Vladimir Bonch-Bruevich was to remember him as having boasted: 'You see, Vladimir Dmitrievich, we can get along without Lenin.'[15] Sverdlov also endeavoured to delay Lenin's return to work.[16] His eagerness stemmed from a zeal to prove that the Bolsheviks were not a one-man political party and from a wish to prevent Lenin from damaging his health by a premature resumption of official duties. Sverdlov's other manifestation of hastiness came with his incrimination of the Socialist Revolutionaries. He had extenuating factors on his side. On the same day as Lenin had been attacked in Moscow, a similar (and successful) attempt had been made on the life of the Cheka's chief in Petrograd, Moisei Uritski. There the assassin L. A. Kannegisser had Socialist-Revolutionary connections, and the Bolshevik central leaders were nervous lest a campaign of killings was being undertaken by a party which had been associated with a revolutionary strategy of assassinations. Kannegisser denied acting on the instructions of the Socialist Revolutionaries; and there was nothing to show that Fanya Kaplan was a Socialist-Revolutionary activist. Sverdlov and his colleagues were ruthlessly seizing a chance to lay collective guilt at the door of a party which had been overwhelmingly more popular that the Bolsheviks in the elections to the Constituent Assembly.[17]

It is extremely doubtful that Kaplan was the wielder of the gun. Her maiden name was Feiga Khaimovna Roitman and she was born in Ukraine, the daughter of Jewish parents, in 1887. In adolescence she became an anarchist. In 1906, while the Russian empire was in revolutionary turmoil, she and her companions prepared explosives to attack the provincial governor-general. The bomb went off accidentally in advance of the attempt. A maid in her hotel was fatally wounded. Roitman was apprehended, put on trial by a field court-martial and condemned to penal servitude for life after her death sentence was commuted.[18]

In prison she went blind; and, although her sight partially returned to her in 1912, she never completely recovered.[19] Kaplan, as she was by then known, was a most unlikely person to be asked to carry out an assassination. When a trial of Socialist-Revolutionary leaders was organised in 1922, testimony was offered that she had indeed been the culprit. But this trial was a disgrace to all standards of jurisprudence. Fictions abounded not only about Kaplan but also about the Party of Socialist Revolutionaries.[20] It is well with the bounds of possibility that a group of Socialist Revolutionaries, working independently of their Central Committee, had engineered the assassination attempt. It is also plausible that Kaplan belonged to them. After her spell in prison before the First World War, she stated that she considered herself 'a socialist with no particular party affiliation'.[21] A liaison with Socialist Revolutionaries might have been acceptable to her. And yet, if she was at the Mikhelson Factory as the member of such a group, the others would surely not have chosen her as the assassin. Sverdlov, however, had made up his mind: Kaplan was to be adjudged guilty. There would be no trial, only an announcement that the death sentence had been carried out. The Party of Socialist Revolutionaries was to be outlawed on the grounds of state treason. Sverdlov wasted no time on Kaplan herself. Neither the Cheka nor the People's Commissariat of Internal Affairs were to be involved. He simply ordered the Kremlin commander P. Malkov to lead her from the detention cell for execution. Her remains were destroyed.[22]

Sverdlov wanted to perpetuate the memory of the assault on Lenin while preventing a cult of the martyr who had allegedly attacked him. The swift dispatch of Fanya Kaplan also had avoided a protracted public examination of the holes in the case for the prosecution.[23] Even Lenin was bemused by the rapidity. When shot, he had turned to Gil and asked: 'Did they catch him or not?'[24] But he did not worry that, despite his assumption that a man had shot him, a woman had been executed. He put the incident completely behind him. Maksim Gorki visited some days later, and found him very phlegmatic: 'Just a scuffle. There's nothing to be done about it. Everyone acts according to his own fashion.'[25] He knew that, even if Kaplan had not done the dirty deed, plenty of others would have been pleased to do it. A thorough investigation of a single assassination attempt would not have eradicated the continuing threat to his life. There were plenty of Socialist-Revolutionaries who would have volunteered to complete the job which Fanya Kaplan had been accused of undertaking.

'PROLETARIAN REVOLUTION AND KAUTSKY THE RENEGADE'

Lenin was too frail to write in longhand; but, being determined to use his unsought leisure to the full, he took on a short-hand secretary[26] and began yet another booklet on Marxist theory: *Proletarian Revolution and Kautsky the Renegade*. His obsession with Karl Kautsky had not eased. Yuli Martov denounced *The State and Revolution* in terms as powerful as Kautsky's; but it was Kautsky who drew the ire of the

Bolshevik leader.[27] What particularly had annoyed Lenin was the publication in Vienna of a 63-page work entitled *The Dictatorship of the Proletariat*. Kautsky for the first time had dedicated an entire work to Lenin and the questions raised by him. The irritable and irritating mode of *State and Revolution* became splenetic. The fact that few copies of Kautsky's work were being bought in Berlin did not reassure Lenin. He proposed that Soviet diplomats should buy up all copies and distribute them to German and Swiss workers who should be encouraged to ensure that the entire printing be 'trampled in the mud'.[28]

Kautsky had contrasted two directions in nineteenth-century socialist thought: the democratic and the dictatorial. He claimed that Marx had never wanted 'the dictatorship of the proletariat' to be unaccompanied by universal civic freedoms. Marx had supposedly meant only that the workers should retain dominant political and economic influence after the socialist revolution. The other social classes would not be disenfranchised, and Kautsky repeated that the Paris Commune – which had earned Marx's approval – had not abolished the voting rights of the middle classes.[29] Lenin retorted that dictatorship meant dictatorship and that Marx knew the meaning of the word.[30] Kautsky rejected this interpretation, he argued, because he abhorred violent revolution.[31] Lenin had a point here. Marx and Engels wrote much on the desirability of violence to transform society whereas Kautsky assumed that, once the German imperial monarchy had been overthrown, the working class could advance to power by parliamentary means.[32] Yet Lenin, too, was not wholly convincing; for it is far from clear that the co-founders of Marxism consistently demanded a formal class dictatorship for the achievement of socialism.[33] Lenin was chancing his arm intellectually. He declared, as if the point was self-evident, that Marx failed to demand the disenfranchisement of the Parisian middle classes in 1871 only because an exodus of them from the capital had already occurred.[34] This was sheer speculation; and, if a calmer consideration of the texts of Marx and Engels had been imposed on Lenin, he would have lost the debate through his over-statements and distortions.

Presumably he calculated that his tirades would distract from his weaknesses in logic and substance. The polemic had started at full blast on the opening pages. Utopian menace was conveyed by language owing much to the German aggregations of Hegel and Marx and by an intolerance reminiscent of Luther, Calvin or Torquemada: 'The working class cannot realise its worldwide-revolutionary aim without waging a merciless war with this renegacy, lack of character, servility to opportunism and unparalleled theoretical vulgarisation of Marxism.'[35] The strongest sections of the booklet lie with Lenin's demonstration that Kautsky had expunged the arguments for violent revolution and dictatorship from his presentation of Marxism. These were merely a starker repetition of *The State and Revolution*. Weakness was most remarkable in Lenin's replies to Kautsky's comments on Lenin himself. Lenin's evasiveness was considerable. His first ploy was to claim that Kautsky idealised 'bourgeois democracy'. Kautsky had allegedly forgotten about the repression of striking workers in the USA and overlooked the secret methods of diplomacy among the imperialist powers.[36] This charge was unfair. Kautsky had always claimed that the existing freedoms of capitalist states needed to be widened and deepened.[37] Lenin was being hypocritical, too, inasmuch as his security troops had recently fired on crowds of workers and his diplomats had made unpublicised deals with the German emperor. His assurance that Sovnarkom's regulations on freedom of assembly were '*a million times* more democratic' than those of capitalist governments was cant.[38] He was being so outrageous because he wanted to influence socialist opinion in western and central Europe. *Proletarian Revolution and Kautsky the Renegade* was quickly translated and dispatched abroad. Lenin pretended that things were happier in Soviet Russia than Kautsky rightly contended. But this distortion of reality was not undertaken exclusively in the interests of the international communism. Lenin was also writing for his own Bolsheviks. They knew the reality of 'Soviet power'. They had suppressed soviets and labour organisations which had turned against Bolshevism. If any of them had doubts about official policies, Lenin's booklet was meant to dispel them. Any rhetorical device was acceptable in this cause.

For instance, Kautsky indicated that the social trends in advanced capitalist societies were moving away from a neat polarisation between 'the proletariat' and 'the bourgeoisie'. Intermediate groups were becoming a substantial segment of the population, and the working class did not constitute the majority of any country. Consequently a 'dictatorship of the proletariat' in Germany would be a dictatorship by a social minority.[39] Lenin's retort was devious. He correctly claimed that not even *The State and Revolution* had explicitly demanded the disenfranchisement of the middle classes in all countries: 'And now it must be said that the question of the limitation of the suffrage is national-specific and is not a general question of dictatorship.'[40] Lenin omitted to add that the same work had urged the investment of all

authority in class-based mass organisations which refused membership
and participation to 'the bourgeoisie'.

He also entirely neglected to confront the implications of the
sociology adduced by Kautsky. The inevitable bipartition of capitalist
societies into two separate classes, the proletariat and the bourgeoisie,
remained axiomatic for him. His booklet, like *The State and
Revolution*, was a believer's exegesis. Kautsky had posed a substantive
question: why did prudence require the disenfranchisement of a
Russian bourgeoisie which by Lenin's own acknowledgement was
weak? Lenin replied only with another question, asking whether
Kautsky had forgotten that Marx and Engels had asserted that
societies were run to the benefit of their ruling classes.[41] Similarly
Kautsky queried the sense of a 'transition to socialism' in Russia on the
premise that a European socialist revolution was imminent. What if
such a revolution, as the Mensheviks had asked in 1917, did not occur?
What were the signs that this revolution was within sight? Lenin's
response gave no substantive exposition, but complained that Kautsky
had broken with Marxism since a belief in the dawn of socialism as
being nigh was a contemporary Marxist commonplace.[42] Lenin
inconsequentially declared that the Bolsheviks had never offered a
precise schedule for revolution in Europe.[43] Kautsky also denounced
the Bolshevik party's dispersal of the Constituent Assembly. Lenin
replied that throughout 1917 he had declared that soviets represented a
higher type of representative political institution than the Assembly.[44]
This was an accurate account of his past statements. But it evaded
Kautsky's other charge that the Bolsheviks had generally given the
impression that they were committed to abiding by the results of the
Constituent Assembly elections.[45]

Lenin sustained his haranguing rhetoric to the end of his booklet.
Kautsky naïvely expected to end world wars without the need for
socialist revolutions.[46] Kautsky had become stupid; he could not
understand that the equalisation of peasant landholdings was not
economically regressive since, in the long term, it would allow the
peasants to aggregate themselves into ever larger units of production.[47]
Kautsky was disingenuous in criticising the Bolsheviks for imposing a
dictatorship of the proletariat upon a largely agrarian country; he knew
very well that the Bolsheviks aimed at an alliance of the urban workers
with the rural poor.[48]

Proletarian Revolution and Kautsky the Renegade made and makes
dispiriting reading for anyone not already an enthusiastic Leninist. The
brighter side of *The State and Revolution*, such as it was, had virtually

disappeared. Offered as a review of Kautsky's booklet, Lenin's chapters in reality evaded the points made by both Kautsky and Martov in recent months. For example, Lenin did not consider the demographic shifts in advanced capitalist countries or the possibility that workers themselves might have different aspirations and interests. He offered no theory of politics in industrial states. Parties, pressure groups, organisational hierarchies, inter-institutional rivalries – which were raised as problems by Kautsky in particular – were overlooked.[49] He did not even mention terror despite its widening application in Soviet-occupied areas. Here a comparison with Trotski is apposite. Trotski announced that intense political conflicts inevitably involve recourse to terrorist methods. This, as he stated in his shamelessly-entitled booklet *Terrorism and Communism*, had occurred in both the English and American Civil Wars. Trotski asserted that the Bolsheviks were merely following precedents.[50] But Lenin wanted to practise terror without theoretical justification or political advertisement. His own booklet was an intellectually thin, self-serving piece of propaganda without the few insights that his forays into political science had displayed in 1917. The leader of Bolshevism had withdrawn into a mental stockade whence he never emerged.[51]

TERROR

The attempt on Lenin's life left him poorly for some weeks. A bullet was removed from his side; the one which was lodged in his skull was thought too dangerous to touch. He had had a lucky escape. The person who fired the shot had come within inches of killing him. He could not return to political meetings until 16 September 1918 – and then only briefly.[52] Meanwhile the All-Russian Central Executive Committee called for reprisals to be taken against the régime's enemies on the day of the shooting. *Pravda* even implied that the bourgeoisie as a class should be exterminated, and Zinoviev repeated the suggestion in Petrograd.[53]

Social échelons higher than the bourgeoisie had gone unmentioned by Lenin; but, out of public sight, he had been scrutinising them. Nikolai II and the Imperial family had been moved around the country since the February Revolution of 1917. On 30 April 1918 they were transferred to the Ipatev House outside Ekaterinburg in the Urals.[54] What to do with the former Emperor was a recurrent question among leading Bolsheviks. As the régime's military encirclement and political isolation increased, discussions became frantic. Trotski fancied a show trial in Moscow; he felt that the Bolsheviks should repeat and improve upon the judicial proceedings mounted against Louis XVI in Paris in 1793.[55] Sverdlov told the Central Committee on 19 May 1918 that a definitive decision was needed about 'what to do with Nikolai'.[56] Exactly what was decided, and when it was decided, has not yet come to light. But a contingency plan was indubitably worked out,[57] and liaison about it between the Central Committee and Ekaterinburg was maintained through Urals Regional Committee members Filipp Goloshchekin and G. V. Safarov. Goloshchekin visited the capital at the start of July,[58] Meanwhile Sverdlov continued to report to central state bodies on developments.[59] Both he and Lenin worried lest the anti-Bolshevik forces, at least those which were not led by socialists,[60] might seek to restore the Romanovs to their throne. A telegram came from Safarov and Goloshchekin on 16 July, which informed the Moscow and Petrograd party leadership that the military situation in the Urals had worsened for the Bolsheviks. The request was made to implement the detailed arrangements made by Goloshchekin on his earlier trip to Moscow.[61] Almost certainly this form of words was a demand for permission to put the contingency plan into effect and kill the Romanovs. In the early hours of 17 July, the functionaries of party and soviet in the Urals woke the Imperial family from their beds, hustled them to a convenient room in the Ipatev House and shot them.[62]

Lenin kept his distance from this act of terror. The pretence was maintained by Sverdlov that the central authorities had merely been informed about the shooting after it had taken place.[63] Lenin did not even comment on the event: through to the end of the year he worried lest the peasants might turn against Sovnarkom as a government of regicides.[64] But the extermination of the Romanovs was to his political liking; and, on a more personal plane, he can hardly have forgotten that it had been Nikolai II's father who had signed the death warrant of Lenin's older brother Aleksandr in 1887. He had never had qualms about terrorist methods if he deemed them pragmatically useful.[65] Nor did he demur from the inauguration, in his absence, by Sovnarkom on 5 September of a Red Terror. The decree was occasioned by the attempt on his life; it was signed by People's Commissar of Justice D. I. Kurski and People's Commissar of Internal Affairs G. I. Petrovski.[66] The fact that Moisei Uritski was assassinated in Petrograd on the same day as Lenin was wounded in Moscow strengthened the suspicion among Bolsheviks that a co-ordinated terrorist campaign was in process.[67]

The Red Terror led to the summary execution of perhaps as many as 1300 prisoners at the hands of the Petrograd Cheka.[68] Bloodletting on a vast scale occurred across the country. Prisons were emptied as prisoners were arbitrarily put against the wall and shot. The institutional tussle between the Cheka and the People's Commissariat of Justice temporarily ceased since Kurski as Justice Commissar had co-signed the decree on terror. Dzierzynski's deputy Martyn Latsis urged his subordinates to take a horrendously simple approach to class struggle in November 1918: 'We are not waging war on individal persons. We are exterminating the bourgeoisie as a class. During the investigation, do not look for evidence that the accused acted in deed or word against Soviet power. The first questions you ought to put are: to what class does he belong? What is his origin? What is his education or profession? And it is these questions that ought to determine the fate of the accused.'[69] Dzierzynski was not as categorical; but as late as May 1920 he called openly for 'the terrorisation, arrests and extermination of enemies of the revolution on the basis of their class affiliation or of their pre-revolutionary roles'.[70] The number of such abuses is as yet unascertained. Countless killings happened, and some were accompanied by physical torture. The Bolsheviks of Nolinsk went so far as to offer a description and justification of gruesome methods of torment in order to terrify the local residents into submission.[71]

The summons to torture was distasteful even to the Central Committee, and a political commission was established on 25 October 1918 to oversee the Cheka's work. Its members were Lev Kamenev, Iosif Stalin and D. I. Kurski.[72] This was a significant choice. Kurski had gained second breath on the issue of the Red terror. As Justice Commissar, he wanted to curtail the Cheka's power in favour of his own Commissariat. Kamenev was appalled by the rapid extension of Dzierzynski's powers. He led a small group of Bolshevik leaders in Moscow who questioned whether the Cheka should be allowed to kill the people it arrested without handing them over for due investigation and trial. Stalin was the commission's only member who could be expected to provide Dzierzynski with unconditional support: he had sent a telegram immediately after the attempt on Lenin's life demanding 'open mass systematic terror against the bourgeoisie and its agents'.[73]

But Stalin was not in a minority among the most influential members of the Central Committee. Lenin had given Dzierzynski firm support in the past and did not withhold it after August 1918. He chose 7 November, the day of celebration of the October Revolution (after the

change of calendar from the Julian to the Georgian), to address
Chekists: 'What surprises me in the wailing about the mistakes of the
Cheka is the inability to place the question in a larger perspective. Here
they are picking on the Cheka's individual mistakes, sobbing and
fussing about them.'[74] A *carte blanche* was written out for continued
excesses. Lenin had been doing this privately before the assassination
attempt. Until midsummer he had joked approvingly about the need
for a policy of social extermination to Isaak Steinberg, a Left Socialist
Revolutionary and People's Commissar of Justice at the time. But
Lenin and Dzierzynski were held in check by Left Socialist-
Revolutionary inhibitions about expanding the range of arbitrary
violence. The schism between the Bolsheviks and the Left Socialist
Revolutionaries freed Lenin's hands in practice. On 26 June, he had
written bluntly to Petrograd: 'Comrade Zinoviev! Only today we have
heard in the Central Committee that the *workers* in Petrograd wanted
to respond to the murder of Volodarski with mass terror and that you
(not you personally but the Central Committee and City Committee
leaders in Petrograd) restrained them. I assertively protest! We are
compromising ourselves: we threaten mass terror even in the
resolutions of the Soviet, but when it comes to action, we put a brake
on the revolutionary and *entirely* correct initiative of the masses. This is
im-pos-sible!'[75]

It was Lenin's understanding that the mayhem wreaked upon certain
social classes regardless of the attitudes of individual members of those
classes would give a salutary lesson that the Soviet authorities meant
business. Failure to undertake a Red terror would only encourage the
Whites to undertake theirs: 'The terrorists will think us wet rags.'[76]
Lenin wanted to get his retaliation in first. Uncontrolled carnage on a
class-based premise was desirable. It was a necessary weapon of the
dictatorship of the proletariat. Lenin had belonged in his youth to
Russian populist groups espousing terrorism. His brother had been
hanged as a terrorist. He had eulogised terror in 1905 as a highly
desirable means of expunging counter-revolution. He had sketched,
briefly, the possibilities of its use in 1917; and, after the October
Revolution, he had installed a terror apparatus. By mid-1918 his itch to
go further was ungoverned.

He was not alone. Zinoviev, after his reprimand by Lenin for being a
softy, pushed for a reinforcement of the Cheka in Petrograd.[77] Stalin
was to load hundreds of ex-Imperial officers in the Red Army on the
Southern front on to a barge on the river Volga with the intention of
drowning them. Only a last-minute telegram from Moscow prevented

their death.[78] Trotski was not much gentler. His method of restoring morale to panicking troops facing the Czechoslovak legion was to introduce exemplary executions; he was also impatient with those who interceded on behalf of persons threatened by the Cheka (unless they happened to be potentially useful commanders for the Red Army).[79] Stalin and Trotski made Lenin seem almost benign. He regularly wrote to the Cheka about politically harmless individuals who came to his attention.[80] A particular engineer or writer or civil servant might emerge blinking to the light of day, after languishing for months in prison, because of Lenin's recommendation. Yet this was justice by whim, and was recognised for what it was by Kamenev. The problem was that Kamenev was outnumbered in the inner counsels of the Bolshevik central party leadership. Only Bukharin agreed with him. *Pravda*, edited by Bukharin, carried a number of critical articles in late 1918. M. S. Olminski was especially hostile to the Cheka. But Dzierzynski continued to protect his apparatus and his personnel with success. Russia was awash with the blood of the Cheka's victims.[81]

Kamenev saw that the key to a reversal of policy lay with getting Lenin to change his mind. The struggle was fought out in the Central Committee. This resulted in a minor victory for the anti-Cheka Bolsheviks: the Cheka had previously gloried in its licence to ignore other institutions. The principle came into usage that the organs of repression should be subordinate to regular supervision by the party. Changes were to be debated in the Central Committee and its inner subcommittees.[82]

Yet it was Dzierzynski who, on 2 October 1918, was asked to draw up a draft code for the Cheka.[83] Kamenev fought back; and, by the turn of the year, he was making some progress with Lenin. On 4 February 1919 the Central Committee determined that the function of sentencing and execution should be transferred from the Cheka to revolutionary tribunals.[84] Bukharin was appointed as a kind of political watchdog over the Cheka's central activities.[85] This was hardly a reversion to due judicial process. Bukharin as an individual could not be acquainted with all abuses, and arbitrary, hasty decisions remained intrinsic to the Bolshevik party's policy. Terror was modified, not abolished. Lenin's speeches were peppered with exculpations of the Cheka. Dzierzynski secured his support in expanding its official powers again (and there had in any case been little change in practice). On 11 June 1919 the Central Committee re-equipped the Cheka with the right to investigate and execute a range of offenders from armed insurrectionaries to cocaine-dealers.[86] Dzierzynski had requested that fraudsters in the state administration and the families of persons found to have gone over the Whites ought also to be subject to summary execution by his officials. The Central Committee baulked only at the inclusion of the families of those joining the Whites. Kamenev's short campaign was resisted.[87]

Under Lenin's protection the terror proceeded undisturbed in the Civil War. He had no more harmonious relationship with any other central party leader than with Dzierzynski. Trotski, Stalin and Kamenev all gave him occasional problems. Dzierzynski was at pains to consult Lenin on his schemes (and Kamenev's opposition made Dzierzynski ask frequently for formal sanction for the Cheka's methods and plans).[88] Thus on 26 November 1919 he requested that a secret instruction should be granted for the organisation of a new Red mass terror – as if such a terror was not in continuous operation. The Central Committee declined to comply.[89]

Perhaps Lenin for once refused to support him adequately on this occasion. But the tension between Lenin and Dzierzynski, if it existed, was negligible. Apparently Lenin felt that the Cheka's affairs were best handled between them rather more informally. A minimum of open discussion was required. Such documentation as has become available indicates how deeply Lenin involved himself. His imaginativeness as an overseer of terror was considerable. At a governmental meeting in August 1920 he passed the following note to a colleague: 'A beautiful plan. Finish it off *together* with Dzierzynski. Disguised as 'Greens' (and we'll pin this on them subsequently), we'll advance for 10–20 versts and hang the kulaks, priests, landowners. The prize: 100,000 roubles for every man hanged.'[90] The Greens were small rural groups of fighters who resisted both the Reds and Whites in the Civil War, and they functioned in their native areas. Lenin wanted mass killings to take place while shielding the Reds from guilt. The official figures on deaths at the hands of the Cheka in 1918-1920 are derisively small: 12,733. The real number may never be known. Some estimates would put it as high as 30,000.[91] The extent of the Cheka's effectiveness in intimidating actual and potential opposition in the Red-occupied areas can only be surmised.

But Kamenev had a point in arguing that a licentious gang of Chekists in each town was not the exclusive and indispensable way to secure acquiescence. Was Lenin acting exclusively out of an intellectual conviction that the Revolution itself would expire unless protected by mass terror? He had personal experience of the Cheka's arbitrariness. For his own cousin, the lawyer Viktor Ardashev, was butchered in

Ekaterinburg in mid-1918 despite innocence of any charges laid against him. Lenin enquired about his whereabouts too late to save him.[92] But not even deaths in his own family deflected Lenin from his policy; and, consciously or not, he even relished the violence. His instructions to the Penza Bolshevik leaders on 11 August 1918 are testimony to this: 'Hang no fewer than a hundred well-known kulaks, rich-bags and blood-suckers (and be sure that the hanging takes place in full view of the people).' He wanted to terrorise the rich, but also to intimidate the very people in whose name he had seized power. For the sake of clarity he added: 'Do it so that for hundreds of kilometres around the people might see, might tremble!'[93] In October 1919, when Petrograd was under threat from White General Yudenich, his plan as proposed to Trotski had been more straightforward but still grimmer: 'If the attack is begun, is it impossible to mobilise another 20 thousand Petrograd workers plus 10 thousand members of the bourgeoisie, set up cannons behind them, shoot a few hundred of them and obtain a real mass impact upon Yudenich?'[94]

WAR AND ARMISTICE

As violence increased in Russia, it was about to decline in the rest of Europe. The Great War was reaching its climax. The Bolsheviks were distant spectators: nothing they did after the Brest-Litovsk treaty of March 1918 directly affected the outcome; Russia had withdrawn from the Eastern front. Yet there was an indirect impact. The German high command, after the treaty's signature, could transfer dozens of divisions to fight the British and French forces. Summer on the Western front was recognised by Ludendorff and Hindenburg as the final trial of strength. Military morale was still high among the German commanders and their troops.

Political confidence remained high among the Bolsheviks about the international situation; their conviction that European socialist revolution was inevitable was undimmed. The Brest-Litovsk treaty had been signed only because the German, French, Austrian, Italian and British popular insurrections against capitalism had been 'delayed'. Lenin had been less taken aback by the postponement than any of his colleagues except for Iosif Stalin; for he had often warned since 1914 that the epoch of European socialist revolution might involve a series of wars, both international and civil, stretching over many years. There might also be a Second World War (and here his glacial intellect was perceptive in contrast with the rhetoric of politicians proclaiming that the Great War would be the last war of any kind).[95] The problem was that no one could predict when socialist revolutions in Europe would occur. Ever since the October Revolution Lenin had impressed upon his party that a precise schedule could not be formulated. In his open letter to 'American workers' on 20 August 1918, he went further: 'We take a gamble on the inevitability of international revolution but this does not mean that we are so stupid as to place a stake on the inevitability of revolution within a *definite* short time.'[96] This was a phrasing he never repeated. He had implied that European socialist revolution was something that he hoped for but could not guarantee. Probably it was clumsy, hasty writing rather than deliberate reflection. Everything else written by him around this time demonstrated a continuing faith in revolution across the continent.

He would have had a harder time keeping his party to toe the line of Brest-Litovsk if the Civil War had not monopolised its energies in the latter months of 1918. The German summer offensive on the Western front was turning into defeat. The Allies took Peronne on 1 September, St Quentin on 2 October and the great industrial city of Lille on 17 October. Already on 4 October the German government enquired about terms for a possible armistice. The Kiel naval garrison mutinied on 28 October; but, although the army's discipline held out, Ludendorff and Hindenburg advised the Kaiser that surrender was inevitable. Wilhelm II abdicated on 9 November and a German republic was proclaimed. An armistice came into effect on 11 November.[97]

These world-changing events made no appearance on the Bolshevik Central Committee agenda-sheet through to the end of the year.[98] There was no decline of interest in Germany; but Lenin and his colleagues could not be certain, at least until the first week of November, that the German military machine was irreparably harmed and incapable of turning its power against Moscow. Communications between Moscow and Berlin were fragile. Few visitors got through from Germany, and newspapers arrived often with several days' delay. The main channel was through the Berlin office of Soviet representative Adolf Ioffe; and his correspondence with Lenin and People's Commissar Georgi Chicherin was the source of the Kremlin's information.[99] Lenin was unconvinced that Ioffe had a proper mastery over the necessary detail.[100] Constantly he urged him in Berlin, as well as Berzins in Berne and Vorovski in Stockholm, to spare no expense to bring about revolution abroad.[101] The problem was the absence of a large communist organisation in Germany. Lenin saw the Spartakusbund, which was a splinter group of the old German Social-Democratic Party led by Rosa Luxemburg and Karl Liebnecht, as the likeliest ally; and Ioffe was instructed to start talks with them on 20 September.[102] These far-left socalists were vital to the international strategy of Bolshevism. The struggle against Karl Kautsky had to be reinforced. Lenin wrote impatiently to Sverdlov on 1 October: 'Things have so "accelerated" in Germany that we too must not fall behind them. But today we have already fallen behind.' Statements on policy had to be prepared very quickly. Lenin sensed that a German October could follow the Russian October of the previous year: 'The international revolution has got nearer *over the past week* to such an extent that account has to be taken of it as an event of the days immediately ahead.'[103]

As opportunities increased in Berlin, Lenin demanded theoretical clarity. He badgered Ioffe and Berzins to secure publication of a German edition of *The State and Revolution*. Simultaneously he demanded that new items by Kautsky and Martov on Marxism, on Bolshevik ideas and on dictatorship should be forwarded to him.[104] Lenin was as game as ever for doctrinal disputation, and upbraided Ioffe for alleged lethargy: 'We should be playing the role of a bureau for work with ideas of an international character, but we're doing nothing!'[105] It was comic of Lenin to think that his abstruse treatise would make much impact on politics in Berlin. Yet in this instance he was not searching for a mass readership. He especially wanted to win over Rosa Luxemburg and other far-left thinkers to his own variant of Marxism; and he assumed that a broad political movement could quickly be formed if they joined his side.

Lenin meant business. On 1 October he wrote confidentially to Sverdlov and Trotski in his staccato style: 'No alliances either with Wilhelm's government or with a government of Wilhelm II + Ebert and the other scoundrels. But we *are beginning* to get ready a fraternal alliance, *grain*, military assistance for the German working masses, for the German labouring millions now that they have started up with their own spirit of indignation (which as yet is *only* a spirit). All of us shall give our lives in order to help the German workers in the cause of advancing the revolution that has begun in Germany.'[106] His words repay scrutiny. A Soviet republic that had a serious shortfall in food supplies was being expected by its leading politician to feed a foreign working class. A 'tenfold' intensification of requisitioning was anticipated by him.[107] Thus the Russian peasant was to give sustenance to both the Russian and the German worker. At the same time Lenin urged that the Red Army should increase the dimensions of conscription 'tenfold'. Accordingly there should be three million troops under Trotski's control by spring 1919. Such plans were tied by him explicitly to the tasks of the 'international workers' revolution'.[108] Brest-Litovsk was but a temporary suspension of his rage to spread his variant of socialism abroad. Peasant revolts against the Soviet authorities were a serious problem in late 1918; but Lenin was willing to take the risk of further alienating his rural population by requisitioning and conscribing peasants ever more intensively.

At last he could throw off restraint. In October he had signed a financial deal with the German government for the delivery of 80,000 tons of coal to Russia;[109] and, in return, he ensured that the Bolsheviks of Ukraine did not try to attack the German troops.[110] The Kaiser's abdication led to the formation of a provisional government under right-wing social-democrats Friedrich Ebert and Philipp Scheidemann; it also included representatives from the Independent German Social-Democratic Party, which had been founded in 1917 by Karl Kautsky and Hugo Haase in disgust at the German Social-Democratic Party's support of the Kaiser. To Lenin it seemed that the developments in Germany in the November were a compressed version of what had happened over several months after the February Revolution of 1917 in Petrograd. A seizure of power by the left-wing socialist radicals was consequently to be encouraged. Sovnarkom regarded the treaty of Brest-Litovsk as a dead letter. It also discarded its supplementary obligations as agreed with the German government on 27 August 1918.[111]

Lenin spoke on Germany for all his colleagues engaged in the Civil War or in other political duties.[112] For him, the collapse of the Kaiser's military and political power proved that the Bolsheviks had been right to overthrow Aleksandr Kerenski's cabinet and inaugurate the epoch of European socialist revolution.[113] Towards the end of December 1918 Lenin scribbled a note to Chicherin as People's Commissar of External Affairs suggesting that the time had come to found a new International, the Third International, which would replace the Second International which – in Lenin's repeated description – had betrayed socialism when most of its member parties had voted war credits to their respective governments in 1914. The long-proclaimed intention to create an alternative left-wing radical organisation was to be fulfilled. Lenin disclaimed personal or chauvinistic purposes. The founding

Congress, he proposed, could be held 'in Berlin (openly) or in Holland (*secretly*), let's say by 1. ii. 1919'.[114] He was buoyed up by the intimations of further revolutionary upheaval. The Kiel mutineers were still in revolt. A Soviet (or Rat) of Workers' and Soldiers' Deputies was created in Berlin. Radical shop stewards became influential amongst the workers in the great factories. Rosa Luxemburg and Karl Liebknecht had been released from prison some weeks before Wilhelm II's abdication: Lenin welcomed them as future comrades in the cause of the Third International and European socialist revolution.

The hand he extended to the Spartakists was surprising in the light of past disputes. Liebknecht, while being motivated by ideas, was not an original writer. Luxemburg by contrast was a fertile theorist and propagandist, and her strategy for revolution differed significantly from Lenin's. Before the Great War she had clashed with him over his prescriptions for clandestine socialist parties, over his emphasis on leadership and hierarchy, over what she described as an underestimation of the potentiality of the 'masses'. She had also criticised Lenin's nationality policy on the grounds that is conceded too much to nationalist aspiration; and with equal fervour she ridiculed his positive attitude to the capacity of the peasantry to help to advance the cause of socialism.[115]

These divergences between Lenin and Luxemburg did not cease in 1917. She continued from her prison cell to have her doubts about the October Revolution. Like the Left Communists in Russia, she regarded Brest-Litovsk as a betrayal of international socialism which would hamper the making of socialist revolution in Germany.[116] She also detested the dictatorial bent of Bolshevism. Universal-suffrage elections, she believed, were intrinsic to the values of socialism; and Bolshevik repression, including terror, was a disgraceful mistake.[117] Nor did Luxemburg warm to the Decree on Land announced by Lenin on 26 October 1917. Her feeling was that the redistribution of agricultural land among peasant households was economically regressive inasmuch as the average size of units of production would be reduced.[118] She retained her objections on release from prison. While Lenin hoped that the Spartakists would form a German Communist Party, Luxemburg wished – if a new party was to be formed – to call it the German Socialist Party so as to dissociate herself fully from the communist Lenin. When the matter was discussed by her comrades on 30–31 December, she and Leo Jogiches were outvoted.[119] The German Communist Party came into existence. Even so, she strove to prevent the inauguration of the Third International for fear of excessive influence being exerted by the Bolsheviks. Once again she was outvoted; but she ensured that Hugo Eberlein, the German Communist Party's delegate to the meeting of communist and pro-communist organisations projected by Lenin in Petrograd, was mandated to make only minimal concessions to the Bolsheviks.[120]

Luxemburg and Liebknecht would have made uncomfortable political partners for Lenin. The faultiness of information about them in late 1918 presumably caused him to drop his ideological guard. He continued to assume, as he had in 1917, that his disagreements with them were trivial in comparison with his agreements. He had always found it easier to make compromises with rival socialists abroad than with those he encountered in the Russian empire. If Luxemburg had been operating in Russia rather than Germany, she would have been under arrest as a subversive. The German Right took the same attitude. A rising against the Berlin authorities was organised by the German communists on 6 January 1919. Gustav Noske summoned the police and the demobilised anti-socialist veterans known as the *Freikorps* to defend the government. Luxemburg thought the rising premature and dangerous. But Noske's soldiers sought her and Liebknecht out. They were murdered on 15 January. The rising was bloodily suppressed. Jogiches, too, was killed a few days later.

Lenin treated them as heroes in death. In February he supported a scheme to bring out editions of the complete works of Luxemburg and Liebknecht.[121] He mentioned them only in the most reverential terms in public. There is no evidence that Lenin's attitude was not genuine. He had pinned his strategical expectations, even after Brest-Litovsk, upon a successful far-left socialist revolution in Berlin, and he had long recognised that Luxemburg and Liebknecht were its likeliest leaders. He may well also have believed that such disagreements as he had with Luxemburg – insofar as he was acquainted with her position – were not insurmountable. Ever the optimist, he probably believed that he could pull her round to his policies on organisation, dictatorship, national self-determination and the peasants. Be that as it may, the murder of Luxemburg and Liebknecht removed a problem that would have attended the creation of the Third International. Furthermore, the suppression of the Berlin Rising ruled out any thought of holding its First Congress in Germany. Instead it would be held in Moscow. Lenin had been urging German far-left socialists to take power; but the sheer amateurism of the Berlin rising, furthermore, must have convinced him that an injection of Bolshevik practicality was vital to a healthy revolutionary movement in central Europe. A further stage in the self-assertion of Bolshevism, its achievements and merits, was heralded.[122]

REDS AND WHITES

Among the faults of the Spartakists had been their lack of organisation and preparation and their underestimation of the forces ranged against them; and Lenin was right to highlight them. With no greater excuse he failed to anticipate the abrupt transformation in the Russian Civil War in the last two months of 1918. The earlier fighting had been mainly between armies subordinate to two socialist administrations: the Sovnarkom of the Bolsheviks and the Komuch of the Socialist Revolutionaries. Trotski and the Red Army had pushed Komuch out of Samara. But then yet another military menace revealed itself: the White army of Admiral Kolchak. His officers abhorred socialism, aiming to restore the social and economic order prevailing before 1917. They were based in the Siberian city of Omsk, and planned to invade central Russia.

Lenin admitted how shaken he was in a telegram to Trotski on 13 December 1918: 'The news from near Perm is extremely alarming. Danger threatens it. I fear that we've forgotten about the Urals.'[123] Kolchak had seized power in Siberia on 17 November. Previously he had been in uneasy alliance with the Komuch administration when it fled from the Volga region. But he quickly rid himself of them. Socialist-Revolutionary leaders in Siberia were arrested. In the territory under Kolchak's control a violent restoration of industrialists and bankers began; and he even expropriated the legally-owned land of local peasants on behalf of landlords whose land was located elsewhere.[124] Bolsheviks and active trade unionists were executed. This was counter-revolution with a vengeance. Meanwhile General Krasnov, the Don Cossack leader, pushed northward to the outskirts of Voronezh. And yet another White force established by Imperial officers under General Denikin – after Kornilov's death – moved upon the towns of the North Caucasus. His Volunteer Army was poised to invade central Russia the following year. The British still held Arkhangelsk, the French Odessa. Furthermore, Ukrainian nationalists under Simon Petliura filled the gap left by the withdrawal of the German forces by proclaiming a Ukrainian People's Republic. A Directory was set up in Kiev. Thus the Soviet republic of Russia was reduced to a territory little greater than the mediaeval principality of

Muscovy. Kolchak, styling himself as Supreme Ruler, grasped his chance. In a rapid movement he threw a large armed contingent at Perm in the central Urals. The Reds retreated in disorder on 13 December 1918. It was the greatest shock to Bolshevik morale since the Czechoslovak Legion's revolt in May. Kolchak looked set to overthrow Lenin.[125]

Yet both the chaos of communications and the country's political dismemberment meant that sudden, unpredicted changes in the military position were inevitable. Lenin's telegram did not reproach Trotski or the Red Army high command. It simply recognised that the Bolsheviks had been caught napping. Obviously the priority was to reinforce the Army in the Perm direction with all possible speed; and Lenin, with Sverdlov as co-signatory, made just this recommendation when the city fell to Kolchak.[126]

Yet these verbal exchanges were confidential: Lenin refrained from public commentary on Kolchak in the winter of 1918-1919.[127] He paid the closest attention to details of strategy and personnel behind the scenes. Even so, he did not treat the emergence of Kolchak and Denikin as a heaven-sent opportunity for propaganda. To be taken unawares was one thing; to ignore the possibility of enhancing the régime's popularity was quite another. The explanation as yet must be speculative. The suggestion that he was altogether too busy with his administrative duties is discountable since he made several speeches and wrote articles in the months after November 1918. If he could discourse on Liebknecht and Luxemburg, why not also on Kolchak? It is possible that he did not wish to sow panic among Muscovites. But this is not wholly plausible. Simultaneously he was allowing a map to be displayed near the Kremlin indicating the exact boundaries of Soviet-held territory. Information about the situation on the various fronts was widely available. Consequently perhaps the conundrum is ultimately resolvable by reference to Lenin's world-view. Since 1914 he had rejected all attempts to make distinctions between reactionaries, conservatives, liberals and anti-Bolshevik socialists; his political universe was Manichean. Kornilov the anti-democrat, for Lenin, had always stood secretly behind Kerenski the democrat.[128] Kolchak was simply a contemporary Kornilov. The coup against the Socialist Revolutionaries in Omsk made no great difference to Lenin's way of thinking, and he wasted scant words on it.

On the other hand, the practical consequences of the capture of Perm by the Whites undoubtedly horrified him. When Kazan fell to the Czechoslovak Legion, Lenin and his colleagues had hardly begun to reform their military and political machinery for war. Perm fell to Kolchak months after the taking of such measures. The Red Army and the civilian institutions had proved inadequate to their responsibilities. Further defeats occurred. The Volunteer Army under General Denikin took Pyatigorsk, an administrative centre in the North Caucasus, on 24 January 1919. Days later he moved into the oil-city of Grozny. The Don Cossacks were meanwhile causing difficulties for the Bolsheviks and their Red forces in the southern cities of the Volga; and the French had landed their naval squadron in Odessa on the Black Sea on 18 December 1918. When Lenin talked expectantly about the rise of German communism, his thoughts were a mixture of belief and and sheer desperation.

It was in this awful winter for Bolshevism that, for the first and last time, he contemplated territorial concessions to the Russian foes of the Soviet state. A domestic version of Brest-Litovsk was considered. The occasion was the conference arranged by the Allies with all the combatant forces in the Russian Civil War on Prinkipo island in the Sea of Marmora. The call went out on 23 January 1919. Georgi Chicherin, People's Commissar for External Affairs, telegrammed on 4 February that the Soviet government was willing to send representatives.[129] The terms approved by Lenin excluded neither the relinquishing of land to the Whites nor even an acceptance of responsibility for debts incurred by previous Russian governments. He surrounded the negotiations in secrecy. Open diplomacy, which had been a Bolshevik objective in 1917 and to a large extent practised in the Brest-Litovsk discussions, had long been abandoned. Lenin wanted no repetition of the searing controversy he had had with the Left Communists. Kolchak and Denikin might know about the Prinkipo offer; the Bolshevik party, apart from a few Central Committee members, were kept in the dark. And it was the Whites, not the Reds, who refused to deal at Prinkipo. They were for 'Russia One and Indivisible', and in any case perceived that any settlement with Lenin would last only so long as he felt too weak to attack them. They needed no lessons on Lenin's wiliness and ideological commitment, and his simultaneous convocation of the Congress of the Communist International put the matter beyond doubt for them.

The situation was less bleak for Lenin than it seemed. Ufa in the southern Urals was re-captured by the Reds as early as 30 December 1918. Kolchak, having taken Perm, was over-stretched and called a halt to his projected advance. To the north, in Arkhangelsk, the expected push against the Reds never happened; internal weakness and the unwillingness of the British to involve themselves to a great extent in the Civil War induced the local leader N. V. Chaikovski to depart for Paris to participate instead in the peace negotiations at Versailles. General Krasnov was repulsed from Tsaritsyn, and his previous readiness to treat with the Germans forced his resignation as Don Cossack leader on 15 February 1919. A southward thrust by Red forces into Ukraine, under the command of V. A. Antonov-Ovseenko, resulted in the seizure of Kiev. In Moscow an American emissary arrived, William Bullitt, to have talks in pursuit of a compromise between Soviet Russia and her enemies.[130]

No Bolshevik could yet be very optimistic. In the phrase of the day, Central Committee members in Moscow 'were sitting on their suitcases' through the winter. There could be no certainty that they would hold Moscow against Kolchak and Denikin, and Bolshevik families had to be ready to flee in an emergency. In March 1919 things took a turn for the worse. Kolchak had re-grouped his forces. Supplies and advice were coming through to him from the British (whose representative, General Knox, stayed by his side). Kolchak's initial target was Ufa. In the middle of the month his troops entered the town in triumph. A flurry of long-distance conversations between Lenin and Trotski led to an agreement that the crisis on the Eastern front was too severe for Trotski to be able to attend the forthcoming Eighth Party Congress. Rumours that Kolchak would soon rule from the Kremlin spread round Moscow. Lenin would have been the prime quarry of the Whites if ever they broke their way through to the capital. Nevertheless both he and his wife put on a brave face in their public appearances. If Trotski could live under the hail of real bullets while travelling in his train, this was the least that Sovnarkom's chairman could do to sustain morale. Indeed Krupskaya insisted on taking greater physical risks than Lenin: in 1919 she was to board a steamship from Moscow to conduct propaganda at the towns and cities on the river Volga.[131] It was a risk that he would never have run himself. As ever, he assumed that everything would go to the dogs if his presence at the helm of party and state were not to be maintained.

FEEDING RUSSIA

There is a recurrent supposition that Lenin resorted to force against the peasantry only under the most extreme pressure of Civil War.[132] This is not sustainable. For, when introducing the Food Supplies Dictatorship in midsummer 1918, he was still unbothered about the counter-revolutionary armies being formed in other parts of Russia: he even wanted to divert the People's Commissariat of Military Affairs into acting as the main agency of grain collection. Obviously he did not think at the time that Trotski would have other tasks, such as the defeat of well-organised armies, to discharge. Economics, not war, impelled him; and he would have moved to a Food Supplies Dictatorship even if there had been no Czechoslovak Legion, no Komuch, no Kolchak, Denikin and Yudenich. Indisputably the treaty of Brest-Litovsk had worsened the situation. Ukraine had been lost to Russia. Yet official opinion was adamant that, even so, there was just about enough surplus grain in the villages to cover the needs of consumers in towns and in those parts of the countryside which traditionally 'imported' agricultural products.[133] Lenin took space in *Pravda* to declare: 'There is enough grain for everyone.'[134]

Yet in the same article he sounded a warning: 'Catastrophe stands before you, it has advanced quite, quite close.'[135] All grain stocks in the Soviet republic had to be obtained by the People's Commissariat of Food Supplies without delay, or else there would be mass starvation. Lenin acknowledged that already there were 'revolts by people tormented by hunger'.[136] To this end he determined upon drawing up a comprehensive official policy. The piecemeal and sometimes contradictory measures of early 1918, he argued, had to give way to a Food Supplies Dictatorship. In Lenin's opinion, the objective had to be the centralisation of food supplies, the unification of the proletariat and the formation of organs of the village poor (and this was written just a few days before the decree on the *kombedy*).[137] The policy of the Central Committee was summarised by him emphatically: 'This means that all grain surpluses belong to the state.'[138] On 4 July Sovnarkom assigned 10 million roubles for the creation of agricultural communes: the transition to socialist ownership and production was to be intensified.[139] But the interests of most peasants, he asserted with equal firmness, would be protected. At the Fifth Congress of Soviets on 5 July he declared: 'It is untrue, and a thousand times untrue, that this is a struggle with the peasantry; and we don't have a disagreement with the middle peasants who have only infinitesimal surpluses.'[140]

On paper the achievements were substantial. By the end of 1918 there were nearly 140,000 committees of the village poor in European Russia; and 7370 peasant cells of the Bolshevik party had been established. 3366 collective farms had been formed in the same provinces. And two milliard roubles of industrial goods were dispatched to the countryside in exchange for the grain obtained.[141] The People's Commissariat of Food Supplies recorded its success. Total state procurements of grain in the financial year 1917-18 were 30 million puds, in 1918-1919 110 million puds. It was still not enough for the subsistence of the population in the Red-occupied areas.[142] Yet the auguries were not good about the peasantry's reaction. The typical effect of the peasant movement had been a redistribution of land, and the overwhelming majority of households had joined what Lenin would call the middling category. If it was true that the country had barely enough surplus grain to survive, then it stood to reason that 'middle peasants' would have to hand over substantial grain stocks.[143] The richer peasants known as kulaks, a diminished proportion of the peasantry, could not supply the entire state's needs. The People's Commissariat was not a sophisticated food-supplies apparatus. Even Lenin, supposedly the party's expert on the social and economic conditions of the peasantry, could define a middle peasant in highly general terms: 'Someone who does not sell his labour power is what we refer to as "middling".'[144] This was not a definition which would easily be applicable in the villages when the 70,000 worker members of the requisitioning detachments arrived on their brief and violent missions. Nor were the committees of the village poor very reliable. Lenin admitted that corruption flourished within them.[145] His own rhetoric did not induce the requisitioners to act cautiously. Class war on the kulaks was demanded. Ruthlessness; no mercy; a fight to the death: these were the common themes of his speeches.[146] Lenin did not want the middle peasants to be alienated; he said this openly, but not often.[147] The detachments were more impressed with the legal requirement that all grain surpluses were to be regarded as state property – and 'surpluses' were no more closely specified than 'middle peasants'.

Without acknowledging his own responsibility, Lenin excoriated the blunder of annoying the middle peasants on 6 August 1918. But his comments were not made public at the time.[148] Conferring with Food Supplies Commissar A. D. Tsyurupa, he finally issued an instruction forbidding the maltreatment of middle peasants on 18 August.[149] He also acted to allow middle peasants to be included in the committees of the village poor.[150] But the depredation of the countryside continued. Most peasants anyway disliked the Soviet government's attempt to introduce open social strife among the peasantry. The committees of the village poor were deeply resented; and yet nothing was done to restrain them. Grigori Zinoviev brought a motion before the Sixth

Congress of Soviets in November 1918 ratifying the transfer of much authority from the rural soviets to these same committees of the village poor.[151] But reports of the damage to the party's reputation done by the committees poured into Moscow. Abruptly, on 4 December 1918, a decree was passed over the signature of Yakov Sverdlov announcing their disbandment.[152]

Deeply implicated in establishing the committees, Lenin kept quiet about the fracas. He hated appearing either silly or apologetic; he had even defended the decision to increase their authority in November 1918.[153] Yet he saw that requisitioning had to be regularised. Nowhere near enough industrial goods were available to get peasants to release their grain voluntarily, and the requisitioning agencies had inadequate training and guidance as to how much grain to seize in each locality. Sovnarkom decided on a modification of policy on 11 January 1919. The essential ingredient was an annual total target of grain, subdivided into individual targets for each province. Subdivisions were to be made at each lower level of government. Every peasant land commune, at the bottom of this system of 'apportionment', was to bear collective responsibility for the rendering of a quota of grain. Severe sanctions were to be maintained for non-compliance; but the policy was designed to end the arbitrary despoiling of the peasantry that had occurred as well as to ensure that grain-deficient provinces were exempted.[154] Only twelve provinces entered the list of provinces to supply grain to the People's Commissariat of Food Supplies, and four Volga provinces under Bolshevik rule were expected to supply three fifths of the total.[155] Nevertheless 260 million puds was considerably less than what was needed to stave off widespread malnutrition.[156] Leading Bolsheviks were turning to an extremely small region to victual both the Red Army and the urban population of 'Sovdepiya'. Mercifully for them, the need to rely solely on Russia was disappearing. On 3 January 1919 the Red forces entered Kharkov in eastern Ukraine. By 5 February they were in Kiev. Sovnarkom's minutes are not detailed on the point; but it may well be that Lenin anticipated a resolution of the crisis in food supplies through the stocks of the Ukrainian peasantry.

Ukraine soon entered the calculations of the People's Commissariat of Food Supplies. Official optimism was restored. As ever, Sovnarkom had only the vaguest idea as to how much grain there was in which province. Guessing wildly, Lenin suggested on 19 February that the 'surpluses for the whole of the Ukraine should be defined at a maximum, for instance, of 500 million puds'. He urged that 'only a fifth or a tenth' should be taken. The rest should be left with the peasants for personal consumption and for the spring sowing.[157] He had begun to learn his lesson that the Civil War might be lost if greater care were not taken with the mass of the peasantry. Even so, decrees on the establishment of collective farms were issued in February 1919 despite the antagonism of most peasants.[158] Urban detachments were ill-informed as to the definition of a middle peasant (as Lenin was told to his face when he addressed the Petrograd Soviet on 13 March).[159] Lenin referred still to peasant revolts against the abuses of the food-supply commissars as kulak uprisings.[160] Much as he had done to pull his party back from disaster, he had not pulled even himself back far enough. Lenin the class warrior prevailed over Lenin the peasant's friend.

Meanwhile he kept up the appearance of being the protector of the workers. He had been wounded, and nearly killed, while addressing the work-force at the Mikhelson factory. But his statements lacked the specificity and incisiveness on industrial policy that he displayed about the party's measures for the countryside. Not for the first time the 'party of the workers' had more to say about the villages than the towns.[161] In the meetings of the Central Committee between the Brest-Litovsk treaty and the beginning of 1918 its agenda barely included the affairs of industry; and, when it did, the topics were not of primary significance.[162] In addition, his public pronouncements on the economy, beyond what he said about food supplies, were vague.[163] He called for discipline, for one-man management, for a rise in productivity, for self-sacrifice in the cause of the Civil War, for support of the party's policies. He did not immediately give up his idea that, since the contemporary advanced economies before the Great War had been operating on a global scale, capitalists should continue to be invited to invest in and reinforce Russian industry. On 16 May 1918, Sovnarkom under his chairmanship asked for a plan to be prepared on 'economic concessions' to be offered to private foreign companies.[164] Lenin was implicitly giving notice that he despaired of a *rapprochement* with Russian capitalism; and now he decided, despite the country's international travail, to attract industrial collaboration and capital investment from foreigners. He repeated this demand on 20 July when the plan remained to be submitted.[165] Evidently his colleagues could see that, during the Great War, substantial participation by even German entrepreneurs was likely to be negligible. Lenin, too, cooled towards the plan; he waited until nearly the end of the Civil War before re-heating his commitment.[166]

The emphasis in policy was shifted. Industrial nationalisation, which had been started with the October Revolution, was intensified. From 28 June 1918 a campaign was in existence to take all large-scale factories and mines into the hands of the state.[167] Sovnarkom took decisions on particular enterprises, and many leading Bolsheviks believed that the party was making a major advance towards socialism. For the former Left Communists, the policy was yet another reason for abandoning opposition to Lenin; it seemed to them that their industrial (as well as commercial and agricultural) recommendations were at last being implemented.[168] A wave of ideological euphoria swept through the Bolshevik party as it had previously in 1917.[169]

Lenin, while not being immune to the euphoria, pointedly refrained from endorsing the notion that the strengthened emphasis on industry was identifiable with the achievement of socialism. As Sovnarkom chairman, he was aware of the dire conditions in reality. It was already clear that the decline in industrial output was unlikely to be reversed. The total recorded for 1918 was down by fifty five per cent on the previous year.[170] Workers were fleeing the towns. The factory workforce dropped from 2.6 million to 1.3 million in the same twelve months.[171] Fuel was becoming so scarce that Lenin contemplated the purchase of coal from the Germans.[172] The drastically-reduced industrial sector experienced a massive loss in productivity. Nor was this any wonder. Hunger drove workers to make articles for personal barter during paid working time; and the exodus of workmates into both the countryside and the Red Army caused further disruption. The anti-capitalist measures of 1917-1918, moreover, had driven owners and resources out of economic activity. In practice, the government's priority was to nationalise enterprises mainly in order to possess the existing stocks of manufacture. A report on progress was already discussed at Sovnarkom on 29 July 1918.[173] Furthermore, guarantees were given to workers volunteering for the Red Army that places in employment would be reserved for them.[174] The life-and-death struggle against the anti-Bolshevik armies took precedence over industrial reconstruction. The fate of the October Revolution hung in the balance.

3 Only One Year

THE PARTY-STATE

Lenin founded a state on principles different from any which had existed. There had been states committed to a single militant ideology. This had been the case not only throughout the expansionist Muslim world in the era after Mohammed's death but also in the countries which rejected Catholicism for Protestantism in the sixteenth century. But no such state had been secular in avowed purpose, totally and aggressively anti-religious. Nor had any of them been dominated, as was Soviet Russia, by a single mass political party. The Bolsheviks were awesome pioneers in this respect as in many others. The 'party-state' was their invention.

They produced this political compound through experimentation. They had a general 'project' of revolution, but no elaborated plan of inter-institutional relationships. On coming to govern in October 1917, they had expected to squeeze power in the party's fist. The penetration of the old 'bourgeois' state by revolutionary means was a declared goal, and the Bolshevik party was determined to direct the process. There was no sophisticated theorising how to act. The assumption was that workers, soldiers and peasants would greet the October Revolution by participating actively in soviets and other sectional organisations. The Bolshevik party would send its representatives to serve and lead these organisations. A departure of men and women from party committees into jobs in the soviets had begun before the seizure of power on 25 October 1917; afterwards it turned into a mass exodus. The soviets had to be staffed quickly with the party's best cadres. Thus Lenin headed Sovnarkom, and local Bolshevik leaders moved effortlessly into the chairmanship of their regional, provincial and urban soviets. Complaints were made that 'party life', so lively in the early months after the monarchy's overthrow in the February Revolution, was declining into quiescence. A few secretaries held each party committee together between committee meetings which were held with increasing infrequency. The party was ceasing to operate as a distinct organisation.[1]

This did not bother leading Bolsheviks so long as the Revolution's triumphal advance continued and the party's representatives behaved harmoniously. The period had ended by the second half of 1918. Already in January and February, the Brest-Litovsk dispute had shaken the complacency of Lenin and his colleagues. Many party committees had challenged the official policy in favour of a peace treaty with the Germans for weeks after its signature; their members in local soviet offices disrupted the flow of governmental business. At the Seventh Party Congress, Yakov Sverdlov as Central Committee secretary had urged the imposition of 'iron discipline' and 'strict centralism'.[2]

No notice was taken of this for several months; not even Sverdlov exerted himself.[3] But it was a straw fluttering in the wind which became a hurricane when the Soviet régime's resources were thrust on to a war footing after the Czechoslovak Legion's revolt in midsummer 1918. Military co-ordination was a stimulus to reconsider the ties between and within institutions. The emergent Soviet state was very ramshackle. Old public bodies were retained and headed by Bolsheviks. New bodies were also formed. The Cheka and the Supreme Council of the National Economy were just two among several. No one, least of all Lenin, gave a second thought to demarcating the functions of all the institutions. Laws, decrees and informal instructions were not meant to offer legislative precision.[4] The people were meant to get on with 'revolution'. Activism was the party's imperative duty. Yet disputes about competence and accountability broke out. These were exacerbated by a staggering nonchalance about procedures at the central political level. In 1918, Lenin and his Sovnarkom colleagues were dispatching plenipotentiaries to bring order to food supplies or to transport. Local organs of administration were overridden.[5] Doing something, even something contradictory to something else being done by a comrade, was regarded as better than doing nothing. Again and again Lenin said he wanted deeds, not promises.[6]

Lenin did not like to delegate power, and he assumed that his personal word as a ruler counted for more than compliance with formal legislative and executive procedures. Always having despised parliamentary democracy, he and Sverdlov issued countless instructions without reference to the bodies whence they derived authority. They co-operated so well that critics charged them with having imposed a 'duumvirate'.[7] They passed important decrees to each other for co-signature. Lenin wrote as chairman of Sovnarkom, Sverdlov as secretary of the Party Central Committee or frequently as chairman of the Presidium of the Central Executive Committee of the Congress of Soviets.[8]

Both men were comfortable wielding power in this informal fashion as well as comfortable working with each other. Trotski was the sole Bolshevik leader with comparable influence in the latter months of 1918. He, too, found power to his liking in the Revolutionary-Military Council of the Republic. The division of responsibilities was a rough-and-ready affair. The Revolutionary-Military Council of the Republic was to oversee the military aspects of the Civil War, and the Council of Labour and Defence would take charge of economic organisation in the Red Army's rear while Sovnarkom handled the rest of governmental business.[9] No particular function, beyond rubber-stamping the wishes of these other bodies, was accorded to the Presidium of the Central Executive Committee of the Congress of Soviets; but the decline in the regularity of its meetings did not prevent Sverdlov from sending out commands in its name. Lenin, Trotski and Sverdlov also relied heavily on consultations among themselves – whether in corridors, on the telephone or by telegrams – in order to co-ordinate the supreme affairs of state. They all of them were centralisers by inclination. They had their disagreements, even disputes. But on the whole they tried to keep them out of the public's gaze. If a chink of light were to appear between the respective policies of the various central bodies, there would be no chance of bringing the chaotic, disobedient bodies to heel. The campaign for centralised control over soviets, trade unions, factory-workshop committees from Moscow continued. Regional, provincial, urban and district levels of administration were to respect the principle of hierarchy.[10]

But this objective was not rapidly achievable. Sverdlov's solution was that the party should insert itself more decisively into the process. He had said as much at the Seventh Party Congress in March 1918. His notion was that party life should be revived and that the committees of the party at each level of government should regularly and closely supervise the several governmental agencies. Not only arbitration but active direction should be imposed.[11] If Lenin with *What is to be Done?* in 1902 supplied the intellectual sperm, then Sverdlov's proposal was the potential organisational egg wherein would incubate the embryo of the new party-state.

But fertilisation did not quickly occur. Party bodies at the centre and in the localities failed to restore the vitality of 1917. The battles by the Volga necessitated the mobilisation of party cadres. Committees of the party perforce operated with ever fewer meetings and full-time staff; and the local party leaderships were drastically reduced in size by the call-ups into the forces. There was also a reduction in Moscow. The

Central Committee provided its own representatives to the Red Army and the governmental and party bodies in the provinces. For example, Zinoviev was left behind in Petrograd and Stalin became political commissar on the Southern front. Only six out of fifteen full members of the Central Committee stayed in the capital in the second half of 1918.[12] Military exigency prevented the central party leadership from gathering regularly. Central Committee members themselves did not much mind; but a different attitude grew in the provinces. It was all very well for Lenin to be complacent. He had inherited and retained a large bureaucratic apparatus, and was the linch-pin of central state discussions. Local Bolshevik leaders were run ragged by both their increasing duties and the loss of administrators to the Red Army. Lazar Kaganovich in Nizhni Novgorod and middle-ranking Bolsheviks such as N. Osinski and T. V. Sapronov in Moscow were prominent critics. They demanded that the party should recover its separate status and impose control over all public institutions.[13] Thus they aimed to streamline activity throughout the state. Without actually using the terminology, they proposed to turn the party into the principal institution of state.

Lenin did not declare what changed his own mind in this direction. Unusually for a matter of this import, he kept mum. Quite possibly the arguments of Kaganovich and Osinski moved him. It is also possible that the commission sent out to the Urals under Stalin and Dzierzynski to investigate the reasons for the ease of Kolchak's seizure of the city of Perm in December 1918 was another. Neither Stalin nor Dzierzynski stinted their denunciation of the overlapping areas of responsibility of local state bodies. Their report called unambiguously for the party to reinforce its institutional control.[14] They must surely have given him a bit of a shock. Before their departure for the Urals he had surmised to them that the Perm disaster was caused by the drunkenness of a single official, M. M. Lashevich.[15]

This dismissiveness of the matter at hand was no longer possible after Lenin had heard from Stalin and Dzierzysnki. And yet the revision of policies and practices was still left by him mainly to others. It is a misconception of the man that he was permanently obsessed by matters organisational; indeed the worry of critics of the Central Committee was that he occupied himself altogether too little with them in general. Kaganovich and Osinski argued in late 1918 that, if the party was to run a centralised state efficiently, it needed to be efficiently centralised itself.[16] This theme had been addressed by Sverdlov at the Party Congress in March 1918;[17] but implementation had been intermittent in subsequent months. Indisputably the central party leadership had treated the rest of the party with a growing brusqueness. Regional party committees were subordinated to Moscow. The Ukrainian Central Committee, which was formally only a regional body within the Bolshevik party as a whole, was forced to accept two nominees from Moscow in autumn 1918 after an unsanctioned Ukrainian uprising against the Germans. Other regional committees suffered similarly or even worse: the Moscow Regional Committee and, after the Stalin-Dzierzynski report, the Urals Regional Committee were simply abolished.[18] But Sverdlov proceeded cautiously below the regional tier. Provincial committees were as yet treated more lightly. Sverdlov recognised the limitations on his resources in manpower and information, and to some extent he still adhered to his old motto for the Central Committee and the Secretariat: 'There is no point in attempting to do the impossible.'[19] By the winter of 1918–1919 his campaign for gradual centralisation was regarded as waywardness at best and incompetence at worst. The critics demanded rapid reform.

Lenin had been involved in particular decisions; and some of them, such as those relating to the Ukrainian Communist Party, had large implications for Bolshevism throughout the old Russian empire. But he refrained from setting an agenda for a broader debate on institutional relationships. The old informality, he assumed, would serve him well enough. Sverdlov, moreover, continued to serve him well too. There had been a plan, drawn up in fact by Sverdlov's wife Klavdiya, to introduce greater formality to the central party apparatus. In summer 1918 she had suggested that a system of Departments be set up in the overworked Secretariat. But husband Yakov saw no urgent need for reform; and Lenin apparently concluded that, if Sverdlov felt that way, then things must be all right.

BOLSHEVISM'S LEADER

This complacency about the Central Committee and its Secretariat was coming under strain by the end of 1918. The infrequency of meetings and the informality of procedures meant that the additional wartime tasks were not adequately discharged. At the same time it was unrealistic to pull back all Central Committee members serving at the front or in the provinces and put them in permanent posts in the capital. Lenin and Sverdlov decided that the solution was to equip the Central Committee with inner subcommittees. This was not without

precedent. The Central Committee after the Sixth Party Congress in
August 1917 had selected a group of eleven members to act in its name
between plenums – and this had been in a period when plenums were
not rare;[20] and, as preparations were put in hand for the October
Revolution, a seven-man Political Bureau was created consisting of
Lenin, Zinoviev, Kamenev, Trotski, Stalin, Sokolnikov and Bubnov.
In practice this body had no discernible impact on the seizure of power
in Petrograd.[21] But the usefulness of inner subcommittees was not
denied, and a further experiment was undertaken in early October 1918
when a 'Bureau of the Central Committee' began to meet.[22] On 16
January 1919 the Central Committee met and established an
Organisational Bureau (or Orgburo) to take charge of internal party
business. The choice of the three members confirmed Lenin's
willingness to leave such administration to others: Yakov Sverdlov,
M. F. Vladimirski and N. N. Krestinski.[23] The Orgburo quickly
became a fixture in the central party apparatus.[24]

The Political Bureau (or Politburo) was also re-instated; its duties
were to oversee the entire range of political, economic and military
policies between Central Committee sessions. As things turned out, the
Central Committee met more often in the first months of 1919 than in
previous months; but this was not an unqualified bonus for Lenin. It
gathered together personalities who had trouble being pleasant to each
other. On 5 February 1919 the Central Committee debated the report
by Stalin and Dzierzynski on the Perm military collapse. Among
Stalin's recommendations was his call for the high command of the
Red Army to be investigated.[25] This could not fail to annoy Trotski
and his friends in the Revolutionary-Military Council of the Republic
who were charged with oversight over the commanders. Central as well
as local practices were put under scrutiny, and the Orgburo under
Sverdlov was instructed to prepare a swift report for the Central
Committee.[26]

Sverdlov alone could not hold Stalin and Trotski apart for very long:
only Lenin could do this; it was one of his principal accomplishments.
Stalin had been appointed as food-supplies commissar in southern
Russia in mid-1918. On 10 July, after observing the situation around
the Volga city of Tsaritsyn, he had cabled to Moscow: 'For the good of
the cause, I must have military powers. I have already written on this,
but received no answer. Very well. In this case I myself, without
formalities, will turf out those commanders and commissars who are
ruining the cause. This is what I'm pushed to do by the interests of the
cause, and of course the absence of a piece of paper from Trotski won't

stop me.'[27] Subsequently, in September 1918, he was confirmed as chairman of the Revolutionary-Military Council of the Southern front. His conduct was overweening in the extreme. He inaugurated a reign of arbitrary violence throughout the Tsaritsyn region. He arrested not only middle-class civilian professionals but also Red Army commanders who had served in the Imperial Army. He intervened in strategical decisions. Despite being a political commissar, he took over operations in the field; and he dominated the work of civilian party and soviet institutions in the locality.[28] He also took exception to Trotski's appointee as front commander, P. P. Sytin. Trotski had had enough by 4 October. 'I categorically insist,' he telegrammed to Sverdlov and Lenin, 'on Stalin's recall.'[29] Next day he declared no less definitely: 'Stalin's actions are disrupting all my plans.'[30] Sverdlov apparently arranged for Stalin to be recalled to Moscow for consultations, and Stalin was persuaded to drop his demand that Sytin should be dismissed. Stalin's party friends in Tsaritsyn were said to have agreed to obey orders from Moscow. In return, Stalin at his own request was elevated to membership of the Revolutionary-Military Council of the Republic.[31]

Stalin's hurt pride was not assuaged. He told Sverdlov that he wanted to resume his responsibilities on the Southern front.[32] A tactful telegram had therefore to be composed by Sverdlov for dispatch to Trotski on 23 October: 'In informing you, Lev Davydovich, of all these statements from Stalin, I ask you to think them over and give me an answer in the first place as to whether you agree to talk things over personally with Stalin, for which purpose he is willing to pay a visit and secondly whether you reckon it possible, on certain concrete conditions, to eliminate the former clashes and arrange to work together as Stalin so much wishes.'[33]

It was Lenin's convalescence after the attempt on his life that brought Sverdlov into such matters, and Trotski began sending top copies of correspondence to Sverdlov rather than to Lenin.[34] Lenin would normally have hated such a loss of personal control, but he was reconciled to this temporary condition by Sverdlov's obvious loyalty. Well as Sverdlov had coped, he had not handled the dispute between Trotski and Stalin as effectively as Lenin would have managed to do. Hostilities were postponed for only a few days even though, for the moment, Trotski had consented to sit down with Stalin to discuss their disagreements. Stalin continued to bombard Moscow with furious telegrams. On 25 October the Central Committee convened under Sverdlov's chairmanship – in the presence of Lenin – to discuss Stalin's claim that there had been sabotage of supplies on the Southern front and that front commander Sytin should be put on trial. The Central Committee turned him down.[35] Stalin found the personal session with Trotski singularly unpleasant. This occurred on the railway between Moscow and Tsaritsyn, and Sverdlov took the precaution of attending. Trotski repeated his objections to Stalin's contravention of policy towards the employment of Imperial officers; he also criticised the appointment of inexperienced Bolsheviks such as Kliment Voroshilov as Red Army commanders. 'They're fine lads!' was Stalin's retort. 'These fine lads,' replied Trotski, 'will wreck the Revolution, which can't afford the time for them to grow up!' Trotski insisted that Stalin's request to rejoin the Southern front be rejected. Sverdlov took Trotski's side: there had to be a limit to the disorganisation.[36]

Yet Stalin was spared total humiliation. The Central Committee meeting of 25 October 1918 ruled that, if Trotski wanted those Imperial Army officers who had been seized as hostages to be inducted into the Red Army, he should ensure that none had belonged to 'the counter-revolutionary movement'.[37] Trotski was also ordered to transfer Sytin to Moscow headquarters; and a technical enquiry into the Sytin affair was to be headed by V. A. Avanesov, an associate of Stalin.[38] Voroshilov, moreover, was to be allowed to remain as a commander on the Southern front.[39] Trotski's ally A. I. Okulov fell out with Voroshilov in December, and this time Lenin came down on the side of Trotski.[40] There was even a perceptible restraint in Lenin's speeches about the basic policy of employing Imperial Army officers. He offered formal approval; but he did not strive hard to protect Trotski from attack by the Tsaritsyn group around Stalin and the rest of what was to become known as the 'Military Opposition'.[41]

The thing was that Lenin appreciated the advantage of not identifying himself too closely with either Trotski or Stalin. The Central Committee's leading members acted freely in their respective areas of responsibility; but Stalin on the Southern front had flaunted his powers more than most. Mayhem had become the norm in Tsaritsyn; the torture and killing of hundreds accused of treason was a sign of the horrors to come in the 1930s. But Lenin, being a committed overseer of terror, mostly turned a blind eye. Stalin offered no threat to his primacy among Bolsheviks. The fact that Stalin sent telegrams about the Red Army not to Trotski but to Lenin and Sverdlov served to bolster Lenin's position; and Stalin obviously enjoyed bragging about his own merits: he needed Lenin's sanction in order to advance his military career.[42] In 1918 Trotski was by far the greater potential rival.

His talent was indisputable. Lenin is said to have commented to him after the October Revolution: 'And what if the White Guards kill you and me? Will Sverdlov and Bukharin be able to cope?'[43] It suited Lenin admirably that Trotski had to impose organisation and discipline in the Red Army. This was looked upon by many party members as dirty work. Lenin, smarting from his mauling in the Brest-Litovsk controversy, contentedly watched disfavour falling on someone else.[44] And yet he did not want the central party apparatus, despite their rivalry, to fall apart. Several Bolsheviks who had been prominent before and even during 1917 failed to cope with the tasks of government. But Lenin wished to preserve the leading group in place, and everyone now knew who the main figures were: Lenin, Trotski, Stalin, Sverdlov, Kamenev, Zinoviev, Dzierzynski and Bukharin. This inner core held sway by 1918–1919, and would supply the major players in the struggle to succeed Lenin.[45]

The outcome of that struggle might have been different but for the unexpected death of Yakov Sverdlov on 16 March 1918.[46] He had greatly over-worked himself and had no reserves of physical resistance when infected with the Spanish influenza. Only Lenin's premature death could have so juddered the politics of the Kremlin. Sverdlov and Lenin had at least tried to make the other leaders work with some semblance of harmony. No one could accuse him of being an intriguer. What made matters worse was that his intense pace of work left him little time to keep written records. His memory for facts and people had been the equivalent of the Secretariat's archives.[47] A rapid reconstitution of the leadership was required, but no obvious substitute for Sverdlov was available.[48] Kamenev was an emollient influence, but was already heavily laden with duties in the Moscow Soviet. Bukharin, who had returned to the Central Committee in midsummer 1918, was preoccupied with the editing of *Pravda*. Neither Kamenev nor Bukharin had the combativeness to control the unruly organisations in the provinces and the armed forces. Dzierzynski had his hands full with the Cheka. Zinoviev was already marked down as the party's choice to lead the Communist International. Trotski was at the front. Stalin, when not causing trouble for Trotski, operated as a troubleshooter whenever and wherever the situation demanded.[49]

Sverdlov's death gave impetus for a re-organisation of the central party apparatus. The Kremlin dyarchy of Lenin and Sverdlov would have been ended in any event. A system of two subcommittees inside the Central Committee had already come into existence, and the introduction of a set of departments in the Secretariat could no longer be delayed.[50] As yet the permanent arrangements were undefined. Lenin anticipated the re-organisation with equanimity. He was pre-eminent in the Central Committee. Thorough discussion and efficient administration were proclaimed as the objectives. But there was also an unspoken aim: the avoidance of unseemly, destabilising disputes of the kind which had involved Stalin and Trotski and had consumed the energies of Sverdlov as intermediary. Lenin desired the intermittent fractiousness to be replaced by unified action in the Civil War.

THE FIRST CONGRESS OF COMINTERN

There were few more famous politicians in the world than Lenin. Only Lloyd George, Georges Clemenceau, Woodrow Wilson and perhaps Trotski equalled him in the public imagination. Nevertheless Lenin's practical impact outside the Soviet republic stayed small; his international diplomacy had been confined to disclaiming sovereignty over western and south-western borderlands of the former Russian empire in the Brest-Litovsk negotiations. And yet he retained a vaulting ambition. He had been ridiculed at the anti-war socialist conferences in Zimmerwald and Kienthal in 1915-1916 when calling for European civil war. After the October Revolution he was taken more seriously; but no results followed. Lenin and his party were held in quarantine by Europe's governments. Adolf Ioffe and other plenipotentiaries who travelled abroad on Sovnarkom's behalf were barely mentioned in daily newspapers outside Russia; and, although Lenin personally copy-edited German-language versions of his own works, they were not widely read. Yet some admirers already existed. The killings of Rosa Luxemburg and Karl Liebknecht had the effect of removing two critically-thinking leaders who might have resisted the penetration of the German Communist Party by Lenin's type of thinking. Even the fact that the German Social-Democratic Party won more seats – 163 out of a possible 421[51] – than any other party in the Constituent Assembly elections of January 1919 and formed a coalition with non-socialist parties had the advantage that, in time, social-democrats could be exposed as having connived in capitalism's survival.

The snag was that Karl Kautsky and the Independent German Social-Democratic Party, which refused to have dealings with the German Social-Democratic Party proper, was also rising in popularity. A contest took place for support from the politically discontented elements in the country's working class. Lenin was thinking flexibly.

Detestation of Kautsky did not discourage him from hoping that a German Communist Party, once formed, might recruit members from the Independent German Social-Democratic Party, and to this end he himself drafted a short article. He noted gleefully that G. Laukant, an Independent German Social-Democratic Party leader, had dissociated himself privately from Kautsky's policies.[52]

This attempt to sow dissent in the leadership of a rival party lay unpublished. On reflection he decided that more harm than good might result at a moment when he and his Central Committee colleagues were laying the ground for a Congress heralded since 1914 in Lenin's declarations: the inaugurative meeting of the Third International.[53] Unlike the Second International, which was avowedly socialist, this would be the Communist International. Lenin had sent a memorandum on 27 or 28 December 1918 to Georgi Chicherin as People's Commissar of External Affairs calling for urgent action, and proposing that the conference should be held in Berlin. The basis of the invitations should be a particular party's willingness to support soviet power and the dictatorship of the proletariat.[54] Precisely why it was in the winter of 1918–1919 that the years-old intention of the Bolsheviks was to be fulfilled is not clear. But probably Lenin had judged it impossible while the treaty of Brest-Litovsk had to be respected on pain of German military retaliation. The immediate aim of a Communist International would be the fostering of revolution in Germany. Lenin also always kept his eyes on developments among Europe's socialists; indeed he had paid more attention to them in the years both just before and during the Great War than to the military, economic and political forces of capitalism'.[55] On 3 February 1919 socialist and trade-union representatives met in the Swiss capital, Berne, to re-establish a Second International which remained the object of Lenin's contempt. It was a divided gathering; but moves were made towards the setting up of a central apparatus as well as towards the drafting of a document for presentation to the forthcoming Peace Conference at Versailles. Lenin was given additional impetus to call a meeting of foreign supporters; and, in accordance with his custom, he would let no procedural nicety get in his way. Forward, to the Communist International![56]

He arranged a meeting to take place on 21 January 1919 between Central Committee representatives, led by himself and Trotski, and foreign communists working in Moscow. These drew up an appeal to revolutionary organisations abroad to collaborate in a founding conference of a new International. Seven foreigners signed the appeal obligingly written on their behalf by Trotski.[57] All but one signed on behalf of parties in eastern and central Europe. The exception, Boris Reinstein, appended his name as representative of the Socialist Labor Party of North America.[58] Lenin had already asked Bukharin and Chicherin to draft a conference plan while he got on with theses 'on bourgeois democracy and the dictatorship of the proletariat' for the conference.[59]

Lenin opened the proceedings on 2 March 1919 by saying: 'In accordance with the behest of the Central Committee of the Russian Communist Party, I am opening the first international communist congress.'[60] Thus he changed the nomenclature from a conference to a congress. The difference lent the proceedings a greater implicit authority; and, by referring to his party as the initiator of the Congress, he emphasised the special role of the Bolsheviks. Lenin and his Russian comrades were pulled up short by the German Communist Party representative Hugo Eberlein who accurately sensed that his Russian hosts would exploit the opportunity to take complete control of the Communist International if a consultative meeting or conference were to be turned into a full-scale Congress.[61] Lenin had a long record of immunity to embarrassment about such dodges. But Eberlein proved stubborn.[62] Lenin in turn was both exigent and conciliatory. He repeated that 'the dictatorship of the proletariat' was crucial. But he added, in order to attract any doubting delegates, that the need for such a dictatorship had become 'comprehensible to the broad masses of workers thanks to soviet power in Russia, thanks to the Spartakists in Germany and analogous organisations in other countries such as, for example, the Shop Stewards Committees in England'. He added, ill-informedly, that he had just read a telegram stating that a Soviet of Workers' Deputies had been set up in Birmingham and that the British government had already given recognition to such soviets as 'economic organisations'. Temporary defeat in Germany was less important than this durable triumph.[63]

Birmingham's clutch of revolutionary socialists would have been surprised by such optimism. Lenin perhaps believed the information he had received; but more probably he was bolstering morale. No delegate (not even Lenin!) had access to accurate data. Ostensibly the First Congress was a victory of international organisation. The thirty four delegates included only seven official representatives of the Russian Communist Party, and the rest hailed from Europe and North America – as well as three from Asia. But the foreign groups they claimed to represent were characteristically tiny. The revolutionary grouping in

France had fewer than a dozen members.[64] Even more to the point: only four delegates had needed to travel to Russia. The remainder were already resident in Moscow; it was laughable to pretend that such persons were not under the control, direct or not, of the Bolsheviks: several were Bolshevik party members.[65]

Eberlein, however, was one of the four delegates who both had a genuine mandate from a serious party and had journeyed from abroad. On the Congress's second day, 3 March, he questioned whether the time was opportune for the Third International's foundation. The Russians were furious, but needed to defeat Eberlein while keeping him in the new International. This involved impressing upon everybody that the International was not their puppet. The contradictions of the records and memoirs of the next two days of consultations indicate the skullduggery at play; loyal Bolsheviks, then and later, wanted to sanitise the dirty work. After tempestuous discussions, Eberlein yielded. On 4 March the delegates ratified their proceedings as the First Congress of the Communist (or Third) International.[66] On the same day Lenin delivered his theses 'on bourgeois democracy and the dictatorship of the proletariat'. The Bolsheviks by then had their tails up. Nothing in the theses was novel for Russia since October 1917; but Lenin sketched ideas which, for the West, were highly unusual. He repudiated bourgeois parliamentarianism, extolling the Paris Commune and the Russian soviets.[67] 'Pure democracy', according to Lenin, existed in capitalist countries neither in the past nor in the present; their civic freedoms were to the exclusive advantage of the bourgeoisie. As an example Lenin cited the brutal killing of Liebknecht and Luxemburg. He followed this with a denunciation of the Independent German Social-Democratic Party for its hostility to Russian soviets and to German workers' councils.[68]

Thus the Third International in Moscow marked itself off from the parties trying to refound the Second International in Berne. Lenin had made the decisive achievement in founding his own International, and wisely refrained from pushing the Bolshevik demands too hard. This was obvious in what he omitted from his theses. There was scant mention of Marx, Engels and Marxism. The theses were taciturn even about communism, about civil war, about spreading the revolution by force of arms. Nor did Lenin discuss the role of the party. There was nothing on centralism, hierarchy and discipline even though these were predominant among his party's priorities at the time.[69] He also avoided an insistence that the Russian soviets should be adopted as a universal model.[70]

The omissions were well-calculated. Hugo Eberlein was kept on board and the passage towards revolution in the other countries of Europe could be anticipated in the knowledge that fraternal communist parties were emerging to collaborate in a worldwide project. Proof of the Russian Communist Party's intention to lord it over the International came with the choice of authors for the Congress's platform, its resolution on the Berne Conference, its theses on the international situation and its manifesto. The first was written by Bukharin, the second by Zinoviev, the third by N. Osinski and the last by Trotski. The platform, accepted by the Congress on 4 March, sketched the proletariat's advance to the inauguration of socialism by breaking with Kautskyism and overthrowing the bourgeois state machine.[71] On 5 March, Zinoviev's resolution on the Berne conference resumed the attack on Kautskyism, retailing the Bolshevik version of the inter-socialist controversies about the Great War and asserting that the Second International currently gave 'service to international reaction'. Zinoviev referred to it as the Yellow International.[72] On 6 March, Osinski delivered theses which castigated the Allies as trampling the principle of national self-determination underfoot and imposing an imperialist peace. The Allies had their own disagreements, and Osinski declared that the League of Nations proposed by Woodrow Wilson was merely a scheme whereby the USA might challenge British and French colonial interests. Capitalism made further armaments races and wars certain.[73]

Trotski rounded off the Bolshevik contribution with a draft manifesto which summarised the deliberations at the Congress in typically vivid and compelling language. His tone was defiant: 'To demand of the proletariat that, like meek lambs, they should comply with the requirements of bourgeois democracy in the final life-or-death struggle with capitalism is like asking a man fighting for his life against cut-throats to observe the artificial and restrictive rules of French wrestling, drawn up but not observed by the enemy.'[74]

The reference to Gallic regulations was recondite and spurious: Trotski seemed to be confusing wrestling with boules. Nonetheless the manifesto was in every other way the Congress document most likely to appeal to socialists abroad. This was the last day of the proceedings. The decision was taken to form an Executive Committee to take charge of the International until its next Congress. Bolshevik hegemony was secured by the proviso that, once a party had declared its allegiance to the International, 'comrades of the country' already resident in Moscow should represent it on the Executive Committee until the party's nominee could take a seat (and the Executive Committee reinforced the Bolshevik position by electing Zinoviev as its chairman).[75] Lenin, having opened the Congress modestly, closed it in similar vein. But there was no denying his triumph as he proclaimed to the world: 'Not only in the East European countries but also in the West European countries – and not only in the defeated countries but also in the victorious countries such as England [sic: R. S.] the movement in favour of the Soviets is spreading further and further; and this movement is nothing other than a movement aimed at the creation of a new, proletarian democracy: it is the most significant step forward to the dictatorship of the proletariat, to the complete victory of communism.' As if regretting an absence of grandiloquence, he added: 'The victory of the proletarian revolution around the entire world is guaranteed. At hand is the foundation of an international Soviet republic.'[76]

OPPOSITION: PARTY AND ARMY

And yet the Bolshevik party, away from the gaze of Communist International delegates, was riven by disputation. Two controversies had broken out. The first resulted from worries about the party's organisational condition, the second from even greater annoyance with official policy on arrangements in the armed forces. Neither dispute was completely public. A show of solidarity was needed in wartime. Yet feelings behind the scenes ran high. Lenin, especially after Sverdlov's untimely death, was blamed for failing to co-ordinate the civilian party apparatus; Trotski was castigated for co-ordinating the armed forces to the detriment of party traditions and personnel. Of the two, Lenin got away the more lightly; and, unlike Trotski, he had not fallen out with any major colleague. Stalin wanted to stab Trotski politically in the back and waited till the Eighth Party Congress for his chance.

At Trotski's request, the campaign in the press against Trotski's measures in the Red Army was restricted. But even this exasperated Trotski, who sent a furious telegram to the central party leadership. His complaint was upheld, and Nikolai Bukharin as editor of *Pravda* was instructed to ban debate from its pages.[77] The campaign about civilian party organisation also reached the press. But it was milder not only in Moscow but also in the provinces. The leading Bolshevik in Nizhni Novgorod, Lazar Kaganovich, insisted that organisational reforms had not been carried far enough. His theses as published in Moscow asserted that 'until now there has been no strong organisational centre'. Instead he called for a system of two inner subcommittees to be installed in the Central Committee.[78] He appeared to be unaware that Lenin and Sverdlov had already initiated such a system.[79] But this would anyway not have satisfied him. What Kaganovich wanted was the strictest centralism. Internal democratic practices, including elections, were to be discarded as unnecessary.[80] No wonder Kaganovich later became a crony of Iosif Stalin! And yet, plainly-spoken though he was, he named no names. I. M. Vareikis in Simbirsk was less restrained. Incensed by Sverdlov's criticism of local party bodies who opposed official policies, he countered that these policies were articulated so vaguely and intermittently as to be next to useless. Guilt should therefore be laid at Sverdlov's door.[81] A further group of Bolsheviks, which became known as the Democratic Centralists, was equally determined to eradicate the organisational malaise. Timofei Sapronov, Vladimir Maksimovski and Nikolai Osinski in Moscow province were prominent among them, calling for the party to be co-ordinated more tightly. The Central Committee was castigated by them for its 'extreme inertia'. And yet, while calling for central planning and functional specialisation, they demanded a return to democratic procedures in the party. Authoritarianism, they claimed, deprived the Bolsheviks of the organisational dynamism that had served them well in the October Revolution.[82]

In public only Sverdlov was mentioned; but privately it was a different story. A sense had been growing in late 1918 that the so-called duumvirate of Lenin and Sverdlov had to be brought to an end. Lenin's prestige, as well as sympathy for him as he convalesced, protected him from direct criticism. But both of them were expecting to be buffeted by complaints at the Eighth Party Congress. No one felt that Lenin did not work hard. Nor could there be any suspicion that Sovnarkom would be more efficiently organised under someone other than Lenin. Yet he had neglected the central party apparatus; and, even when he had embarked on reforms with Sverdlov's help, he had not deigned to inform the party in the provinces.[83] Even so, those who criticised him most strongly gave him the benefit of the doubt. Osinski was to write to him after the Congress acknowledging that he was the only conceivable supreme leader for the party. Lenin was gently chided not so much for lacking organising talent as for omitting to take measures to support himself with a carefully-co-ordinated team of organisationally-talented personnel.[84]

The figure of Trotski by contrast evoked outright resentment. His early anti-Bolshevik career had led many to demur at his recruitment to the party in mid-1917. He had been the source of much friction, too, in the Brest-Litovsk controversy.[85] But his activity as People's Commissar for Military Affairs since spring 1918 had given the greatest offence. He conscripted Imperial Army officers. He enforced the ban on party committees in the Red Army. He restored aspects of the discipline and organisation of the Imperial Army. He rode around on horseback as if he were a traditional commander-in-chief. He sanctioned the shooting of the communist activist Panteleev for cowardice in the face of the enemy.[86] While no one questioned Lenin's sincerity, Trotski came widely under suspicion as the cuckoo in the Bolshevik nest. Trotski, unlike Lenin,[87] chose to engage in dispute rather than hide behind the collective decisions of the Central Committee. Trotski admitted in 1919 that 'Bonapartism' might arise in the revolutionary army; but the more acute danger to the Soviet state, he averred, stemmed from Bolsheviks in the armed forces who were incompetent or obstructive.[88] Such was his confidence that he asked the Central Committee for permission to absent himself from the Eighth Party Congress and return to deal with the emergencies at the front.[89]

Trotski had mentally cocooned himself. Lenin and Sverdlov had largely supported his particular decisions as People's Commissar for Military Affairs; but they had refrained from commenting often on those particular issues agitating his critics. They themselves had fulminated against kulaks, landlords, priests, factory-owners and bankers. They had sanctioned the execution of the former Emperor. They could not bring themselves to express a kindly attitude to the Imperial army officers. Lenin did not disavow Trotski's policy; on the contrary, he spoke several times in the winter of 1918–1919 in favour of the enlistment of 'bourgeois specialists' in the Red Army.[90] But Trotski had had to persuade him hard. Apparently it came as a surprise to Lenin to learn that the Reds had had to induct no fewer than thirty thousand Imperial officers in order to keep armed forces of any kind in the field. Thereafter, according to Trotski, Lenin supported Trotski.[91]

As late as 13 March, however, Lenin avoided antagonising Trotski's critics and referred to them at a meeting in Petrograd as 'belonging to the numbers of the most dedicated and convinced Bolshevik-Communists'.[92] Yet he coupled this with support for Trotski's policy. A set of theses was composed by Trotski on 20 February *en route* to Petrograd and, on their publication five days later, became the Central Committee's official proposal for submission to the Eighth

Party Congress.[93] On 14 March, still not having departed for the front, Trotski chanced his arm by getting the Central Committee to agree to prohibit leading Bolsheviks in the Red Army from attending the Congress unless a special request were to be made.[94] In Trotski's anticipated absence the Central Committee chose G. Y. Sokolnikov as its rapporteur on the military question.[95] Objections had been made by political commissars against what they regarded as an attempt to gag them. Trotski denied that there had been a trick of any kind. But he had to give way on the practical demand: his opponents were given the right to stay in Moscow for the Congress.[96] In addition, Lenin further assuaged Stalin's feelings by recommending his appointment as People's Commissar for State Control (even though this was passed only on a split vote). Stalin and Trotski barely concealed their mutual hostility. It was becoming almost automatic for them to oppose each other's requests for personnel transfers (as indeed occurred at the same meeting of the Central Committee).[97]

Stalin also adroitly encouraged Trotski's adversaries outside the Central Committee. The informal name for them was the Military Opposition. Some wanted greater party influence in the Red Army and hated the Imperial officers. Stalin and his associates Kliment Voroshilov and Semen Budenny fell into this category. Other members of the Military Opposition, such as V. M. Smirnov, by contrast demanded the 'democratisation' of the armed forces and disliked Stalin's approval of centralisation and hierarchy. Still others came to the Military Opposition directly from the Left Communists who had opposed the treaty of Brest-Litovsk. Sergei Minin, who had befriended Stalin in Tsaritsyn in mid-1918, was the most prominent such individual.[98] But the higher purpose of defeating Trotski brought them to terms. That they meant business was proved by the decision of a disconcerted Central Committee to put 'the military question' at the top of the Congress agenda.[99] By returning to the front, Trotski was showing revolutionary dutifulness and personal arrogance at the expense of political sense. Lenin would not have made the same mistake.

THE EIGHTH PARTY CONGRESS

The Eighth Party Congress assembled after supper on 18 March 1919. Lenin delivered a eulogy of the late Yakov Sverdlov.[100] His political concerns quickly emerged. International relations had dominated the previous Party Congress, and most party officials had been swept into military work in subsequent months. Yet Lenin told the 263 voting delegates that the crucial current question was the party's attitude to the 'middle peasantry'.[101] Only then did he mention the foundation of the Third International.[102] Descent into the usual squabbles over the presidium, the mandate commission and the official agenda ensued. Lenin was curt with refusals to serve on such bodies: 'You can't decline, comrade Muranov. You'll only hold up the Congress with this.'[103] But the atmosphere was lightened when, speaking first in German and then in French, he invited foreign communists to join him on the platform. Bolsheviks applauded thunderously.[104]

There were shouts of 'Long live Ilich!' as he delivered the Central Committee's report.[105] He showed no mercy, even retrospectively, to the opponents of the Brest-Litovsk treaty, accusing them of 'an incorrect and non-Marxist' viewpoint.[106] These included not only Left Communists but also the Mensheviks and Socialist Revolutionaries. Yet he also reckoned that a flexible policy towards the other socialist parties needed to be maintained. He did not rule out the possibility that a number of their members might come over to Bolshevism. But he still speculated that Dzierzynski might need to put them against a wall and shoot them.[107] The party had also had to feel its way in building a Red Army. Experimentation had been necessary: Marx and Engels had offered no specific doctrine. Lenin argued that to repudiate the use of 'bourgeois specialists' would be infantile.[108] At last he had openly came off the fence on to Trotski's side. The Soviet republic, he asserted, had to avail itself of the expertise available from the legacy of capitalist culture. He even claimed that, until spring 1918, the régime's measures in many ways carried through a bourgeois revolution. Thus the Decree on Land expropriated the gentry but left the kulaks untouched. Lenin suggested that it was only with the creation of the committees of poor peasants that the rural dimension of the October Revolution entered its 'proletarian' phase. Why was he so proud of this? These same committees had been denounced in December 1918, and Lenin even now stated that the anti-kulak campaign had battered the middle peasants.[109] Essentially he was claiming that policies had been right and implementation faulty. Lenin remarked: 'Organisational activity has never been a strong side of Russians in general and Bolsheviks in particular, and meanwhile the main task of the proletarian revolution is precisely an *organisational task*.'[110]

This indirect defence of the Central Committee was attacked by local leaders resenting the slights delivered to lower party bodies.

Democratic Centralist N. Osinski made criticisms, and a brief discussion ended with an endorsement of the central leadership's political but not its organisational leadership.[111] Lenin was spared a further bruising by the lateness of the hour, by his prestige and by the Congress's knowledge that the mastermind of the Secretariat, Yakov Sverdlov, was no longer alive to answer the accusations.

The second session, next morning, was opened by Nikolai Bukharin with a report from the commission writing the party programme.[112] His words were curiously bland until he came to the national question. Citing Stalin's speech to the Third Congress of Soviets in January 1918, he proposed a formula offering 'the self-determination of the labouring classes of each nationality'.[113] This formula reflected a narrowing of Lenin's ideas since before the Great War, when he had advocated national self-determination in general. Yet Bukharin, who had never disguised his distaste for concessions on the national question, had not got everything his way. The agreed draft programme stated that any proposal of secession from the Soviet republic would need to take account as to what phase of 'historical development was occupied by a given nation'.[114] Bukharin had exhaled no hostility towards Lenin. But his inoffensiveness was not reciprocated: Lenin breathed fire and brimstone in his complementary report. Firstly, he insisted that the programme should describe Russian capitalism in its early as well as its advanced stages. This was no quibble. Lenin wanted the programme to state that the wartime dislocation had induced massive economic regression. Bukharin's wafflings about 'finance capitalism' annoyed him.[115] Lenin particularly asserted the 'right of nations to self-determination'; and, noting that Bukharin appeared to accept the application of this notion to industrial societies such as Germany, Lenin reminded the Congress that the German working class had not become politically 'differentiated' in its entirety from the German bourgeoisie and that any referendum of German workers would not necessarily result in a vote for socialism.[116]

This was a neat dissection of Bukharin's argument. But the knife was double-edged: it also cut back into Lenin's suggestion that a proclamation of the right to national self-determination would speed up the installation of socialist régimes. But Lenin was a master of rhetorical distraction. Turning to Bukharin, he asked whether he had forgotten about the Bashkirs. Lenin affirmed that the granting of an ethnically-based autonomous administration (which he hoped to repeat in relation to the Kirgiz, Uzbeks, Tajiks and Turkmens) was the most effective way to secure support for socialist policies and for a diminution of the influence of the mullahs.[117] He ended on a high note, suggesting that a policy of national self-determination in Poland was already yielding fruit. Warsaw workers were supposedly adopting communist policies. He acknowledged that 'a decree has not yet been issued for all countries to live by the Bolshevik revolutionary calendar', but insisted that the prospect of European revolution had not vanished.[118]

Debate on the party programme was resumed in the evening. Georgi Pyatakov, Lenin's oldest Bolshevik opponent on the national question, attacked him. Finnish independence, granted by Lenin to Svinhufvud in December 1917, was castigated as a fiasco. No socialist revolution had resulted from it.[119] Pyatakov was even more anti-nationalist than Bukharin and denounced even the slogan of 'the self-determination of the labouring classes of each nationality'. He denied, for example, that Ukrainian workers should have the right to prevent union with Russia if soviet republics were already to have sprung up in Austria and Germany. A single economic centre ruling across a unified socialist space would be essential.[120] L. B. Sunitsa agreed with Pyatakov that the interests of 'the worldwide combat organisation of the proletariat' should be paramount.[121] Even N. Osinski, who approved of Lenin's formulation, accepted it only as a 'demonstrational slogan'.[122] By this he meant that it was a useful means of fooling non-Russians that the party was more favourable to national self-determination than it really was.[123] Only Central Committee colleague Aleksei Rykov supported Lenin unequivocally.[124] Lenin, of course, did not intend to facilitate demands for separation from Russia by non-Russian nations. But, unlike Osinski, he refused to admit this even in the privacy of the Party Congress. His main adversary in any case was Pyatakov. As Lenin put it, 'Come across any communist and you'll discover a Great Russian chauvinist!'[125] Furthermore, the rest of the Congress's agenda was long and time was pressing, and Lenin was spared the risk of putting his formulation to a vote. Instead a commission was set up, including both Lenin and Bukharin, to finalise the draft programme.[126]

On 20 March, Zinoviev reported on the Communist International. He told the Congress about the news from Munich and predicted a German socialist revolution was maturing.[127] Zinoviev roused the Congress by claiming that the Russian Communist Party had won the right to exercise ideological leadership over all far-left socialists, and his report was unanimously approved.[128] G. Y. Sokolnikov, reporting on the military question, had worse fortune. He referred to the system of political commissars in the Red Army as a success and maintained that it would not be sensible to sack the officers conscripted from the old armed forces.[129] Trotski was not present, but had supplied theses for the Congress.[130] An opposing report was delivered by V. M. Smirnov, who spoke to his own theses. The tsarist style of discipline; the privileges of many officers; the restricted authority of political commissars like himself; the absence of collective decision-making; the party's fragile control over the Red Army: these were again his points of objection.[131]

The diametrical opposition of viewpoints induced delegates to hand the matter over to a special section of the Congress for preliminary discussion. This was a very rancorous debate. Trotski was routinely denounced.[132] Sokolnikov and others struck back, but it was a lost cause. 37 out of 57 participants voted for Smirnov and against Trotski.[133] This was a massive defeat for the Central Committee. Sokolnikov, who had merely been carrying out the instructions of Lenin and Trotski, wanted no further part in the matter. He had no military experience and rued his involvement in the debate; and, together with the minority of the section, he walked out.[134] The fifth session of the full Congress met late on 21 March to deal with the shambles.[135] Lenin determined to stay clear of the dispute if at all possible. S. I. Aralov, Trotski's subordinate in the Revolutionary Military Council of the Republic, spoke on his behalf on the situation on the war fronts.[136] Then came the debate on the Trotski-Smirnov disagreement. Smirnov had already had to make compromises. In particular, the majority of the Congress section had rejected his demand for collective decision-making.[137] But this amendment stemmed from a desire to reinforce discipline and initiative in the Red Army; no attempt was being made to let the Central Committee down lightly.

Nerves snapped when A. I. Okulov, another of Trotski's staff, condemned the Bolshevik leaders on the Southern front who had notoriously imprisoned 'military specialists' on a river barge rather than admit them into their forces.[138] Next to speak was Southern front commissar Voroshilov, who described cases of sabotage by the Imperial officers and told the Congress that, if he had hearkened to Lenin's advice, the rapid occupation of the Ukraine by the Reds would not have occurred.[139] Both Voroshilov and Stalin, moreover, disingenuously stressed their acceptance of military specialists in principle; and Stalin added that he disapproved of those of Smirnov's theses which were likely to undermine strict military discipline. Stalin refrained from criticising Lenin; indeed he contrived to avoid direct criticism of the Central Committee's position.

Yet his disagreements with Lenin were evident. Ignoring Lenin's call for reconciliation with the middle peasants, Stalin stressed what a danger was posed by them. They revolted in the rear, they were recalcitrant conscripts. Force alone could keep them on the Red side.[140] Lenin waded in. He was airily dismissive of the talk of Smirnov and his supporters about the 'autocratic-feudal' regulations in the armed forces. He also supported Trotski, affirming that Trotski's policy and the policy of the Central Committee were one and the same. Turning to the Southern front, he acknowledged that he had occasionally fallen out with Stalin and that Stalin had not always been proved unjustified in his views.[141] The sting came in the tail. Lenin revealed that the Bolsheviks on the Southern front had lost 60,000 men in battles against forces which were numerically inferior by far. A more rational use of political commissars would have saved lives. His accusation stopped just short of implicating Iosif Stalin.[142] But everyone knew that Stalin had stirred things up behind the scenes. Lenin himself comported himself with decorum, admitting that he was 'not only not a military specialist but not even a military person'. Lenin repudiated Stalin's implied charge that the leadership of the Red Army was thwarting the Central Committee's will. Trotski's name had to be cleared, and Lenin did this without compunction.[143]

If Stalin restrained his criticisms, Smirnov felt no such inhibition and derided Lenin for his 'military innocence'.[144] He also took a final swing at Trotski before his own amended theses were read out to the Congress.[145] But his effort was in vain. It was the theses of Trotski and Sokolnikov that, on reflection, the Congress chose to adopt as a basis for its resolution. Lenin had cast in his lot with Trotski, and the delegates were not inclined to rock the boat in wartime.[146]

A five-man commission was established at the sixth session of the Congress on 22 March to finalise the Trotski–Sokolnikov composite motion. Stalin had played his hand cleverly enough to be selected for it as a member of those 174 delegates (against 95) who had voted on Lenin's side.[147] Quickly the Congress moved to Zinoviev's report on the organisational question. He came before the Congress after sustaining quite a verbal battering in the sessions of the closed organisational section in the previous two days. N. Osinski in particular had claimed that, while Lenin and Sverdlov had been acting as the Central Committee, there had been 'no political line'. Policy had been made on the hoof; systematic deliberation and communication had been absent.[148] Fellow Democratic Centralist T. V. Sapronov repeated the charge.[149] L. M. Kaganovich, despite feeling that the Central Committee erred through too frail an attempt at centralism, railed at Osinski as being insincere.[150] Osinski, retorting that Lenin himself had admitted that 'personal politics' had been developing, focussed on the bureaucratic phenomena in party and government and demanded a return to the elective principle. But his main recommendation was simply that a majority of Central Committee members should belong to Sovnarkom.[151] Sapronov supported him: he complained that too many abuses of power were reversible only by face-to-face pleadings with Lenin, who would then intervene directly. Far too many unaccountable organs had been established.[152] And this time Kaganovich, adherent of a neat chain of command, agreed with the Central Committee's critics.[153]

Zinoviev's speech to the full Congress repeated his message to the organisational section; and, in the seventh session that evening, critics in turn repeated their complaints. But Zinoviev was helped by the news from Hungary. A Soviet republic had been proclaimed in Budapest.[154] Kamenev then reported for the commission on the party programme and went over the amendments made to the draft produced before the Congress. Lenin, before the start of the Congress, had wanted the party to declare a commitment to 'the freedom of secession for nations in reality'; during the Congress debates he had advocated the same freedom but had refrained from using the same terminology.[155] In commission he compromised with Bukharin on his formulation, stating that 'colonies and nations with unequal rights' should have the right to secession.[156] This was a fudge. Lenin could claim that it indicated a commitment to self-determination, Bukharin that the reference to unequal rights was not applicable in the areas under the party's control (since the Soviet Constitution guaranteed national equality). When Pyatakov rose to force a vote on his own critical amendment, he lost. The programme was accepted unanimously.[157]

Yet the 'national question', which did not appear on the Congress's agenda, remained contentious. The gap between Lenin and Bukharin (and Stalin) had not been bridged, and the bruising disputes of 1920–1923 would show how wide it was.[158] A fudge also occurred on the military question. Reporting back from the Congress, E. M. Yaroslavski (who disliked Trotski) spoke warmly in favour of Trotski's theses and said that he had never in any case objected to them in general principle.[159] The Trotski-Sokolnikov motion was then passed unanimously and with only one abstention.[160] The amendments in commission had been few. A couple of Trotski's provocative sentences had been excised.[161] But Sokolnikov had been compelled to make further concessions. Clauses were introduced on the need for 'centralised party-political control' over the Red Army; for the promotion of 'proletarians and semi-proletarians' to command posts; for political commissars to have the right to have disciplinary sanctions over commanders; for a reduction of the old-style military regulations; for the establishment of a Political Department of the Revolutionary-Military Council of the Republic under the leadership of a member of the party's Central Committee.[162] The net result was a compromise. The party was to be placed at the core of military organisation; and, although Imperial army officers were no longer to be rejected as on the Southern front, the rights of political commissars under the party's supervision were enhanced. This compromise was pleasing to Lenin; but Trotski, on learning how proceedings had gone, was furious: the dispute was not yet at an end.[163]

The whole Congress showed that the mood of party officials, central and local, had to be taken into account if the existing central leadership was to keep the party actively on its side. Lenin understood this; Trotski did not. But even Lenin failed to follow things as closely as he had needed. The question of the middle peasants, which he had declared to be the crucial question for the Congress, had barely been discussed; and such discussion as had taken place was frequently inimical to Lenin's demand that these peasants should be treated gently.[164] Reporting for the Congress agrarian commission, he repeated that '*no acts of violence* [italics in original]' against them were permissible.[165] He rebuked those who wished to coerce the rural population into a system of socialist collective farming. Only when the régime had 100,000 first-class tractors at its disposal, he asserted, would it be conceivable that most peasants would accede to this; and he continued: 'But in order to do this it is first necessary to conquer the international bourgeoisie, it is necessary to force it to give us those tractors; or else it is necessary to raise our productivity to such a point that we can provide them ourselves.'[166]

The briefest of debates followed. Among the speakers, a certain Panfilov criticised Lenin's pessimism and especially recommended collectivisation for the prosperous agricultural communities of Ukraine.[167] This was in line with contributions made by V. V. Kuraev and others behind the scenes in the commission. A greater emphasis on class struggle and socialist collective farms had been frequently demanded.[168] Lenin had not been without support,[169] but had had to speak robustly to bend the commission his way. Its members knew that, in the final analysis, theirs was not the item at the front of the

Congress's attention. Kuraev therefore acceded to Lenin's insistence that the middle peasant question should dominate the draft proposed by the commission.[170] The Congress then passed the motion 'on the relation to the middle peasantry' unanimously.[171] Lenin announced the results of the Central Committee elections. As usual he headed the votes. His concluding remarks emphasised the universal assent greeting motion after motion. By exaggerating the party's unity, he hoped to bring it about in reality. The fissiparous political tendencies had to be overcome. The Whites had to be defeated. No hint of military crisis was given by him: it was as if the Central Committee had not enjoined Trotski to confront Kolchak. Lenin brightly assured the Congress: 'We are convinced that *this will be the last heavy half-year.*'[172] The Hungarian socialist revolution pointed the way to the future. 'The beast of international imperialism', he affirmed, was expiring. 'This wild beast will perish and socialism will conquer throughout the world!'[173]

THE PARTY PROGRAMME

The development of Lenin's political ideas ought not to be assessed exclusively through books he wrote such as *What Is To be Done?* and *The State and Revolution.* For the programme accepted by the Eighth Party Congress was predominantly his programme. He wrote the main draft and chaired the Congress commission which accepted it as its basis for discussion; and it was this draft, too, that was debated and sanctioned by Congress.[174] He proof-read it for publication as if he were the sole responsible author. He took his usual care, noting the persistent misspelling of 'exploitation' and explaining the word's origins to the offending print-worker.[175] The programme offers insight into the kind of society which he wanted to build. Not since *The State and Revolution* had he produced so comprehensive a medium-term statement, and his commitment to it was to outlast the Civil War.

The preamble declared that the October Revolution had 'realised the dictatorship of the proletariat'.[176] There was a discreet abandonment of the idea, as proposed by Lenin in 1917, that workers and poor peasants would jointly rule Russia.[177] The proletariat was to rule alone. Its victory in all capitalist countries was affirmed to be as inevitable as the immiseration of the working class had been under capitalism.[178]

Revolutionary wars could be anticipated as the struggle between socialism and capitalism intensified. The rise of the Third International and the démise of the Kautskyite 'centrists' was forecast.[179] The programme sketched out several tasks 'in the general political area'. The Soviet state had purportedly led the way in legislating for 'a higher form of democratism'. No apology was made for depriving the middle class of its political rights. The Programme maintained that the civic freedoms offered to workers by certain capitalist states were more formal than real. 'Proletarian democracy' was supposedly different.[180] Attention was drawn to the recallability of soviet deputies as well as in the abolition of the division of legislative and executive authorities. The priority, in Lenin's words, was to 'attain a further rapprochement of the organs of power with the labouring masses'.[181] This was all confident stuff (which the commission, on Bukharin's suggestion, had asked Lenin to insert in the draft).[182] Yet it was pragmatic too: the programme emphasised that the 'broad masses' of the population did not match the urban factory workers in their cultural level and revolutionary preparedness. Since a shortage of working-class administrators persisted, the retention of the 'specialists' from the régimes of Nikolai II and Aleksandr Kerenski was essential. 'A partial rebirth of bureaucratism' had resulted.[183] But an eventual solution would be obtained through 'the gradual attraction of every single member of the entire labouring population into work in the administration of the state'.[184]

Both the Congress commission and the Congress had few objections until they examined the clauses on the 'national question'. The rights of national self-determination and secession, which Lenin had demanded, were obfuscated in the final version: this was the single major defeat he suffered in the discussions on the party programme.[185] But his efforts ensured that the programme was not without potential appeal to the non-Russian peoples, even if Marxist jargon was used: 'Proletarians and semi-proletarians of the various nationalities' were to be drawn into collaborative activities. 'The national feelings of the labouring masses' were to be respected. No nation should have privileged status over the others.[186] The constitutional arrangement to be made at the end of the Civil War was to be a 'federative unification of states organised according to the Soviet type'.[187]

Sections on military, judicial, educational and religious policy followed. Lenin's original draft had been written in the heat of the controversy between Trotski and the Military Opposition, and had avoided mention of the Red Army.[188] The Congress commission, however, insisted on filling the gap at least in general terms. A clause was inserted on the need to encourage the promotion of workers and peasants to positions of command. The abolition of the elective principle in the armed forces was also defended.[189] The judicial section was more uplifting, prescribing that delinquents should henceforward be punished not by loss of liberty but by public dishonour and compulsory labour on behalf of society. On the other hand, legal procedures were scoffed at. Where the necessary decrees were not in place, judges should simply be 'guided by a socialist consciousness of justice'.[190] In education, the programme called for compulsory, free schooling for all children through to seventeen years. Facilities were to be made available to adults who had not been to school.[191] Religious training was to be banned from educational premises and the party was to campaign for 'the complete withering away of religious prejudices'. But this was to be handled sensitively lest persecution of believers should increase religious fanaticism.[192] Lenin managed to effect a blend of clear intention and reassuring rhetoric which he had failed to obtain on the national question. The programme's principal objective was the creation of a society of highly literate and publicly active citizens.

The economic section was more detailed than the others. Lenin aimed at 'the maximum unification of the entire economic life of the country in accordance with a single state plan'. This would involve 'the greatest centralisation of production' and the inducement of small-scale artisanal enterprises to form bigger and bigger conglomerates. The transformation was to be entrusted primarily to the trade unions, whose functions would move from the traditional defence of ordinary workers towards control over production. Thus 'a struggle against the bureaucratisation of the economic apparatus of Soviet power' would be waged. Central planning was repeatedly insisted upon, and the mobilisation of every man and woman capable of work was to be undertaken.[193]

A steep rise in productivity was projected. This would necessitate 'systematic work on the re-education of the masses' and 'the creation of a new socialist discipline'. Shortage of managerial talent would be a temporary disadvantage. The party would need to employ 'specialists', who had abandoned organised sabotage against the régime, for the foreseeable future; ultra-radical proposals to sack them were to be rejected. The immediate introduction of 'full communism', implementing the principle of 'to each according to his needs', was not possible; only the first steps away from capitalism could be undertaken.[194] Nowhere was this more obvious than in agriculture. The programme boasted that 'large-scale socialist' farming had begun; but there was still a long way to go before socialism would underpin the agrarian sector. The priority in the short term would be to reform the peasant land communes by getting rid of strip-field allotments, supplying improved seed-stocks and increasing agronomic assistance. No mercy would be shown to the kulaks. Their resistance to the government's policies would be suppressed and the campaign would be continued against their 'exploitative impulses'. Meanwhile the middle peasants would be courted so as to bring about their 'steady and planned involvement in the work of socialist construction'. The programme specified that the current breakdown in trade between town and countryside, which had brought the country close to destruction, exemplified the need for general economic and cultural differences between urban and rural conditions to be eliminated.[195]

Trade, too, had to be subjected to state planning and direction; and all citizens were to belong to 'consumer communes' so that the distribution of goods could be accomplished with efficiency. Co-operatives should be transformed into agencies for 'communist development'. Banking was to be monopolised by the state and turned gradually into 'a central accountancy for communist society'. In the longer term, money would fall into desuetude and the state budget would become the budget for the entire economy of the country.[196]

A range of social reforms was projected. A massive housebuilding scheme was announced to banish cramped and insanitary conditions from the scene. The eight-hour working day was to be reduced in the case of miners and others doing dangerous jobs to six hours. Greater protection for women at work was anticipated. Unemployment was to be eliminated. Nevertheless child labour ought to be abolished immediately. An inspectorate to be established to supervise the implementation of all governmental decrees.[197] Universal free health-care was promised. Campaigns against alcoholism and venereal disease were to be launched. Thus an inspiriting vista of projects was sketched. Blame for delays and reverses was placed directly upon the effects of the Great War and the Civil War. Capitalism was blamed for the outbreak of both. Yet the word went forth. The Soviet régime begged for the support of the so-called labouring masses. Workers and poor peasants were to be the major future builders of socialism as well as the major beneficiaries. Capitalism's demise throughout Europe was at hand. Lenin had produced a programme reflecting the grand designs of a Bolshevism which, put on the rack of the Civil War, lifted its eyes to the future tasks of peacetime. The renovation of society in entirely reconstructed material circumstances was anticipated. Communism was glimpsed on the horizon.

The fudgings of the party programme should not go unremarked. No reference to the one-party state, to the Red Terror, to the Cheka, to the imposition of a uniform official ideology, the persecution of other political parties, to the forced-labour concentration camps. The bland picture of law-breakers being shamed in public but not losing their liberty was offensively at variance with reality. Not only current practice but also intentions were slurred over. Policy on the national question was portentously grand and extremely vague. Similarly, the objective of influencing the middle peasants by persuasion rather than by force was stated without indicating what would happen if persuasion failed. Throughout the programme there are fine general goals but little specification.

Grim passages also are impressive. Throughout the programme there was praise of 'the dictatorship of the proletariat' and scorn for any form of socialism hostile to it. Eulogies of revolutionary justice, allowing the Bolsheviks and their supporters to feel unrestricted even by their own legislation, marked out a strategy for the party in the post-war epoch. Lenin wanted to show confidence in the durability of the Soviet régime in Russia and the surrounding regions. Mass participation in administration would be encouraged, and the participants would be enlisted in the struggle for socialism. If there is a single word that dominates the programme, it is struggle. Class struggle, struggle against the counter-revolution, struggle with imperialism. The state, increasingly run by the so-called masses, was to make its role all-pervasive. It was to direct industry, agriculture and commerce in the transition towards a communist framework of life. Bulwarks against the deployment of power in a manner undesirable even to the Bolshevik party are considered still more casually than in Lenin's *The State and Revolution*. The division of powers between legislative, executive and judicial arms of government is crudely mocked. Such maladministration as existed is attributed to officials from the pre-October period with a petty-bourgeois mentality. The dominance of the state, extruding all other forms of influence on public life, is recommended by Lenin and his colleagues in a spirit tantamount to the nightmare entertained in Thomas Hobbes's *Leviathan*.

4 And Ours Shall Be the Victory

THE MOVING FORTRESS

Accounts written solely from official records can be seriously misleading. A history of the principate in the Rome of Augustus would be defective if based mainly on his decrees; and classical Athens is barely comprehensible if the archaeological evidence, as in monuments and inscriptions, is used to the exclusion of eyewitness reports. This caution needs to be applied with the same rigour to more recent times. The decrees of the Bolsheviks in the Civil War must not be treated as an accurate gauge of reality. Few states in history had announced punitive sanctions as severe as the Russian Socialist Federative Soviet Republic. Nor were Lenin and his colleagues pusillanimous in the exercise of repression. Merciless struggle, monolithic unity and and the strictest discipline were catch-phrases of Bolshevik public life. Yet practical implementation was patchy. The legislation, moreover, tended to become more severe as previous laws, already themselves severe, had proved ineffectual.

There can equally be no doubt that the Bolsheviks were violent on a massive scale even if not as comprehensively as was their officially-stated intention. Kolchak's spring offensive was awaited with disquiet in 1919: the Red terror was intensified. With his 110,000 men, Kolchak had the largest of the three White armies. After the Eighth Party Congress, Lenin and his colleagues informed local Bolshevik bodies that an 'extraordinarily threatening danger' was posed from the east. In fact the sprawling lines of the Whites allowed Trotski and Commander-in-Chief Vacietis to re-group their defences. The Reds mounted a counter-offensive on 28 April. Ufa, which had fallen to Kolchak in mid-March, was back in Red hands on 9 June. Admiral Kolchak, now recognised by General Denikin as Supreme Ruler, won no further major battle. The Reds took Perm on 1 July, Omsk on 14 November. The White army fled in chaotic fashion and mid-Siberia was returned to Bolshevik rule. Kolchak had overlooked his personal safety, and was captured and interrogated. In February 1920 he was executed on orders from Moscow. Lenin had spent the previous months calling for the forces of Kolchak to be fought and pursued without mercy; but he did not want to appear responsible for Kolchak's summary liquidation.[1]

His reasons are perplexing. He gave orders that any future official explanation should suggest that local Bolsheviks were responding to a local emergency. This was very like what he had done about the murder of the Imperial family in July 1918. It is improbable, however, that he feared the peasantry's hostility on the grounds of having killed a popular military hero. Nor is he likely to have worried that, if the Reds even then lost the Civil War or if an anti-Bolshevik crusade from abroad succeeded, similar treatment might be meted out to him in retaliation; for he knew his deeds had already made him a marked man[2] It may simply be that he wanted to persuade other White units to surrender of their own volition.[3]

General Denikin on the Southern front became the most acute threat to the Reds.[4] To the Eastern front political commissars, fighting Kolchak, Lenin had written on 29 May 1919: 'If we haven't conquered the Urals by the winter, I consider the doom of the Revolution inevitable.'[5] But the series of telegrams he was to produce for the Southern front were even more strident. In politics, he was always keen to assert a single overriding priority at any given moment. He acted the same in warfare. In October a previously obscure White army under General Yudenich moved out of Estonia towards Petrograd. Lenin refused to accept that Yudenich should be taken seriously. 'It's clear,' he cabled to a Petrograd Soviet which did not share his viewpoint, 'that the Whites' offensive is a manoeuvre to distract our pressure upon the south.'[6] As Yudenich's offensive proved difficult to resist, however, Lenin had to consider how many forces to transfer northwards. On balance, he was even willing to give up Petrograd without a fight. In 1917 he had criticised Aleksandr Kerenski for planning to let the city fall into German hands;[7] now he argued that it would be no great loss. Returning to Moscow, Trotski upbraided Lenin; and he found support not only from his sympathiser Krestinski but even, to his surprise, from Stalin. Lenin gave way, but not before precious time was lost in securing Petrograd's defences. Commander-in-chief S. S. Kamenev made precisely this complaint, and Lenin on 22 October acknowledged that a mistake had been made.[8] On the previous day he had heard that Tsarskoe Selo, twenty kilometres from Petrograd, had been occupied by Yudenich. But the line held. The Red forces, substantially reinforced, drove his 15,000 troops back. By mid-November, Yudenich's retreat had reached the Estonian border and his campaign was in tatters.[9]

Earlier spats had occurred among Politburo members; but Lenin had avoided involvement. The principal disputants were Trotski, Zinoviev and Stalin. On 25 March 1919 Zinoviev had complained to the Central Committee that Trotski was ignoring the compromises on 'the military question' agreed by the Eighth Party Congress; and Lenin was asked to write to Trotski for redress.[10] But Trotski was worried by other military factors. He urgently wanted to clear his name in regard to the execution of commissar Panteleev; he also drew the Politburo attention to widely-felt resentment among Russians in the Red Army who felt that Jews and Latvians found it easy to secure posts in the rear rather than at the front. Trotski called for an ethnic redistribution of manpower.[11]

Yet Trotski was playing the game too hard. He supported the sacking of S. S. Kamenev as commander of Red forces on the Eastern front despite the remonstrations of Stalin. He continued to run the Revolutionary-Military Council from his special train, thereby escaping a degree of control from Moscow. He was unabashed about his support for ex-Imperial army officers. Already in May 1919 there had been signs that Lenin thought S. S. Kamenev to have been treated shabbily.[12] Matters came to a head at the Central Committee plenum on 3-4 July. Lenin, with reservations but also with decisiveness, took the side of Stalin and Zinoviev. The Revolutionary-Military Council was relocated to Moscow; and S. I. Gusev, one of Trotski's critics, was appointed to its membership. To Trotski's annoyance, S. S. Kamenev was appointed Commander-in-Chief (and, for a few days, Vacietis was put under arrest on suspicion of treason).[13] Trotski left the meeting in a fury. Nevertheless Lenin would not go all the way with Stalin. The policy of employing Imperial army officers, which Stalin opposed,[14] was retained. Lenin emphasised this in an open letter on behalf of the Central Committee on 9 July. He also called for an end to the officer-baiting that had occurred in Petrograd: a hidden reference to Stalin's activity; and he repudiated Stalin's request to excise the relevant passage.[15] Yet Stalin did not walk away totally without satisfaction. An official decision on 14 July indicated that the influence of political commissars was to be increased at the expense of officers. He had won much of the post-Congress argument.[16]

Trotski had asked to step down as People's Commissar for Military Affairs on 5 July. Only the unequivocal countermandment of both the Politburo and Orgburo dragged him back to normal work. The same session also expanded his scope to run specifically the Southern front.[17] Red offensives had been resumed in March, April and May 1919, but were all repulsed. In late June, Denikin's forces seized Kharkov and Tsaritsyn. On 3 July, as the Bolshevik Central Committee was having its frantic meeting in the capital, Denikin issued his Moscow Directive. His commanders were instructed to advance north along the Volga and through Ukraine with all speed. Meanwhile Denikin occupied Kiev and Odessa on 23 August, and such was his success that Orel was under his occupation by 14 October. He was 350 kilometres from Moscow, and Lenin was not minded to deflect manpower to protect Petrograd.[18]

Yet this was the extent of Denikin's success. A staunch Red counterattack was launched and by mid-November was proving successful. By 16 December 1919 Denikin had lost Kiev. The retreat became a rout. Tsaritsyn was re-taken by the Red Army in January 1920, Ekaterinodar in March. The remnants of Denikin's Volunteer Army evacuated themselves from southern Russia to the Crimean peninsula. Kolchak was dead. Yudenich was a refugee in Estonia. Hopes that the White administration in Arkhangelsk, with its British protectors, might pose a military threat to Petrograd proved illusory. The Bolsheviks and their Red Army, almost to their own surprise, had pulled off victory in the main theatre of conflict over the Russian empire. Lenin celebrated enthusiastically. It was a victory won at much greater cost than the triumphs of the October Revolution. And yet he was unforthcoming about the Civil War.[19] He and the Politburo had had no time to draw breath since 1918. How Lenin evaluated the capacities of Kolchak, Denikin and Yudenich is unclear. Possibly he gave them no thought at all. He must have recognised his own luck. His government started the Civil War holding Moscow and Petrograd and, therefore, the surest links of communications and transport with the rest of the country. The bulk of the population also lived under Bolshevik rule.[20] Furthermore, he fought the war politically as well as militarily. He was determined to use the sensitivities of the non-Russians to maximum advantage despite his own party's suspiciousness about his policies; and, chaotically though his state was organised, it had the edge over the various White administrations.

But what a manoeuvrer he was! Having had little but trouble from the Cossacks since 1917, he spotted that they were falling out with Denikin by 1919. Very well, then: Bolshevik propaganda should be diverted towards attracting their support![21] And how he could dispense with allies when their usefulness was over. Both Nestor Makhno and Nikolai Grigorev in Ukraine had fought alongside the Red Army with their irregular local peasant forces. But they and Lenin had no illusions about each other. Once Denikin was defeated, they fell into dispute.

The Red Army ruthlessly secured dominance over its rivals. Not that it failed to make strategic and organisational mistakes. There were plenty of them, and Lenin's misjudgement about Petrograd was simply the one he was personally and primarily responsible for. But he had made fewer than most of his colleagues; and those, like Kamenev, who foresaw difficulties more clearly than he, would never have led the Bolsheviks to the party's satisfaction.

GATHERING THE LANDS

It had been the ending of the Great War rather than any success against the Whites that had first brought Lenin and his colleagues back to deliberations on the 'national question' in the former Russian empire. The German military collapse left a vacuum of power in the previously-occupied lands. Soviet republics had quickly been established in Estonia, Lithuania and Belorussia, Latvia and Ukraine. The Constitution of the Russian Socialist Federal Soviet Republic (or RSFSR) drawn up in summer 1918 was extremely unspecific; and even debate at the Eighth Party Congress had avoided specifying what relations were to be pursued among the various republics.[22]

Nevertheless the beginnings of a policy, while not being advertised, were already in place and were about to be extended. The creation of independent Soviet republics had been initiated by Lenin. Lest there should remain any doubt he had sent a telegram to I.I. Vacietis, Supreme Commander of the Red Army, on 29 November 1918 insisting that such a proliferation would 'remove the opportunity for the chauvinists of Ukraine, Lithuania, Latvia, Estland [i.e. Estonia: RS] to regard the movement of our units as an occupation'. Otherwise, Lenin added, the troops of the Reds would not be treated as 'liberators'.[23] Lenin worked closely with Stalin, who was still the People's Commissar on Nationality Affairs, on all these matters. Sovnarkom charged Stalin with the task of drawing up decrees recognising the new Soviet republics.[24] The central party leadership, moreover, was already exercised by geo-strategical considerations. In the winter of 1918–1919, Adolf Ioffe was sent to Belorussia to persuade local Bolsheviks that the RSFSR's interest would be served by a line of 'buffer republics' between itself and powerful states to the west.[25] Their immediate re-incorporation into an undisguisedly Moscow-based state might instigate an even more British and French anti-Bolshevik crusade than at present. Lenin kept a rein on policy. Leading local

Bolsheviks in each Soviet republic were not easily reconciled to their own declarations of independence. The Latvian Petr Stucka and the Lithuanian V. S. Mickevicius-Kapsukas, both being former Central Committee members, were put under pressure to become 'separatists'.[26] Another local leader, V. G. Knorin of the party's North-West Regional Committee, maintained that the Belorussians were not a nation and that official policy engendered nationalism.[27]

But these Bolsheviks did not control the Red Army. Without Lenin's assistance, they could not conquer their own countries. The policy of Lenin, Stalin and Trotski had therefore to be accepted. Nikolai Krestinski on 11 January 1919 had been asked by the Central Committee to clarify relations between the central party apparatus on the one hand and the newly-formed republican governments, republican party bodies and even the People's Commissariat of Nationality Affairs on the other.[28] But the only published elucidation was the Party Congress decision to treat the Ukrainian, Belorussian, Lithuanian and Latvian Communist Parties as regional party organisations subordinate to the authority of the Russian Communist Party in Moscow. Republics could have formal independence only so long as republic party bodies were strictly controlled by the Central Committee and its Politburo in Moscow.[29]

That a close formal link between the RSFSR and the other Soviet republics (and not just between party bodies) should be forged had been decided, but was not announced. The Central Committee on 16 January 1919 had secretly ordered Bolsheviks in Belorussia to inititate negotiations for a 'union' of all the republics, including Russia.[30] Evidently Lenin did not want to be seen as an initiator. The fiction of non-intervention by Moscow in non-Russian affairs had to be maintained. It was several weeks after the Party Congress before policy was further defined. The push for tight unification had grown even in the central party organs. For example, the Politburo on 23 April 1919 resolved to ask the Ukrainian Bolshevik leadership to ascertain how best 'a fusion of Ukraine with Soviet Russia might be arranged'.[31] Such language indicated that Lenin was yielding now to the arguments of the Stuckas and the Mickeviciuses. His change of stance is not explained in the Politburo minutes; but probably he sensed that the military threat from the West had disappeared. Germany was subject to the Treaty of Versailles. In March 1919 the British decided to withdraw their troops from northern Russia. Furthermore, the Bolsheviks in command of the other republics were not always sensitive to national traditions – and often they carried through measures in total defiance of local society.[32] For example, the Ukrainian Bolsheviks had harassed the so-called middle peasantry and tried, in places, to impose collective farming by force. Consequently Lenin may well have judged greater centralisation of authority to be less risky than letting the local Bolshevik-led governments enjoy much autonomy. Not that Lenin ever needed great encouragement to centralise! Consideration was given on 12 May to a plan for the 'unification' of the RSFSR and the Ukrainian Soviet republic with single People's Commissariats for Military Affairs, the Railways, Finances and Labour as well as a single Supreme Council of the National Economy.[33]

Ukrainian Bolshevik consent was also to be sought; and yet, even before treaty documents were signed, Lenin approved a directive to the party leadership in Kiev stipulating that 'the People's Commissars of the RSFSR should become People's Commissars of the Union with the People's Commissariats of Ukraine as their regional plenipotentiaries'.[34] Still an attempt was made in public to hide these centralist realities. Full integration of all Soviet republics was not yet anticipated. Consultations proceeded with Bolsheviks in the other republics. Instead, on 1 June 1919, a draft resolution was taken from Lev Kamenev at the Politburo in favour of a 'military-economic union' of Russia, Ukraine, Latvia, Lithuania and Belorussia.[35]

This kind of union fell a long way short of political fusion or even federation. But only on paper. The Politburo controlled the entire party and, despite occasions of serious disobedience, the Civil War witnessed a strong insistence of authority on local Bolsheviks and consequently on republic governments. In August 1919 Christian Rakovsky, chairman of the Ukrainian Sovnarkom, was brusquely ordered by the Politburo to close down several People's Commissariats and to dispense with a Ukrainian Council of Defence and Labour.[36] A contrast is sometimes drawn between Lenin and Stalin on basic aspects of the national question. This is wishful thinking. The differences were wholly of secondary importance. Lenin liked to finesse the appearance of policy to a greater extent than Stalin. He also strove to offer minor titbits as concessions to non-Russian national opinion. Typically he wrote an open letter on 28 December 1919 stating that it was up to the workers and peasants of Ukraine to determine 'exactly what federative link' to have with Soviet Russia.[37] No such statements were made by Stalin, Trotski or Zinoviev. But Lenin was disingenuous. He had no intention of holding a plebiscite on secession, on federation, on one-party rule or on anything whatsoever. He was not even going to allow free debate inside the Ukrainian Communist Party. By the end of 1919 he was stamping hard on the chest of local political life, and went on doing so until his own physical breath deserted him.

Yet there was an issue which, while not having a primary significance, mattered a lot. Stalin as People's Commissar for Nationality Affairs was only biding his time as he supported the formation of a military-economic union. Naturally he had no objections to particular further measures which increased the power of Moscow *vis-à-vis* the republics. But his inclination in the longer term was to create a blatantly unitary and centralised state which would differ in structure from the former Russian empire only in granting regional autonomy to areas such as Ukraine.

What Stalin had in mind was the extension of the principle of the Bashkir republic which was already part of the RSFSR. Since the beginning of 1918 it had been party policy to set up administrative enclaves wherever a non-Russian nationality lived in large numbers. This was discovered to be easier said than done. The first large enterprise was the project for a 'Tartar-Bashkir republic'. It was planned by Stalin's Commissariat as early as 18 March 1918, but the battles with the Whites in the Volga region and the Urals rendered it impracticable for a whole year. This was not the only trouble. Relations between Tartars and Bashkirs left much to be desired.[38] Furthermore, the Tartars against the expectations of the Bolsheviks proved to be aggressively self-assertive. Presumably Lenin and Stalin worried also lest too large a Turkic-speaking enclave might result; and they thought it better to foster the creation of not one large but two smaller enclaves. In March 1919 the decision was taken to form an autonomous Bashkirian republic. The Bashrevkom still caused problems. It clashed with the 'Russian' Provincial Cheka in Ufa, and Stalin was called in to mediate between them in September.[39] Then a dispute erupted with the Kirgiz Revkom, which had been set up in July, over territorial boundaries. The clashes persisted into October, and again the Politburo had to step in. As if this was not enough, the exiguous Bolshevik cadres in the Tartar-inhabited lands could not be counted on to support the formation of a Tartar Republic along the model of Bashkiria. The Politburo resolved on 13 December 1919 that only with their sanction would the republic be established.[40]

The basic problem was that, as the Mensheviks had warned the Bolsheviks before 1917, the former Russian empire was a quilt of interstitched nationalities. No single ethnic group lived alone in a clearly demarcated zone; and, as often as not, the attempt to designate such zones aggravated inter-ethnic tensions. There was some compensation for the Bolsheviks. Stalin in 1920 was applauded at the Politburo for suggesting that poor Chechens in the North Caucasus should be rewarded with the land of locally-expropriated Cossack 'kulaks'.[41] The policy was judged to be so successful that it was ordered to be applied, with appropriate modifications, throughout 'the East'.[42] Bolshevism had a deficiency of party cadres in the North Caucasus and Central Asia. In trying to rally support among the resident non-Russians, the Politburo judged that its appeal would be greatest among the lower social strata within them.

Yet this same device was fraught with dangers. Mirsaid Sultan Galiev, a rare Bolshevik from Tataria, had come to believe in the necessity of a huge Turkic-speaking socialist state being carved out of the Russian empire, larger even than the ill-fated Tartar-Bashkir Republic. He also wanted aspects of Islam to be grafted on Bolshevik thought.[43] The Politburo on 26 August 1920 was to refuse him permission to attend the Congress of the Peoples of the East in Baku.[44] Lenin manifestly wanted to resolve the 'national question' within tight parameters. A maverick such as Sultan Galiev might turn into a Soviet Ataturk. In addition, the non-Bolshevik members of the Bashrevkom proved even more intractable in 1920 than in 1918–1919. Some who rebelled against Sovnarkom were put under arrest and, on Stalin's recommendation, transferred to Moscow prisons.[45] The old empire was a mass of turbulent ethnic conflicts. By 1920, too, as the end of the Civil War hove in sight, the reconquest of the Transcaucasus became possible. An Azerbaidzhani Soviet Republic would be declared in April, an Armenian Soviet Republic in November. Nor would the announcement of a Georgian Soviet Republic be long delayed.[46] Being so closely involved both as People's Commissar and as Politburo expert, Stalin concluded that enough was enough. A RSFSR incorporating the various Soviet republics on the Bashkirian model was his proposed solution. Stalin's knowledge of the question was gaining respect among fellow central party leaders.

Only Lenin seriously opposed him. To Lenin, it was self-evident that a fictional federation disguising a real centralist state was massively preferable to an overtly centralist state. The perturbations with the Bashkirs would be trivial in comparison with those likely to be unleashed by the Ukrainians. The alliance between Stalin and Lenin on the 'national question' which had held firm against criticism at the Seventh Party Conference of April 1917 and the Eighth Party Congress of March 1919 was beginning to break apart. Both men had adjusted their opinions in the light of experience; but this led to a parting of the ways. Stalin was moving further and further away from pragmatic compromise with nationalist opinion among non-Russians; and Lenin could not be indifferent to the danger this involved: Stalin had positioned himself much closer than before to the conventional attitudes of the Bolshevik leadership at central and local levels. A clash between Lenin and Stalin might be postponed, but not permanently avoided.[47]

WAR LEADER

Lenin was one of the few leaders to stay in Moscow throughout the Civil War. The only other Central Committee member not to venture forth from the capital was Nikolai Bukharin, who was *Pravda*'s editor; even Krestinski and Kamenev, who spent most of their time there, were given occasional secondments elsewhere. Just once Lenin took a trip to another Russian city after the capital's transfer to Moscow in February 1918: this was his sojourn in Petrograd in July 1920 for the start of the Second Congress of the Communist International.[48] Lenin had no metropolitan prejudice. But he had an exceptional inclination towards centralism, and assumed that his presence in Moscow was crucial to the smooth running of the central political machinery. He considered his contribution to the war effort irreplaceable. An avoidance of physical danger was consequently essential. Since before the Great War he had carried a Browning pistol.[49] After the February Revolution of 1917 he had undeniable reason to guard against assassination; but in neither of the attempts on his life in 1917–1918 did he remove the firearm from its holster. Duckshooting was the nearest he came to experience of armed combat in the Civil War. He visited no front. The nearest he came to a Red Army conscript was on Red Square when greeting a parade commemorating the October Revolution;[50] and his contact with commanders was limited to conversations in the Kremlin, more often than not by telephone.

It is striking how little the conditions of the Civil War entered his speeches and articles. The same had been true in the Great War; and his notes on the theories of von Clausewitz, made by him in 1915, had indicated no great empathy with the sufferings of soldiers.[51] The clichés of wartime reportage passed him by. In mid-1917 he had adduced a chance meeting with an old peasant woman in a *Pravda* article.[52] No such anecdotes appeared in his journalism in the Civil War. Old peasant women in 1918–1920 would have provided him with little in the way of politically supportive anecdotes.

The impression should not be given that his life was entirely cocooned. More than once his chauffeur Stepan Gil was flagged down by Moscow policemen and the official Kremlin limousine fired upon. This even occurred when Lenin, after the arrest of the Left Socialist-Revolutionaries in July 1918, visited their headquarters. He tried to keep a residual contact with ordinary daily existence.[53] As always, he talked to visitors to Moscow who were fellow party members; he also continued to receive groups of peasants who, as once they had brought their grievances to Nicholas II, picked out Vladimir Lenin as the new 'little father'. Despite all the posters and newspaper photographs, however, Lenin's image was not well-known among Moscow's inhabitants. This had been crudely proved on 19 January 1919. Lenin and his sister Mariya were being driven by chauffeur Gil to the Sokolniki district on the outskirts of Moscow to visit his wife Krupskaya. As they approached the nearby railway bridge at around six o'clock in the early evening darkness, a small gang of men leapt into the middle of the road. Lenin and Gil assumed that they confronted yet another police check. Nothing could be further from the truth. The gang members were robbers. Lenin was relieved of the contents of his pockets, including his Browning pistol. The thieves put a gun to his head so as to impel his co-passengers to collaborate. Lenin was not completely intimidated. Rather he was astounded, and shouted out to them: 'My name is Lenin.' The expected reaction was not forthcoming. The gang not only did not recognise him; they did not even think that the name was of any significance. When he demanded to see their official documents, they retorted: 'Criminals don't need official documents.'[54]

They then ejected everyone from the official limousine and sped off in it. Lenin had further humiliation in store. He and Mariya turned up at the building of the Sokolniki District Soviet only to discover that even there no one knew what he looked like. The robbers had absconded with his passcard! Eventually he was believed, and Dzierzynski was summoned to Sokolniki to hear Lenin's complaints about the Cheka's level of efficiency. Within days the 'bandits' were arrested. They sought mercy on the grounds that they had assumed they were robbing someone calling himself Levin rather than Lenin.[55] Thus they intimated that they thought their victim to be Jewish. This was not taken as an extenuating circumstance. After all, the Bolshevik party was committed to the eradication of anti-semitism (and, although the fact was not bruited, Lenin was anyway part-Jewish by descent). The robbers were executed. Lenin joked about his surrender of pistol and wallet to the gang in terms borrowed from the lexicon of Marxism: 'Such a compromise was akin to our compromise with the bandits of German imperialism.'[56]

This was self-parody; but it conveyed the combative posture of his leadership. A less ironic example of his militancy occurred in an argy bargy over the command appointments in May 1919. Lenin's telegram to Trotski ran as follows: 'In connection with the coded telegram from the three commanders of the Eastern front I propose we should appoint [S. S.] Kamenev as front commander, remove Kostyaev and appoint Lashevich instead of Aralov. Send a reply about the plenum. I fear that Stalin will not be able to make it for the twenty fifth [of May: RS], and it is harmful to drag you away. I therefore make a proposal for the plenum's postponement and for negotiations to take place over the telegraph.'[57] He could also turn on the pressure on military administrative bodies. Once the strategy was fixed through discussion with Trotski and the Red Army commanders, he harassed officials to implement decisions. A telegram to Kiev, also sent in May 1919, minced no words: 'I repeat my request to telegram me twice weekly about the actual assistance to the Donbass. I insist on the fulfilment of this request. Don't lose the moment of victory over Grigorev, don't let go a single soldier from those who fought against Grigorev. Put out a decree and bring into effect the disarming of the population; shoot on the spot in any case of a hidden rifle.'[58] Sometimes he jabbed even at Trotski: 'I'm extremely staggered by your silence at a moment when, according to information received albeit not yet verified, a break-through in the Millerovo direction had widened and assumed the dimensions of an almost completely irretrievable catastrophe.'[59]

Yet his interference was limited mainly to emergencies; he recognised that Trotski, Stalin and other Bolshevik commissars at the fronts had to take decisions without automatic detailed consultation with Moscow. His own greatest contribution came through his chairmanship of the central party and government bodies which presided over the war effort. Lenin was the motor of the political machinery. He mobilised concerted effort. He ensured co-operativeness – not an insignificant achievement in the light of the contempt shown to each other by Trotski, Stalin and Zinoviev. He was a co-ordinator of people and institutions.

In 1919 he dominated the affairs of Central Committee and Politburo. In accordance with arrangements made in the previous year, the central party bodies constituted the apex of the state's deliberative and decision-making mechanisms. The Politburo exerted the most powerful influence in the Kremlin. It directed foreign policy, guided the Communist International, laid down economic and social policy, supervised the work of all state institutions and controlled military strategy. No party or governmental body came near to it in importance. The Orgburo, which had been established as a parallel inner subcommittee of the Central Committee to handle organisational questions, yielded to the insistence that the Politburo should control appointments to the most important party and governmental posts.[60] Lenin habitually chaired Politburo sessions. No official title was accorded to him; but he was the unchallengeably pre-eminent member of the central party apparatus. And, through the Politburo, he intervened frequently in cases of disagreement among Central Comittee colleagues. They had learned to trust him. Not even the Politburo could meet regularly; Trotski, Stalin and Zinoviev were usually distant from Moscow. He sent telegrams to them, asking for their opinions on items on the Politburo agenda.[61] None of them could complain that major decisions were made without prior deliberation. His aggressive telegrams caused no offence. Lenin's colleagues appear to have treated them as reassurance that someone in the Kremlin cared about them and their work.

If he made his major impact upon the war effort by means of the Politburo chairmanship, his contribution was also great to state institutions. Chief among these initially was Sovnarkom. It was in the collegiate deliberations of the People's Commissars that Lenin managed to put flesh on the bone of Politburo decisions. After Sverdlov's death the legislative work of the Central Executive Committee of the Congress of Soviets became even more of a formality. Sovnarkom's decrees gained in importance; and Lenin ensured that the Politburo's wishes were not merely sanctioned but also elaborated before public announcement. Few decrees with a specifically military implication in any case went through Sovnarkom. Instead they were saved for the Council of Workers' and Peasants' Defence, especially if they touched on matters of supply to the Red Army. The Council was an adjunct of Sovnarkom; its chairman was Lenin.[62]

In an average day, which was extremely busy, Lenin sought to impose the Politburo's will on a state which was woefully chaotic despite its aspirations. Winning the next battle and getting basic supplies to soldiers and workers was as much as he could realistically aim at. This he achieved only in part. Few colleagues questioned but that he did as well as anyone might have done in the circumstances. At a joint session of the Politburo and the Orgburo it was suggested, on 29 April 1919, that he should write leaflets for distribution to peasants.[63] (It was a perennial criticism, since before the Great War, that he wrote too much for sophisticated Marxists and too little for ordinary folk.). But compliance was not enforced. A source of greater irritation was his practice of doing things through the Politburo even when there were enough Central Committee members currently in Moscow to make a quorum; but nothing was done about this until the end of 1920 (when Politburo members were in dispute with each other).[64] On the whole, he was given the benefit of the doubt. His supreme position in Soviet politics was accepted as necessarily deflecting him from such tasks. The co-ordination of the Politburo, Central Committee, Sovnarkom and the Council of Workers' and Peasants' Defence was extraordinarily taxing; and he did it with suitable modesty. He neither received nor asked for any special title.

There was an element of hypocrisy here. Aleksei Rykov was appointed 'dictator for military supply' in mid-1919; it was a noisome appellation which annoyed Rykov.[65] But Lenin was among several central party colleagues who insisted. He was imposing upon Rykov something which he would have resisted for himself. Lenin's refusal of titles, awards and celebrations was to some extent a self-regarding tactic. He wanted everyone, including the closest associates, to perceive him as lacking all personal ambition and lust for power and renown.

Not that the modest persona he cultivated in public was entirely artificial. Lenin was genuinely devoid of vanity. He abhorred the ceremonials of the tsars; he despised the pomp and sartorial carefulness of Western liberal and conservative leaders as well as the moderate socialists who emulated them. And, if he had lived to witness it, he would have been both appalled and amused by the strutting behaviour of Mussolini and Hitler. Lenin was a fellow of simple habits. He drank little, ate plainly, took walks around the Kremlin. Only a few perks came his way. He went shooting in the forests with leading Bolsheviks. He had his personal chauffeur, and servants cleaned the Kremlin apartment he shared with Nadezhda Krupskaya. He had a large library in his Kremlin office; his requests for books from Moscow libraries and from bookshops abroad were given priority. When convalescing, he could use the Gorki sanatorium thirty five kilometres from Moscow. Yet the little time he spent away from Moscow and political leadership was far from being non-political. His only friends were Bolsheviks.

Nearly all were comrades rather than friends. Inessa Armand still loved him, but was rarely in Moscow. He let few people close to his innermost feelings. Such comforts as were available to him from his position as head of government were anyway regarded by Lenin as enabling him to concentrate upon the consolidation of the October Revolution.

EXPORT OF REVOLUTION, SIEGE ECONOMY

The activities of Lenin and his associates in 1919 demonstrate that, after the treaty of Brest-Litovsk, the party still adhered to its objective of European socialist revolution. The Hungarian Soviet Republic's formation was greeted warmly in Moscow. Its leader Béla Kun was to reveal, indiscreetly, that considerable financial assistance reached him in Budapest and that Lenin had been the instigator of its provision.[66] Lenin also wished to supply military assistance to the extent that the Red Army was capable. On 21 March he cabled to General Vacietis: 'The advance into part of Galicia and Bukovina is necessary for contact with Soviet Hungary. This task must be accomplished more quickly and soundly, but no occupation of Galicia and Bukovina is necessary beyond the limits of this task.' He then added: 'The second task is to establish a link with Soviet Hungary along the railways.'[67] The limit on Lenin's willingness to deploy force was the contemporary threat posed by Admiral Kolchak in the Civil War. On 13 May he encouraged Kun by sending a telegram indicating that 'yesterday Ukrainian armed forces, having beaten the Romanians, crossed the river Dniestr'.[68] He and the rest of the Bolshevik leadership had been equally cheered by the communist seizure of power in Munich. A Bavarian Soviet Republic was declared in mid-April. In northern Italy, especially Turin, workers' councils were being established with the participation of local communists. It was beginning to look as if the predictions made by Lenin in 1917 were coming true. 'However heavy the situation,' he claimed before the Moscow City Soviet, 'we can confidently say that we will defeat international imperialism.'[69]

Already, however, the Hungarian and Bavarian Soviet Republics appeared fragile, and Lenin sensed that the Hungarian comrades were too reckless for their own good. On 23 March he insisted that Kun should avoid a 'naked imitation' of the October Revolution in Russia.[70] Romanian troops advanced in the direction of Budapest in the second fortnight of April. Kun pleaded in vain for Red Army detachments.[71] The most that Lenin, Chicherin, Trotski and the generals would allow was the dispatch of forces to menace the Romanian forces from the rear;[72] but a full-scale invasion was ruled out. The Bavarian Soviet Republic was suppressed in early May. On 18 June, Lenin advised Béla Kun to open negotiations with the Allies rather than fight on hopelessly.[73] Kun was torn between unrealistic ambition and despair; he was also rancorously, unfairly accusing Chicherin and Rakovsky of abandoning him. Lenin defended his colleagues; but the sole counsel he could give was as follows: 'Hold on for all you are worth, and ours shall be the victory.'[74]

Lenin was wrong about this: the Hungarian Soviet Republic was overthrown by late August and Béla Kun fled to Moscow. Yet Lenin was right in his caution about international relations in the Baltic region. Not only did he and Chicherin aim to avoid giving offence to the Allies; they also strained to minimise the involvement of the independent states in the anti-Bolshevik military operations of the year. The Estonian, Latvian and Lithuanian communist governments established in the winter of 1918–1919 quickly collapsed. Estonia resumed its independence from Moscow in February 1919. The Lithuanian Soviet Republic, proclaimed in January, was merged with the Belorussian Soviet Republic into the so-called 'Litbel'; but it was crushed in April, partly as the result of a Polish incursion. By May the Latvian Soviet republic had also been disbanded. As the Red Army concentrated upon Denikin, the Politburo sought peace with the Baltic states. Its members were prodded by Chicherin into considering a settlement. The matter came before the Politburo on 11 September, and it took all the pressure that Lenin could muster to secure a decision to end the condition of war with Latvia and Lithuania as well as with Finland. Estonia was not yet considered for inclusion in the process, presumably because Yudenich remained on its territory. Lenin's difficulty lay in countering the arguments of the 'native' communist leaders of the Baltic region who wanted to keep their respective countries on the agenda of revolutionary expansion. But Lenin pulled the Politburo to his pragmatic viewpoint. Political and military prudence prevailed.[75]

The Estonian question continued to divide the Politburo. Trotski demanded the Red Army's right to invade the country if its government gave sanctuary to Yudenich (as was to happen in mid-November).[76] Chicherin opposed on the grounds that such a policy would destroy the impression, eagerly cultivated by Soviet diplomacy, that the Russian republic was uninterested in extending socialism to foreign states on the point of a bayonet.[77] It was a matter of public appearance; Chicherin was not hostile in principle to military conquest, but judged the moment politically inappropriate. Initially he had Lenin's support.[78] But subsequently Lenin agreed with Trotski that Yudenich should not only be driven back from Petrograd but also be sought out and liquidated as a military force.[79]

But not even Trotski wanted the reconquest of Estonia; and, once Yudenich had been defeated, negotiations with the Estonian government were undertaken. By late December Estonian independence had been recognised; by early February 1920 there were full diplomatic relations between Tallinn and Moscow. A breach in the wall of international capitalism, Lenin felt, had been obtained. The Allies were not as easily wooed as were these former provinces of the Russian empire. Even so, there were signs of a breakthrough. Lloyd George questioned the practicability of the Allied economic blockade from September 1919. The treaty of Versailles had been signed in June, and imposed a huge indemnity upon Germany. The subsequent treaties of St Germain and Trianon had broken up the Habsburg lands into separate states. Militarily, too, it was very punitive. Quite what might soon be inflicted upon the Soviet régime was open to guesswork. Through summer 1919 Lenin kept a discreet silence about Allied intentions.[80] He must have been relieved that his dire predictions about the imperialism of the United Kingdom and France in 1917 were not fulfilled.[81] He may well have been momentarily putting his eggs in the basket of European revolution and hoping for success in Hungary and elsewhere. Whatever he was thinking, he knew that a purely Russian programme of action would not bring salvation. Events in Europe had to have their own dynamism. For this reason he could hardly fail to breathe a sigh of relief when, in April, the French began to pull back from Odessa. Still more encouraging was the decision of the Supreme Allied Council in January 1920 to lift its blockade of Soviet Russia.[82]

Just as he had not highlighted the danger from the Allies in mid-1919, so Lenin eschewed any welcome for the lifting of the blockade. He had no wish to appear to be at the mercy of foreign states. But he wished also to make maximum use of the situation: the official policy of Sovnarkom in 1918 to seek concessionnaires abroad to sink capital into Russian industry was resumed. Precisely this was said by Lenin in an interview with the *Christian Science Monitor* in September 1919.[83] At the same time he jotted down an open letter to American workers justifying such a démarche.[84] Nevertheless, knowing the unpopularity of concessions and being busy with a thousand other duties, Lenin left it to the People's Commissariat of Foreign Trade to draw up a detailed plan in January.[85] The incumbent supreme official was Lev Krasin, who submitted theses on concessions to Sovnarkom under Lenin's chairmanship on 20 March 1920.[86]

So what on earth was Lenin up to? His commitment to European socialist revolution, strong as it was, was subsumed under the priority for the survival of the Russian Socialist Federal Soviet Republic. This had never disappeared from his calculations; and, to his satisfaction, it had also become the viewpoint of most of his Left Communist opponents of 1918. Lenin and his colleagues were disappointed by events in Munich and Budapest in 1919. They still expected that a fraternal régime would emerge somewhere in Europe. The communist political advances in northern Italy were encouraging, and the set-back in Germany was not reckoned to be permanent. Lenin perceived that the punitive terms of the treaty of Versailles could not but help the cause of the Communist International in Germany. At the time he behaved cautiously, barely commenting on the treaty.[87] And in any case he wanted to ride two horses at once. If European socialist revolution was still his hope, he was equally determined to attract capital investment in Russia from foreign entrepreneurs. The contradictions in this dual policy did not worry him. Likewise he would aim to procure security for his party and state by playing upon the divisions of interest among the 'imperialist powers' around the world. Ultimate optimism was accompanied by short-term manoeuvring and compromise. Lenin was a stealthy, sinuous politician.[88]

Nowhere was he more subtle than in his statements on the Soviet economy. In 1917 he had often explained his project for industry and agriculture; in 1919 he judged it best to maintain the reticence observable in the previous year. The single topic attracting generous comment was the food-supplies situation; and he mentioned his passion about the country's electrification but twice in the year after the Eighth Party Congress.[89] For the rest of the time he dwelt on generalities: nationalisation, forcible procurement, centralisation and discipline.[90]

His stance was calculated for public effect. In the Sovnarkom and the Council of Labour and Defence he was highly active and highly vocal. He was sensitive to the run-down of industrial output. The priority was not yet reconstruction of factories and mines but the maintenance of those which might be crucial to the war effort. The Red Army needed guns and munitions. For this reason, special attention was given to the armaments plants in Petrograd and Tula. Strikes broke out all over the areas controlled by the Russian Soviet republic. The laws became ever more severe; but they reflected the weakness of the authorities.[91] The Politburo, recognising the need to keep at least the acquiescence of the working class, was horrified by work-stoppages in Ivanovo-Voznesensk – the main textile city. The People's Commissar of Food Supplies, Aleksandr Tsyurupa, was instructed to divert grain to bring the strikes to an end.[92] In general the Politburo – as well as all the state agencies which were subordinate to it – maintained the development of policies from 1918.[93] Nationalisation of industry descended from large-scale enterprises down to small factories and even mere workshops. Sovnarkom's decrees entrusted an increasing authority in the Supreme Council of the People's Economy. And yet the collapse of factory and mining output accelerated. The official industrial value in 1919 was merely forty four per cent of what it had been in the previous year.[94] Desperate People's Commissars were driven to allowing temporary remissions in the ban on private trade in food. The sack-men who brought grain into the cities were supplying a half of the urban diet even when their activities were illegal.[95]

Nevertheless there was no relenting in the policies of party and government. No faction in the party called for change apart from the emerging Workers' Opposition. The Left Communists no longer existed as a separate group. The centralising and nationalising tendencies were entirely to their liking: they had lost the diplomacy of Brest-Litovsk but won the economics of Civil War. The Military Opposition had no particular opinion of industry, agriculture and trade; and this was true also of the Democratic Centralists. Even the Workers' Opposition, led by Aleksandr Shlyapnikov, had yet to elaborate their proposal. Shlyapnikov wanted to provide workers and peasants with greater control over production and distribution in the economy. He emphasised the role to be played by the trade unions as a counterweight to the Bolshevik party. But it was a sign of Lenin's confidence that he refrained from comment on Workers' Oppositionist notions.[96]

Initiative in foreign and military affairs came often from Lenin, but not in relation to the economy in 1919. Trotski inaugurated the debates in the central party leadership. He it was who, on 15 January 1920, instigated the formation of 'labour armies' out of peasant conscripts who were expecting to be demobilised as the Civil War's end drew within sight. In Trotski's view, the methods which had won the War should be applied to peacetime economic reconstruction. It was therefore crucial to apply military discipline to the workforce.[97] Stalin went along with Trotski's argumentation and became leader of the First Labour Army.[98] Lenin ostensibly felt likewise. But he chose his words carefully when supporting the labour armies. In a speech to the Moscow Provincial Party Conference on 13 March 1920, which was censored heavily in the report by *Pravda*, he gave his approval to the labour armies only reservedly. He argued that the very size of the Red Army made rapid demobilisation impossible. Consequently, according to Lenin, the troops should be retained under military discipline and deployed for economic duties.[99] This was a long way from endorsing labour armies as a main durable agency of post-war reconstruction, and exemplified the disjunction between the thinking of Lenin and Trotski. Militarisation of labour, for Lenin, was a regrettable necessity and not a policy to glory in.[100]

Lenin and Trotski gave their speeches on the issues without naming each other in dispute; the tone was comradely. In the Central Committee, however, tempers flared. In February 1920 Trotski put forward yet another proposal. This time he suggested that the dire shortage of bread in the towns could be solved only by removing certain regions of the country – Ukraine, the Don and Siberia – from the system of forcible grain requisitioning. The situation in the Urals had convinced him that peasant hostility to the régime would otherwise increase beyond control.[101]

Trotski did not imply that his proposed reform was to be permanent. Nor did he fail to stress that it should be restricted to certain regions; and he also insisted on the desirability of introducing collective farms and compulsory labour in them – and, despite his later attempt to gloss over the fact, he did not envisage the project of labour armies for battle-hardened Red conscripts as an alternative to his proposals for agriculture. On the contrary, they were complementary to each other. Force was basic to his perspective on both urban and rural economic reconstruction.[102] And yet, to his astonishment, the Central Committee debate was furious. Grain requisitioning was the cornerstone of Bolshevik wartime policy: the idea that a private market in wheat and rye might return was anathema to the party's leaders. Lenin was so infuriated that he accused Trotski of supporting 'Free Trade-ism'.[103] The vote went against Trotski by eleven to four. Thereby a chance was lost to restore the exchange of goods between town and countryside. Trotski was badly shaken by his experience. He never ceased to believe that the Central Committee had been wrong to reject his proposal, and took a bitter pleasure a year later when his persecutor Lenin instigated a reform of food-supplies policy remarkably similar to his own.[104] But on this occasion Trotski did not fight his corner. Lenin had won the debate, and Trotski chose to concentrate on his work in the Red Army and areas of economic policy where he could get Lenin to compromise with him.[105]

LENIN AND RELIGION

Among the subjects which had been aired at the Eighth Party Congress had been religion. Surveys carried out in the mid-1920s were to show that the great majority of the Russian population remained Christian by belief; and the Bolsheviks knew that in the peripheral zones of the old empire – in the Ukraine, the Baltic region, Georgia and Armenia – devotion to national denominations had been unaltered by the calls of the party to abandon the faith. The Muslim populations of Azerbaidzhan, central Asia and the Volga region were deeply attached to their religious customs. Most citizens of the Soviet republic ruled over by the godless Lenin were believers.

After the October Revolution he had taken a lead in the government's measures. His Land Decree at the Second Congress of Soviets had expropriated all the landed property of the Russian Orthodox Church, and his Basic Law on the Socialisation of the Land in February 1918 had confirmed this.[106] The intention was that, by undermining the economic resources of religious institutions, popular belief in God (or god, as Lenin put it) would be foreshortened. Other measures, too, were put in hand. Civil marriages and civil divorces were discussed in Sovnarkom and passed into law.[107] Lenin had gone through a Church marriage ceremony in Siberia in 1898, giving Krupskaya a copper ring made by a local artisan.[108] He now broke the legal link between wedding ceremonies and religion. At first the Orthodox Church kept out of politics; but on 19 January, when the Germans seemed likely to overrun Russia and eliminate Bolshevism, Patriarch Tikhon pronounced an anathema on Sovnarkom. This was not a call to arms: priests were instructed to undertake only passive resistance.[109] The régime intensified the pressure. Lenin on 23 January 1918 signed a Decree on the Separation of the Church from the State and School from the Church. This forbade the Church to hold property and prohibited its involvement in general schooling. It could no longer own even its cathedrals; and, on 19 April 1918, the People's Commissariat of Justice established a Liquidation Department for the purpose of nationalising the Church's property.[110] Tikhon bowed before superior physical force. On 25 September 1918, after the Red Army had turned back the Czechoslovak Legion's invasion, he enjoined his fellow believers to recognise the authority of the Soviet state so long as its orders did not contravene the dictates of their consciences. He refused to send blessings to the White armies in the Civil War.[111]

Tikhon wanted the Reds to be defeated and did not withdraw his anathema on them; but his aim was to facilitate the Church's survival until such time as Lenin's government fell from office. Lenin appreciated the potential of the Patriarchate as a focus for anti-Bolshevik opposition. But he, too, acted cautiously. On 20 October 1918, at the First All-Russian Congress of Women Workers, he argued that excessive zeal in the extirpation of 'religious prejudices' would be counterproductive. 'The masses' would only split into separate camps, and the party would lose support.[112] At the Eighth Party Congress in March 1919 he suggested that the Bolsheviks would merely give rise to fanaticism if offence was given to the beliefs of Christians. Atheism had to be disseminated tactfully so that 'an actual liberation of the labouring masses from religious prejudices' might occur.[113]

This attitude to ordinary Russian Orthodox believers was counterparted by a savage persecution of the Church's leaders. Lenin was cunning. Tikhon was spared imprisonment because of the likely popular hostility; but other servants of the Church were less fortunate. According to figures released by Tikhon, twenty eight bishops and thousands of priests were killed between 1918 and 1920. Even 12,000 ordinary believers were arrested during religious devotions and executed.[114] It is highly improbable that Lenin strongly disapproved. He disguised his attitude, presumably for fear of infuriating the faithful. He rarely spoke about the Orthodox Church in the first three years of his rule; those speeches at the Congress of Women Workers and at the Eighth Party Congress were the sole major examples. He and his fellow leaders desisted from reconsidering their policies on the Orthodox Church once the decrees of 1918 had been issued.[115] Behind the scenes, Lenin blatantly fomented anti-religious violence. A telegram from him to the Penza Soviet Provincial Executive Committee on 9 August 1918 may well be the tip of a bloodstained iceberg: 'Received your telegram. It is necessary to organise a reinforced guard from specially trustworthy people to carry out a merciless mass terror against kulaks, priests and White Guardists; to lock up doubtful types in a concentration camp outside the town. Get an expedition in motion. Telegraph about implementation.'[116]

The Russian Orthodox Church was the one remaining institution capable of rallying most ethnic Russians against Sovnarkom and was singled out for maltreatment by the Cheka.[117] Lenin and Dzierzynski took a different attitude to the other Christian denominations. This self-restraint was entirely a matter of *Realpolitik*. As early as 1903, at the Second Party Congress, Lenin had brought the 'sects' to the party's attention. Their grievances against the Romanov autocracy, he argued, should be used by Marxists as a means of strengthening the struggle against Nikolai II. The party should campaign for freedom of conscience for all denominations; and Lenin's friend V. D. Bonch-Bruevich, an expert on the sects, was encouraged to write pamphlets explaining how the egalitarian ideals of early Christianity could be implemented only by a state committed to Marxism.[118]

Even so, Lenin did not publicly refer to the sects at all in the Civil War. He mentioned Judaism and Islam only rarely. He took the trouble to oppose antisemitism by recording a speech, 'On the Pogrom Slandering of the Jews', on a new-fangled gramophone disc.[119] But only a few thousand Russians had gramophones and the speech was not carried by any newspaper.[120] Lenin's attentiveness was little greater towards Islam. On 20 November 1917 he and Stalin had co-signed a proclamation to 'all labouring Moslems of Russia and the East' which guaranteed their freedom to worship;[121] Lenin also warned at the Eighth Party Congress in March 1919 against offending Muslim sensibilities, and declared that the influence of the mullahs in central Asia was even greater than the influence of priests in Russia.[122] But otherwise he avoided the topic of religion. Not even at the Second Congress of the Communist Organisations of the Peoples of the East, on 22 November 1919, did he expatiate on his views.[123] The reasons for this failure can only be guessed at. But one factor must surely come into the reckoning: this is that the Bolsheviks were already regarded by many Russian Orthodox Christians as a gang of marauding Jews. There was no disguising the fact that persons of Jewish origin were the largest ethnic group in the Central Committee; and even the non-Jewish members of the Central Committee were, by a majority, non-Russian. Almost certainly Lenin did not want to inflame Russian popular opinion by siding too openly with religious believers who did not belong to Russia's national church. His decrees of 1917 and the Soviet Constitution of July 1918 had promulgated freedom of conscience in the Soviet republic. This, he must have felt, was already enough.

Not that conditions were pleasant for these other religious believers – be they Christian sectarians, Jews or Moslems – in the Civil War. The separation of the Orthodox Church from the state had been greeted by them as a sign that the discrimination against them practised under Nicholas II and not entirely removed even by the Provisional Government had been abolished. Yet the interlude came to an end. The various decrees in 1918 on property, on schooling and on the propagation of religious faith were applicable to them as well as to the Church of Tikhon; and, as the Red Army asserted control in areas where the population held to their traditional religion, there were frequent barbarities.

In Lenin's defence it could be said that religious persecution was not confined to the actions of the Reds. The Whites treated non-Christians appallingly and antisemitism was a prominent aspect of their ideology.[124] Most Jews preferred to live under Lenin than under Kolchak. In any case his target for persecution was not the generality of believers but their organisations, buildings and official representatives. If he had wished to direct the Red terror against all believers, he would have threatened the lives of all but a minority of the population. Bishops and priests were indeed to be found ministering to the forces of the Whites. Lenin was fighting a Civil War; he would rather over-repress than risk leaving opponents the chance to counter-attack.[125] Nor was he the most avid advocate of militant atheism among the Bolshevik party leaders. In discussions over the Constitution in summer 1918 he had supported the formal right to conduct 'religious propaganda'. P. I. Stucka, People's Commissar for Justice, had led a group which regarded Lenin's position as unnecessarily indulgent to religion in general.[126] Lenin won the day. Even so, he continued to have to protect his position against Bolsheviks with ideas more extreme than his own. His words on religion at the Eighth Party Congress had been meant to restrain comrades such as Nikolai Bukharin who hankered after a more militant set of measures.[127]

All these extenuating factors notwithstanding, Lenin was a harrier of organised religion. Any gentleness towards it was based on pragmatic considerations. Any relief of persecution was only temporary. Religion, for him, had always been a 'a sort of spiritual pocheen in which the slaves of capital drown the image of man and their demand for a life more or less human'.[128] All contemporary metaphysical faiths were therefore 'organs of bourgeois reaction serving the defence of exploitation and the stupefying of the working class'.[129] Thus the

Romanov autocracy had needed not only hangmen but also priests to maintain its power.

These words were written before the First World War; but, although Lenin avoided such language after 1917, his sentiment was unchanged that religion was the opium of the people. The 'drug' was as widely used at the end as at the beginning of the Civil War; the Reds had merely assured themselves that the various faiths were unable to promote active resistance to the régime. But Lenin had yet to determine how his government should tackle the question of religion. Lenin's tirades against 'metaphysics' were made not against religious belief but rather against those Marxists who, in his view, had moved away from the materialist conceptions of Karl Marx. He sensed a particular potential menace in the growing attractiveness of the works of the ex-Bolshevik Aleksandr Bogdanov (whom Lenin since 1908 had charged with the 'heinous' offence of philosophical idealism) to some of his close party colleagues.[130] His own version of Marxism, he assumed, was sufficient to provide the ethical foundations of an entirely new social order. In a speech to the Third Congress of the Komsomol, on 2 October 1920, he stated: 'We reject any such morality taken from a supra-human, supra-class conception. We say that it's a deception, that it's a swindle and a blocking-up of the minds of workers and peasants in the interests of landlords and capitalists. We say that our morality is entirely subordinate to the interests of the class struggle of the proletariat.'[131]

THE NINTH PARTY CONGRESS

No Party Congress had met in so triumphal a spirit as the Ninth. Lenin, welcoming the 553 voting delegates to the Bolshoi Theatre on 29 March 1920, exulted: 'The internal development of our revolution has led to the greatest, quickest victories over the enemy in the civil war and, because of the international situation, these victories have turned out nothing less than a victory of the soviet revolution in the weakest and most backward country, a victory over united global capitalism and imperialism.'[132] Expectations rose about central Europe. A report had just come through that 'the Berlin radio station lay in the hands of the German workers.'[133] In fact the Bolsheviks had yet again been misinformed. Yet they did but hope. Lenin gave the Central Committee's political report, emphasising that the Politburo 'had resolved all questions of international and domestic policy'.[134] A furious denunciation of the Allies and all their works followed. But he stressed that certain capitalist powers were starting to reconsider their attitude. Latvia had made peace proposals. Finland wanted to agree on a demarcation line. Even Poland was making pacific overtures.[135] Yet Lenin did not delude his listeners; he declared that these 'small states' would be unable to make peace with Bolshevism unless the Allies, their creditors, gave permission. But he urged that Bolsheviks in the meantime should look on the bright side and get on with 'the peaceful tasks of economic construction'. The bourgeoisie had taken and kept power in their revolutions without prior administrative experience, and the workers would be able to cope equally well.[136]

Nikolai Krestinski followed Lenin with the Central Committee's organisational report. But at the second session, on 30 March, the Central Committee was rebuked.[137] Most speakers tacitly concluded that Lenin had placed excessive stress on the need for one-person leadership. But where did the need end? He was tweaked by T. V. Sapronov, the Democratic Centralist: 'In that case I put the question to comrade Lenin: just who is it who will be appointing the C[entral] C[ommittee]?'[138] Sapronov prophesised that the result would be 'the dictatorship of the party bureaucracy'.[139] He added: 'If you follow this system, do you reckon that therein will lie the salvation of the revolution?'[140] Only when L. M. Kaganovich pleaded for greater centralist severity did the tirades against Lenin relent.[141] B. M. Volin and others praised the Central Committee.[142] Trotski, turning to the Ukraine-based opponents of the central party apparatus, questioned their own efficiency by claiming that, out of every hundred activists they mobilised to the Red Army, 'five went and ninety deserted.'[143]

Krestinski did not trade insults,[144] leaving it for Lenin to summarise the case for the Central Committee. Sapronov was accused of over-gorging himself on theory. 'It is necessary,' declared Lenin in sprawling chunks of rhetoric, 'it is necessary to be able to grasp that we are now faced with *a practical task*, that we must deal with the *businesslike* task of the quickest victory over collapse and ruin with all the forces, with the genuinely revolutionary energy, with the uncompromising zeal with which our best comrades – the workers and peasants in the Red Army – defeated Kolchak, Denikin and Yudenich.'[145] Too much theory, too little action: it was a cheeky attempt to turn defence into attack. And it worked: a majority of delegates voted to accept the joint reports of Krestinski and Lenin.[146] At session three, the same evening, Trotski kept up the non-apologetic style with his report on 'economic construction'. There had already been accusations that Aleksandr Shlyapnikov and other party figures seeking to defend workers' rights tended to be given jobs in the provinces or abroad so as to get them out of the way. Trotski did not play down his ideas before the Congress. He asserted that 'elements of compulsion' had to be incorporated in official labour policy. There should be 'militarisation' of the trade unions. Better an individual good technician running a factory than a collective of elected but unqualified workers.[147]

Trotski was followed by opponents, including People's Commissars N. Osinski and A. I. Rykov, who spoke against one-person leadership, non-electivity and militarisation.[148] Rykov was irritated at Trotski's jibe at him as military supplies 'dictator'.[149] At the fourth session, on 31 March, Sapronov mentioned the personnel transfers in the Ukraine.[150] Trotski was implicitly criticised again when Milyutin urged that the single economic plan should not be a pretext for commissars from the Red Army to acquire civilian jobs.[151] But Lenin repaid Trotski's assistance to him. In particular, he charged Rykov and Milyutin with omitting to supply the Congress with sufficient statistical information to prove their case. He also quoted from his 1918 pamphlet *The Current Tasks of Soviet Power*.[152] He evidently saw no threat to the Trotski-Lenin alliance on the economy; and Trotski felt sure enough of their relationship to admit that, under pressure from Lenin, he had excised the more centralising side of his theses.[153]

Bolshevism's two outstanding leaders presented a united front, not least on one-person leadership and on the need for a 'general state economic plan'. V. M. Smirnov comically asked what would happen to Trotski if Lenin took over the government singlehandedly.[154] Further teasing followed to the end of the fourth session and, that evening, at the fifth.[155] Trotski struck back. V. V. Kosior, he concluded, 'not only reads inattentively but also reads poorly'. Central Committee member M. P. Tomski fared no better: 'I regretfully have to say that comrade Tomski, who receives all the books, has been weaker on these questions than everyone, weaker even than comrade Osinski if this is possible.'[156] The wrangling continued until exhausted delegates voted to hand the draft resolution over to a commission for further editing.[157] At the sixth session on 1 April it was Bukharin who introduced the debate on the trade unions. The same questions of hierarchy, discipline and command re-imposed themselves. Bukharin, who together with Evgeni Preobrazhenski had just published his textbook *The ABC of Communism*, took Shlyapnikov to task as if he were an absent pupil. Shlyapnikov's wish to hand over economic management to the trade unions overlooked the indissoluble bond of politics and economics. According to Bukharin, the party could not afford to abandon its role in economic leadership.[158] The trade unions would have managerial responsibilities. But Bukharin argued that they should fulfil them after having been transformed into state institutions. 'Statification' was the party's objective. Without referring to the controversy kicked up by Trotski, Bukharin acknowledged that the time was unripe for them to be turned into agencies of state; his report was a call for little to be changed in the short term.[159]

The status quo would not do not only for Workers' Oppositionist leaders like Y. O. Lutovinov but also for M. P. Tomski as the party's appointee as chairman of the All-Russian Central Council of the Trade Unions.[160] They saw that the rags of trade union authority were about to be worn thinner. But their appeals fell on deaf ears. Bukharin's draft resolution was accepted as Congress policy.[161] Lenin left things to his colleagues according to the pre-arrangement of the Central Committee. Tiredness was setting in. Radek's report on the Communist International was delivered without accompanying debate in the evening; and on the next day, 2 April, the delegates reduced discussion on the co-operative movement and on political organisation by establishing separate sections to compose drafts for submission to Congress.[162]

Both were fraught affairs. Kamenev smoothed feathers in the organisational section. The draft resolution avoided most of the difficulties raised by the Democratic Centralists and the Workers' Opposition, and concentrated on the registration and indoctrination of rank-and-file party members. Passed unanimously by the section's commission, it was ratified on the nod by Congress at the opening of the eighth session on 3 April.[163] Lenin had less reason to thank his colleagues in the other section. The discussion on the co-operatives involved the whole basis of wartime economic policy. V. P. Milyutin, usually on the right in the politics of Bolshevism, secured the section's approval for theses demanding the nationalisation of co-ops and their transformation 'in a socialist direction'.[164] His démarche was a reminder that even the more cautious Bolsheviks were yet Bolsheviks: Milyutin overlooked peasant attitudes to nationalisation. Krestinski made this very criticism.[165] At this point Lenin, who had heard of the spat only the night before, intervened against Milyutin whom he accused of being impractical and ignorant of Lenin's ideas.[166] Milyutin retorted that Krestinski had played unfair by appealing to 'authorities'. This was the squeal of someone recognising that he would lose. But it was an accurate assessment of Lenin's status: the Congress reversed the section's choice and took Krestinski's draft theses as the basis of its resolution.[167]

Trotski momentarily took a leaf out of Lenin's book and avoided unnecessary controversy. But on 5 April, at session nine, his report on 'the transition to the militia system' was heard respectfully as he mapped out his vision for the Red Army in what everyone thought to be the imminent period of peacetime reconstruction. Trotski kept clear of the disputed themes of the Eighth Party Congress: relations between party and army; military specialists; executions of communists. For once, Trotski adopted Lenin's technique of being vague in order to gather support at the time and have the freedom to act as he wished later. The Congress, opting not to open debate, unanimously accepted his draft resolution in its entirety.[168]

No Party Congress had gone so smoothly for Lenin. On 5 April he addressed its last session. The Central Committee elections had taken place, and he had retained his place with totally predictable ease. Twenty full places had been allocated. Lenin was unconcerned that leaders closer to Trotski than to him – A. A. Andreev, E. A. Preobrazhenski and I. N. Smirnov – had entered since the previous year. Stasova's failure to keep a place, moreover, was a loss to him. But others who had not been elected at the Eighth Congress included A. I. Rykov, J. E. Rudzutak and F. A. Sergeev: each of them preferred Lenin to Trotski.[169] In any case this was not a Central Committee of factions. Disagreements and compromises were frequent, amicable and natural. Lenin confidently roused the Congress with his final oration. He declared that the 600,000 party members would 'work as one man after establishing a tighter link with the economic organs and the organs of the trade unions'. This seemed too tame for a closing speech, and he knew how little attention had been paid to the broadest aims of the party at the Congress. It was quite the most introspective Congress since before 1917. No one had picked up Radek's report on the Communist International in subsequent proceedings. Nor did anyone complain that the agenda had not even included the 'national question' in the lands of the Russian empire. Finishing his remarks on the economy, Lenin triumphantly proclaimed: 'We shall manage to resolve this problem just as victoriously as we resolved the military problem, and shall proceed quickly and firmly to the victory of the Worldwide Socialist Soviet Republic!'[170]

5   The Tar in the Honey

THE POLISH–SOVIET WAR

Civil wars are notoriously messy wars. The military campaigns between the North and the Confederacy in the USA in 1861–1865 had a brutal neatness; but they were exceptional. When a state collapses into internal war, cross-cutting tensions and enmities are typically released. The civil war in England, Scotland, Wales and Ireland in the mid-seventeenth century is an example. National, regional and confessional as well as social and economic divisions became sharper and cut deep tranches of lasting embitterment into the attitudes and practices of the combatant armies.

The 'Russian' Civil War was similarly complex, equally bitter. The year 1917 witnessed not one uniform revolutionary process but a multitude of variegated revolutions, and the ensuing years saw the outbreak of many intersecting civil wars. In 1918 the Bolshevik-led Reds had fought against the armies assembled by the Socialist-Revolutionaries in the Volga. By the end of the year this conflict had been superseded by a struggle between the Reds and the anti-socialist forces of the Whites. Russians fought with Russians. The peasantry's hostility to taxation and conscription induced thousands of peasants to go into the nearby woods and fight off all outsiders. These 'Greens' hated Reds and Whites indiscriminately. Nor were the various campaigns exclusively a Russian affair. The first great campaign after the October Revolution was the invasion of the Ukraine by Bolshevik-led troops in December 1917. It was re-invaded by the Reds in 1918 after the German defeat by the Allies. There was also much fighting between the various non-Russian peoples. Border disputes raged among the Armenians, Azeris and Georgians; and the violence involved adjacent states. The Turkish government sent its forces into territory claimed by Georgia. Military intervention in the former Russian Empire was not confined to major powers such as Germany, France, the United Kingdom and the USA. All sides were enmeshed in large civil wars within the Civil War.

Poland was another complication. In December 1919 the Supreme Allied Council called for a frontier to be drawn between Russia and

Poland (which was to be named the Curzon Line after the British Foreign Secretary). Yet the Polish prime minister, Ignacy Paderewski, claimed that the borders of the first independent Polish state since 1795 required historical and demographic debate. The Bolshevik commitment to European revolution, too, exacerbated the situation. No Polish or Soviet leader seriously expected that conflict of some kind could permanently be avoided. In 1919 the Polish forces had helped to demolish the 'Lit-Bel' Soviet Republic and entered Vilnius as conquerors. In addition, conflicts had occurred between Polish and non-Bolshevik Ukrainian forces. Negotiations in the autumn between Sovnarkom and Paderewski were aborted by mutual mistrust; and the Polish military commander Josef Pilsudski held talks with the ousted Ukrainian nationalist leader Semion Petlyura for a war to be fought to establish a border federation of Poland and Ukraine in opposition to the Soviet republic of Lenin and Trotski.[1]

After a winter's preparation, Pilsudski struck in spring 1920. The campaign was brief. Kiev was under Polish occupation on 7 May.[2] Such seizures of power had happened so often in the Ukraine in the previous years that Lenin was not unduly disconcerted. Bolsheviks were enjoined by him to treat 'the new adventure with utmost tranquillity'. His explanation of Pilsudski's motives was curious. Lenin maintained that the Poles were primarily seeking to lengthen the line of contact between Moscow and Berlin and thereby inhibit a German socialist revolution. It did not occur to him that Polish developments were predominantly autochthonous.[3] But Lenin's judgement, eccentric as it was, revealed what was in his own mind. Despite having insisted on the signing of the Brest-Litovsk treaty in 1918, he had never forsworn the export of Soviet revolution on the point of Red bayonets should a suitable opportunity offer itself.[4] Other Bolsheviks who had advocated the same treaty were not immune from a subsequent compulsion to prove their revolutionary credentials by advocating risky ultra-leftist putsches. Zinoviev, who had an additional stain on his record for having opposed the October Revolution, was to behave in this fashion when calling for a German communist seizure of power in 1923. But Lenin had no need to demonstrate the genuineness of his radicalism. He acted in mid-1920 as he would have done with or without Brest-Litovsk. For him, the treaty of 1918 had always been a manoeuvre that was a temporary necessity. Pilsudski's incursion gave him the chance he had awaited.

Throughout May 1920 the Politburo was gathering military and political personnel to form a Western front against the Poles. Trotski was given oversight of the forthcoming campaign, and Stalin was attached to its southern sector with Budenny's cavalry units which had been recalled from other war zones.[5] The Red Army moved swiftly. Fierce but brief battles took place in the approach to Kiev, resulting in defeat for the Poles. By 10 June, Pilsudski had been forced to evacuate the Ukrainian capital. His forces were pursued and harassed by the Reds. Negotiations with the Lithuanian government produced an agreement for a joint Red and Lithuanian attack on Vilnius, which fell on 14 July. The Reds pressed on and took Grodno, and by this success they approached the moment of decision; for immediately ahead of them lay the notional Curzon line. Any further movement would have indicated a will to invade territory recently declared to belong to Poland by the Allied Supreme Council. The Bolsheviks would be disclosing a desire to use their armies to envelop Europe in political disturbances and insurrections.[6]

The British Foreign Office sent a telegram to Moscow on 11 July calling for the Curzon line to be respected.[7] The Bolshevik Central Committee assembled for a plenum on 17 July. Participation was high: seventeen full and candidate members attended, and Stalin was the sole figure from the Politburo who was absent. The Polish-Soviet war was far from dominating the agenda. Deliberations on both the Second Congress of the Communist International and several wrangles over personnel preceded the item on the telegram from Lord Curzon. The decision was to reject the British request. Chicherin was told to reply to Curzon in kind and Trotski to draw up a suitably rousing public proclamation; and the Secretariat was instructed to mobilise all Poles in the party for deployment on the Western front.[8] The Commander-in-Chief of the Western front, Mikhail Tukhachevski, received the political sanction he had wanted. On 23 July he issued the order that the Red Army should cross the river Bug and occupy Warsaw.[9] On the same day the Polish Bureau of the Central Committee appointed a Provisional Polish Revolutionary Committee. It was to be chaired by Julian Marchlewski; his colleagues were to be Feliks Dzierzynski, Feliks Kon, Edward Prochniak and Josef Unszlicht. This act showed that the Bolsheviks aimed at more than hot pursuit in order to teach Pilsudski a lesson. The Provisional Polish Revolutionary Committee, or Polrevkom, proclaimed the removal of the country's existing cabinet and issued decrees on land, industry, administration and security in line with Bolshevik policies in Russia since 1917. The inclusion of Cheka leaders Dzierzynski and Unszlicht showed that no mercy would be shown. The Polrevkom shifted its headquarters westwards as the Red

Army advanced. Dzierzynski awaited his triumphant return to Warsaw.[10]

Inside the core of the Bolshevik central leadership there was a sharp reversal of the roles played in the Brest-Litovsk dispute. Trotski, especially after his inspection tour of the troops, urged caution; Radek was even more dubious as to the reception the Reds would receive from Polish workers and peasants.[11] Both had opposed a separate peace with Germany in 1918. Lenin, who had insisted on avoiding war at that time, had become its most committed advocate. By coincidence Stalin, too, had moved to a pro-war position alongside Lenin; but even he had worries about the invasion. His particular concern was lest the Reds at both front and rear were inadequately organised, inspirited and co-ordinated. Lenin was the sole fire-breathing enthusiast.[12]

Thus it would not be too far-fetched to argue that, if the attack on Kiev had been more a war of Pilsudski than of the Polish government, the advance on Warsaw came predominantly from Vladimir Lenin. This was not the first time that, in contrast with his own party's left wing, he overestimated the willingness of foreign workers to disregard the patriotic summonses of their governments. This intra-party phenomenon was observable throughout the Great War. His perception of the significance of nationalism was acute in relation mainly to the territory of the old Russian empire (whereas the Bolshevik left tended to have fuzzy vision here).[13] In any case he was not wholly devoid of corroborating data. Reports of restlessness among the workers of both Warsaw and Berlin were not absent in summer 1920. Lenin was not entirely stupid in supposing that the political situation was more fluid than his more cautious colleagues, despite their closer contact with the Red Army, intimated; and, because he was in Moscow and they were at or near the front, he was well-placed to push his policy on them. They, moreover, shared the assumption that the October Revolution in Russia would expire unless fraternal revolutionary states were established elsewhere in Europe; they had also become loath to challenge Lenin's general judgement: by 1920 it was accepted in the Central Committee that he had been right about the October Revolution and the treaty of Brest-Litovsk. The idea that his intuition might be fallible was becoming heretical.

His main difficulty was with the men in the Polrevkom who had a more leftist attitude to politics than he. So far from wanting to hand the land over to the Polish peasantry as had been done in Russia, Marchlewski aimed to nationalise it and set up collective farms. Lenin was furious. A chance might be lost to keep the sympathy of the peasants as the Red Army advanced.[14] Nor, on the other hand, was this proponent of state terror entirely convinced that the Polrevkom would take the brutal measures against the gentry, the clergy and the old régime in Poland that he thought vital. All through the summer he urged an expansion of terrorism.[15] On 19 August he sent a message to Radek which showed how his worries about the land and the terror coalesced: 'I beg you, go direct to Dzierzynski and insist that the gentry and the kulaks are destroyed ruthlesslessly and rather more quickly and energetically, also that the peasants are effectively helped to take over estate land and forest.'[16] For not even Lenin, despite his unbridled optimism, thought that the Red Army with its northern sector under Tukhachevski could occupy Poland and unaided set up a socialist administration. The aim was to help the Polish workers to help themselves, and then to move on to Germany. In late July 1920 it looked to Lenin and to many governments in the West that he might well succeed.

'THE INFANTILE DISEASE OF"LEFTISM" IN COMMUNISM'

In April and May 1920, in advance of the Second Congress of the Communist International, Lenin composed a pamphlet of thirty thousand words. He wrote it out as usual in longhand; the experience of trying to dictate his thoughts to a duty secretary, which had briefly been forced on him after the attempt on his life in mid-1918, had been uncongenial. Despite his many other commitments, he made time to do things in the way he liked.[17]

The pamphlet began with a declaration: 'At the present historical moment, the situation is precisely that the Russian model displays something – and something extremely essential – to *all* countries about their inevitable and not distant future.'[18] The October Revolution showed, he argued, that socialism required 'the most merciless war' to be waged by the proletariat against the bourgeoisie. This in turn necessitated 'the unconditional centralisation and strictest discipline' of the proletariat; and the proletariat's leadership, the party, had also to adhere to 'the strictest centralisation and iron discipline'.[19] The Bolsheviks in Lenin's opinion had been placed in an excellent position to learn the necessary lessons early. The harshness of the Romanov monarchy had forced Russian socialist theorists into becoming émigrés and thus brought them into contact with the rest of the world's latest ideas, and the years before 1917 saw the Bolsheviks test these out intensively in a variety of activities: illegal and legal work; small party groups and mass organisation; parliamentarianism and terrorism.[20] Lenin's argument was that the Bolshevik tradition had not been leftism for its own sake. Mistakes had been made. Lenin recalled the boycott of the First State Duma in 1906 and the initial refusal to sign a peace treaty with the Germans in 1918.[21] (This was also a piece of self-promotion: Lenin had wanted both to enter the Duma and sign the peace.) The point was that Bolshevism had had to cure itself periodically of an affliction he called 'the infantile disease of leftism'.[22]

According to Lenin, compromise between revolutionary élan and practical prudence had been at the heart of official party policies under his leadership. There was some truth in this; but it neglected Lenin's periods of recklessness and intransigence. His summons for insurrection at all costs and without delay in autumn 1917 was a classic instance. This is exactly what was best known about him among the Communist International delegates already assembling for the Congress in Moscow. Lenin wanted to describe the less rumbustious episodes of the past. His détour into the history of his party drove home the message to left-wing elements in the Communist International's parties that the Russian Communist Party, the only affiliated party which had seized and kept power, had achieved its ends by avoiding ultra-leftist sloganeering.[23]

Among his targets were the communists of Germany. The recently-formed German Communist Party had already lost its left-wingers, who had established the German Workers' Communist Party. Within the German Communist Party itself there remained a left-wing faction highly critical of the official leadership. The malcontents argued that insufficient effort had been given to involving the working class in the running of the party. As a result, they said, a 'party of leaders' had emerged rather than a 'mass party'. The German left-wing communists aimed at a dictatorship of the proletariat wherein the proletariat held direct power.[24] Many also questioned whether party activists should bother with work in trade unions. They placed a premium on political propaganda and organisation undertaken exclusively in the party.[25] Lenin was scathingly realistic: 'We can (and must) begin to construct socialism not from human material which exists in fairy-tales and is specially created by us but from the legacy bequeathed to us by capitalism.'[26] Then he dealt with the contention of the German leftist faction that parliaments were 'an historically and politically redundant' arena of revolutionary struggle.[27] Lenin repeated his pre-1914 argument that, while parliamentarianism would not produce a transition to socialism, no party should pass up the opportunities afforded by Dumas and Reichstags for propaganda.[28] Compromises were a necessity for mature revolutionaries in quest of power. Permanent flexibility was required. Lenin maintained that it was Kautsky, Bauer and other opponents of communist parties who held to fixed and unalterable strategical schemata. Here was a typical polemical flourish. The ultra-leftism inside and outside the German Communist Party was identified by him with the Kautskyism which was considered a heresy throughout the Communist International.[29]

The German Communist Party as a whole – and not just its leftists – was called upon by Lenin to be more flexible. The German Independent Social-Democratic Party, which included Kautsky in its leadership, was riven by factionalism, and its left-wing sections had approached the German Communist Party for co-operation. The German Communist Party, in Lenin's opinion, had wrongly rejected these overtures. He claimed that, between the February and October Revolutions, his policy had been to manoeuvre and compromise in relations with the Mensheviks so as to detach their 'best workers' from them.[30] This was an astonishing claim for the protagonist of total irreconcilability.[31] But Lenin's distortion of the history of 1917, with which the non-Russian parties of the Communist International were ill-acquainted, served current political ends. A Soviet Germany was his primary foreign objective. But realism was essential. Lenin insisted that, as the Bolsheviks had had to accept the treaty of Brest-Litovsk, so the German comrades might even have to acquiesce in the treaty of Versailles for a lengthy period.[32]

This was argumentation *à l'outrance*: no aspect of international relations was more fiercely criticised by communists, Russian or German, than the Versailles treaty. The test of the German Communist Party's seriousness about obtaining power was its capacity to accept the necessity of harsh compromises. The same was true of the nascent communist movement in the United Kingdom. The British party had yet to be formed, but already left-wing socialists such as Sylvia Pankhurst and Willie Gallacher had turned their backs on parliamentarianism. Lenin did not wish to discourage sympathisers. He conceded that their revolutionary mood was 'cheering and valuable'. But moods, he added, are inadequate for the preparation of an advance on power.[33] He proposed that Gallacher and his friends should enter parliamentary politics and even effect an accommodation with the British Labour Party. His reasoning was that the British Labour Party held the affections of most working-class people in the United

Kingdom whereas the British communist movement had scant support. An electoral pact would enable the communists to gain a few parliamentary seats. Lenin asserted that similar deals had been done between Bolsheviks and Mensheviks before 1917.[34] This was yet another overdrawn analogy. A Bolshevik-Menshevik coalition had been formed in 1906 because most Bolsheviks and Mensheviks desired it; they did not come together because a newly-formed Bolshevik faction wanted to become more influential by means of association with a more popular Menshevik faction.[35] Lenin added that 'the conditions for a successful proletarian revolution were clearly growing' in Britain. If this were so, he did not explain why his intransigence towards the Mensheviks in 1917 was inappropriate in the case of Pankhurst and Gallacher.[36]

Lenin admitted that the British Labour Party might reject any overtures from British communists, but he asserted that even a rejection would raise the prestige of communism among the working class.[37] This dubious prediction ignored the difficulties that a Communist Party of Great Britain would experience in recruiting members if it forswore a role as rebel against the political status quo. He also vastly underestimated the hostility to his own world-view which had taken root among Labour Party leaders. They were bound to show the door to communists seeking a pact with them.

Nevertheless *The Infantile Disease of 'Leftism'* was a milestone in the development of international communism. It showed how confident Lenin had become. His style was hectoring and condescending. Many communist leaders in Europe were not political novices; and yet Lenin lectured them as from a professorial chair. He patronisingly referred to their politics as being childlike. He was claiming, not too subtly, the wisdom of the patriarch; and, whenever he indicated past mistakes made by the Bolshevik party, he adduced the rashness of his own Bolshevik opponents. Apparently he had never been in the wrong. He also played on the assumption that no one would have the knowledge or presumption to challenge his tendentious exposition of Bolshevik party history. Plainly he wished to subject all Communist International parties to firm discipline. Thus British communists should not be allowed to abstain from parliamentary elections.[38] His ambition to supervise the other parties endured after the book went to press in Petrograd. News came through that the German Communist Party had split into two factions and that the communist sympathiser in the Italian Socialist Party, Amadeo Bordiga, had come out against putting up parliamentary candidates. In a hastily-written appendix, Lenin excoriated these tendencies as being precisely what he had warned against in the book's earlier pages. Ultra-leftism, wrote the quintessential ultra-leftist of 1917, had to be disowned by the Second Congress of the Communist International in Petrograd.[39]

THE SECOND CONGRESS OF THE COMMUNIST INTERNATIONAL

Delegates to the Second Communist International Congress congregated in Moscow in summer 1920 and, in deference to Petrograd's status as the birthplace of the October Revolution, they took the train to the north and assembled in the Smolny Institute on 19 July 1920. Grigori Zinoviev spoke for the International's Executive Committee. A funeral march was played in memory of comrades who had died in the struggles for revolution in central Europe.[40] His report exhibited delight that the Independent German Social-Democratic Party, the French Socialist Party and the American Socialist Party had broken with the Second International. Zinoviev enjoyed the refracted light of the October seizure of power (which he had opposed at the time). In particular, he called upon member parties to accept the organisational rules proposed by the Bolshevik party.[41]

A prolonged ovation greeted Lenin as he rose to deliver the report on the world political situation. His words caused a certain surprise. In his view, the Great War had added to the list of the world's colonies. Germany, Austria-Hungary and Bulgaria had been reduced 'to what is the equivalent of colonial status' by the treaty of Versailles; and Russia, too, had suffered in like fashion.[42] Of the major pre-war powers, only USA and Britain were economically independent any longer. France, despite being co-victor in the war, was a debtor nation. Even Britain's foreign indebtment had mounted; and the collapse of the ' "mechanism" of the world capitalist economy' meant that the USA also could 'not buy or sell'. Supposedly, the fall in American working-class living standards made the growth of a 'revolutionary mood' inevitable.[43] Lenin erroneously asserted that the British Independent Labour Party was seeking affiliation to the Communist International.[44] In addition, Lenin expatiated on German developments. Otto Bauer's pamphlet *Bolshevism or Social-Democracy* was criticised as being a central European variant of Menshevism. It was no such thing. For Bauer contended that Bolshevism, while being suited to the peculiar conditions of Russia, ill-befitted the rest of industrial Europe. The fact that Lenin overlooked this was an index of his determination to avoid Bauer's arguments in hope of attracting support from Germans and Austrians who might otherwise ignore him.[45]

The 'opportunism' of foreign parties supporting the Second International, he maintained, was explicable by the benefits accruing to the 'labour aristocracy' from imperialism.[46] This was a greater obstacle to communism's advance than left-wing 'infantilism'. The Communist International would be able to bring the sincere but misled leftists of central and eastern Germany to their senses.[47] Giacinto Serrati from the Italian Socialist Party congratulated the Red Army on a campaign that was going well against the Poles.[48] Karl Reinhardt, speaking for the Austrian Communist party, expressed revulsion about the barbarous repression of Béla Kun's Soviet republic in Hungary.[49] But it was Julian Marchlewski from the Communist Workers' Party of Poland that made the Congress look closely at the current military campaign in Poland. While suggesting that a Polish Soviet republic would eventually emerge, he did not exclude the possibility that German volunteers would intervene against the Reds: 'We still face an uphill struggle.'[50]

Marchlewski's speech, however, was brief and rather abstract. Delegates were waiting on events. A map was pinned to a wall to display the Reds' daily progress.[51] The second session was delayed for four days while Lenin and his Russian colleagues concentrated on the Polish war. On 23 July, Zinoviev offered the report on the role and structure of the communist party, urging that the current techniques of Bolshevism be adopted everywhere. He advocated centralism, discipline, hierarchy and careful vetting of recruits to each communist party; and, unlike Lenin, acknowledged that the 'dictatorship of the proletariat' in practice involved 'the dictatorship of the communist party'.[52] Debate at last became heated. Jack Tanner, a leader of the shop stewards' movement in Britain, objected to the dictatorship of a minority.[53] Such worries induced Lenin to intervene with the point that only the minority of any class joins a party and that, in the case of the communist parties, this minority is the class's political vanguard. The proletariat had to be led, and Lenin noted that Tanner had not denied this. Moreover, he insisted that the Congress should formulate a policy mandatory for all member parties of the Communist International.[54] The Bolshevik leaders manipulated the proceedings with cunning. Trotski spoke next, announcing that the Polish government that very day had sued for peace. The Congress was exhilarated, and delegates were inhibited from protesting against Zinoviev's theses.[55] Nor did it harm Lenin's interests at the Congress that the entire third session, which followed on 24 July, was given up to disputes among the foreign parties.[56]

Back he came at session four with a report he would not trust to any colleague: on the national and colonial questions. He had not forgotten his problems with the Bolshevik party at the Eighth Party Congress in March 1919.[57] Yet he did not quite get a clear path from the Communist International delegates. The colonies of the European powers had predominantly non-industrial and pre-capitalist economies, and Lenin had usually called on his party to support 'bourgeois-democratic liberation movements' in them. The Indian delegate M. N. Roy thought this indulgent to the indigenous bourgeoisies of the colonies. The tendency was for them to accommodate themselves to their imperial masters. Roy, unlike Bukharin in 1915–1917, spoke from direct experience; and Lenin gave way to him. His modified submission to the Communist International Congress demanded that support be given to the 'revolutionary movement' in colonies and not to the 'bourgeois-democratic liberation movement'.[58]

Lenin at this juncture made a major addition to his own Marxist strategy; the fact that Lenin did this *en passant* at a Communist International Congress has left the importance of his words little noticed. But a crucial lacuna in his thought was being filled. As yet he had never explained how socialism would be introduced to countries which were not already capitalist. At the Congress he stated for the first time explicitly that 'the Communist International should advance and theoretically establish the proposition that, with the assistance of the proletariat of the advanced countries, the rest of the countries can move over to the soviet system and – through certain stages of development – towards communism while by-passing the capitalist stage of development.'[59] How this would occur he even now did not venture to say. 'Practical experience,' he opined reassuringly, would give the answers.[60] At all costs he wanted to avoid an opening of past polemics among Russian socialists. Back in the 1890s he, like his fellow Marxists in Russia, had urged that Russia had to go through more or less the same course of economic and social development as Britain, France and Germany. Capitalism, Lenin maintained, could not be leapt o'er. It had to be undergone and survived. Only subsequently could there be socialism.[61] In mid-1920, faced with Communist

International comrades from entirely non-industrialised countries, he had had to re-think his strategy. The result was an unadvertised attack on his own pre-revolutionary assumptions.

This intellectual shift was made without reference to Russia. In 1917 he had still been contending that capitalism already existed to a very large extent in the former Russian empire. After the October Revolution he admitted that vast sectors of the economy had been untouched by capitalism. In central Asia and northern Siberia there were social groups which had not known even feudalism.[62] But it was not until 1922 that he came to apply this revision of his Marxist understanding to his own country.[63]

Nor did Lenin yet try to link his newly-developed thinking to his practice in 1917. The strategy of the Bolshevik leader in the October Revolution was replete with inchoateness and contradictions; but, at least in some respects, it was premised on the capacity of a Russia which was not fully industrialised to move directly, even if gradually, towards a socialist order.[64] This, too, was a linkage made by Lenin only in 1922. Consequently, at the Congress, he also studiously ignored Karl Marx's speculative musings in the 1880s. In particular, Marx had written letters of encouragement to the Russian agrarian socialists (or *narodniki*). Marx had insisted that there was no uniform 'Marxist' theory of stages; and that, if socialists were to obtain and hold power in contemporary non-capitalist Russia, they might even be able to inaugurate a socialist society based on the peasant land communes. His proviso was that such a revolution would require support from proletarian revolutions in the economically-advanced countries of the West.[65] Not a breath about this left Lenin's lips. To his dying day he refused to advert attention to the mutual admiration of Marx and the *narodniki*. For Lenin, it was *de rigueur* to present himself as the most orthodox Marxist; and he was untroubled by the fact that this necessitated playing fast and loose with the contents of Marx's correspondence with Russian nineteenth-century agrarian Marxists.[66]

Debate continued into the fifth session on 28 July with reports by delegates from Asia. The 'national question' in the states of Europe with large national minorities interested the Congress less than the 'colonial question' in the rest of the world.[67] A consensus had arisen that the new communist parties in the colonies should preserve their independence from other anti-imperial political groups. Evidently, if the Communist International wanted such parties, it had to give them a rationale beyond helping the indigenous bourgeoisies to power. The ideological liaison between Lenin and Roy was disrupted momentarily by Serrati's awkward comment that words such as 'backward' were undefined and amenable to chauvinistic and pseudo-revolutionary interpretation.[68] Serrati had made an accurate observation, altogether too accurate for the liking of Zinoviev who called it 'very uncomradely'.[69] Zinoviev's snub did the trick: Congress voted unanimously for the proposed theses with just three abstentions.[70]

Next day, at session six, Zinoviev reported on the conditions of admission to the Communist International. Radek followed him with an attack on the Independent German Social-Democratic Party.[71] Foreign parties at the Congress were subjected to pressure by Bolsheviks in sessions seven and eight; but the German Independents Crispien and Dittmann were singled out for such treatment by others too.[72] Crispien stood up to it, castigating Bolshevik attitudes to revolutionary terror and to the peasant question.[73] Belatedly, on 30 July, Lenin joined in. He took Crispien to task for failing to accept the need for the dictatorship of the proletariat and for terror. He also complained about his delay in breaking with Kautsky: almost a capital offence in Lenin's eyes.[74] Zinoviev's theses gained overwhelming endorsement.[75] On 2 August it was the turn of Bukharin at session nine. The Bolsheviks had selected him to deliver the report on parliamentarianism. It was an ironic choice in the light of Bukharin's reputation for hostility to the use of parliaments by Europe's socialists in the Great War;[76] and Lenin relished hearing him declare that communists had to use parliaments as instruments of political struggle. Amadeo Bordiga gave a counter-report, stating that no parliament could serve at all as a means of 'liberating the proletariat'.[77] Without waiting for Bukharin to reply to Bordiga, Lenin returned to the platform in the following session. He objected that Bordiga was willing to overlook one of the few opportunities for agitation and organisation available to revolutionaries in advance of a revolution.[78] The theses of Nikolai Bukharin won a thumping triumph.[79]

In sessions eleven and twelve there was acceptance of Radek's report on trade unions.[80] Not until 4 August, in session thirteen and over two weeks into the Congress, was a report offered by a leader who did not come from the Bolsheviks. This came in the debate on the agrarian question. The *rapporteur* was Julian Marchlewski. Officially he represented the Polish delegation; but he had belonged to the Russian Social-Democratic Labour Party before 1914 and had lived in Moscow intermittently since 1918. He did not even deliver his report in person. Following the Red Army's advance, he had been appointed to the Polish provisional revolutionary government and had left for Poland.

His report was given by Ernst Meyer, who admitted that the words were based on 'the theses of comrade Lenin'.[81]

Lenin recounted his experience with the Bolshevik party in 1917, when he had initially hoped to incorporate the principle of land nationalisation and, after criticism, had had to remove this particular demand from his theses.[82] The confession guaranteed success for the report. It was a lively debate. Italian delegate Antonio Graziadei had implicitly criticised Marx's prediction of a steady concentration of capital in agriculture, resulting in the disappearance of the peasantry, as having been proved wrong.[83] Such heresy was attacked by the Bolshevik Grigori Sokolnikov. A reverential tone was stipulated when Marx and Engels were being cited. Unanimous acceptance of Meyer's report ensued.[84] Delegates moved on to discuss the statutes of the Communist International at session fourteen that evening. Diplomatic considerations entrusted the report to a non-Russian: there had been criticisms that the Russians were ruling the Congress. The Bulgarian Christo Kabakchiev was asked to propose statutes which, by empowering the Congress to set up a highly centralised structure for the Communist International, would lend still greater power to the Bolsheviks.[85] David Wijnkoop from the Netherlands was not taken in. He declared that the International's leadership would turn out to be simply an expanded Russian Executive Committee.[86] Paul Levi had suggested Germany as the location of the Executive Committee, and Wijnkoop said he had no objections to Italy or Norway.[87] But John Reed spoke up for Russia.[88] Wijnkoop found scant support; the statutes, presented but not written by Kabakchiev, were adopted unanimously.[89]

Business was dispatched at session fifteen on 5 August. Zinoviev's report on workers' councils, which included a call for dictatorship, was passed virtually without debate.[90] On 6 August the same briskness was observable. Sylvia Pankhurst, a British communist leader, held up things by objecting to the instruction that she and her comrades should affiliate their organisation to the British Labour Party. After all that Lenin had said about Europe's 'social-chauvinists' and his schismatic behaviour in 1917, the British comrades were as much mystified as annoyed.[91]

Lenin made his last appearance at the Congress in order to drum comrade Pankhurst back into line. His argument was that the British communists were in danger of remaining a sect and needed to enter the mainstream of the labour movement in order to canalise it towards communist goals.[92] Sylvia Pankhurst's resistance was in vain. By a vote of 58 to 24 the British communists were told to join the Labour Party.[93] By the closing rally on 7 August 1920 the Bolsheviks could look back on a Congress where no attempt at any basic alteration of their imperious proposals had been successful. It was a triumph for Bolshevism and for Lenin in particular. The deference verged on the embarrassing. Willie Gallacher from Scotland, taken to task by Lenin in *The Infantile Disease*, told the Congress: 'I have found my name mentioned in it in connection with my activity. I have taken this rebuke as a child takes the rebuke of a father.'[94] Perhaps young Willie had his tongue in cheek. But the general tone was anyway deferential towards Lenin. The Bolsheviks had taken power; they had won their Civil War; they were bursting through to Poland and, with luck, would soon be in Berlin. Such unpleasantnesses as existed about them would presumably be mollified by more cultured socialist revolutions abroad. Lenin and friends had breached the walls of global capitalism. Factory owners and bankers were the world's worst sinners whereas the Bolsheviks could be brought to repent their ways. Long live the October Revolution!

CULT OF A STATESMAN

Unforced acclaim for Lenin came from the Soviet and foreign delegates at the Communist International Congress. Yet official propaganda about him had also been made since the October Revolution.[95] Increasingly the central party leaders recognised that their policies would have a greater impact on society when refracted through the prism of an outstanding political figure. Lenin, as leader of party and government, was the obvious subject. It was perceived that a riposte had to be made to the propaganda of the White armies. Street posters in the regions occupied by Kolchak and Denikin had depicted him as the embodiment of evil. Often Lenin, alongside Trotski, was depicted as a Jew. His grandfather on his mother's side had indeed been Jewish.[96] But the anti-Bolshevik portraitists did not know this; their intention had blatantly been to stir up hostility to the Bolsheviks by playing on popular antisemitism. As for Lenin, he did not advertise his ethnic ancestry. Neither his Jewish nor his Kalmyk forebears were mentioned in public.[97]

Information about him was studiously filtered by the party's propagandists. A cult of Lenin was in the making. *The Communist Manifesto* had stressed that class struggle was the essence of revolutionary action; and, in the 1850s, Marx had written extensively on the impact of broad social interests on the fortunes of great leaders. This attitude was superseded after October 1917. The Bolsheviks pulled down the memorials to Russian emperors, replacing them with hastily-commissioned busts and statues of protagonists. Marx, Engels and Bakunin were favourite examples.[98] There had anyway been a tradition within Bolshevism to accentuate the need to train individuals to supply the leadership for the achievement of socialism. The Bolshevik revolutionary hero belonged to the party's imagery.[99] Its rationale for focussing attention on the living Lenin was provided by Mikhail Olminski, who had written a biographical piece on him for a Moscow Bolshevik newspaper in mid-1917 and who in 1918 called for Lenin to be studied as the incarnation of 'the colossal revolutionary proletarian collective'.[100] By then the Bolshevik press had been lavishing regular praise on the party's chief. A poem in his honour had been published in *Pravda* as early as 29 October 1917.[101] An official photograph was taken of him in January 1918 and reproduced extensively.[102] May Day was celebrated in the same year by Demyan Bedny, a Bolshevik versifier, with a paean entitled 'To The Leader'. Among Bedny's extravagances was the claim that Lenin's writings constituted the Holy Bible of Labour.[103]

The attempt on Lenin's life in August 1918 was followed by outpourings about his preciousness to the party. A sentimentalised account was written by Grigori Zinoviev, who asserted that Lenin had undergone penury in Switzerland in service of the revolutionary cause.[104] Descriptions of him by others used Christian symbols. Lenin was said to have been 'crowned with thorns of slander'; and L. S. Sosnovski maintained in a Petrograd newspaper that his survival of a Socialist-Revolutionary attack proved that there was something beyond the normal about him: 'Lenin cannot be killed.'[105] Elena Stasova, who had served before Sverdlov as Central Committee secretary, wrote somewhat less disingenuously: 'Don't you know, even then I had the same confidence that he would recover, and I simply had not a shadow of doubt that it would be so: even though my reason was worried by the bad external signs my soul remained calm and declared to me that our Ilich would be preserved.'[106]

Lenin did not encourage this overtly. Always embarrassed by the fuss made of him, he could also become irritated by it. In March 1919 a seventeen-year old girl, Valentina Pershikova, defaced a portrait of him and was arrested by the Tsaritsyn Cheka. Lenin demanded her release, saying that she should be proceeded against only if she was a counter-revolutionary.[107] His fiftieth birthday in April 1920 was celebrated altogether too splendidly for his taste. The poet Vladimir Mayakovski wrote a poem, 'Vladimir Ilich', that generations of Soviet schoolchildren had to learn by heart. Lenin did not enthuse; his attitude was succinctly depicted as follows: 'I don't belong to the admirers of his poetic talent, although I quite admit my incompetence in this area.'[108] An evening gathering was held by his Politburo colleagues. Eulogies were delivered by Kamenev, Bukharin and Stalin. Lenin made his excuses and left in the middle of the proceedings. (His departure itself was used cultically in order to indicate how ordinary a fellow he was.)[109] He continued to avoid taking grandiose titles, remaining mere chairman of Sovnarkom and making no attempt to be called prime minister or premier; he still led discussions of the Central Committee and the Politburo without any formal designation that marked him off from his colleagues. It pained him that anyone could think otherwise. Adolf Ioffe, who had lost his seat on the Central Committee at the Eighth Party Congress in 1919, charged him with accruing excessive authority. Others had put it more crudely by stating that Lenin had become a dictator. 'You're mistaken,' he retorted, 'in repeating (several times) that "the C. C. [Central Committee: RS], c'est moi". This can be written only in a condition of great nervous irritation and exhaustion.'[110]

Yet the Bolshevik party leader and Sovnarkom chairman did protest too much. He did not stop his supporters from naming one of the 'agitational trains' in his honour; and, while he fastidiously continued to refer to the Lenin factory as 'the former Mikhelson factory', he did not seek a restoration of the nomenclature.[111] If he had wanted to eradicate the cultic paraphernalia, no one could have stood in his way. But he weakly demurred, and sometimes even nurtured the growing cult, insisting upon participating in a *subbotnik* on May Day in 1919. This was a scheme whereby everyone was encouraged to do a full day's extra work without pay. Digging the ground in the Kremlin compound was his job for a few hours. The next day's newspapers, as he must have anticipated, extolled his dedication.[112]

His tacit calculation must have been that the publicly-fostered veneration was a political asset which he could not afford to discard. It helped the Soviet state and, whenever he was challenged by his colleagues, it assisted him. And yet he can hardly be accused of overdoing things on his own behalf. On his return to Russia in 1917 he had been inventive in fashioning his message and his image under the scrutiny of public opinion. He did not stop trying to identify himself with the working class after the October Revolution. 'We, the workers' continued to be one of his rhetorical flourishes; its autobiographical inaccuracy for the son of a distinguished provincial civil servant who had passed his noble status on to him was overlooked. Lenin also went on wearing his workman's peaked cap, which had been effective in winning popularity at mass meetings in 1917.[113] And, despite the worries about his security, he continued to make occasional speeches at workplaces and to mingle with the groups of factory workers. Furthermore, he appreciated the potency of modern mass media enough to agree to be filmed walking around in the grounds of the Kremlin with his personal assistant Vladimir Bonch-Bruevich after recovering from the assassination attempt. Lenin decided, too, to put some speeches on gramophone records. In 1919 he specially wrote six short pieces and delivered them in a specially-constructed studio.[114]

These were pioneering events in the history of politics and the media only in retrospect: their impact at the time was negligible. The newsreel was hardly a success. It had been weeks after his arrival in Petrograd in 1917 before Lenin acquired an ease before crowds, and he never learned how to relax in front of the camera. He was nearly as diffident on the records of his speeches: his stilted diction gives no impression of the oratorical zest witnessed by audiences in these years. More to the point, the Russian film industry was in its infancy and supplies of celluloid and other equipment were small in the Civil War; and only a tiny proportion of the population owned gramophones.[115]

It is true that his name was appended at the bottom of most laws and decrees, and that his articles were carried regularly by *Pravda* and *Izvestiya*. His photograph was more common in the public domain than anyone else's. And yet the Soviet republic had a predominantly agrarian economy, was poorly served by its network of transport and communication and had been battered by the effects of the Civil War. Knowledge about Lenin was perforce restricted. The ubiquitousness of the 'Lenin cult' was therefore a mainly posthumous phenomenon. After the failure of a gang of armed robbers to recognise him in 1919, Lenin was unlikely to overestimate the impact of official propagan-da.[116] Nevertheless the situation was not static. Not only many workers but probably even more peasants held him in affection. The old tradition whereby a village would send one of its elders to the capital to seek an audience with the emperor was continued with Sovnarkom's chairman. Lenin was becoming as much 'the little father' to the peasantry as Nicholas II.[117] This phenomenon did not mean that most peasants were consciously pro-Bolshevik. The countryside witnessed revolts against the Reds throughout the Civil War and immediately afterwards. But approval of the Land Decree of 26 October 1917 persisted; and, almost certainly, the popular notion had not died that political and economic problems were caused not by the ruler but by his advisers at court.

In reality Lenin was crucially responsible for several policies which aggrieved the peasantry. But he was not universally perceived in such a fashion. The Land Decree was popularly known as 'Lenin's Decree'. Fondness for him among broad strata of society was to increase still further in 1921 when he introduced a New Economic Policy which permitted a limited revival of the private grain trade.[118]

Even the fact that this permission was extracted from Lenin against the resistance of his prejudices was not counted against him. He escaped a fair verdict on his record. It is as if he was venerated despite himself. His personal modesty gave the impression to many who met him at Party Congresses or at Kremlin audiences that he was a truly a fitting ruler in the era of mass politics. Visitors overlooked evidence pointing in the opposite direction: his middle-class background; his dogmatically intellectualist outlook; his willingness to order the deaths of thousands of people, including workers and peasants, who stood in the way of his party's demands. Lenin was not an ordinary Russian. Lenin did not share the aspirations of ordinary Russians. In most ways he was disappointed that Russians were not more like the Germans! But enough Russians were unaware of his general attitude for him to appear as a demotic tsar. It was a paradoxical result for a revolutionary who, as a youngster, had started to think about politics when his older brother had been hanged for trying to assassinate the emperor Aleksandr III and eradicate tsarism from the Russian land. Lenin had dedicated his own life to the achievement of a communist society. He was being placed on a pedestal of esteem at a stratospheric height above the eyes of the common man and woman.

THE NINTH PARTY CONFERENCE

To leading communists, at home and abroad, he was equally heroic; but some of them also found him extremely enigmatic. Paul Levi, the theoretician of the German Communist Party, had been startled by his encounter with the Bolshevik leader at the Second Congress of the Communist International. Levi thought that, if a non-communist government in Berlin were to go to war against the Allies, his own party should refrain from involvement.[119] Lenin, however, remonstrated that German communists should even form what he called 'an unnatural bloc' with the extreme political right in such a contingency. The ex-army officers under Wolfgang Kapp, who had attempted to seize power in March 1920, should be welcomed as partners. According to Lenin, Kapp and his associates differed from Russian counter-revolutionaries in the crucial respect that they were determined to overthrow the treaty of Versailles.[120] A German anti-Allies campaign would therefore be a war of national liberation. Once it had been won, the German Communist Party in turn would resume the political offensive against the German bourgeoisie.[121]

That Lenin should have impressed this upon Levi was remarkable enough: the advocate of 'European civil war' in 1914–1917 had become the supporter of a *Burgfrieden* between the German bourgeoisie and working class.[122] Even more stunning was the timing of his argument. At that moment the Red Army was thrusting its forces into Poland. Not only Warsaw but also Berlin was its objective. Lenin sensed that the long-awaited pan-European revolution was imminent. A seizure of power by Italian communists seemed likely to him, and he had written to Stalin in July that Bukharin and Zinoviev agreed with this assessment.[123] Lenin was already thinking about the practicalities: 'My personal opinion,' he confided, 'is that for this purpose it is necessary to sovietise Hungary and perhaps Czechia and Romania too.'[124] Such grandiose thinking about the political map of Europe was not altogether lightheaded. Northern Italy at the time was convulsed with working-class strikes and factory occupations. Nor was Lenin oblivious of the difficulties. In particular, his altercations with Levi showed a recognition that socialist revolution in Germany might be more difficult to bring about than elsewhere. And his strategical deviousness was reminiscent of Stalin's Nazi-Soviet Pact of 1939. For Lenin was willing to do a deal with the kind of militarists who would become Nazis by the end of the decade.[125]

In the meantime there was no more enthusiastic proponent of the invasion of Poland than Lenin. This required an all-out military effort, and Trotski objected that the Reds were simply in no fit condition for such an exhausting task.[126] Stalin, too, warned against the nationalism of Polish workers; for him, Lenin exaggerated the ability of the Red Army to detach the Warsaw working class from support for patriotism.[127] Kamenev was out of the country, on a mission to London. Polish comrades, including the same Jan Marchlewski who had been seconded for the invasion from the Communist International

Congress, sensed that a mistake was being made.[128] Karl Radek, an astute observer of central European politics, also tried to dissuade Lenin.[129] But on a rare visit from the front to Moscow, Trotski could find only Rykov to back his own opposition to opening an offensive; and Rykov came over to Lenin's side once the invasion had been started.[130] If the Brest-Litovsk treaty was one man's peace, this was one man's war.[131]

It went disastrously wrong despite early successes. The two Red sectors fought independently of each other. Stalin in the south aimed at Lvov while Tukhachevski drove onwards, in the north, in the direction of Warsaw. This dispersal of effort caused chaos.[132] But in any case the Poles rose against the Reds in a massive national effort. They assumed that the Bolsheviks were internationalist in ideology but Russians in intention. This notion was given credence by the summons of the anti-Bolshevik General Brusilov, in retirement since 1917, and to all Russian officers to rally to the Russian flag in the country's hour of need. Furthermore, the lines of communication and supply for the Red Army were overstretched. Trotski had anticipated that the Poles would prove more redoubtable than Kolchak, Denikin and Yudenich. At the battle of the Vistula, in mid-August 1920, he was proved completely correct.[133]

Throughout the campaign Lenin had thrust the Red Army into an aggressive posture. Lord Curzon, British Foreign Secretary, had proposed peace along prescribed boundaries between Soviet Russia and Poland on 12 July.[134] For Lenin this necessitated simply a 'mad reinforcement of the attack on Poland'.[135] Trotski's counsel in favour of peace negotiations was overturned.[136] Lenin demanded that a militant manifesto should be issued.[137] The British in mid-August had tried to lean on the Polish authorities to accept Soviet peace terms (but Lloyd George was unaware that these would involve the setting up of a workers' militia and the redistribution of the land among the peasantry). Lenin was determined to press on to Warsaw and then to Berlin. He noted with satisfaction in mid-August that the Reds had reached the borders of East Prussia.[138] On the same day he telegrammed sarcastically to his forces: 'The Commander-in-Chief does not dare get nervous. If the *military* department or the Commander-in-Chief *does not refuse* to take Warsaw, it is necessary *to take it.*'[139] The battle of the Vistula brought the ruler in the Kremlin to his senses. European revolution was not, after all, going to be exported on the point of Red bayonets. The Bolsheviks themselves would have to sue for peace. The Soviet-Polish war had ended in catastrophe.[140]

At last the lid placed on internal Bolshevik disputes was blown off. The pressure-cooker had been under dangerous strain all year, and the start of the Ninth Party Conference on 22 September 1920 was watched nervously by the central party leaders as the 116 delegates with voting authority assembled.[141] The military situation exercised all minds. Unusually the right of making the first report was given to a non-member of the Bolshevik party: the obscure Polish communist Wladislaw Ulanowski. His words made plain the extent of the catastrophe that had befallen the Red Army.[142] Ulanowski's presence was intended to help Lenin and his colleagues to rebut criticism for ordering the advance on Warsaw.

Lenin was fortunate that scarcely any delegates knew that he was the main instigator of this advance. In his political report on behalf of the Central Committee he argued that the peace terms proposed by the Soviet government in January 1920 had been interpreted by the Polish government and its friends as a sign of weakness. This was the motivation, according to Lenin, for Pilsudski's incursion into the Ukraine. The advance on Warsaw, which Lenin described unreservedly as a 'war of offensive', showed how wrong Pilsudski had been. Small states like Estonia and Georgia, despite what was called by Lenin their bourgeois orientation, had made peace with Moscow. Lenin rightly noted that 'all Germany was on the boil' as the Reds attempted 'the sovietisation of Poland'. The objective had been to 'feel out with bayonets'. The decision had been taken at the Second Congress of the Communist International, but had to be kept secret since so many participants were 'nationalists and pacifists'. But all ended in disaster. Lenin admitted that the Poland's 'readiness' for revolution had been overestimated. He also conceded: 'I absolutely in no way in the slightest pretend to knowing military science.' Lenin allowed that diplomatic mistakes might have been made. And yet he insisted that military victory had been at least a possibility. He complained about the refusal of the German communists to link up with the 'German Kornilovites'; and he continued to ignore the fact that Polish workers as well as 'petit-bourgeois elements' had risen up against the Red Army invaders. Even in defeat there had been gains. In Britain the revolutionary cause was gaining working-class support through the 'Committee of Action'. The Bolsheviks could sue for peace from a position of strength.[143]

In the heavily-abridged version of his speech in *Pravda*, which appeared fully a week later, he avoided terms such as 'sovietisation of Poland' and 'war of offensive'. Nor did he refer to his astonishing advice to the German Communist Party. He maintained, moreover, that the Soviet economy was improving and that the anti-Soviet alliance of Poland, France and the Russian Whites was being disrupted by conflicting aims. If the Polish government refused Moscow's terms, war would be resumed and would result in a Red victory. At the Conference, by contrast, he acknowledged that a winter campaign would cost too many lives.[144] Lenin, by means of *Pravda*, was seeking to deceive foreign embassies into believing that the Red Army could and would fight on regardless.[145] There were other reasons for self-censorship in print. Subsequent speeches referred to his indications about the series of mistakes made in the Polish campaign.[146] Delegates who had come to the Conference to rebuke the central party leadership as a whole witnessed a verbal brawl between two individual leaders, Lenin and Stalin. The proceedings looked as if they were running out of control.

Kamenev, whose speech was also edited for public consumption, kept clear of personal unpleasantness when reporting to Conference on the international situation. He had just returned from a diplomatic visit to England, and was able to emphasise that the decisions on the Polish campaign had been taken in his absence.[147] This neatly removed him from the dispute between Lenin and Stalin and from the controversy as to whether the order to march on Warsaw should ever have been given. Kamenev was listened to attentively. His had been the first trip abroad by a major Bolshevik figure since before the October Revolution (and it is worth noting by comparison that Lenin, an inveterate traveller before 1917, made no foreign excursion for the rest of his life; indeed he travelled no further than from Moscow to Petrograd on any particular occasion). Kamenev warned that the Committee of Action in England was constituted by anti-Bolsheviks.[148] He was pouring cold water on the interpretation of the situation abroad given earlier by Lenin. He did this so decorously that few delegates can have appreciated the extent of the anti-Lenin criticism in the Central Committee. Trotski was similarly equivocal in his report on the military fronts. Only hints of his worries were offered. He reminded the Conference that the danger from Wrangel was as great as had been posed by the Polish armed forces, and that other fronts still existed in the Soviet republic: in the Caucasus, in Turkestan and by Lake Baikal.[149] While announcing support for the original determination to go for Warsaw, he accentuated the dangers involved. To be a revolutionary was to take risks. The Red Army had in fact been routed; but, according to Trotski at the Conference, this had been unforeseeable (even though he had, months beforehand, foreseen it).[150] He explicitly refused to sound an optimistic note. If a winter campaign was necessary, so be it. Yet Trotski wanted, if at all possible, peace on the Western front.[151]

Trotski made plain that he held Stalin responsible for some 'strategical mistakes'.[152] He had not contended that the whole scheme to press on to Warsaw had been erroneous. The Politburo was sensitive on this score, and Béla Kun was introduced at the Conference's second session to declare on behalf of Hungarian communists that the invasion of Poland had very nearly brought communism to central Europe.[153] Central Committee member Karl Radek refused to gag himself on this matter, declaring that the advocates of invasion had grossly exaggerated the revolutionary inclinations of workers in Germany, France and Britain; he implicated Lenin in the blame.[154] Radek loosened the tongues of others. M. M. Khataevich asserted that the central leaders had been intoxicated by their previous military successes.[155] K. K. Yurenev accused the Central Committee of having offered 'a policy of impressionism'. The likely reaction of Poles had not been properly explored, and the Red Army had been poorly equipped and led.[156]

Felix Kon, member of the Polish Revolutionary Committee, described the invasion as ill-prepared.[157] He revealed that the central party leaders and not Polish communists such as Kon had taken all the crucial decisions. D. V. Poluyan boiled over at this point: the invasion had been a blunder from start to finish. Polish nationalism had been totally ignored.[158] S. K. Minin, serving as political commissar with the First Cavalry Army, charged Lenin with evading basic questions.[159] Similar accusations were made by following speakers;[160] and I. I. Khodorovski added that the directive for an advance on Warsaw would never have been issued if central leaders had kept contact with local party committees.[161] Bukharin was put up to deflect the flak. Invoking Marx and *The Communist Manifesto*, he declared that policy should be based upon the priority to foster worldwide socialist revolution. Bukharin threw a foul punch with the claim that Radek's imprecations meant he was 'crossing over to a Kautskyite position'. Revolutionary wars were correct in principle; revolutionary crises were growing in Italy and elsewhere. The revolutionary administration of Russia was right to attempt to stimulate the outbreak of European socialist revolution.[162] Stalin, too, defended the Central Committee; but he acknowledged that a lack of co-ordination had damaged the campaign.[163] Dzierzynski, who had been said to have questioned the thinking behind the invasion, stepped forward to rebut this (even though there was much truth in it!).[164] Radek once more insisted that the attitude of the Polish workers had been misjudged.[165] At this point Kamenev defended the Central Committee with an original argument: namely that the intention had been to stimulate a German socialist revolution and that geography entailed a march across Poland regardless of the Polish working-class's attitude to the Red Army.[166]

But there was no avoiding the central fact: miscalculations had been made and had led to a defeat (or 'expanded negative victory', as Radek put it in a parody of Bukharin's extraordinary description of economic collapse as 'expanded negative production').[167] Nerves were snapped when Trotski blurted out a critique of Stalin's activities. Stalin, according to Trotski, had misled the Central Committee into believing that the Polish army retreating towards Warsaw was incapable of further resistance.[168] Lenin joined the assault on Stalin. The implication was that Stalin had been ambitious to take command of the entire Red campaign.[169] Not since his condemnation of Kamenev and Zinoviev for alleged political black-legging before the October Revolution had Lenin made so personal an attack on a colleague. The Conference descended into shambles as the second session closed at 11 o'clock in the evening.

Next day, on 23 September, Stalin insisted upon the right to reply to Lenin and Trotski. Neither Lenin nor Trotski deigned to respond. Stalin had not denied that he had been responsible for strategical and operational blunders, but informed the Conference – and here he touched a sensitive spot for Lenin – that he had expressed doubts about the campaign when it had first been contemplated.[170] In order to save the leaders from further embarrassment it was decided to move to the next item of business, Krestinski's organisational report for the Central Committee. The statistical information was accompanied by a complaint that local party committees seldom appreciated the strains of work in Moscow. Shortage of personnel, caused by mobilisations and ill-health, was perennial. Krestinski had tried to take provincial grievances seriously, and wanted to defend himself in advance.[171] This did not save him. Democratic Centralists T. V. Sapronov and K. G. Zavyalova made their usual complaints.[172] Political departments were bitterly resented. If Stalin had suffered worst on the first day, Trotski was now put under threat since he was the principal advocate of such departments. Lenin, escaping much censure in the debate on the Polish campaign, continued to evade blame in discussions of Krestinski's report. The rancour was directed at others. Perhaps Lenin would not have offended so many fellow Bolsheviks even if he had been given one of the 'dirty' jobs in the Red Army done by Trotski and Stalin. But he had given out the jobs, not received them.

His wish to stand above unnecessary controversy was displayed in the ensuing debate 'on the immediate tasks of the party' in the fourth session on 24 September. Zinoviev stated bluntly: 'The chief conclusion of the proletarian revolution is the need for an iron, organised and monolithic party.'[173] A split between the top and the bottom of the party was rejected by him as nonsensical exaggeration. Insofar as problems of authoritarianism existed, Zinoviev maintained, they were attributable to the objective pressures exerted by the party's post-October functions in government and military command. He reminded the Conference that Lenin had warned that communism was not achievable overnight and that economic and political inequalities in society would persist for an epoch. Zinoviev argued that unequal conditions would prevail in the party in the same years.[174]

Dispute flared up, and Zinoviev was the target of invective. Sapronov reiterated his complaints: about the organisational reprisals against the Democratic Centralists; about the secrecy surrounding the discussions of the local committees as well as the central party apparatus; about the authoritarian methods rampant throughout the party. Bureaucratic centralism reigned.[175] Zinoviev was fortunate inasmuch as his critics were divided. The Democratic Centralists thought the standpoint of the Workers' Opposition, which called for working-class rank-and-file party members to have a decisive impact on policy and for the working class as a whole to control all economic production and distribution, was demagogy. Y. K. Lutovinov and the Workers' Opposition replied that the Democratic Centralists behaved no differently from supporters of Lenin in their local party committees.[176] The exchanges between Sapronov and Lutovinov eased Zinoviev's task. He also proffered a resolution which went some way towards the demands of those who attacked him. He expressed concern about the decline of electivity to party offices and of open mass meetings of local party organisations. He envisaged the establishment of 'control commissions' in the party to ensure that abuses would be eradicated.[177] But Lenin intervened only briefly, opining that the Central Committee's attackers were not so much demagogic as simply exhausted.[178] The fact that this was not regarded as condescension demonstrates his prestige.

Even so, he was rather complacent in strongly implying that internal party reform was of little consequence at a time when factory workers were under-fed and Red Army soldiers were worn out by campaign after campaign.[179] Sapronov reasonably questioned whether the proposed changes in the party would be implemented.[180] Zinoviev shared Lenin's coolness about the reform, but the fury of his opponents had induced him to disguise his feelings. Lenin had very nearly destroyed the effectiveness of Zinoviev's duplicity. What saved the two of them was the limitation on time for further debate. The motion had to be handed over to a commission of elected delegates, including both Zinoviev and Sapronov, for elaboration.[181]

Zinoviev had survived his ordeal, but not without inadvertently unhelpful assistance from his revered leader. Next day started with the sixth session's discussion on the Second Communist International Congress. The report by Zinoviev was self-congratulatory. He boasted that the Central Committee had had the Congress on its agenda for the previous three months; and that most problems at the Congress had related to decisions on which foreign organisations were to be allowed to join. He teased Radek for having wanted to exclude all non-Marxist groups;[182] but he simultaneously accentuated the Central Committee's aim to keep tight control of the Communist International. The initially-proposed nine conditions for membership had been increased to twenty one for this purpose.[183] Furthermore, Zinoviev had no doubts about the correctness of the decision to invade Poland. He recalled that, in the corridors of the Congress, he had canvassed non-Soviet participants to take more active steps to support the Bolsheviks. 'Hands off Russia!' was too passive a slogan.[184] He referred frequently to Germany. A seizure of power there by socialists continued to be regarded as crucial to the flourishing of the Soviet régime, and Clara Zetkin was invited to address the Party Conference in connection with recent developments. Zetkin had in the past been on poor terms with Lenin; her refusal to release the funds from the Shmidt legacy before the First World War, when she had been one of the legacy's three trustees, had mightily annoyed him.[185] By 1920 she had become an admirer of the Bolshevik leader. So reliable a foreign supporter was useful in rebutting the objections by Conference delegates themselves to the waging of the Polish campaign.[186]

Radek was like a terrier. Snapping away at the heels of Zinoviev and – not so discreetly – Lenin, he noted how the caution of the Bolshevik central party leadership about the possibility of imminent socialist revolution in Europe had changed abruptly into extraordinary optimism as the Red Army advanced into Poland. This transformation on the spur of the moment resulted from a new mood in Moscow, but was no basis for assessing the international situation.[187] Radek defended himself against a previous charge that, out of sectarianism, he had allied himself with anti-Zetkin German communists not wanting to invite non-communist leftist socialists to the Komintern Congress. This, he stated, was untrue; and he added that Lenin's own *The Infantile Disease*, published shortly before the Congress, had had the purpose of pushing away those leftists who were not entirely adherents of Bolshevik party policies. If Lenin's idea had been to attract as many leftists to Moscow as possible, why attack Anton Pannekoek and others so viciously in print? The problem was the absence of a fully-considered policy deriving from broad discussion rather than from command from on high.[188]

At last someone was infringing party decorum: 'I know this isn't a popular thing, to speak against this or that line of the Central Committee, all the more if it is Vladimir Ilich who is predetermining the line.'[189] The blame for overestimating the chances of immediate success for European socialist revolution was laid at Lenin's door. Bukharin tried to rehearse the arguments already put by Zinoviev while Lenin kept silent.[190] The end of the Conference's sixth session gave the central party leaders an intermission to consider how to handle Radek's attack. In the evening the seventh and last session began. N. Osinski, a Democratic Centralist, exculpated the Central Committee of political charges and declared that the failiure of the Warsaw offensive stemmed from personal tensions among Trotski, Stalin and Smilga.[191] Radek, however, refused to shut up. Accused of unwarranted pessimism, he reminded the Conference that it had been leaders such as Kamenev and Zinoviev who had opposed the Bolshevik seizure of power in October 1917.[192] The wrangling between Radek and Zinoviev continued for some minutes. Then Radek, having managed to tell a few home truths, let the matter rest. Zinoviev, despite being the Central Committee's *rapporteur*, let Kamenev proffer the motion of support for the Central Committee's conduct in relations with the Communist International; and even Kamenev was diffident enough to get Bela Kun to co-sign the motion with him.[193]

The shambles continued. Zinoviev's commission to formulate a resolution on 'the current tasks of the party' had not met. Permission was obtained for the commission to present a version to the Central Committee within two days.[194] Lenin's political report, which had opened the Conference, was not even voted upon. This had not happened since before the October Revolution. Even more extraordinary was Lenin's absence from the last session. Zinoviev was left to draw the proceedings to an end: 'Young comrades who happen to be participating in a Conference for the first time must be told that in no case whatsoever should it be concluded from the fact that one or another comrade has come out against another that we have major disagreements or arguments which prevent friendly work.'[195] But where was Lenin? According to Zinoviev, news of a Polish military counter-offensive had just come through to Moscow.[196] Perhaps Lenin was detained at his Kremlin telephone or was conferring with the Red Army command; he was not so cowardly as to avoid unpleasantries from an audience. Whatever the reason, he and his associates had been given a mauling by their fellow delegates that they would not forget.

NOTING BUKHARIN

Lenin would have paid little heed to the Conference in any event. For, as the threat of renewed conflict with Poland receded in the following few days, he turned to questions of Marxist theory rather than Conference resolutions. Naturally his duties as Sovnarkom chairman cut back his time for writing. Nevertheless he sustained a passionate interest in Marxism. It provided relief from the difficulties of the day; but it also remained a crucial means for him to interpret the world and rationalise his policies and behaviour. Thus, however overworked he became, he regularly used his prerogative to order any book he liked from any Russian library and to acquire foreign publications from the country's official representatives abroad. But his bibliophilia did not signify intellectual open-mindedness. He had always had strong preferences and dislikes; and, after the turn of the century, he had never seen the point of expending energy on the notions propounded by other parties both socialist and anti-socialist. In his own party, the rival acceptable theorists became fewer. Schisms among Russian Marxists before 1914 led him to cease to show respect for Plekhanov, Trotski, Martov, Maslov, Zhordania and Bogdanov. Then came the Great War. Lenin broke with most socialist parties in the rest of Europe; and he wrote no large work without a section criticising Karl Kautsky. It is true that practically all prominent Bolsheviks, including those of a practical bent like Stalin, had pretensions as Marxist theorists. Kamenev and Zinoviev had several books to their credit. Trotski, moreover, had returned to Lenin's side and was a political thinker of distinction among Bolsheviks. Nevertheless Lenin paid them little heed, reading their books but not adjusting his ideas much in reaction.[197]

The single Bolshevik who figured in his mind as a commensurate theorist was Nikolai Bukharin. Lenin had followed his career in the Great War with almost fatherly care. His *protegé* had disappointed him, in 1916, when their views on the strategy for socialist revolution had diverged. But in 1917 they agreed about more than they disagreed about. This continued to be the case after the October Revolution. Lenin was to remark in his so-called 'testament' in December 1922 that Bukharin was 'the most valuable and greatest theoretician in the party'.[198]

And yet Lenin, while acknowledging Bukharin's gifts, had doubts whether he understood Marxism. Bukharin was not unique in incurring such suspicion. It will be recalled that Lenin in his notebooks in 1916 had asserted that 'not one Marxist has completely understood Marx in the past half-century'.[199] Thenceforward Lenin felt himself to be the only true propagator and developer of Marxism in the twentieth century. He never stated this. But his critical remarks in the margin of Bukharin's book *The Economics of the Transition Period* indicate that he had not changed in his self-perception.[200] The problem, according to Lenin, was the influence of Aleksandr Bogdanov upon Bukharin. Bogdanov and Lenin had fought a political and philosophical battle in 1908-1909, ending with an organisational schism between their respective supporters in the Bolshevik faction. Lenin had several cardinal objections to him. Bogdanov had denied the existence of the 'external world' independently of human cognition; he had introduced non-Marxist ideas, especially from neo-Kantianism, to his analysis of social phenomena; and he had refused to accept that Marx's *Capital* was an unchallengeable building block of knowledge, and had derided the attainability of absolute truth.[201] On only one of these objections did Lenin later change his mind. In 1915-1916, writing in his own *Notebooks on Philosophy* he came to see that absolute truth was an impossibility.[202] But otherwise he retained his anti-Bogdanovist animus, and Bogdanov's name appears more often than any other in the expletive-laden commentary by Lenin in the margins of Bukharin's book.[203] Lenin had forgiven Bukharin his alleged anarchism in the Great War (and indeed had recognised that the allegation was unfounded).[204] He had forgiven him his Left Communism in 1918.[205] And now to find that the heterodoxy lay deeper, that Bukharin was a crypto-Bogdanovist! The discovery was unbearable! The heresy must be rooted out, and Bukharin brought to his senses!

Bukharin's style was bad enough. It was full of meandering syntax and waffly terminology. Lenin adopted an ironical stance: 'Ooof! Oh!

Watch out!'[206] He had a point. Lenin himself wrote in the jargon of contemporary Marxism, often with tedious prolixity; but he would never have allowed himself to refer, for example, to wartime economic collapse as 'expanded negative reproduction'[207] or to the effects of Bolshevik policy in 1918–1920 as 'the resurrection of industry in a socialist formulation'.[208] Lenin offered dozens of emendations to this stylistic archness, and generally criticised Bukharin for 'playing at definitions' and 'playing with concepts'.[209]

The 'Old Man' of Bolshevism felt that substantial questions, too, were at stake. Bukharin's terms gave him away as a believer in false gods. The book's introduction asserted that Marx's ideas exhibited 'a method whose heuristic value has only now risen to its full gigantic height'.[210] This plaudit seemed dispraise to Lenin, and his reaction besmattered the page: 'Only "heuristic value"?? And not reflecting the objective world? [This is] "shameful". . . agnosticism!'[211] Marx, in Lenin's estimation, had to be revered as a theorist innocent of error. Bukharin's remaining chapters evinced further manifestations of Bogdanovism. He frequently implied hostility to Lenin's cherished notion that the 'external world' exists independently of human cognition.[212] Picking some bits of Marx while discarding others and even incorporating ideas from non-Marxist thinkers, Bukharin had committed the crime of eclecticism.[213] There were only two acceptable founts of wisdom: Karl Marx and Friedrich Engels. Bukharin had betrayed the faith, and Lenin offered summary judgement. Bukharin, he proposed, was guilty of subjectivism, of solipsism, of agnosticism.[214] Lenin continued to contend that, in philosophy, a dyke separated materialism from idealism. Bukharin had allegedly moved over to idealism. His position on the far bank from Lenin was indicated in a 'scholasticism of terms contradicting dia[lectical] mat[eralism] (i.e. Marxism)'.[215] Lenin closely read and annotated Bukharin's book, but he abbreviated his comments in order to slake his intense annoyance.

Supposedly Bukharin, the party's most widely respected theoretician after Lenin, was not even a pukka Marxist. Lenin tried to sugar the pill. He emphasised how much he liked the 'excellent' chapter on 'extra-economic compulsion';[216] and he also put comments like 'true' and 'sehr gut' at various earlier points in the book.[217] Even several of Bukharin's definitions were to Lenin's liking. The phrase that state power was 'concentrated and organised social force' appealed to Lenin. He warmly greeted the description of the state in general as 'the broadest organisation of a class where all its force is concentrated, where the instruments of pressure and repression are concentrated.'[218]

Lenin's *recensio academica* contained the following headline: 'A spoonful of tar in a barrel of honey.'[219]

Yet who but a fool would sup from such a barrel? However lightly Lenin tried to let Bukharin down and however enthusiastically he affirmed that the book contained only a 'small inadequacy' (and needed only twenty to thirty pages excised),[220] the fundamental criticism was not withdrawn. The passages admired by Lenin were confined to his observations on the desirability of strong state power in enforcing revolutionary order. These alleviated Lenin's concern lest Bukharin should go over not only to Bogdanov's philosophy but even to his political recommendations; for Bogdanov had always condemned the violence and illegitimacy of the October Revolution.[221] Nevertheless there were worrisome aspects to the book even in relation to the level of current party policies. These aspects were but lightly drawn, but Lenin was alert to them. In the first place, there were Bukharin's repeated positive references to 'sociology': always a term spat out by Lenin.[222] Unlike Bukharin, Lenin regarded twentieth-century sociologists as bourgeois apologists who harmed the socialist cause. Bukharin by contrast found some of their ideas inspiring. He was no different from Lenin in insisting that the ultimate key to social analysis was class. But he also saw sense in breaking classes down into 'groups' and 'groupings'.[223] For Lenin, this was tantamount to recognising that sociologists such as Max Weber and Roberto Michels who had accentuated the importance of status over economic condition had been right and Karl Marx and Friedrich Engels wrong. Heretical and incorrect notions on society and economics would inevitably result.

Lenin's views on epistemology and ontology were sincere, but crude and unconvincing. His powerful intellect had not been fully engaged with the problems he chose to assess so magisterially, and his prejudices were by now so barnacled as to leave no hope for removal.[224] Bukharin's ideas, too, were confused and over-confident; but at least he sought to take account of social sciences as they had developed around the world since the death of Marx and Engels. Lenin was undaunted: in September 1920 he determined to re-enter the philosophical fray by sanctioning a second edition of his 1909 philosophical philippic *Materialism and Empiriocriticism*. He made no more than minor modifications in a text which affirmed all his objections to the world-view of Aleksandr Bogdanov.[225]

The introduction written for this new edition mentioned Bogdanov; but Bukharin was an equal, if unnamed, target as Lenin renewed the intra-Bolshevik dispute on philosophy.[226] Lenin was motivated not only by the intellectual issues but also by their connection with current political discussions in the party about the working class. Among the objects of his concerns was the mass organisation known as Proletkult. This organisation had been founded by Bogdanov as an instrument whereby the working class might independently establish its own 'proletarian culture' and supplant the prevailing 'bourgeois culture'. Its claim to have 400,000 active members was probably exaggerated. But the Bolshevik party's claim to have hundreds of thousands of working-class members was accompanied by the acknowledgement that most of them had no active role in party life. Above all, Proletkult disliked the tutelage exercised by the party over all mass organisations. Workers, according to Bogdanov, had to take charge of their own present and future affairs; and he tied these recomendations to his viewpoint on ontology and epistemology.[227] This was anathema to Lenin as a strategy of revolutionary change, and he derided Bogdanov's ideas on 'proletarian culture' as themselves being 'bourgeois and reactionary'.[228]

The necessity for the working class to undergo cultural development after the October Revolution had been asserted by Lenin in *The State and Revolution* in mid-1917.[229] But he wanted the party to direct the development, and his experience since the October Revolution reinforced this strong tendency in his thought. Bukharin, too, supported the notion of the party as the vanguard of the working class and the central party apparatus as the vanguard of the party. He had repeated this notion, so repugnant to Bogdanov, in his *Economics of the Transition Period*; his passages on the theme attracted plaudits from Lenin.[230]

Yet Bukharin had his own vision of a 'proletarian culture' none the less. He wanted culture under socialism to break decisively with the culture of the bourgeoisie, which he deemed inimical to socialism and to the interests of the working class. No art or even science, to Bukharin's mind, was innocent of ideological orientation.[231] Bogdanovism was detectable here, as Bukharin acknowledged.[232] Lenin tried to intimidate Bukharin back into line. His attack was indirect. Since Bogdanov professed a tight link between his own epistemological and political standpoints, Lenin tried to undermine Bukharin's attitude to 'proletarian culture' by enquiring provocatively about his attitude to philosophy. In particular, he asked for Bukharin's reaction to the second edition of *Materialism and Empiriocriticism*.[233] Bukharin refused to play Lenin's game. He also suggested that, instead of raking up a controversy with Bogdanov that was a decade old, Lenin should do everyone the favour of reading what Bogdanov had written more recently.[234] Lenin in turn refused. This was partly because he felt he already knew enough about Bogdanov; it was also because he, no less than Bukharin, hated to be deflected from what he regarded as a major current practicality. Bukharin's talk about the urgency of fashioning a totally new form of society with a comprehensively new culture seemed utopianism to Lenin. The cultural objectives of the moment, it seemed to Lenin, ought to be less ambitious: literacy, account-keeping and administrative capacity. Their attainment would massively improve the chances of putting the country on a path to economic reconstruction. The spectre of hunger had to be driven away.[235]

Bukharin would not yield. On 9 October 1920 he wrote to Lenin: 'I personally consider that to "conquer" bourgeois culture in its entirety, without destroying it, is as impossible as "conquering" the bourgeois state.' This statement essentially accused Lenin of attitudes to revolution espoused by his deadly enemy Karl Kautsky.[236] Lenin, keeping unusually calm at such sniping, retorted algebraically: '(1) Proletarian culture = communism; (2) it is carried out by the RCP [Russian Communist Party: RS]; (3) class-proletarian [power? RS] = the RCP = Soviet power. Are we all agreed on this?'[237]

On the cultural front, however, Bukharin would not yield. And, as the Politburo under Lenin's influence proceeded to bring Proletkult organisationally to the heel of the Soviet state, Bukharin declined to speak on the Politburo's behalf. 'On the Proletkults', a central party circular sent out on 1 December 1920, was written without the assistance of either him or any other sympathiser of the movement such as Anatoli Lunacharski.[238] The disagreement with Lenin impelled Bukharin into an intense bout of reading (which was beyond Lenin's capacities since he could hardly cope with his governmental and party duties in any case). Like Lenin in the epistemological controversy of 1908–1909, Bukharin wanted material to confound his adversary. The result was the book *Historical Materialism*, which was to appear in 1921. On a single major point of philosophy he was at one with Lenin: namely that the world exists independently of human cognition and that any alternative suggestion was solipsistic.[239] But on other points he differed. He did not treat Marx as unchallengeable; he continued to adduce not only Bogdanov but also militant anti-Marxists in support of his argument; he repeated that a 'proletarian' science and culture was needed to replace 'bourgeois' science and culture.[240] A row over

Bolshevik cultural policy was in the making. That it did not take place in the winter of 1920–1921 is attributable to the onset of the most dangerous political crisis confronting the party since the October Revolution. Workers went on strike, soldiers and sailors mutinied, peasants revolted. The mind of Bolshevism confronted the matter of popular rebellion.

6 Less Politics!

Bolsheviks wanted the Soviet state to guide all public and private institutions in their expanding republic. Direct and comprehensive dominance was their objective. This is so familiar a notion from later communist and fascist history that the effort has to be made to consider how unusual it was at the time of the October Revolution and Civil War. Bolshevism invented it. Many earlier rulers had wanted and obtained autocratic power; but none had wished to subjugate each and every institution to its will. Even the Romanov monarchy had granted rights and privileges to favoured bodies, groups and individuals. Not even the most absolutist among the Russian emperors had envisaged total control as their objective.

The Bolshevik party had expounded such an ambition soon after the October Revolution, and elaborated it in its party programme at the Eighth Party Congress in March 1919. Yet the totalitarianism of intent was not matched by reality. Orderliness and compliance with the central party leadership's commands had increased, but institutions operated disobediently on occasion. To some extent this flowed from the confusions of Civil War; and the absence of a reliable network of communications and trained personnel were a further obstacle to the construction of an all-pervasive state. Even among Bolsheviks there were inhibitions about the desirable scope of the state's pretensions. The October Revolution was meant, in Lenin's words, to introduce a dictatorship of the proletariat. The fact that the party had used violence against the working class had not eradicated a feeling among Bolsheviks that the interests of the workers should be protected. A residual belief existed that trade unions in particular should, within limits, fight for the rights of 'the labouring masses'. These limits were narrow. Only the Workers' Opposition contended that the the unions should not entirely accept the party's hegemony. Leading Bolshevik trade unionists, such as Central Committee member Mikhail Tomski, were comfortable with the notion of a one-party and one-ideology state. But it was also supposed to be a workers' state, and Tomski and his friends resisted the reduction of the unions to being mere transmission-belts for the conveying of the party's instructions to the working class. The eruption of the strike movement, which had never been extinct in the Civil War, convinced Tomski that greater pressure on the working class would have disastrous consequences for the régime.[1]

This was not Trotski's opinion. If the state belonged to the workers, he maintained, the traditional purposes of trade unions were redundant. Instead the unions should become primarily agencies of economic production. This amounted to the 'statification' of the union movement –and Trotski did not evade the term in his pronouncements.[2] He had proselytised for labour armies and for the extension of central state economic planning; and he did not hide his distaste for the Ninth Party Conference's criticisms of the 'political departments' which had replaced the trade unions on the railways. Trotski, People's Commissar of Military Affairs, requested the militarisation of Soviet public life. He would not take the Party Conference's reprimand lying down.

That this should be his reaction was a sign of unrivalled ability to throw away his advantages. Stalin was licking worse wounds from the Conference. Trotski's continuation of his challenge to party policy distracted attention from Stalin's humiliation and re-focussed attention on Trotski. Lenin despaired of his Politburo and Red Army colleague. Unlike Trotski, he felt at ease with the Conference's decisions. There had been assaults on Lenin's management of both the Polish campaign and the party's internal affairs, and a resolution had been passed on the need to reform party organisation. Lenin coped with the Conference by putting it out of his mind as soon as the delegates went home. The establishment of a Central Commission, for example, would not deflect him in any way from his purposes. The burden of day-to-day decision was heavy. The Poles, victors at the battle of the Vistula, had to be watched carefully even though negotiations were in progress. The Entente powers were unpredictable. The Red Army was a shambles, and minor mutinies were occurring. Industrial conflicts broke out. The peasants of Russia and the Ukraine were taking up arms against the Soviet authorities. Food supplies to the towns were at a critically low level. In Lenin's estimation, these were the issues requiring urgent attention. He felt that Trotski had lost a sense of perspective if he insisted on a theoretical discussion of the role of trade unions in a socialist state.

Yet the contrast drawn by Lenin between Trotski and himself was not fair. For a start, Trotski was resting his case on practicality as well as theory. He argued that economic reconstruction would succeed quickly only if workers were to forgo the conventional bargaining practices with their employers and to submit to rigorous labour discipline in an industrial and mining sector under central state control. In Trotski's opinion, the working class of 1917 no longer existed. The closure of enterprises; the migration into the villages; the malnutrition and disease in the towns; the conscription into the armed forces: all this had led to a collapse in the size, morale and political 'consciousness' of the working class. The state had to take command and, when necessary, coerce the workers into co-operation with the requirements of economic reconstruction.[3]

Lenin, however, had luck inasmuch as his policy neither necessitated an unsettling change in the measures of the day nor confronted particularly fearsome adversaries; for the Democratic Centralists and Workers' Opposition did not much trouble him. Nor was Trotski alone in his propensity to lunge into theoretical abstraction at the drop of a hat. Lenin, as he had shown in controversy after controversy before the Great War and would show again in the foreign-trade discussion of 1922, was even more likely to act in such a fashion.[4] Trotski for once outdid him. He wanted change and wanted it fast. His abrasiveness towards the Democratic Centralists and Workers' Opposition did not cease, and he remained unapologetic about the political departments which had been castigated at the Ninth Party Conference by many local committee men who otherwise supported the Lenin–Trotski leadership.[5] Nor did Zinoviev's attempt to rally these discontented supporters at the Ninth Conference give him pause for thought.[6] Trotski, convinced of his correctness, took his ideas to the lion's den: the Fifth All-Russian Conference of Trade Unions. His speech on 3 November 1920 set out the following basic proposition: 'The administrative-economic apparatus is nothing but the union's production organ, i.e. its most important organ.' In case this jargon had mystified his listeners he added that the unions should replace their obligation to protect the immediate interests of their members with an overriding commitment to the raising of productivity. They should be production unions, not trade unions in the conventional sense.[7]

Yet his words served to strengthen hostility to him. He was brave, but also unwise: he exposed himself to the charge of disregarding the party's supreme political role. The Central Committee met for a three-day session starting on 8 November. Lenin would tolerate him no more. Tomski returned from the Conference of Trade Unions, where he had officially represented the Bolshevik Central Committee, and fulminated against Trotski. Lenin not only condoned this but gave himself the licence to make 'exaggerated and therefore incorrect "onslaughts"'.[8] On his recommendation, Trotski's theses on the trade unions were rejected by eight votes to seven.[9] It was a narrow victory. Pressing their case, Lenin and his group proposed counter-theses which were accepted by ten votes to four.[10]

But at this point something odd happened: a so-called 'buffer group' emerged consisting of several Central Committee members. They were fearful lest a split in the party's leadership might endanger the régime, and some also felt that a compromise between the two leaders was desirable. These included several who were no friends of Trotski: Kamenev, Zinoviev, Rykov, Artem and Tomski. Kamenev was forever trying to make oil mix with water in Bolshevism.[11] But Zinoviev was not a reconciler and Tomski had had a blazing polemic with Trotski at the Congress of Trade Unions;[12] Rykov had been the butt of Trotski's sarcasm at the Ninth Party Congress;[13] Artem had previously hugged close to Lenin.[14] There were also adherents of the buffer group who were sympathisers with Trotski to a greater or lesser extent. These were on the 'left' of the Bolshevik political spectrum: Bukharin, Dzierzynski, Krestinski, Radek and Serebryakov.[15] Thus ten Central Committee members out of nineteen, including some who were absent, resolved to hold the two protagonists apart. Lenin was forced to back off. The speech he was scheduled to make to the Conference of Trade Unions was cancelled by order of the Central Committee. Zinoviev was charged in his place with making a 'businesslike and not a polemical report'. The Central Committee forbade its members to 'bring the disagreements into open discussion' and elected its own trade union commission under Zinoviev's chairmanship.[16]

The commission's composition was balanced equally between Lenin and Trotski. Lenin was represented by Rudzutak, Trotski by himself. The other members came from the buffer group: Rykov, Tomski and Zinoviev.[17] But the equality of treatment was a mere show. On substantive trade-union questions the composition would leave Trotski in a minority of one; and, if Rykov was far from Trotski's standpoint, Tomski and Zinoviev were still more distant.[18] Zinoviev, moreover, was a slippery opportunist. His espousal of moderate reform at the Ninth Party Conference in September 1920 was unaccompanied by implementation in his own political base in Petrograd.[19] Like all the Bolshevik leaders, he had a genuine ideological commitment. But he was untrustworthy in day-to-day politicking. His choice as commission chairman was a red rag to a bull.

Trotski refused to participate in the charade. Nor did he accept the Central Committee's recommendation for the 'degeneration of centralism and militarised forms of work' in Tsektran to be reversed.[20] The Waterworkers' Union was infuriated to the point of explosion by his intransigence. The matter came before the Central Committee on 7 December. Zinoviev took the side of the Water-workers' Union and demanded the reselection of Tsektran's leadership. This time he was more aggressive than Lenin. Yet his assault on Trotski was rejected by those who, unlike Zinoviev, stayed within the buffer group. Lenin had gained a new ally in the person of Zinoviev. Rykov, too, voted on his side.[21] But the buffer group's remaining members held firm despite the defections. Bukharin emerged as its leader. His views on trade unions were summarised in the slogan of 'workers' democracy in production'. In reality he no more intended to provide unionists with greater influence than did Trotski. The slogan obfuscated Bukharin's will to impose a priority for the raising of productivity at the expense of workers' bargaining rights and immediate material interests.[22] But the stand-off between Lenin and Trotski meant that his reduced group held the balance of power in the Central Committee; and, although not all of the group's members liked his specific slogan, it was sufficiently vague to allow them to force it through as Central Committee policy. This was a position akin to Trotski's in the Brest-Litovsk dispute in early 1918. Lenin was as annoyed with Bukharin in 1920 as with Trotski two years previously. He and his supporters insisted that a Party Congress should be convoked within a couple of months to resolve the disagreement one way or another.[23]

FRONTS, POLICIES, SITUATIONS

The Ninth Party Conference, while discomfiting all Politburo members including even Lenin, failed to tie them down to many specific changes of policy; but it certainly had pushed economic questions to the top of the agenda. The figures of industrial output were depressing. In 1920 Russian enterprises produced only fourteen per cent of the total achieved in 1913. Agriculture, too, was in a disastrous condition. Even if allowance is made for the fact that the Soviet régime controlled a territory smaller than the former Russian empire, a grain harvest of forty six million tons was poor. Transport was in chaos. The towns had been depopulated by disease, malnutrition, conscription and the flight to the countryside. But the villages were hardly better off, and in central and northern Russia, where requisitioning had been hard throughout the Civil War, they were a great deal worse. As the Reds moved southwards in September and October to concentrate their military efforts upon General Wrangel, debate began about the ways available to reconstruct the economy of Russia and the peripheral regions of the former empire.

The most radical proposal for changing policy in the Bolshevik party had come from Trotski in February 1920. It had not been debated outside the Central Committee; and Trotski, once worsted by Lenin's continued support for comprehensive grain requisitioning, dropped the matter.[24] But at least Trotski had tried to face the economic facts. Lenin remained extraordinarily complacent. For the four months following April 1920 he made no major statement on the economy.[25] There was no comparable period, previous or subsequent, when he remained silent about agriculture, industry and trade. He continued to chair Sovnarkom and the Council of Labour and Defence so that the appalling evidence of collapse in industry and agriculture came regularly before him.[26] The Second Congress of the Communist International and the invasion of Poland had held his attention. As he came to recognise the crisis for what it was, Lenin persisted with existing measures. War Communism had to work better. It was Kalinin, not Lenin, who insisted on 14 September that the Politburo should establish a commission of enquiry into the conditions of the peasantry.[27] Lenin stuck to the grain requisitioning, to the labour armies, to a virtual state monopoly in industry; he also reiterated his commitment to attracting concessionnaires into the Russian economy. More generally, he adhered to the objective of formulating a 'single economic plan' for the country.[28]

Visiting peasants, however, did not let Lenin forget them.[29] In mid-October a certain Belyaev told him at an open meeting that the state's behaviour reminded him of the folk-story of the goat, the ram and the lynx. By pitching the workers against the peasants, Lenin was setting up a situation like the fight between the goat and the ram, in which the lynx, whom Belyaev likened to world capitalism, could be the beneficiary.[30] Lenin's defence of official policy was not quite as dogged as usual. He emphasised that the grain levy had been lowered in central Russia (even though he added that it had been raised in the south).[31] Lenin hoped to indicate that the Politburo was mindful of the peasantry's distress. Still more remarkably, he omitted to declare an anathema on free trade; and this lacuna characterised his public statements until late December.[32]

Evidently he was less sure of himself than earlier. The last campaign between the Reds and the Whites was drawing to a close. Wrangel exploited the moment of the Soviet invasion of Poland to break out of the Crimea in June 1920. His forces pushed into Ukraine. But the Red Army was re-grouped against him after the Polish débâcle. By early November he was back in Crimea and was forced to evacuate all his forces abroad. General Wrangel never returned to his native land. Lenin rejoiced. This was natural, but his complaint that the threat from Wrangel had been neglected in the summer was less justifiable: he himself had harassed his central party colleagues into concentrating on Poland.[33] An armistice was agreed between Poland and the Russian republic in October. Negotiations continued and were far from easy. But the Politburo was willing to make what Trotski sarcastically described in anticipation as 'a collaborationist peace'.[34] Claims were abandoned to much territory in what had been Soviet Ukraine and Soviet Belorussia. By March 1921, the details had been worked out and the diplomats met to sign the Treaty of Riga. A peace settlement was also agreed with the other Baltic states; and Sergo Ordzhonikidze, who wanted to move the Red Army over the Azerbaidzhanian border into Persia, was strictly countermanded.[35] The military extension of the network of Soviet republics was to be halted in a southerly as well as a westerly direction. Both Turkey and the United Kingdom, with her Asian possessions and interests, had to be re-assured that Red bayonets would not be carrying Bolshevism to other countries.

This gave Lenin the chance to re-think War Communism. Reports from the People's Commissariats of Food Supplies and Agriculture came to him and his colleagues in early December 1920.[36] Both revealed a crisis growing more acute. Lenin edged his way towards a new agrarian policy. He did not trumpet it. His talent for sloganeering was reserved for another hobby-horse of the moment: the introduction of electricity to factories and other work-places. In a memorable phrase he claimed: 'Communism is Soviet power plus the electrification of the entire country!'[37]

But what he also had in mind was something that drastically challenged the principles of current policy. This was the proposal, which he jotted down in advance of the Eighth Congress of Soviets, to reward individual peasant households for any increase in their productivity.[38] In the Civil War the Bolsheviks had exacted taxes, grain and conscripts from village communes as a whole. When they paid anything to the peasantry, the payment also was made to communes. Compensation on an individual basis was thought to smack of indulgence to the kulak; and, even though the committees of the village poor were disbanded in Russia in December 1918, class struggle in the countryside remained the state's conscious objective. Let us be clear about Lenin's new thinking. He was not suggesting free trade; he was not aiming to abolish the state grain-price monopoly. Yet he intended to give incentives to any peasant household which raised its level of production above the local norm. Nor did he stipulate that better-off categories of the peasantry would be excluded from the scheme. This was not capitalism, but it was not much like War Communism either. Discussions took place in the Central Committee.[39] Opinions were divided, and Lenin and Preobrazhenski were instructed on 20 December to draft a resolution on the agrarian question presentable to the Eighth Congress of Soviets.[40]

On the same day Lenin gave a report to the Bolshevik fraction on foreign concessionnaires. He argued that they would not only assist economic recovery but also divide the Soviet régime's enemies among themselves. For example, the granting of privileges to American entrepreneurs in Kamchatka would set the USA against Japan.[41] Lenin reminded his audience: 'A question such as the existence of the Soviet republic alongside capitalist countries, a Soviet republic surrounded by capitalist countries: this is such an intolerable thing for capitalism that any opportunity will be grasped to resume war.'[42] The threat from abroad could not be resisted effectively by military means. The political division of world capitalist imperialism was vital. Lenin laid emphasis, as regards the threat from the west, upon improved relations with Germany. He was willing even to offer 'food-supply concessions' to Berlin. The idea was that, if given access to abandoned land in eastern Ukraine, German entrepreneurs would introduce tractors to the country's agriculture.[43]

This extraordinary suggestion caused dispute. Not only the Workers' Opposition but many other Bolshevik speakers saw concessions as a betrayal of the Revolution, the proletariat, Marx and communism.[44] Lenin had greatly misjudged the adaptiveness of his party. Having been late in perceiving the dire condition of the economy, he had failed to prepare the minds of his fellow party activists before the Congress of Soviets. He had improvised, and learnt to his cost that even a modification of War Communism through profit-based rewards and foreign concessions would be difficult to achieve. The Congress opened on 22 December 1920. Lenin trimmed his report on behalf of

Sovnarkom of those aspects which had been most contentious. Nevertheless it was impossible entirely to avoid conflict. The proposals for a system of rewarding individual peasant households rankled. Foreign concessions were unpopular. Disagreements in the Central Committee about the trade unions were being aired at the Congress of Soviets; and Bolshevik delegates had to be carefully courted if the Congress was not to turn into a fiasco. The wartime pressures for party unity were waning. Strife returned to the Bolsheviks with a vengeance. In vain did Lenin propose that 'the best politics henceforward will be less politics'. His stress upon the need for a 'single economic plan' failed to reassure everybody. Even his call for a scheme to bring electricity to the entire country gained little applause.[45]

What saved him from humiliation was the unreadiness of Bolsheviks to undo him in front of the small number of Mensheviks, Socialist Revolutionaries and Left SRs at the Congress. The Bolshevik party's monopoly was not yet total, not quite. Solidarity of some basic kind with the party leader was essential. Furthermore, it did Lenin no harm that these other socialist parties were asking for a reform of economic policy more basic than Lenin's proposal. Chief among these demands was the replacement of grain requisitioning by a graduated tax-in-kind set at a lower general level of procurement. The remainder of the harvest would be left with the peasants, and they would be allowed to trade it on the open market.[46]

Lenin dissociated himself from such an abandonment of War Communism. He railed against peasants who became involved in what the Bolsheviks called speculation. Free trade in grain was ruled out.[47] But Lenin was still not out of the woods. Polemics on the agrarian question were almost inevitable even when Bolshevik delegates to the Congress were on their best behaviour. On 24 December, Lenin repeated to a Bolshevik fraction meeting that a turn towards 'the peasant individual economy' was required.[48] He shelved his contentious (and unrealistic) project for German farmer-concessionnaires; but he continued to scoff at the existing collective farms. Their ability to generate agricultural recovery, in his view, was negligible.[49] Even Lenin, however, was taken aback at the vituperative discussion which ensued. Despite his best efforts, the Bolshevik fraction at the Congress rejected the Lenin-Preobrazhenski proposals on the grounds that they favoured only the kulak. The Central Committee's motion was repudiated. Lenin was angry. Party discipline had been infringed. The Central Committee met in the emergency on 27 December, and Lenin described in graphic detail how truculent the Bolshevik delegates had been towards him. The fraction's attitude was condemned, and 'the personal rewarding of industrious peasants' was again defended. Lenin was empowered to go back to the fraction to re-assert the policy of the Central Committee.[50]

And the Central Committee also offered compromise. The priority was to become the recompensing of the industrious commune rather than the industrious individual household; and no household using 'kulak-type' methods should be eligible for reward.[51] Lenin was jaunty.[52] He acknowledged that, in practice, it was difficult to distinguish between an 'industrious peasant' and a kulak. But he simply maintained that the decisions in particular communes should be left to the peasants.[53] This was skimpy advice; and, as if recognising the political and intellectual weakness of his position, he declared that the Central Committee would anyway no longer treat this as a matter of discipline. Fraction members could, he said, vote according to conscience.[54] This humility did the trick. The fraction fell into line with the proposed compromise.

The gruelling debates were not terminated when the Congress ended on 29 December 1920. The controversy about the trade unions raged through the New Year in public.[55] In the Politburo, unbeknownst to the rest of the party, there persisted the dispute about concessions. Interested senior party officials were invited to the session of 16 February 1921 to debate whether to sign a deal with foreign entrepreneurs willing to take a stake in the oil industry. The acrimony was such that the Politburo opted, by five votes against four, to prohibit an open 'party discussion'.[56] The Central Committee duly took up the case on 24 February. Once again there were bitter exchanges. Lenin was forceful in his contention that the oil-wells in Baku in Azerbaidzhan and in Grozny in the north Caucasus were in such ruin that 'extreme measures' such as the introduction of foreign concessions were vital. Even so, it was only by eight votes to six that the plan was accepted in principle by the Central Committee; and, as a sop to the critics, Lenin had to agree to Aleksei Rykov being asked to investigate how the Soviet republic would go about independently reconstructing the oil industry if the attempt were to be made.[57]

All was turmoil for Lenin, including his more intimate life. The dearest friend from the pre-revolutionary era, Inessa Armand, had been in the south of the country convalescing. On leaving Kislovodsk in the north Caucasus, however, she contracted cholera and died. Her corpse was conveyed by train to Moscow's Kazan Station at three o'clock in the morning of 11 October 1920. Lenin was present and followed the coffin through the cold, snow-laden streets. No death since his mother's had hurt him so deeply. Angela Balabanova witnessed the scene: 'I never saw any human being so completely absorbed by sorrow, by the effort to keep it to himself, to guard against the attention of others, as if their awareness could have diminished the intensity of his grief.'[58] Lenin and Inessa probably had a sexual liaison of some kind before the Great War, and the emotional tie persisted. Recalling the earliest stage of their friendship, Inessa had written to him: 'At that time I was not completely in love with you, but then, too, I loved you greatly. Even now I could cope without the kisses; just to see you and talk with you would be a joy – and this could bring pain to no one.'[59] Her passion was undisguised: 'I kiss you strongly.'[60] Her correspondence scarcely suggests an entirely platonic relationship; and, when she went on a trip in February 1919, she left behind a sealed letter to Lenin, to be opened in the event of her death.[61] Shortly before she died, she confessed to having 'an intense feeling' only for her children and for Lenin.[62] Whether Lenin reciprocated her attitude to him is not known for certain. But a residue of tenderness persisted, and for a time he was emotionally overwhelmed by her death.

THE 'TRADE UNION DISCUSSION'

It had taken the crisis among the party leaders for the Central Committee to resume its importance. The Politburo had previously been formulating policies, the Orgburo and Secretariat handling administrative business with little interference. Even so, the Central Committee was not influential for very long. On 24 December it finally gave permission for debate to be opened on the trade unions;[63] and its members, instead of sitting in semi-permanent session as during the Brest-Litovsk controversy, took their respective cases to the rest of the party to make their case. Trotski's impatience had proved ungovernable. Next day he brought out his pamphlet, *The Role and Tasks of the Trade Unions*, for presentation to the Eighth Congress of Soviets. He ignored requests to wait until the Party Congress.

This pamphlet asserted that the fate of the Revolution was in the balance. The rights and activities of trade unions were a foil for broader deliberations on centralism, hierarchy, electivity, social rights and economic development in a socialist state. Overt political battle, which quickly became known euphemistically as the 'trade union discussion', commenced on 30 December under the gaze of the Bolshevik party fraction at the Congress of Soviets. Lenin and Zinoviev stood together against Trotski. Bukharin tried to place himself between them; but the weight of his arguments was evidently less unfavourable to Trotski than to Lenin and Zinoviev.[64] At any rate this was not merely a bilateral struggle. Shlyapnikov, too, entered the fray; but, if the Central Committee members were agreed on anything, it was that the Workers' Opposition had to be crushed. Lenin concentrated his fire on Trotski. Not for the first time he declared that few issues of general principle divided them. The notion that trade unions should help to raise productivity had been settled at the Ninth Party Congress in March 1920.[65] But Trotski had given himself up to abstractions: 'Why is the working class to be defended, and from whom, since the bourgeoisie doesn't exist and the state is a workers' state?' Lenin declared that the working class still needed unions to protect its interests.[66] After contemptuously dismissing both the buffer position and the Workers' Opposition, he urged support for a set of theses on the unions drawn up by fellow Central Committee member Jan Rudzutak. He had overlooked them when Rudzutak had offered them to the Fifth All-Russian Conference of Trade Unions a month previously; but these now became the official Leninist platform.[67]

Lenin emphasised, in an off-the-cuff remark, that the Soviet state was 'not a workers' but a workers'-and-peasants'' state. He did not argue this through to the end. Bukharin obviously thought that he detected a theoretical gaff, and made an interjection to Lenin's speech: a rare occurrence by 1920.[68] It was one of those nice points of Bolshevism. Before the October Revolution, Lenin had called for the inception of the 'dictatorship of the proletariat and the poorest peasantry'.[69] Bukharin noticed that 'workers'-and-peasants' state' as a formula did not stipulate that only the poorest peasants would serve as the proletariat's fellow holders of power. But Lenin disdained to enter debate on the topic.[70] His own intention – and again we have to guess in the absence of hard evidence – was to stress that party policy had to take account of the fact that the urban working class constituted only a small proportion of the population.[71] But he sensed that Bukharin might attack him on the grounds of this formula; and, instead of defending it, he went on to the offensive by suggesting yet another formula and stated that 'ours is a workers' state with *a bureaucratic distortion.*'[72]

Lenin had come upon a formula that would see off his adversaries: it conveyed pride in the results of the October Revolution while indicating that the workers had a continuing need of protection by trade unions. It also involved a shift in emphasis towards the standpoint taken by Zinoviev and Rudzutak. Lenin exploited the advantage he held through having a majority in the commission on trade unions set up by the Central Committee. The commission completed a draft decree for the Tenth Party Congress, and Lenin and his colleagues signed their approval of it on 14 January 1921. These included nine Central Committee members and a further member of the trade-union commission, and the document became known as the Platform of the Ten. Quickly it was followed by the issuing of rival platforms by the buffer group, the Democratic Centralists, the Workers' Opposition and lesser groupings.[73] Much bargaining went on. Lenin's surge continued and Bukharin made overtures to Trotski. A compromise was reached whereby the buffer group would campaign with Trotski so long as he ceased to advocate the retention of labour armies.[74] It did them little good. Trotski had started with considerable support in Moscow, Petrograd and the provinces. But by early February 1921 even the Urals Regional Committee, where his popularity was at a peak, had moved away from him.[75] On Lenin's side, the campaigning was done mainly by Zinoviev who pursued Trotski across the country on whistle-stop tours like those which became typical of American presidential campaigns. Weeks before the Tenth Party Congress it was obvious that the Platform of Ten had won.

But Trotski could have no complaints. Despite having most Central Committee members on his side, Lenin could not manipulate the administrative levers of a Secretariat staffed by Trotski's sympathisers: Krestinski, Serebryakov and Preobrazhenski. Nor did Lenin's attempt to demonstrate that Trotski and Bukharin misunderstood Marx's doctrines make much difference.[76] The underlying explanation is that Lenin stood for party unity and was able to portray Trotski as a splitter. Trotski's advocacy of militarised trade unions was also resented for its diminution of the authority of the party. The record of his anti-Bolshevism before 1917 was not forgotten. Trotski reacted by claiming that Lenin's indulgence to the unions was a rhetorical ploy. To a large extent Trotski was right (even though it is equally true that Lenin was hostile to the extreme anti-unionism of Trotski). And yet Bolsheviks in the localities faced conditions which could no longer be handled exclusively by command and violence. Industrial strikes were growing in number and intensity. Trotski could not explain how he would stop them without bloodshed.

Shlyapnikov was Lenin's next target. The Workers' Opposition was organisationally loose and politically diffuse. Yuri Milonov, the Samara provincial party leader was unwilling to call for the abrogation of the party's dominance over the soviets and trade unions; and E. N. Ignatov, a Bolshevik official in Moscow, wished to supply the soviets with the right to veto appointments in the trade unions. Both baulked at the request of Shlyapnikov and Aleksandra Kollontai for an equitable division of powers among party, soviets and trade unions. The necessity of coming to the Party Congress with an agreed platform intensified debate among sympathisers of the Workers' Opposition. The result was a triumph for Shlyapnikov and Kollontai.[77] But in the party as a whole this mattered little. The freedom of the Lenin-versus-Trotski controversy was not extended to Shlyapnikov. Zinoviev, pseudo-prophet of internal party democracy since September 1920, clamped down on Workers' Oppositionists in Petrograd. They were entrenched in a few cities such as Samara and Nizhni Novgorod, where they gave more generous treatment to their opponents than they themselves received elsewhere.[78] Lenin castigated Shlyapnikov as an anti-party syndicalist and his ideas as a 'syndicalist deviation' from Bolshevism.[79] Lenin ignored the evidence. Shlyapnikov did not want to abolish the Bolshevik party; his platform was not designed to entrust the working class with untrammeled power. He was not a syndicalist, and Lenin knew it. Yet Lenin, having been patient with his party critics until the Eighth Congress of Soviets in December, had his blood up. Not only Shlyapnikov but also Bukharin, who had said that ultimately the trade unions should be turned into bodies controlling the entire industrial sector, were denounced for having supped with short spoons with syndicalism.[80]

Lenin introduced a philosophical dimension to the discussion: always a sign of his irritation. Bukharin, in order to show that Lenin's case on the trade unions was one-sided, had taken a paradigm from the physical world. Thus a glass on any table could be defined as a cylinder or equally well as an instrument for drinking. Lenin interjected that its definition might also include its capacity as an object to be thrown. Such sarcasm prefaced a recitation of Bukharin's sins:he failed to understand Marxian dialectics, indulged in eclecticism, had not read Hegel and showed ignorance of Plekhanov. Oh dear! Comical as this is as a response to Bukharin's perfectly ordinary and innocent turn of speech, it was written in earnest: 'In parenthesis it is appropriate to note for the benefit of young party members,' asserted Lenin, 'that *it is impossible* to become a conscious, *real* communist without studying – and truly *studying* – everything written by Plekhanov on philosophy since this is the best of the entire international literature of Marxism.'[81]

TOWARDS THE NEW ECONOMIC POLICY

The 'trade union discussion' prolonged the diversion of the leadership's attention from problems which had begun to be addressed, however imperfectly, at the Ninth Party Conference of September 1920. A Politburo decision was taken on 28 January 1921 enjoining Trotski and Zinoviev, who were on an investigatory mission for the Council of Labour and Defence in the Urals, to relegate questions about the trade unions to the background.[82] The crisis in food supplies was at last put at the top of the official agenda. Yet this could hardly be counted as a virtue. Failure to secure grain for the towns would have left urban Russia to starve; and in any case the policy of requisitioning all seizable harvest surpluses remained intact.[83]

The dangers for Bolshevism were on the increase. Strikes by factory workers broke out throughout urban Russia. Demands for an end to the one-party state, to authoritarian work discipline, to food shortages and to the grain-picket squads were commonplace. Bolshevism was losing a dangerously large section of the social class that provided the rationale for the October Revolution.[84] Rumblings were heard also in Kronstadt, where the naval garrison was sick and tired of Lenin's régime. The same grievances were aired; and, although the Mensheviks and Socialist Revolutionaries moved among the sailors, the impetus to mutiny was no more the exclusive result of their agitation than it was amidst the working class. Resentment of Bolshevik political and economic policies within a garrison that had supplied the shock troops for the party in 1917 was reaching boiling point. In addition, the possibility existed that Petrograd workers and Kronstadt sailors might combine their rebellious energies.[85] In the countryside there was a fast-spreading blaze of anti-Bolshevism. Provinces in the Volga region, in Ukraine and in western Siberia were consumed by peasant revolts.[86] All patience with the Reds had gone. The peasantry hated the continuation of the forcible requisitioning of food, the imposition of labour duties and the military conscription of their young men; and their discontent was clearly focussed on the Bolshevik party and its commissars.[87] The Socialist Revolutionary A. S. Antonov, a local leader, put himself at their head and incurred Lenin's wrath as having manipulated the minds of Tambov's peasants.[88] But the peasants would have risen even without an Antonov. They were determined to secure justice for their cause, and offered a still greater threat to Lenin and his associates in 1921 than they had to Kerenski in 1917.[89]

The Politburo met again on 2 February 1921. Trotski and Zinoviev had left for their inspection of the economic situation in the Urals, and their absence gave an enhanced role to Bukharin. Lenin, Kamenev and Stalin agreed with him that the People's Commissariat of Food Supplies under A. D. Tsyurupa had destroyed the capacity of agriculture to recover in several provinces. A decision was taken to 'point out to com[rade] Tsyurupa that the political situation and the uprising of the peasants absolutely demands the most serious attention to the rapid implementation of a food-supplies price discount in places where the peasants are especially suffering from the bad harvest and are in especially severe need as regards feeding themselves'.[90] Siberia and the Caucasus were discussed;[91] but it was Tambov that caused trepidation in the Politburo. Military force was to be sent there in strength; and, presumably out of distrust of Tsyurupa, the Orgburo was to co-ordinate the various efforts.[92]

At first sight it was a bit rich of Lenin to harass Tsyurupa. The policy of the People's Commissariat of Food Supplies, and the quotas it administered to particular provinces, had been regularly scrutinised by Politburo and Sovnarkom.[93] Even so, Tsyurupa's distaste for the changes proposed by Bukharin was real. The Politburo felt that he had to be brought into line. It is also clear that the striking workers and mutineering sailors did not yet unduly bother Lenin and his associates. The impetus for reconsidering general party policy came from the peasants in revolt. Almost all the debates at the Politburo on 2 February revolved around the clash between the peasantry and the régime. The danger areas were growing in number; the Politburo was agitated not only about Tambov but also Kursk, Orel, Penza, Pokrovsk, Samara, Saratov and Voronezh.[94] Industrial products were to be distributed 'for political reasons as the first priority'.[95] In other words, the wish to be reconciled with the peasants stemmed from fear about the party's destruction and not from philanthropical concern. Equally interesting is the lack of Lenin's prominence in the debate. It had been Bukharin who had raised the topic, and Preobrazhenski who was entrusted with drafting a set of practical measures. Preobrazhenski was to complete his labours by the evening and consultations were to take place with absent Politburo members Trotski and Zinoviev.[96]

And yet, although a psychological gap had been crossed on 2 February, a vaster ideological chasm lay ahead. Emergency relief and emergency repression might work in the short term. But Preobrazhenski's remit did not include the one policy which would be the minimum reform acceptable to the peasantry: the abandonment of requisitioning the entire grain surplus in favour of a tax-in-kind fixed at a level low enough to allow peasants to trade a part of their stocks in local markets.[97] Since the October Revolution the tendency of Bolshevik policy had been in the direction of reinforced state regulation of the economy. Private enterprise was a pejorative term in the party. An ideology which had been solidly anti-entrepreneurial before 1917 had become diamond-hard in the Civil War.

But Lenin had been shaken into re-thinking his own attitudes more and more deeply. He had taken detailed notes on grievances expressed at a special meeting of non-Bolshevik peasant delegates at the Eighth Congress of Soviets on 22 December 1920.[98] In addition, he visited certain villages in Moscow province: Yaropolets on 14 November 1920 and Modenovo on 15 December 1920.[99] Moscow province was not the whole of the Russian republic; but at least he could directly witness rural conditions in a fashion that he had avoided in the Civil War. Peasants also streamed into the capital seeking an audience with the Soviet leader throughout the winter of 1920–1921.[100] Quite what these various visitors proposed to him, and how directly, is discernible only partially. Their memoirs were to be written within a political environment that brooked no criticism of the Bolshevik party and Soviet government; and, in any case, the nature of his office was bound to deter people from speaking frankly even to a man of Lenin's renowned approachability. At his meeting with peasants at the Eighth Congress of Soviets, for example, apparently no one urged the replacement of requisitioning with a tax in kind set at a lower level of procurement.[101] Only the Menshevik and Socialist Revolutionaries at the Congress proper made this demand.[102] The first Bolshevik official to do so in Lenin's presence was V. N. Sokolov. In a private audience late on 2 February, Sokolov as member of the Siberian Revolutionary Committee predicted disaster unless a substantial lowering of requisition-quotas was quickly announced and the peasantry was permitted to trade its resultant grain surplus.[103]

Did Sokolov finally change Lenin's mind? The answer is not known. At a conference of metal-workers on 4 February 1921 Lenin merely hinted at the direction of his thought. He phrased himself in Marxist abstraction, dwelling on the 'relations of the workers to the peasants' (whereas the real problem was the state's relationship with the peasants).[104] He wandered round the topic, expressing worry lest the peasantry, impoverished and starving, might follow the example of Hungary in 1919 and fall 'under the power of the gentry landlords'.[105] This argument was specious: Russian and Ukrainian peasants lit no candles for the departed landowners. But the outlandishness of his words signalled the urgency of the situation; and when he touched on future policy *vis-à-vis* relations between workers and peasants, he heralded the introduction of new measures: 'We are not against a revision of these relations.'[106]

The meaning of this still very vague utterance was clarified at the Politburo on 8 February. Four full members were present: Lenin, Kamenev, Stalin and Krestinski. Trotski was in the Urals with candidate member Zinoviev; and candidate members Bukharin and Kalinin did not attend despite being in Moscow at the time.[107] It was at this meeting that Lenin, having listened to a report by Deputy People's Commissar for Agriculture N. Osinski, wrote his 'Preliminary Rough Draft of Theses Concerning the Peasants'.[108] It was the most historic discussion since the Brest-Litovsk controversy of 1918. Lenin's jottings were the basis of what became known as the New Economic Policy. A tax in kind, set at a lower level of procurement than had been sought in the previous year, was to be instituted. The aim was 'to expand the freedom of the cultivator to use his surpluses over and above the tax in local economic exchange'; and to ensure that the fiscal regulations rewarded peasants who increased their output.[109] This astonishing reversal of policy was made without any prior deliberation in public. Lenin's draft was scribbled out on a single sheet of paper and handed to a working party consisting of Kamenev, Tsyurupa and Osinski. These were to report back to the Politburo after a fortnight.[110] No Politburo resolution was recorded on the proposed change of policy; and Lenin, in contrast with his behaviour in the Brest-Litovsk discussions, held back from joining this crucial working party. Knowing that a proposal to 'expand the freedom of the cultivator' was antithetical to the mood of the party, he acted stealthily before the Party Congress. The intra-party discussions in early 1918 had nearly broken up the party. Already the Bolsheviks were at sixes and sevens about the trade unions; and, at a moment of peasant revolts, Lenin had to handle his collapsible party with extreme care.

The proposed tax in kind would not be implemented gently; there would on the contrary be intensified violence against the peasantry. Politburo meetings throughout February decided the personnel and practical measures needed to crush the resistance to Bolshevik party power.[111] The menace was perceived that, if the tax in kind were to be given publicity before the beginning of the spring sowing, the peasants would hide grain stocks from the People's Commissariat of Food Supplies so that profits might be made later. The country needed the grain immediately.[112] Peasants were not to be given everything they wanted. The 'Preliminary Rough Draft' fell far short of restoring the private commercial rights of the pre-1917 period. A free national market was not envisaged.[113]

On 16 February 1921 the Politburo decided to sanction a press debate on the pros and cons of a tax in kind. A cautious approach was maintained: the participants would be lesser Bolsheviks and not the party's leaders.[114] Next day *Pravda* carried an article by P. Sorokin and M. Rogov in favour of a new tax;[115] a riposte from V. Filippov appeared shortly afterwards.[116] By 18 February the Politburo commission chaired by Kamenev had produced a draft decree. Several amendments had been made to Lenin's sketch. The commission called for the tax level for the country to be set at 350 million puds of grain.[117] This was only a sixth lower than in the previous year under the requisitioning policy. The rationale for so high a level is unclear. Tsyurupa's dislike of the reform may have had its effect; or perhaps it was calculated that the recent conquest of the Transcaucasus and parts of the Ukraine would make the task of the tax collectors much easier. Another amendment balanced the original intention of encouraging agricultural production with a concern to protect the interests of the poorer peasants.[118] The Politburo convened on 19 February. Tsyurupa's objections were argued so forcefully that the commission report was forwarded to Central Committee members.[119] Neither Lenin nor anyone else in the Politburo looked on the reform with enthusiasm, and no one wanted to incur unpopularity for pushing it through without the consent of most party leaders. The Central Committee duly met on 24 February, and accepted the commission report.[120] The Rubicon was crossed. Both the tax in kind and the permission for peasants to trade their grain surpluses were to be rapidly introduced.

The decision was as yet secret. The Politburo, while keeping Sovnarkom in the dark about its deliberations,[121] set up another commission on 19 February. Its members were technical experts on the policy and statistics of food supply: N. I. Muralov, P. I. Popov and the awkward Tsyurupa. These proceeded to excise 'local economic exchange' from Kamenev's earlier draft. Their aim was to restrict the peasants to bartering with the People's Commissariat of Food Supplies, which had access to the warehouses of the state-owned factories.[122] It was a blow for the consensus achieved in the Politburo; but even Lenin, while disagreeing with Tsyurupa, had opposed the re-emergence of middlemen who would take grain for sale in other towns. In addition, the Red Army was to quell revolts and to supervise the spring sowing. The state's civilian organs, too, were to increase their regulation of the agrarian sector of the economy. The People's Commissariat of Agriculture was instructed by Sovnarkom on 22 February to draw up long-term plans for submission to the State Planning Commission. An entire economy run from Moscow remained the objective.[123]

Nevertheless Lenin might not have reconciled the Party Congress to the tax in kind if popular rebellions had not intensified. It was by no means universally accepted in the party that a lowered level of state-procured grain would alleviate urban food-supply difficulties; and the vehemence of the Bolshevik fraction's reaction to the much milder proposal for agrarian reform made by Lenin and Preobrazhenski at the Eighth Congress of Soviets lingered in the Politburo's memory. And yet, as the Politburo assembled on 28 February, the grievances of workers and sailors could no longer be ignored. Strikes and food shortages shook the minds of all Bolsheviks in Moscow. The Moscow situation was so serious that Trotski, who had just returned from the Urals, was appointed as 'chairman of the defence committee of the city of Moscow'.[124] Suddenly it was recognised that rural revolts were not the only ones which could bring down the government. Zinoviev had meanwhile returned to Petrograd to find even worse difficulties. The Kronstadt naval garrison was in constant agitation. Strikes broke out in Petrograd, and an anti-Bolshevik leaflet campaign had been organised.[125] The Politburo called in the Cheka. Arrests of active Mensheviks and Socialist Revolutionaries, including those who were factory labourers, were demanded. The Politburo recalled Dzierzynski immediately to Moscow to take charge again of the Cheka.[126]

This scale of opposition to the party had not existed since spring and summer 1918. On 2 March the Kronstadt garrison, having been disobeying orders for two whole days, arrested their pro-Bolshevik commanders and political commissars. Mutiny had erupted with a vengeance. And yet deliberations on the proposed tax in kind were held over until the Central Committee plenum of 7 March 1921.[127] A last-ditch effort was made by opponents of reform. The original advocates of the tax were denounced by some Bolshevik activists as being

Socialist Revolutionaries (as indeed Sokolov had once been);[128] and the tax was said to involve a re-installation of 'bourgeois relations' in the economy (as in fact it did).[129] From Bolshevik leaders in the Ukraine, including the entire Ukrainian Central Committee, there had come a protest that a tax in kind would impede the People's Commissariat of Food Supplies from extricating any grain whatsoever from the peasants at a time of an anti-Bolshevik peasant revolt across the southern provinces. Food-supply officials were being slaughtered.[130]

But Lenin held firm. Writing to Trotski on 3 March, he had argued that such revolts were evidence for the case 'not against the tax but in favour of a strengthening of military measures'.[131] Nor did he fail to emphasise that the contents of the Ukrainian Bolshevik protest had acknowledged that the local working-class population already demanded such a reform so that they could barter with the peasantry.[132] The Central Committee in Moscow fell into line with the Politburo's recommendations. On 7 March its plenum set up yet another commission to prepare yet another draft decree for the Party Congress. This time Lenin took charge, becoming commission chairman. The other members were Kamenev, A. D. Tsyurupa and G. I. Petrovski.[133] They restored the clause on 'local economic exchange' which had been removed by Tsyurupa. Peasants were to receive the freedom to barter with citizens in the nearest town as well as with the officials of the People's Commissariat of Food Supplies.[134] Tsyurupa was defeated. Lenin had pushed through a reform by methods different from those used in his victory over the Brest-Litovsk treaty. Caution, consultation and the cultivation of willing allies had done the trick. Now, at the moment of triumph, he would go before the Party Congress with the support of the most influential figures in the Central Committee. Personality alone had not worked its magic. Without the drastic worsening in circumstances in February and March, he might have been as unsuccessful as at the Eighth Congress of Soviets. But it is equally true that, if Lenin had not headed the campaign for reform, the proposal would probably not have reached the agenda sheet of the Tenth Party Congress.

LENIN'S COHORT

The party remained in a condition of shock at the divergence between Lenin and Trotski over the trade unions. There were many children in the country who grew up thinking that the October Revolution had been led by an individual called 'Lenintrotski'.[135] In 1918, during the Brest-Litovsk dispute, Lenin and Trotski had avoided trenchant mutual criticisms.[136] The world at large assumed that an identity of viewpoint characterised their work in the Civil War. The wrangles of 1920–1921 were all the more astounding. The London magazine *Punch* carried a detailed pen-and-ink sketch of Trotski brawling in an office and knocking askew a wall-picture of Lenin.[137]

Trotski had been reckless. He knew he was talented and let everyone know it. He could write as well as Tocqeville and Burke; he could orate like Demosthenes and Churchill (and without their need for textual self-preparation); he could organise a war-machine with the skill of Ludendorff. Not satisfied with his superiority, he treated his comrades with disdain.[138] Only Lenin was recognised by him as equally talented as himself: the rest of the Central Committee were subject to his airy dismissiveness; and, coming into a room of commanders and political commissars, he was quite capable of letting his cloak fall to the ground and leaving someone else to pick it up.[139] He was tall by Russian standards and handsome; he took scrupulous care of his sartorial appearance.[140] He could not bring himself to commune with his colleagues on their level. He scoffed at the plodding demeanour of provincial party leaders like Vyacheslav Molotov. And, when Molotov retorted that not everyone could be a genius, Trotski refused to act graciously.[141] He read French novels at Central Committee meetings when the proceedings bored him – as often they did.[142] As a day-to-day politician, he was his own worst enemy. He had thousands of admirers; and some of these, like Nikolai Krestinski and Adolf Ioffe, were Central Committee members. But consultation was not his style. It never occurred to him that others might not admire him and might even regard him as threatening to become the October Revolution's dictator.

Lenin and Trotski knew that such a menace was not as acute as it appeared. Trotski had been asked by Lenin in the October Revolution to become People's Commissar for Internal Affairs. He had refused; for he felt that his Jewish background would make him an inappropriate choice in a country where anti-semitism was rife. He had been reluctant to accept the request to take over the People's Commissariat of Military Affairs in 1918; and he later noted how the White armies had used his Jewishness as political ammunition in the Civil War.[143] Trotski implied a need to operate within a team in order to have an impact. To be sure, he may have been exaggerating concern about his ethnic origin in order to avoid receiving certain posts.[144] Furthermore, his readiness to turn the party upside down in pursuit of his preferred policies was demonstrated by the 'trade union discussion'; and his behaviour after Lenin's death hardly betokens a person reluctant to inherit the position of dominant party leader.

Nevertheless in the winter of 1920–1921, while Lenin enjoyed the appearance of good health, Trotski fought him over policy only; there was no attempt to reduce Lenin in importance. But the controversy seriously marred both their relationship and his reputation in the party. Trotski was undoubtedly putting a sincere case, and he was right to argue that the trade-union question touched on almost every aspect of the party's strategy: state power, economic reconstruction, workers' rights, local self-government; but he should also have known that the average party official, tried and tested in the heat of the military conflict of 1917–1920, felt that debate was a luxury which was ill-affordable by the Bolsheviks. Less talk, more action! Scarcely a month passed when Lenin omitted to make such a comment. Trotski could have learned with advantage from Lenin's refusal to give ideological hostages to fortune. Trotski admitted that what he sought was a properly-working 'bureaucracy'.[145] Lenin wanted the same objective, but omitted to say this directly: the term was repugnant to the Marxist tradition. The distrust of Trotski grew. Nothing was known in public about his refusal of posts because of his Jewish ancestry. Instead the talk among Bolshevik party officials was that, with his power-base in the Red Army, he might become the Napoleon of the Soviet régime. Bolsheviks thought much about the precedents in the history of the French Revolution. Trotski's non-Bolshevik past and his abrasive treatment of the party in 1918–1920 gave grounds for the fear that a Bonapartist counterrevolution might be undertaken under his leadership.[146]

Lenin meanwhile gained from his evident wish to deflect the party from a damaging discussion. He put a year of disastrous activity behind him, and his role in the party as the healer of political wounds was reinforced. Even Aleksandr Shlyapnikov in the Workers' Opposition spoke respectfully about him (whereas Shlyapnikov's abhorrence of Trotski was so intense that he refused to make common cause with him in 1923 when Trotski at last spoke in favour of internal party reform).[147] Moreover, little love was lost between the Workers' Opposition and the Democratic Centralists. Shlyapnikov's ideas were regarded by Sapronov as a deviation from Marxism. Lenin's motley adversaries used their strongest venom in attacking each other. It was as if the sole way open to them to prove that they were still loyal Bolsheviks was to refer affectionately to 'Vladimir Ilich'.[148]

Lenin gathered up this windfall of luck; but he also made the fruit tumble from the tree by shaking it. He restricted his own participation in the verbal free-for-all. A few jests were made by him at Trotski's expense. If the trade unions were so badly run, he suggested, how about letting Trotski and Krestinski take them over in a new duumvirate.[149] But this was hardly strong invective, and it only became public knowledge when Zinoviev divulged it. Zinoviev hurried round the major party organisations on Lenin's behalf, talking stingingly about the People's Commissar for Military Affairs. Those Bolsheviks who had been at the front in the Civil War, he emphasised, had scant understanding of conditions and possibilities in the rear.[150] Lenin's reference to Krestinski touched a raw nerve. There was an obvious danger that Trotski would make privileged use of the Central Committee Secretariat. Lenin would have certainly have done so if he thought he could have got away with it. Krestinski was on Trotski's side in the controversy; and Preobrazhenski and Serebryakov belonged to the 'buffer group' headed by Bukharin.[151] This group, forced to come off the fence dividing Lenin and Trotski, scared Lenin in 1921 by deciding initially in favour of Trotski.[152] And yet the Secretariat kept an impartial stance while its troika took Trotski's part. There was no undercover campaign, no Trotskyist faction. Zinoviev's men tried to pretend that skulduggery was afoot. F. F. Raskolnikov (who headed the political administration in the Baltic fleet) claimed that the rumour had been put about that 'Trotski and his supporters wanted to drive us to prison, hard labour and iron bars.'[153] Zinoviev's platform, more than Lenin's, conceded that appointmentism was a problem in the party. In fact the Petrograd party organisation was directed with negligible regard for democratic procedures. But Zinoviev was a capable demagogue and discerned the weakness in the defences of his opponents.[154]

Trotski's unwillingness to trade insult for insult was matched only by his aversion to political compromise. Lenin revelled in verbal ambiguity. He even wriggled out of announcing his own platform – which was unpredented in the party's debates – by encouraging a young and obscure trade union official, Jan Rudzutak, to produce a form of words congenial to his group.[155] At last, as defeat approached, Trotski yield a little. Bukharin and the 'buffer group' delivered the ultimatum that they would not back him unless he revoked his ideas on 'labour armies'. At a time of strikes and mutinies there could be little prospect of prolonging their existence, and Trotski complied. But it was too little, too late. Party organisation after organisation, despite Trotski's visits to them in person, came over to Lenin's side. Weeks before the Tenth Party Congress Lenin had won the 'trade union controversy'.[156]

His victory required consolidation by changes of personnel. Lenin restrained his associates from taking heavy revenge upon Trotski, and argued that only two thirds of the seats in the new Central Committee should be saved for themselves.[157] Such magnanimity was not to everyone's taste. A cabal of fifteen leading 'Leninists' was addressed by him as the Congress gathered in Moscow. Here Lenin put the case that Trotski should be included on their slate for election since he would be in a permanent minority in the Central Committee and disabled from causing a split in the party. He also recommended that Shlyapnikov and Kutuzov from the Workers' Opposition become full members (and Lutovinov, Medvedev and Kiselev as candidate members); and, from the Democratic Centralists, he suggested that Sapronov should be given a seat. But Lenin also insisted that the main supporters of Trotski should be removed; Krestinski, Preobrazhenski, Serebryakov and I. N. Smirnov would be pushed out from the Central Committee and its inner subcommittees.[158] Simultaneously there would be promotions for his supporters. Lenin must already have had it in mind to give full membership in the Politburo to Zinoviev in return for his part in Trotski's defeat, and discussions were under way to fill the Secretariat with officials who had taken Lenin's line in the winter of 1920–1921.[159] In addition, Lenin planned to call a meeting of all those who agreed with him on the trade unions. Stalin, who had returned to his inner counsels, queried whether this would not be interpreted as factionalism. Lenin was amused: 'What's this I hear from a died-in-the-wool old factionalist?!'[160] He refused to take his position as father of the party for granted. As he had done in the years before 1917, he assembled his confederates around him and made his dispositions on a factional principle.

THE TENTH PARTY CONGRESS

The Tenth Party Congress was opened by Lenin in the morning on 8 March 1921. Celebratory speeches were made by representatives of the Georgian, Armenian and Azerbaidzhani Communist Parties which had recently become the ruling authorities across the Transcaucasus.[161]

717 voting delegates attended. At a time of gathering crisis in Russia there was a need to infuse the Congress with optimism; but it was equally urgent that delegations should be made aware that their experience of particular local problems was shared nationally. No one should leave the Congress thinking that the policies of the Civil War could be maintained.

At the evening session Lenin delivered the long-awaited Central Committee political report. Unusually he admitted that a mistake had been made in 'our advance, our excessively swift advance virtually as far as Warsaw'.[162] Rather than using the royal plural, he was shamelessly shifting responsibility to the entire Central Committee. He added that the party leadership, in procuring much more grain than in the previous year, had been erroneously motivated by a 'desire to increase the hand-outs to starving workers'. This was an intriguing admission to be made by the architect of the dictatorship of the proletariat, and no wonder *Pravda*'s résumé of his speech did not mention it.[163] Urban working-class consumers, he implied, had been treated too generously. The reconquest of Ukraine and Azerbaidzhan had made coal and oil available to a government which proceeded to distribute it too generously; and a further blunder was committed in failing to requisition the grain in the areas where the harvest had been most successful: Siberia and the north Caucasus. Instead the state authorities had taken stocks from peasants whose 'surpluses were not great'.[164] And, to compound things, the demobilisation of 'a peasant army' had been undertaken too fast. Thousands of unemployed, exhausted conscripts returning to the villages took up 'banditry'.[165]

Lenin's implicit argument was that the peasantry's capacity to destabilise the authorities had been underestimated. The Central Committee report was a confession of blunder after blunder. But he tied it to an aggressive posture for the future. Lenin declared that the factional disagreements in the Bolshevik party were an intellectual luxury. Castigating the Workers' Opposition as 'a syndicalist or semi-anarchist deviation', he asserted that Shlyapnikov's ideas might prove menacingly attractive to the peasants.[166] The Kronstadt uprising was a case in point. Lenin described it as a 'petit-bourgeois counter-revolution' more dangerous than the White invasions of Kolchak, Denikin and Yudenich.[167]

His plea for unity and orthodoxy was intended to sugar the pill of the various unpleasant measures he had yet to defend at Congress. A trade agreement with the United Kingdom was a pressing requirement. So, too, was the party's acceptance of the desirability of foreign capitalist concessionaires taking a stake in Soviet industry. The leasing out of oil wells in Grozny and Baku would secure necessary technology and revenues.[168] Even so, general recovery would be a matter 'of many years, no less than a decade and – in view of our devastated condition – probably even more'.[169] An economy based on large-scale units of production would not quickly be achieved. The state would have to deal with small-scale producers, especially in agriculture, for a lengthy period. It had been on these grounds that the Central Committee had opened debate on the replacement of grain requisitioning with a graduated tax in kind. Lenin stressed that such a tax had been introduced into law in October 1918, but had proved impractical in the Civil War. He also assured his audience that the party leadership had not gone soft. 'The peasant,' he stated with a chilling directness that was withheld in the subsequent report in *Pravda*, 'must starve a bit so as thereby to relieve the factories and the towns from complete starvation'. Inside the four walls of the Congress hall Lenin declared that force would be widely used.[170]

Lenin sat down after nearly two hours of oration. Krestinski's organisational report on behalf of the Central Committee, which lasted over an hour, was bureaucratically perfunctory by comparison.[171] The real drama lay with Lenin's strategical change since the previous Congress. Solts's report for the Central Control Commission was simlarly unexciting.[172] Nobody could overlook the momentousness of the occasion. In the words of I. I. Skvortsov-Stepanov, Lenin had set the programme for the proceedings.[173]

At the Congress's third session on 9 March the attacks on 'Vladimir Ilich' began. Aleksandr Shlyapnikov resented his jibe that the existence of the Workers' Opposition had led to the revolts against the authorities. Rather the reverse was true according to Shlyapnikov. Popular discontent had induced him and his supporters to call for an alteration of the party's policies. Lenin's attitude to the Workers' Opposition would only cause further disunity.[174] Shlyapnikov's words quickly proved prophetic. Osinski, for the Democratic Centralists, agreed with Lenin that syndicalism had grown as a force in the party.[175] No love was lost between the Workers' Opposition and the Democratic Centralists. Nor was Lenin immune from criticism. L. S. Sosnovski, a supporter of Trotski in the trade-union controversy, quipped that Lenin had barely mentioned the workers. Unlike Trotski, Sosnovski criticised the new grain policy as a 'capitulation before the petite bourgeoisie'.[176] Back came Yuri Milonov for the Workers' Opposition, claiming that Lenin as Sovnarkom chairman regarded obstruction of his government's will as being both petit-bourgeois and harmful.[177] Back came D. B. Ryazanov from yet another angle. It was his contention that the strict line on the trade unions accepted by Lenin at the previous Party Congress was responsible for stimulating working-class discontent.[178] Furthermore, a certain Rafail denied that the trade-union controversy had been the luxury depicted by Lenin. In Moscow, as he pointed out, 'the arch-democrat Stalin' had been organising Lenin's faction as if an internal party war were being fought. The dispute had by no means been gentlemanly.[179]

Krestinski had got off lightly. The reason was not that tensions in the party had weakened but rather that it was already obvious that Trotski had lost the trade-union discussion. Lenin was the undoubted party leader and was held responsible for all existing trends. When the time arrived for Lenin to respond to his critics, he was ill-disposed to compromise. Picking up Shlyapnikov's enquiry as to why People's Commissar Tsyurupa had not been arrested for his recent decisions, he feigned horrified astonishment (as if Lenin had not similarly called rhetorically for the incarceration of close colleagues).[180] That evening, at session four, Lenin's report was approved by 514 votes against 47 for the Democratic Centralists and 45 for the Workers' Opposition.[181]

A vibrant debate on agitation and propaganda ensued, introduced by Evgeni Preobrazhenski (who, like Krestinski, was a supporter of Trotski). Lenin did not participate; indeed he did not re-appear at the speaker's lectern until three days later.[182] He had made his plans on politics and economics clear. He had attracted some criticism, but not as much as might have been expected. Until the debate on the trade unions he would retire from the fray. Apart from anything else, there was the response to the Kronstadt revolt to organise, and he needed to confer amicably with Trotski (who was about to return from an emergency investigative trip to Petrograd).[183] Perhaps he also worried lest the the coalition of the Platform of Ten should fall apart. No topic was more likely to bring this about than the 'national question', which was the very next item on the Congress agenda. The official report was delivered by Stalin. With the recent conquest of the Transcaucasus in everyone's mind, Stalin stressed the party's objective of equal rights for all nationalities; and he expatiated a bit on the tendency of several Russian Bolsheviks to indulge in 'Russian Great-Power chauvinism'. Stalin took the chance to reply to a scathing article about him by Georgi Chicherin in *Pravda*. His tone was angry. Among Chicherin's mistakes was a favouring of the slogan of national self-determination! Stalin noted that, as a result of discussions at the Eighth Party

Congress, the slogan no longer figured in the party programme. He affirmed, moreover, that the right of secession had been retained in the programme.[184]

This last point was tosh. The programme referred to secession only indirectly, and Stalin and his friends had been among those who had seen to it in 1919 that no unambiguous statement had been made.[185] Furthermore, Lenin in 1921 would indubitably have been annoyed by Stalin's dismissiveness about national self-determination. The slogan remained dear to Lenin.[186] Not that Stalin was criticised by Georgi Safarov, who gave an opposing report, for illiberalism. Instead Safarov, like most speakers, was scathing about Stalin's avoidance of practical detail.[187] Some speakers from 'the borderlands' went further than this. V. P. Zatonski from the Ukraine argued against the creeping Great Russian chauvinism and stated that Stalin seemed to deny that any republics independent from Moscow were conceivable. He also confessed that he himself, a Bolshevik leader, failed to understand the precise nature of the treaty between Soviet Russia and Soviet Ukraine.[188] Anastas Mikoyan and Mikola Skrypnik, too, complained about Stalin's vagueness.[189]

Lenin might well have joined Stalin's critics – and this omission was to make his dissatisfaction with Stalin all the more abrupt and tumultuous in the following year.[190] Stalin for his own part perceived that greatest unease abided among yet other delegates that too many concessions were being made to the non-Russian nationalities; and, by repudiating the charge that he was 'artificially implanting' national consciousness in areas where it previously barely existed, he also eluded a confrontation with the delegates from the borderlands. He thereby gave the impression of being closer in thinking to Lenin than was strictly true.[191] Furthermore, a ruling from the chair cut short the discussion and a drafting commission was formed.[192] The next debate, initiated on party structure in the sixth session on 11 March by Nikolai Bukharin, was equally contentious. Still Lenin kept himself out of the way. Criticisms were made almost identical to those offered at the Party Conference in September. Democratic Centralists and Workers' Opposition were to the fore; but this time they were opposed by several delegates who suggested that the central party leadership had been altogether too indulgent to them.[193] Yet even the Party Congress could not isolate itself from external events. All minds were focussed upon Kronstadt. The formal agenda of the Congress was suspended in the next three sessions, and it is claimed that no verbatim record was kept. Lenin played his part again. Measures were formulated with his assistance to ensure the military and the political reliability of Red

Army units. Dzierzynski provided information from the files of the Cheka.[194] Up to 140 Congress delegates volunteered to stiffen the army units sent across the frozen waters separating Petrograd from the island of Kronstadt; and, on Dzierzynski's suggestion, delegates from Samara and Saratov provinces were instructed to go back and deal with their rebellious peasants.[195]

Nothing was left to chance, and Lenin on the same day as the last of the emergency sessions penned drafts of his two motions on the syndicalist deviation and on party unity.[196] In the first motion, the Workers' Opposition was condemned for is allegedly anti-Marxist ideas; in the second, factional activity in general was banned on pain of expulsion from the Central Committee for any faction's leader (and from the party for the faction as a whole). This assault, even if not previously planned in detail, was made almost inevitable by the difficulties posed in Kronstadt and the Volga region. After this intervention, the debate on party structure was resumed. Bukharin was ridiculed for knowing little about his subject.[197] Yet Kronstadt had shaken everyone. Even the Workers' Opposition, as Aleksandra Kollontai stressed, supported the bloody suppression of the rebellious sailors and had sent its volunteers.[198] There was an overwhelming vote for Bukharin's theses: 369 against merely 23 for the Workers' Opposition and nine for the Democratic Centralists.[199]

At session twelve, on 14 March, Zinoviev opened the debate on the subject which had engaged party leaders in previous months: the trade unions. Nothing new was said. Trotski, who had by then got back from Petrograd, followed him. He emphasised that in February 1920, so far from being unorthodox as a Bolshevik, he had put forward a version of economic reform not totally dissimilar from the current proposal to abolish grain requisitioning; he revealed also that Lenin at the time had accused him of 'Free Trade-ism'.[200] But Trotski did little to promote his case on the unions beyond asserting that the Central Committee's motion was so lacking in fluency that Lenin could not have scrutinised it closely.[201] The debate had had its sting half-drawn by the situation outside the Congress. The Workers' Opposition and the Democratic Centralists had their say, but briefly. Lenin was not pressed unduly hard when he spoke on Zinoviev's behalf (although he did not desist from charging Trotski with having broken Central Committee discipline with his unleashing of the trade-union controversy).[202] Trotski retorted very reasonably that he had infringed no disciplinary code; he quoted, too, Lenin's statement at the Ninth Party Congress against the 'rubbish' spoken on behalf of democratic practices in the trade unions.[203] It was a nice historical point that did him no good. As he went down to the expected defeat, he lamely declared that the trade-union resolution would not survive in effect through to the Eleventh Party Congress. Zinoviev, naturally, disputed this hotly; and the Congress voted a trouncing victory to the Platform of Ten.[204]

Yet another closed session was held that evening, devoted to deliberations on elections to the Central Committee. The results were announced the following morning at session fourteen. 479 delegates voted. All 479 votes were cast to confirm Lenin's membership. Out of the other Politburo members, Stalin came sixth in the Central Committee list, Trotski a humiliating tenth and Zinoviev – who had been the peripatetic champion of Lenin's line on the trade unions in the winter – an even more distressing eighteenth.[205] Lenin had not been guiltless of polemical distortion in the trade-union controversy; but he had genuinely tried to stop its happening in the first place. His unanimous election to the Central Committee was his reward.

Only then did Lenin step forward with the Central Committee report on the end to grain requisitioning. He affirmed the question to be 'primarily political'. In a phrase which was becoming conventional, Lenin suggested that the nub of the matter was 'the relation of the working class to the peasantry'.[206] At present the peasants were discontented, and Lenin added: 'Classes cannot be tricked.' The 'final success' of socialist revolution in the Soviet republic still depended on the timely outbreak of revolutions 'in one or several advanced countries'; but a second and equally important prerequisite was the creation of an 'agreement' between the proletariat and the mass of the peasantry.[207] This was mealy-mouthed rhetoric evading any mention of one-party dictatorship. Yet it was also a forceful assertion, before an audience not known for its friendliness to the peasants, that policies had to be changed drastically. He dropped all pretence: 'What is freedom of circulation? Freedom of circulation is freedom of trade, and freedom of trade means a return to capitalism.' But immediately he added the reassurance: 'We can permit free local circulation to a decent extent without destroying but in fact strengthening the political power of the proletariat.'[208] Any communist who thought the country's economic base to be reconstructible within three years was fantasising. Existing collective farms were examples of how not to run an economy.[209] It had to be recognised that the proposed reform of policy would strengthen the emergence of 'kulakdom'. But needs must![210] Lenin asked the Congress, which by then was eating calmly out of his hand, to refrain from discussing details. It should instead, he urged, take a decision in principle and in favour.[211]

Tsyurupa, still unconvinced but resigned to Lenin's victory, offered a co-report. His gripes were that the new as well as the old policy depended on the same method of calculation and collection of tax even if the targets were set lower; and that the government lacked accurate statistical information on which to base any targets whatever.[212] Tsyurupa objected mainly to the private trading and to the encouragement of rural co-ops.[213] He also implicitly challenged Lenin's assumption that the new policy would somehow be more orderly in implementation. War communism in its technocratic manifestation spoke with the voice of Tsyurupa.[214]

Two speakers followed in Lenin's support, including Evgeni Preobrazhenski: the Bolshevik Left contained many who saw that some reform was urgently necessary. But then M. I. Frumkin, who worked under Tsyurupa in the People's Commissariat of Food Supplies, argued that Lenin's proposal would condemn workers to death by starvation. He castigated private trade, and reminded the Congress that the attempt to apply a tax-in-kind in 1918 had failed.[215] Lenin's summary speech at the end was characteristically combative. He acknowledged that a danger existed from 'petit-bourgeois' agricultural and indeed industrial producers if his policy were to be accepted. In one of his boldest strokes, he replied that large-scale industry would be reconstructed largely through injections of foreign capital. Lenin, the denouncer of global capitalist imperialism, even contended that the policy on concessionnaires was an attempt to form 'a bloc with the capitalism of the advanced countries'.[216] Undoubtedly, in the light of the hostility shown to his policy in subsequent months, he was to regret this improvised remark. It was tantamount to stating that the October Revolution should search fondly for fraternal capitalist régimes. This would have made a nonsense of Bolshevism. He proceeded successfully to the final vote. His motion was accepted. And yet he may have been disappointed. The number of delegates who supported him against Frumkin was not recorded.[217] Furthermore, D. Z. Manuilski declared that the Ukrainian delegation offered only very conditional support for the resolution. It would strike a blow at the committees of the village poor in Ukraine. Manuilski demanded that Lenin's policy should be accepted only with the proviso that it could be substantially modified in response to local conditions.[218]

Lenin had handled the Congress superbly. He had shown initial aggression; he had then lain low while his adjutants moved among the delegates and the import of his programme was considered. He had made an appeal for unity in the face of a tremendous economic and political crisis; and he had slipped his proposal to terminate grain requisitioning to the end of an overloaded agenda. No one else could have done this. Kamenev would have been booed off the platform. Trotski had covered himself with too much controversy. Lenin was vital to the re-orientation of policies. And he handled his role with the aplomb of a man who knew his position in the party to be stronger than anyone else's.

At session fifteen the same evening it was Kamenev's turn to report on 'capitalist encirclement'. His points were succinctly made. A further world war could be expected. The principal belligerents, he wildly predicted, would probably be 'England and America'. Only an uprising of the proletariat in those countries could prevent such a war.[219] Kamenev forbore to pick up Lenin's impromptu call for a 'bloc with the capitalism of advanced countries'. But the necessity for manoeuvres in foreign policy was stressed. Pursuit of a trade agreement had to be resumed. It was Kamenev's contention that, with Russia's re-entry into the world economic system, capitalism's own post-war recovery would be prevented.[220] And yet even he, the leading figure on the Bolshevik Right, took a stern view. He called for rapid re-arming for the future defeat of 'countries which are economically much richer'.[221] Such a statement allowed him to return to a stirring defence of the central party leadership's decision to make Baku in Azerbaidzhan into the first centre for oil concessionaires.[222] He was harassed by Anastas Mikoyan, who was equally keen to continue his criticism of Stalin when the draft resolution of the commission on the national question was presented at the end of the session. The commission had incorporated a little more detail, but substantially Stalin's original report was retained. Mikoyan was voted down.[223]

Most of the main decisions had been taken before the last session on 16 March. Zinoviev's report on the Communist International was typically triumphalist. Then, in the closing minutes, Lenin quickly introduced the two debates on party unity and the anarcho-syndicalist deviation. Not an inch to the Workers' Opposition was given by him.[224] Karl Radek had a presentiment of the threshold being crossed in the history of the party: 'I have the feeling that there was perhaps being established here a rule which can be turned against anyone as yet unknown.'[225] Even Radek, in his light-hearted fashion, recommended acceptance of Lenin's motions. Both were passed by overwhelming votes.[226] The Central Committee's other reports and proposals were swiftly given similar treatment. Kamenev declared the Congress at an end and the delegates sang the *Internationale*.[227]

7 The Rifle and Sickle

DEVELOPING THE NEW ECONOMIC POLICY

There are many examples in history of governments embarking on reforms without intuition about the potential repercussions. Often a relentless process is begun. It is doubtful that Henry VIII anticipated the full consequences of disestablishing the pope's power over the Church in England. Even Martin Luther was unaware of the ecclesiastical revolution he was unleashing when calling for the papacy's transformation.

When Lenin's party introduced a grain tax and permitted the trade in surplus stocks held by peasants, however, no such illusions prevailed. The Bolsheviks were Marxists; they also had come through a Civil War which, in their estimation, had been won by measures on production and distribution which had marked a movement towards socialism. No Bolshevik leader regarded the New Economic Policy (as Lenin started to call it from May 1921)[1] as anything other than a retreat forced upon the party by the peasantry's discontent. The genie of capitalism had been released back into the economy. Every Central Committee member approved this with reluctance, taking it for granted that a resurgence of private commerce would strengthen the social forces in the country hostile to the Bolsheviks. Karl Marx's *Das Kapital* had taught them that, where economics lead, politics eventually follow. Having defeated the bourgeoisie by force of arms after the October Revolution, they were deeply annoyed that capitalist tendencies would rise up again in peacetime. Unease and irritation were expressed in dozens of written queries passed up to Lenin at the Tenth Party Congress. The Congress's resolution, while breaking with forcible grain requisitioning, was indefinite on many significant details. What was to be done about industry, about artisanal workshop, about co-operatives, about sowing quotas?[2] Well as he had managed the Congress, Lenin had also had much luck. The revolt of the Kronstadt sailors during the Tenth Party Congress prevented the irritation from being manifested in too unruly a fashion; the incentive to rally around the Central Committee was irresistible.

The Central Committee and its Politburo would have to elucidate its policy rapidly if an impact on the opinion of the peasantry was to be made before the spring sowing. The party's organs rather than Sovnarkom or its various adjuncts took virtually all the major decisions on the New Economic Policy. A Central Committee plenum met on the Congress's last day, and appointed the new Politburo. Lenin, Kamenev, Stalin and Trotski kept their places; but Krestinski, who no longer had a seat in the Central Committee, gave way to Zinoviev. Vyacheslav Molotov was to lead the Secretariat together with V. M. Mikhailov and E. M. Yaroslavski.[3] None of these, however, was appointed to the Central Committee's commission, to be chaired by V. P. Milyutin, for the elaboration of official measures.[4] Lenin did not want to be identified as the sole architect of the reform which, from May 1921, was regularly known as the New Economic Policy. Connoisseurs of his style were able to recall that in 1918, despite having being the protagonist of a separate peace treaty with Germany and Austria-Hungary, he insisted that others in the Bolshevik party leadership should go out to Brest-Litovsk to do the signing. Certainly he could plead pre-occupation with other business which was being reported to him: the Anglo-Soviet negotiations; the Kronstadt and Tambov revolts; the attempted seizure of power in Berlin by the German Communist Party with their 'March Action'; the worsening conflicts in the Soviet trade union leadership; industrial strikes in Soviet Russia; dissent in the Bolshevik party; the activities of the Mensheviks and Socialist Revolutionaries; the establishment of 'Soviet power' in the Transcaucasus. Even so, the choice of priorities for his close participation was his prerogative. He wished to ensure that the entire Central Committee was responsible to the New Economic Policy. Milyutin, moreover, had taken his side in the pre-Congress discussions: the drafting details could safely be left to him. In the mean time pressure was put upon the commission to work fast. Milyutin could build on the drafting already done in the Politburo, Central Committee and Congress; and, after showing his project to Kamenev and Tsyurupa for their comments, he was able to come before the fully-attended meeting of the Politburo on 18 March.[5]

Lenin was in the chair.[6] The Politburo wanted further changes to be made to Milyutin's draft. In particular, the meeting – undoubtedly with Lenin's approval – demanded that the new tax would be levied on individual households, not on whole communes. In addition, the draft was to be modified so as to specify that 'local exchange' would involve the re-opening of the old bazaars and markets.[7] Thus commenced the broadening of the contents and language of reform which continued through the rest of the year. Dread terms like 'markets' had previously been avoided.

On 19 March the Politburo looked at a manifesto to be directed at the peasants. It was a masterpiece of political appeal, promising the permanent removal of landlordism and expressing regret that grain requisitioning had been made necessary in the Civil War. The manifesto committed the government to buying industrial products abroad so that it would be worthwhile for the peasantry to maximise their sown area in anticipation of trading it later in the year. The grain tax, moreover, would be set at a lower level than the wartime requisitioning target; and, while the poor peasants were guaranteed continued material support, the manifesto assured the rest of the peasantry that efforts to increase harvest would be rewarded. The fiscal level would be announced before the sowing.[8] Only at this stage did the central party leadership make its intentions fully public. The central party apparatus had deliberated secretly before the Congress, and occasional articles in *Pravda* had indicated what was afoot. The Congress had ratified the general proposal for reform. The central party apparatus had scrutinised and sanctioned the details. Only when this process had been completed was either the Central Executive Committee of the Congress of Soviets or Sovnarkom involved. The party monopolised power not only in theory but also in reality; the supreme issue on the agenda of Soviet politics was not to be devolved to the formal state authorities until policy had been fixed by the Bolshevik leadership.

Then the legislation came thick and fast. Mikhail Kalinin presented the Politburo-approved decree to the Central Executive Committee of the Congress of Soviets on 21 March.[9] The original plan for Lenin and Kalinin to do this jointly was discreetly dropped.[10] Lenin was staying out of the highlight. He also kept back from belonging to the party's new commission on the grain tax set up by the Politburo on 25 March. Instead the commission's chairman was to be Kamenev.[11] Further vital decisions were recommended by its members. The aim was for state bodies to procure between 300 and 350 million puds of grain through the tax.[12] This would not include the Ukrainian harvest. In fact the commission resolved to maintain wartime-style requisitioning in Ukraine.[13]

Thus the potential region of greatest grain surplus in the Soviet-ruled republics was to be exempted from Lenin's reform. The antagonism of the Ukraine-based Bolshevik leadership, already expressed at the Tenth

Party Congress, may have had an influence;[14] but probably Kamenev and his colleagues – with Lenin in agreement in the background – were themselves worried about a resurgence of Ukrainian private trade before the completion of the transfer of land from gentry and rich peasants. The Ukrainian agrarian revolution was in an early stage. The Bolshevik party's fear of kulak-led resistance to its authority was so strong that even the Ukrainian equivalent of the committees of the village poor, abolished in Russia in December 1918, remained in existence until the mid-1920s.[15] The Politburo generally accepted Kamenev's recommendations. The sole objection was made to the level set for the grain tax outside the Ukraine: further consultation led to its reduction to 240 million puds of grain.[16] The commission was divided over the question of extending trading rights to urban retailers. Bolshevik leaders before and during the Party Congress had considered ideas on reform limited to bartering between the peasant producer and both the state procurer and the individual consumer; private traders had not been envisaged. The Central Committee discussed the division in the commission, and ruled in favour of those who wanted to allow a private retail trade.[17] An important linguistic modification was also made. The words 'buying and selling' were affirmed as being words for the party to popularise (even though the Politburo also intended to punish any peasant found to have sold more grain than would allow him to sow enough in the spring).[18]

Still Lenin kept his head down. It was another of the party's agrarian specialists, V. V. Kuraev, who wrote bluntly in *Pravda* on 27 March 1921:'We must *review all* questions of our agrarian, peasant policy'.[19] Not until early May 1921 did he given a lengthy printed exposition of his views.[20] Lenin, a more than willing public speaker in normal times, delivered only four speeches in the ten weeks after the Party Congress. Just one of these, which was a report to a meeting of party secretaries in Moscow province, focussed upon the New Economic Policy.[21] Distraction by other governmental business can hardly explain his avoidance of the topic. Lenin was lying low.

Yet behind the scenes he was deeply involved in official decisions, chairing both Politburo and Sovnarkom.[22] Sovnarkom continued to oversee the arrangements for the sowing committees;[23] and Red Army units, including cavalry, were deployed to ensure that the sown area reached a maximum.[24] Furthermore, the decision to set the tax level as low as 240 million puds of grain did not solve the difficulties of fiscal planning. There was conflict between the People's Commissariat of Food Supplies and the Central Statistical Administration in the estimation of the grainstocks available; and Lenin, with his expertise in the geography of agriculture going back to his 1899 book *The Development of Capitalism in Russia*, was naturally drawn into arbitrating.[25] Much of this effort was guess-work; for the statistics of both sides were chaotic and unreliable. The result could be horrendous for particular provinces. V. A. Antonov-Ovseenko, sent by the Politburo as political commissar to suppress the Tambov peasant revolt, wrote to Lenin in alarm at the quota assigned to the local authorities.[26] The Volga region was the major source of grain as identified by the Politburo in its discussions.[27] The reform was therefore still a tremendous gamble by Lenin; it might cause more problems than it solved. As yet it was restricted to commerce and taxation. Nothing was yet intended to alter the government's programme on industry, finance, transport, management, labour and planning. The focus remained on the countryside.

It was a self-limitation which could not long endure. The economy was collapsing. Lenin, in the sole speech to the Moscow party secretaries, reported his own astonishment at a report he had received from comrade Korolev which revealed that, in Ivanovo-Voznesensk province, 'no more than six factories have been working and not one of these work continuously for a whole month'.[28] Inflation was steep and getting steeper. Food supplies were still below the necessary minimum for subsistence in most towns and cities, and early indications about the forthcoming harvest were not encouraging. Factory production in 1921 was a fifth of the total registered before the Great War. Coal output fell to 31 per cent, steel to four per cent, pig iron to three per cent. Transport remained in crisis: only three tenths of the pre-war freight load was carried in 1920–1921.[29] In these circumstances the New Economic Policy would rapidly have to be expanded if the Soviet authorities were to extricate themselves from disaster.

CONQUEST OF EMPIRE

At the Tenth Party Congress and subsequently Lenin had demanded a union between workers and peasants. And yet his private thoughts were not so kindly about the peasantry. His first plan for the speech to the Party Congress on agrarian reform in March 1921 assumed that a 'peasant counter-revolution' was occurring against Bolshevism.[30] He could not say this at the Congress without casting a shadow on the party's claim to be defending the interests of the mass of the population. He even jotted down a reminder to himself to 'gloss over in the press "the interrelationships of the proletariat and the peasantry"'.[31] But his predominant intention was to suppress revolts in the villages. Gentle towards the peasants he met, Lenin was brutal in his dispensations of policy.

His frantic supervision of military actions, no less than the discussions in the Politburo about the development of economic policy, distracted him from considering what kind of constitutional settlement should follow the ending of the Civil War. By far the greatest proportion of the lands of the Romanovs had been reconquered; but the precise relations to be established among the several Soviet republics, including Russia, had yet to be decided. Repression was at its most intense in the grain-producing areas of Russia. Mikhail Tukhachevski was recalled from the Western front against Poland to conduct operations against the peasants of Tambov province. Simultaneously troops were assembled for assaults on rebels elsewhere in the Volga region, western Siberia, Ukraine and the southern Russian provinces on the Russo-Ukrainian border.[32] Lenin was deeply involved. A Politburo session under his chairmanship instructed E. M. Sklyanski, Trotski's deputy, to put pressure on the Red high command to get on with the task of 'suppressing banditism'.[33] The ruthlessness anticipated by Lenin at the Tenth Party Congress was repeatedly requested. In this tense situation no quarter would be offered to the Mensheviks and Socialist Revolutionaries. Any of their leaders discovered in Moscow and Petrograd were to be arrested on sight; the fitful existence allowed to their parties in the Civil War was to be terminated.[34] Nor should any trace of the Kronstadt mutiny be allowed to endure. The most prominent mutineers were shot, and thousands of ordinary sailors were to be transferred to a 'disciplinary colony' whence few returned.[35] Propaganda would, Lenin hoped, eventually redress the discredit into which the Bolshevik régime had fallen. But force was the key to survival. First suppression, then economic reform.

The violence applied in the Volga region was paralleled in areas of non-Russian populations. A revolt of Bashkirs had occurred in May 1920. Azeris, too, had risen against the Bolsheviks in the same month; and the Politburo discussed the weakness of the party's power in Baku well into 1921.[36] Armenians had followed the Azeri example in February 1921. And the Georgians, who were the most recently-conquered nation of the Transcaucaus, simmered with disaffection from the authorities imposed by the Red Army under Sergo

Ordzhonikidze. In central Asia a revolt burst out among Moslems who rallied to rebels known as the Basmachis.[37] The Bolsheviks had alienated the non-Russians to a lesser extent than had the Whites in previous years; but this led no party leader to think that the 'national question' had been solved. On the contrary, the lands of the former Russian empire were seething with political unrest among the various nations and ethnic groups. Debate had sooner or later to be joined about the entire constitutional settlement to be imposed.

There was an assumption in the Politburo that some kind of federalism was required. But how this would be realised was undecided. The conquest of the Transcaucasus had meant that the Russian Socialist Federal Soviet Republic (or RSFSR), Ukraine and Belorussia were joined as independent Soviet republics by Azerbaidzhan, Armenia and Georgia. Bilateral treaties were signed between the RSFSR and the three new republics across the Caucasus mountains along the lines already established with the others.[38] But the preferred long-term ties among all six Soviet republics were not specified. In December 1920, when the latest treaty had been signed between Russia and Ukraine, 'federal' was struck from the draft describing the Russo-Ukrainian relationship.[39] Almost certainly the temporising was caused by disagreements among central party leaders. Already in June there had been a spat between Lenin and Stalin.[40] Lenin wished to form a federation of Russia, Ukraine and other republics whereas Stalin wanted to incorporate these other republics in the RSFSR with rights of 'autonomy' of the type inaugurated with the Bashkir Republic in 1919. Several such republics were established within the RSFSR. The largest by far was the Turkestan Republic (which was at the centre of the revolt of the Basmachi). To treat Ukraine in such a way, according to Lenin was 'chauvinism'.[41] Russia and its Bolshevik leaders had to go out of their way to demonstrate their anti-nationalist credentials; and he was annoyed that his nearest major ally in the party on these questions had turned against him.

The dispute had ramifications for policy throughout Europe. For Lenin, the addition of Ukraine to a federal multinational state would merely have been the prelude to the additions of Poland and Germany. In midsummer 1920 this had been a matter of urgent policymaking as the Red Army prepared itself to march on Warsaw. For Stalin, this was naïve inasmuch as neither the Poles nor the Germans would 'ever enter a federation on the principle of the rights of Ukraine'.[42] There were further possible distinctions here. Perhaps Stalin, unlike Lenin, was also aiming to have as strong and large an RSFSR as possible so as to act as a counterweight to a future Soviet Germany; but Lenin the Russian was less Russocentric than Stalin the Georgian, and he was apparently untroubled about a Soviet federation in Central and Eastern Europe which might not be dominated by Russia.

Stalin was difficult to face down. His expertise was beyond question. He remained People's Commissar for Nationality Affairs, despite demanding to resign on 24 November 1921, and had been used by the Politburo to supervise decisions about the borderlands in general and the Transcaucasus in particular during the Civil War.[43] In previous debates on the 'national question', moreover, Lenin had met intense opposition from the party on the grounds that he excessively indulged nationalist opinion.[44] Stalin himself had been criticised for this at the Tenth Party Congress.[45] Lenin could not count on defeating Stalin's constitutional project in open party debate. For the while neither man wanted such a debate, and their disagreement was kept secret in the central party leadership. There was anyway much consensus between them. Their ideas on federalism were confined to the governmental institutions. Both continued to insist upon a strictly centralised, unitary party. The Central Committee, its Politburo and its Orgburo in Moscow were to instruct and control all party bodies throughout the republics, and these 'local' bodies were to direct the republican governments as Moscow demanded. A tacit understanding therefore emerged between Lenin and Stalin that other more pressing matters of politics and economy should engage their attention: the fractiousness of the 'trade union controversy' was considered an ill-affordable luxury.

Not that the affairs of the non-Russian nationalities were overlooked by Lenin. He was especially solicitous about events in the Transcaucasus, and on 3 March 1921 had instructed Ordzhonikidze to avoid simply repeating what had been done in Russia since the October Revolution. The region's peculiarities had to be taken into account. Initially Lenin, the lifelong harrier of the Mensheviks, advocated the quest of 'an acceptable compromise' with the Georgian Menshevik leader Noi Zhordania.[46] Ordzhonikidze and fellow members of the Caucasian Bureau (or Kavburo) in Tbilisi must have blinked when reading the telegram. Such advice from Moscow at a time when the Russian Mensheviks were being thrown into the prisons of the Cheka!

Lenin had changed his mind about Zhordania, and continued to restrain the Kavburo. On 14 April 1921 he sent an open letter to 'the communist comrades of Azerbaidzhan, Armenia, Georgia, Dagestan and the Mountain Republic' demanding that local conditions be respected. A 'slower, more cautious and more systematic transition to socialism', according to Lenin, should be undertaken than in Russia. His reasoning was not just that the region was predominantly agrarian or that Bolshevik rule was under threat. He also asserted that the Transcaucasus could act as a conduit for trade between the Soviet republics and the West. Foreign concessionnaires should be welcomed. In this direction he was in favour of the creation of 'a tight union' among the peoples of the region.[47] Neither Stalin nor Ordzhonikidze was pleased to be tolerant to their native country. A tightly unified Transcaucasus unquestionably appealed to them. Ordzhonikidze secured a single regional transport policy and interfered in a variety of matters relating to foreign trade. He re-shuffled personnel, making use of party activists sent to him by Stalin and the Orgburo in Moscow. His appearance on a white horse in Tbilisi was thought offensive: Ordzhonikidze ruled, and liked to be seen to rule; and he was as infuriated as Stalin himself in July 1921 when Stalin, on a rare visit to Georgia, was heckled at a public meeting.[48] The rest of the central party leadership, too, wanted to hold the republics of the Transcaucasus to heel. On 3 April 1921 a Politburo decision was taken to require them to submit any treaties with Turkey to Moscow before ratification.[49] Their formal independence must not go their heads. Thus it came about that Ordzhonikidze, with Stalin's full support, sought to reinforce control over each republic by constraining them within a Transcaucasian Federation. In August 1921 this became the official policy of the party's Kavburo.[50]

The Transcaucasian Federation idea had the Central Committee's support and was due to come before the Politburo on 29 November. Lenin backed it in principle, yet deemed implementation premature. He wished to restrain the Kavburo, and proposed that further discussions be undertaken with party members and 'the worker and peasant masses' in the region. Even Lenin envisaged that the discussions would last no longer than 'several weeks' (and he was persuaded by Stalin that this could safely be re-phrased as 'a certain period of time').[51] The Politburo approved the proposal despite a furious objection by Budu Mdivani on behalf of the Georgian Central Committee.[52] The feet were cut from beneath him by the device of getting a far from reluctant A. F. Myasnikyan, who had a leading role in the Armenian Bolshevik leadership, to appear at the Ninth All-Russian Congress of Soviets in December 1921 to demand the Transcaucasian Federation's creation.[53]

Still there was no deliberation as to the permanent arrangements to be made among the RSFSR, Ukraine, Belorussia and the proposed

Transcaucasian Federation. Stalin wrote to Lenin on 13 January 1922 repeating his commitment to the incorporation of all of them within the RSFSR. But he denied wanting to do this quickly. It was certain unnamed comrades, according to Stalin, who demanded immediate action.[54] Whether he was being disingenuous is uncertain. Possibly he was content to see the Transcaucasian Federation, which was promulgated despite Georgian Bolshevik resistance on 12 March, come into existence before moving on to a grander constitutional project. Complaints from Georgia continued to reach Moscow, and the problems of other republics did not cease. Clashes between the Central Committee in Moscow and the Bolshevik politicians of Ukraine had occurred since 1918. In a memorable rebuke, Stalin after the Brest-Litovsk treaty had told V. P. Zatonski to stop 'playing at governments'.[55] Not all the holders of power in Kiev were ethnic Ukrainians. Christian Rakovski, a Bulgarian, and Mikhail Frunze, a part Romanian, were as determined to keep the Central Committee at bay as were natives of the republic such as Mikola Skrypnik. The attempt by Moscow to break up Ukraine into separate economic areas was resented.[56] On 11 March 1922 the Ukrainian Politburo complained to the Central Committee in Moscow about a series of infringements of the republic's rights as embodied in the treaty with the RSFSR.[57] This republic, great in industry and agriculture, was always a source of worry for the Bolshevik party. The Politburo repudiated the complaint; but Frunze still placed it on the Politburo agenda on 11 May 1922. A commission was established under Frunze's chairmanship to offer recommendations on the future relations between Ukraine and the RSFSR.[58]

Stalin resented this interference. He was not only an avid centraliser who imposed Moscow's policies on the peripheral regions; he was also the leader most often called upon by Moscow to mediate in conflicts between one region and another. The spats over the territorial limits of Bashkiria in 1919 were followed by several others within the RSFSR; and, most notoriously, a menacing disturbance broke out between the Azerbaidzhani and Armenian Soviet republics over the ownership of Nagorny Karabakh. In 1920 the Politburo had ruled in favour of Armenia, but in 1921 Nagorny Karabakh – despite being heavily populated by Armenians – was handed to Azerbaidzhan.[59]

Sooner or later, however, Stalin and Lenin would clash over Stalin's project for 'autonomisation'. Stalin obviously felt that reason was on his side. At that time he was not the harrier of the non-Russian nationalities he became in the 1930s. He supported the use of native-language schooling and fostered local cultural development. He promoted non-Russian Bolsheviks to high office. He spoke against privileges enjoyed by any one nation.[60] Furthermore, his duties as People's Commissar for Nationality Affairs left him in no doubt how frail the Bolshevik party was in the non-Russian republics. Bolsheviks were few in number, were usually disproportionately drawn from ethnic Russians as well as from persons who had joined the party late in the Civil War.[61] The arguments for letting republican Bolshevik organisations take full charge of their respective republics were not self-evident. To Stalin it must have seemed that Lenin had not thought out a responsible party policy. Lenin had been proved wrong before in Stalin's eyes. Until 1917 he had claimed it possible to run a great multinational state without the recognition of one language for state business. He had also promised to offer the right of secession to non-Russians. In 1920 he had underestimated the nationalism of the Poles.[62] Stalin knew that his convalescent colleague would been annoyed by the autonomisation project; but he expected that eventually he would concede ground just as had happened over the Transcaucasian Federation. The will to retain the peoples of the Soviet lands subject to the party's power and policies, by force if the need arose, was common to both men. Stalin was therefore unprepared for the intensity of Lenin's hostility when it revealed itself from autumn 1922.

INTERNATIONAL RELATIONS

Both Lenin and Stalin at any rate knew that the 'national question' was inseparably linked to issues of foreign policy. In September 1920 the Congress of Peoples of the East had been organised so as to advertise the virtues of the treatment of non-Russians in the Russian Socialist Federal Soviet Republic to the rest of the world; and in the discussions of 1921–1922 the argument was put, especially by Christian Rakovsky, that exemplary tolerance should be shown by the Central Committee towards the various Soviet republics so as to make Bolshevism an attractive alternative in the eyes of national minorities in the states established in eastern Europe since the treaty of Versailles.[63] The linkage with the same question was perceptible also with the development of policy on 'concessions'. The introduction of American oil companies, if it occurred, would result in the handing over of virtually all large-scale Azerbaidzhani industry to the mercy of foreign capitalism.[64]

The Politburo was perplexed as to how to develop a line which would simultaneously enhance territorial security, facilitate the spread of socialist revolutions and attract investment from foreign capitalists. The defeat at the battle of the Vistula had led to a revision of foreign policy. Lenin rightly believed that, however successful they were with these important but lesser states, it would be progress with the Allies that would determine the Soviet régime's survival. Yet this attitude exaggerated the control exerted by the British, French and Americans over the countries bordering on the former Russian empire, but not to the point that it was entirely ludicrous. Lenin had hopes for a rapprochement with the USA, and such was his gullibility that he was tricked by a commercial mountebank called Vanderlip who claimed that, if granted the timber concession in Kamchatka in the Far East, he would guarantee that the American administration would take a pro-Soviet orientation.[65] About the French, who were owed vast sums of money since before the October Revolution, Lenin harboured no illusions. The greatest diplomatic effort was put into a resumption of trade links with the British. Lev Kamenev had spent several weeks in London in 1920 – not always to the best diplomatic effect: his call on the Mile End Road for the arming of English workers disconcerted Lenin almost as much as it infuriated Lloyd George.[66] Nevertheless the British cabinet took a benign view and, despite further disagreements, the negotiating process went well; and Lenin looked forward to adding the United Kingdom to the smaller states of the Baltic as his country's trading partners. Not only two-way commerce but also an inflow of foreign investment through concessionaires were his stated objectives.[67]

Lenin also knew that nothing could be counted upon in advance. In public he had argued, on 6 December 1920, that Russian participation in world trade was necessary for economic recovery everywhere.[68] Whether he believed this is doubtful. In the 1890s, let us recall, his economic works denied that the capitalist industrial development of a large country crucially depends upon its access to all world markets; and such a position would hardly have led him to contend that Russian raw materials were absolutely indispensable for the United Kingdom with its huge overseas empire.[69] Nor did he give up the hope that 'world revolution' would come to the rescue of the RSFSR and the allied Soviet republics; indeed no assertion of this possibility was made by him between the Tenth Party Congress and the end of 1921.[70]

This emphasis was strengthened by the failure of the 'March Action' undertaken by the German Communist Party, on the initiative of Béla Kun and other representatives of the Communist International, to overthrow the elected German government and seize power in the last week of March 1921.[71] Paul Levi had questioned this strategy, but difficulties with his comrades led to his resignation from the German communist leadership. The March Action was swiftly suppressed by army and police in Berlin. The planning behind the fiasco was minimal. Bukharin sympathised with the German communists; but, inside the Executive Committee of the Communist International, it was almost certainly Grigori Zinoviev who gave official sanction to Kun's activity. Zinoviev suffered the embarrassment of having 'black-legged' against the Bolshevik party in the October Revolution; he over-compensated for this in the Communist International by zeal for foreign socialist adventures (which may also explain the roisterings of his fellow alleged black-leg Kamenev in London in 1920). Levi excoriated the Action, and was expelled from the German Communist Party.[72] At the time Lenin did not comment. Nor is there much evidence that he was involved in the Communist International's decision. Lenin's diary in March was filled with considerations about the tax in kind, the Georgian operation, the Kronstadt and Tambov revolts, the arrangement of foreign concessions, the trade treaties, the Tenth Party Congress. Even if he were to be shown to have known in advance about the Action in Berlin, he evidently was not its long-range supervisor.

The episode shows how even Lenin did not control his colleagues over all policies. By his own estimation, socialist revolution in Germany was a prerequisite for the full achievement of socialism in Russia. Equally Lenin's political distance from the March Action demonstrates the intensity of his pre-occupation with the multifaceted crisis confronting the Soviet state. Survival, not expansion, was his current priority. He subsequently refrained from criticising Zinoviev, Radek and the German leaders over their blunders, but notably also failed to endorse them. At any rate, his behaviour towards Germany in the rest of the year concentrated more on trade with the German bourgeoisie than on the revolutionary potential of the German proletariat.

On the last day of the Tenth Party Congress, on 16 March, an Anglo–Russian Trade Agreement was signed in London. Both a Soviet–Turkish treaty and a Soviet–Persian treaty came into effect in the same month, and a provisional trade agreement was made with Germany on 6 May.[73] The search for concessionaires was paramount.

Undeterred by the dispute about Baku and Grozny oil, Lenin pushed for east Ukrainian coal as a further possible concession. 'It is ultra-desirable,' he wrote to Trotski, 'to give up a quarter of the Donbass (+ Krivoi Rog) to concessionaires.' The opposition, according to Lenin, was supposedly motivated by 'Donbass patriotism'.[74] In fact the hostility to concessions stemmed not only from local pride but also from distaste for the re-introduction of large-scale capitalism from abroad. The basis of the New Economic Policy was found wanting by many party officials, activists and ordinary workers. A furious discussion took place at the Fourth Congress of Trade Unions in May 1921, and Lenin was obliged to attend to justify concessions.[75] He was undismayed that the conditions imposed by the Soviet authorities upon any concessional contract were more restrictive than those available in other countries. Even so, he had to admit that no profitable concessions were brought into being in 1921 – or even, as he was later to note, in 1922.[76] In retrospect the most successful démarche was in the direction of military rather than commercial co-operation. On 10 October 1921 Lenin wrote to Trotski approvingly about the negotiations in progress with the German high command.[77] Permission was to be granted for German forces to train and for German army equipment to be developed on Soviet soil; and the Red Army was to be involved so as to secure its own benefit. This 'commercial and military concession', as Lenin called it, was so useful to Berlin as a secret means of evading the clauses of the treaty of Versailles that it was retained throughout the decade.[78]

This complicity with the friends of Ludendorff may be taken as evidence that, on balance, he was assuming that the collapse of Western capitalism was not imminent. Nevertheless Lenin was often known to play two games at once. It is equally possible that he was ready to be surprised. The German high command, in other words, was better than nothing, but the agreement would be torn up just as soon as the German communist leaders succeeded in emulating the October Revolution. But a bird in the hand was worth two in the bush. Soviet Russia was on the edge of the abyss. The economy was a shambles and the Red Army, as Trotski never failed to remind the party, required re-training and re-equipping.[79] A palliative was vital if the anticipated panacea was temporarily out of stock.

Yet the central party leaders were also exercised by Marxist theory; the question arose about the prospects for international capitalism if there might be no European socialist revolution for several years. About the inevitability of such a revolution there was no disagreement.

This remained an article of faith (and perhaps also of desperation since a lengthy permanent absence of fraternal socialist régimes abroad was thought to make a crusade against Bolshevism a distinct possibility). Lenin unusually kept aloof from the debate among his colleagues. His pamphlet *On The Food Tax* and his subsequent speeches to the Tenth Party Conference, in May 1921, concentrated on domestic economics and politics at the expense of the international situation except insofar as he mentioned concessionaires.[80] His proposals for Baku, Grozny, Donbass and Kamchatka were contentious, and he may have judged it unnecessary to cause further dispute by raising doubts about the imminence of socialist revolutions in Europe. It is just as plausible that he simply thought the issue to be a distraction. Lenin's favourite assertion that the Bolshevik party should focus on practical tasks and should give up its chattering carried the implication that theorising should be kept in the background. Certainly this is hard to square with his own frequent disquisitions on 'state capitalism', on Bukharin's philosophical position, on trade unionism under socialism.[81] Yet Lenin frequently tried to have his cake and eat it too. But perhaps in these crucial months his supreme desire was to try out projects in practice before making hasty conclusions. The evidence about the prospects of the major capitalist powers was patchy and ambiguous. Lenin preferred to get on with government and to leave speculation to others.

Zinoviev had no such self-restraint. In line with his encouragement of the March Action, he argued that capitalism was already in deep crisis and that the harassment of the European labour movement signalled the fearfulness of the European bourgeoisie.[82] Bukharin was on Zinoviev's side, but he in turn was opposed by Trotski.[83] For Trotski, capitalism was achieving a certain temporary equilibrium to the extent that an upsurge in industrial production and trade was likely.[84] This involved a re-jigging of political alignments. Bukharin had supported Trotski in the trade union controversy only to join Zinoviev a few months later, and Zinoviev was Trotski's perennial antagonist. 'Left' and 'right' were no longer easily definable terms among Bolsheviks. As if to prove the point, Trotski found himself accused of having forgotten 'the perspectives of international revolution'.[85] Rumblings of the dispute were audible throughout summer and autumn 1921.[86]

The Politburo wanted to avoid open dissension on the scale of the previous winter. For example, Lenin's main speech at the Ninth Congress of Soviets on 23 December was magisterially unconnected with the Trotski-Zinoviev debate. On international relations, Lenin spoke in the most general terms to the difficulties of the labour movement abroad; but, although he talked about the inception of a crisis in world capitalism, he used vague language and implied no criticism of Trotski. His continuing keenness on trade with the West would suggest that, like Trotski, he considered that Western economic stabilisation was on the cards.[87] In future years Lenin's reticence was to be exploited by official party spokesmen as an indication that he advocated the long-term 'peaceful co-existence' of socialism and capitalism around the world with struggle being limited to ideological, non-violent competition. Such was to be the interpretation of Nikita Khrushchev. Textual corroboration was exiguous: the best adducible evidence was a comment reported from a private interview given by Lenin to the Moscow correspondent of the *Christian Science Monitor*.[88] Even then, Lenin is recorded as having mentioned co-existence without breathing anything about its being peaceful. In addition, Lenin's open letter of April 1921 to party comrades in the Transcaucasus adumbrated a policy of 'co-habitation' with the capitalist West. Yet this can even less convincingly be taken as a commitment to long-term peaceful co-existence. Lenin himself put inverted commas around 'co-habitation', thereby signalling his recognition that an eventual violent clash between socialism and capitalism was probable.[89]

Nor did his letter go beyond economic parameters. The political irreconcilability of the Soviet régime and the capitalist West was a foundation stone of his world-view. Events were in flux. Toning down Trotski's presentation, Lenin at the Ninth Congress of Soviets characterised capitalism with the following words: 'What has been achieved is a certain fragile equilibrium'.[90] Those Bolsheviks who thought that political as well as economic compromises should be made with the major capitalist powers he regarded as madmen. Chicherin as People's Commissar of External Affairs, for instance, secretly enjoined him to introduce universal suffrage. An electoral curia for 'parasites' (or the former middle and upper classes) would not put the party's power at risk and yet would induce foreign capitalists to invest in the Soviet republics.[91] Lenin counter-suggested that Chicherin should be sent off to a sanatorium to recuperate mentally.[92]

To Lenin's mind, trade links should be restored only if the gains of the October Revolution and the Civil War were not damaged. Perpetual international isolation would be arduous. 'And yet,' Lenin enquired ponderously at the Ninth Congress of Soviets, 'is such a thing at all conceivable that a socialist republic could exist in capitalist encirclement? This is inconceivable neither in the political nor in the military sense. That it is conceivable in the political and military sense has been proven: it's already a fact.'[93] This confidence that Bolshevism could survive was to be treated by Stalin after Lenin's death as proof that Lenin had believed that the building of socialism could be completed even in conditions of capitalist encirclement. No such thought crossed Lenin's mind or left his lips even though he increasingly behaved as if 'European socialist revolution' was not immediately in prospect. Lenin had been discussing only the régime's survival rather than the implementation of all the tasks described before October 1917 in *The State and Revolution*. In the mean time the Politburo was urged by him to manoeuvre carefully. Lenin's wish to play off one capitalist power against another was to the fore. The recently-signed treaties were an encouragement; nothing had had to be given away in internal politics. He and the Politburo had admittedly bowed to Turkey's preference that Soviet Azerbaidzhan rather than Soviet Armenia should own Nagorny Karabakh.[94] But the state order of all Soviet republics remained intact despite such territorial re-arrangements. Similarly, as the price of the Anglo-Soviet trade treaty, he had had to promise to suspend anti-capitalist propaganda in Britain and her empire. But this was a compromise easily made. The Communist International was not formally under Moscow's control and could go on conducting propaganda in its own name; and, of course, the treaty in no way stipulated a dismantlement of the so-called dictatorship of the proletariat in the RSFSR and the other Soviet republics.[95]

'ON THE FOOD TAX '

Lenin sought to clarify the New Economic Policy with a pamphlet. In the weeks after the Party Congress he wrote *On The Food Tax*; he finished it on 21 April 1921 and dispatched it to the printers for rushed publication.[96] This exposition of party policy was not meant for the peasants to read. On the contrary, it was aimed at active party members in Moscow and the provinces. In elucidating his own intentions, Lenin had to work hard to keep fellow Bolsheviks on his side. *On The Food Tax* was a vital aspect of his campaign to convince the party.

It was partly for this reason that, when calling for the discontinuation of earlier measures, Lenin chose to accentuate aspects of continuity. Apparently the New Economic Policy was old hat. Referring to his disputes with the Left Communists, he dedicated over a quarter of the pamphlet to word-for-word quotations from his 1918 pamphlet *On 'Left-Wing' Infantilism and on Petit-Bourgeois Tendencies*.[97] His main point was that 'state capitalism' was no bad objective in a country where small-scale private production was the predominant form of economic activity. Lenin claimed that the dangers were avoidable. The premise that 'the workers and peasants' held power in Soviet Russia was false, but it was also an article of Bolshevik faith; and Lenin maintained that the supposed reality of a government based upon popular consent would ensure that state capitalism would not lead to an abandonment of the socialist commitment.[98] The small traders, the peasants and the industrial artisans constituted the most numerous segment of the economically-active population. Being divided into tiny production units, they were difficult to control without resort to force. State capitalism by contrast was amenable to registration and direction. It also competed against and beat down the small-scale producers; it would do socialism's job for it.[99] Large-scale economic organisation and up-to-date technology were prerequisites for the building of socialism. Lenin repeated that the agreeing of 'concessions' with foreign entrepreneurs would make an important contribution to the resources of the Soviet state. The entrepreneurs would admittedly take their profits, but the lower social classes would eventually gain benefit from the diffusion of modern machinery, management and training.[100]

The argument that this strategy merely restored his strategy of 1918 was not entirely misleading: industrial concessions had been an objective of party and government even in the Civil War. But Lenin's words involved, too, a deal of obfuscation. After the October Revolution he had retained and strengthened the state grain-trade monopoly; in spring 1921 he was insisting on its abolition. Private commerce was essential to the New Economic Policy, and he knew about this contrast full well.[101]

It was also incorrect of him to assert that the New Economic Policy repealed measures induced solely by the exigencies of Civil War. Several measures could in fact be traced back to the October Revolution. Of course, there had been armed struggle ever since 25 October 1917. But the greatest intensity of Civil War came in the second half of 1918, when massive state control and ownership had already been introduced. Picking up a term in growing use among Bolsheviks, Lenin urged that the economics of 'War Communism'

1 (*above*) Lenin chairs Sovnarkom, 17 October 1918.

2 (*below*) Lenin speaks at the unveiling of a monument to Marx and Engels, 7 November 1918.

3 (*above*) A reluctant Lenin making a recording of one of his speeches, 29 March 1919.

4 (*right*) Lenin stirs the Red Square crowd, May Day 1919.

TROTSKY – LIMITED.

Our Mr. George. "GOOD MORNING, GENTLEMEN. I'M AFRAID I'VE CALLED ON YOUR BUSY DAY."

5 (*left*) The magazine *Punch* considers the factional strife between Lenin and Trotski in the 'trade union controversy' of 1920–21.

6 (*above*) Lenin prepares himself during a session of the Second Comintern Congress.

7 A determined Lenin, photographed at the time of the war with Poland, July 1920.

8 Sketch of Lenin by N. Altman.

9 Lenin and Stalin meet in summer 1922.

10 Lenin at Gorki, preparing to tackle the Politburo on the Georgian question, August 1922.

11 Poster for the Fourth
    Congress of Comintern,
    1922.

12 Lenin at Gorki, summer
    1923.

13   Lenin in his bath-chair, August 1923.

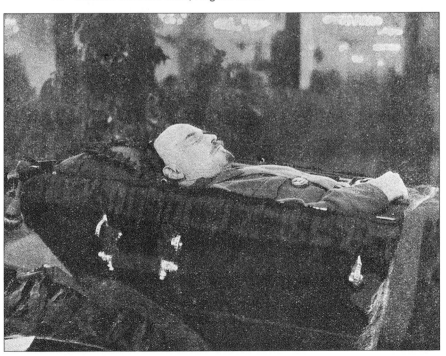

14   Lenin lying in state in the Hall of Columns.

15 (*above*) Lenin's coffin on Red Square on the day of his funeral.

16 (*right*) Front page of *Gudok* newspaper, 24 January 1924. Caption in top-right hand corner reads: 'Lenin is dead, but his cause is alive. It is the will of the working class for victory over the old world of enslavement.'

should be put aside.[102] This was poor history, cunning politics. He foresaw the party's reluctance to abandon ultra-centralist state economic intervention, and he wanted to disseminate the idea that the New Economic Policy simply restored measures that had once had the general concurrence of Bolsheviks. At the same time it allowed him to suggest that this same New Economic Policy, which was a retreat from socialism in some ways, was also a further advance towards it. In Lenin's presentation, the end to grain requisitioning would eventually facilitate the inauguration of 'correct socialist product-exchange'.[103] Utopianism still filled his pages. Probably it was sincere. Quoting his words from May 1918, he reiterated that the Soviet republic's society displayed a variety of stages of social and cultural development, stretching from patriarchal economy based on barter through to modern socialist economic forms. In 1921 he proposed that even a 'direct transition from patriarchalism to socialism' was not impossible. The nomads of the central Asian steppe might undergo just such a transformation. The principal obstacle, according to Lenin, was the weakness of the Soviet state's technical resources, especially in electricity power-stations.[104]

Lenin still wrote as a confident social engineer. He indicated a wish to produce 'a uniform economic plan for the entire state'.[105] He castigated 'the abuses of those who have crawled over to the communists: the old state officials, the landed gentry, the bourgeois and the rest of the swine'; he urged the sanctions he had recommended for speculators in 1918: 'Here what is needed is a terrorist purge: try them on the spot and, unconditionally, shoot them.'[106] He had largely stopped bothering with arguments put forward by non-Bolsheviks; but on this occasion he considered the case against terror put by Martov the Menshevik and Chernov the Socialist-Revolutionary. In Lenin's view, his critics were merely 'lackeying assistants' of the White armies who were enlisted to ease the organisation of a 'White Guard terror'. This monstrous accusation was accompanied by the asseveration that terror was inevitable in all countries experiencing profound social crises: 'There is not and cannot be a middle ground, a"third option".'[107]

Thus his deadly intolerance did not cease in 1921: the widely-entertained notion that Lenin conceived the New Economic policy as involving a relaxation in the social atmosphere for everyone who took no part in politics is badly mistaken: Lenin still breathed fire. But at least one large group of people was spared the usual threats: the so-called speculators. '*It is impossible* to distinguish speculation from "correct" trade,' Lenin added, ' if speculation is to be understood in the politico-economic sense. Freedom of trade is capitalism, capitalism is speculation: it would be ridiculous to close our eyes to this.'[108] The New Economic Policy would fail unless capitalism returned to flourish in a legal framework. Lenin wanted this understood from the start: capitalist practices had to be accepted in post-war economic reconstruction. And yet he would not have been Lenin if he had not simultaneously snarled at capitalism. Any theft, any evasion of state control and accountancy should be punished. Sovnarkom was already working on draft legislation to define what was and what was not to be allowed in private enterprise. He continued in like manner when he considered the Kronstadt mutineers and their 'cloudy slogans of "freedom"'. He utterly denied that the Bolsheviks had been in any way to blame for the revolt, and he noted the comfort taken in the events on Kronstadt by Mensheviks, Socialist Revolutionaries and Kadets.[109] No quarter should be given to these parties. Their present ploy was to pretend that they had dropped politics and to lie low; but no mercy should be shown: 'prison' was the place for them.[110]

Turning to peacetime tasks, Lenin declared that 'bureaucratism' affected all corners of the state's activities. It was worse in his opinion in Moscow than in the localities. He attributed this to the social composition of officialdom. The party had to continue to use the so-called specialists from the administration of the Romanovs and to engage further thousands of persons from the urban lower-middle class.[111] Lenin stressed that the Bolsheviks themselves had to accept different attitudes to work if they were not to 'become bureaucratised'. He recommended that leading members of People's Commissariats should be transferred from Moscow to rural district soviets. He expected that dozens of such personnel would 'enthusiastically' meet such an invitation.[112]

This passage demonstrated a growing concern of his. But his remedy was hopelessly inadequate; and, in recommending it, Lenin showed himself to be out of touch with those many Bolshevik leaders who by now enjoyed and wanted to prolong their life of privilege and power in the capital. But there was no self-doubt in him. He proceeded also to brush aside long-winded doctrinal discussions: 'Less dispute about words! We have sinned to a boundless extent in this connection until now.'[113] Action was the priority. Bolsheviks had to buckle down to their own education: 'We must not be scared to admit that here there is still *much that can and must be learned from the capitalist*.'[114] Lenin also urged his party to accept that, in the immediate future, the benefits of the New Economic Policy would accrue to the lower middle class, especially to the peasants, rather than to the workers. This was embarrassing for the Bolsheviks, who prided themselves on being the 'vanguard' of the working class; but conditions in the towns could not be improved until trade with the villages, which necessitated material incentives being given to the peasantry, was restored.[115] The repugnance of workers for the re-introduction of foreign entrepreneurship was also to be overruled.[116] And yet Lenin was adamant: the New Economic Policy was indispensable. He summoned the party to foster the co-operative movement among the peasants. He conceded that co-ops, while helping the rural population to buy goods more cheaply, encouraged 'petty-bourgeois, capitalist relations'. But by encouraging larger units of economic activity, they would consolidate state capitalism. Consequently they were a means of accelerating the 'transition to socialism'.[117]

Lenin insisted that victory for socialism in Russia and Europe could not be thwarted forever. Progress might be impeded, and it remained Lenin's contention that it would take decades before socialism could be attained in Russia. A foreshortening of the possible time-scale was conceivable only if socialist revolutions broke out beforehand in countries like 'England, Germany, America'.[118] Lenin left the topic at that. He entirely omitted to explain how state capitalism would be turned into socialism. The New Economic Policy offered a starting point and a destination; it did not provide a route. Much as he had clarified his intentions, Lenin had not dealt with the underlying strategical quandary of the agrarian reform. He tried to brazen things out. As he had done in the past when faced by an internal party difficulty, he used the old trick of attacking the other socialist parties in Russia. None of them, he asserted, really knew what it wanted at the moment. They were large in number, but they were vacillating. The Bolsheviks were few, but they were united: 'And we know what we want. And for that reason we shall win.'[119]

THE TENTH PARTY CONFERENCE

And so Lenin began to resemble a door-to-door salesman who, having sold an article to his customers one day, finds himself pursued down the street by them the next. *On the Food Tax* had been offered to them as a guarantee that the article was genuinely serviceable: instead it added to the wrath of the customers. Information about disquiet was

freely available to the central party leadership. Opinion among
Moscow Bolsheviks was very agitated; the City Party Committee
secretary P. S. Zaslavski was still reporting late into the summer that
the fellow party members under his control hated the reform ratified at
the Tenth Party Congress.[120] The concern was that the anger at the
New Economic Policy was not confined to oppositionists but was a
widely-held feeling in the party. If further evidence was needed, it was
supplied by the proceedings of the Fourth Congress of Trade Unions in
mid-April. Mikhail Tomski, who had supported Lenin in the 'trade
union discussion' and headed the Central Council of the trade union
movement on behalf of the party, was deputed to present a motion in
line with official party policy. This he did. But David Ryazanov
pointed out that Tomski's motion did not include a reference to
'proletarian democracy' in the trade unions despite its acceptance by
the Party Congress. Tomski gave way.[121] But Lenin, when he heard of
this, was infuriated. Ryazanov's amendment, while formally unobjec-
tionable, stressed the need for trade union leaders to be elected and for
trade unions to be responsive to the aspirations of their members. In
Lenin's view, this was but a short step from a campaign to overturn the
New Economic Policy by favouring the workers at the expense of the
peasants. Tomski was withdrawn from the Central Council; and Lenin
and Stalin replaced him at the Congress of Trade Unions and, after
cajoling the Bolshevik fraction, secured a repeal of Ryazanov's
amendment.[122]

This was not the end of the matter. At the Central Committee he
barked that Tomski had betrayed the trust reposed in him. Lenin
stunned his colleagues by invoking the Party Congress resolution on
party unity and demanding the exclusion of Tomski from the Central
Committee and even the party itself.[123] But a technical problem had
existed for Lenin: namely that the Congress resolution on party unity
laid down no procedure for expelling a Central Committee member.
Resourcefully and angrily Lenin proposed to convoke a joint meeting
of the Central Committee and the Central Control Commission as a
sort of court to try Tomski. Dzierzynski as a supporter of internal
party discipline backed Lenin. And yet Lenin felt he had to back down
since he had 'only an insignificant majority' in the Central Committee
for such ruthlessness against Tomski. A commission of Stalin,
Dzierzynski, Frunze and Kiselev was set up to investigate the affair.[124]

Quietly the matter was dropped, and Lenin was left to allow his ire to
expire. What had been shown beyond contradiction at the Fourth
Congress of Trade Unions was that booklets and *Pravda* were going to

have an inadequate effect. The New Economic Policy was a massive jolt to the party. The Tenth Party Congress had given its approval; but, on drawing second breath, probably most party leaders and activists in the localities felt that the basic arguments had been given insufficient ventilation. This most doctrinally-obsessed of political parties needed its practical measures to be vetted for ideological rectitude. The Party Congress had been an important and gigantic advance in this direction; but the goal had not been reached. Consequently an extraordinary assembly was deemed necessary. Two months after the Party Congress it was determined to hold a Party Conference. The announcement was made on 11 May.[125] Perforce the Conference's organisation was hurried and ramshackle; but Lenin was reconciled to its necessity. He had come to recognise that an even further extension of the New Economic Policy was vital. It could not be imposed without the co-operation of the party leadership in Moscow and the provinces. The performance at the Party Congress had to be repeated at the Party Conference. Once more the individual performance of Lenin would be crucial. If the birth of the New Economic Policy was secured by the Congress, it was the Conference which would guarantee its paediatric care.

The Tenth Party Conference was the scene of altercations so furious that the official minutes of the proceedings included only the reports of the official spokesmen and their concluding speeches. The debates were withheld from publication (and, in the Soviet period, scholars were inhibited from revealing much about them).[126] 239 delegates assembled in the Sverdlov Hall of the Kremlin on 26 May 1921 to hear their leadership's account of themselves.[127]

Lenin's opening report summarised his recently-published pamphlet *On The Food Tax*; he moved through its points with a few explanatory remarks. He was brisk, confident and imposing. But opposition was inevitable: the Politburo had arranged things so that four accompanying reports should be given before discussions might be opened. V. P. Milyutin reported on small-scale industry, L. M. Khinchuk on agricultural co-ops, A. I. Sviderski on food supplies and E. A. Preobrazhenski on finances. These took so long that Sviderski and Preobrazhenski had to wait until the second session on the same evening before they could speak.[128] A united front was shown to a large extent. This comforted Lenin since Khinchuk and Sviderski had not been completely happy with the abolition of grain requisitioning and Preobrazhenski remained worried that the measures were more favourable to kulaks than was desirable.[129] It was also noticeable that the parameters of the New Economic Policy had been expanded. Milyutin suggested that, as the country waited for large-scale industry to be reconstructed, manufacturing enterprises of small and medium size should be transferred back to private entrepreneurs.[130] They had the flair and local knowledge to produce for the peasants, and their activity would restore the cycle of trade between town and countryside. Preobrazhenski added in his contribution that monetary measures were necessary to put a brake on inflation.[131] Their words were like extra chapters to Lenin's booklet; they constituted a case for New Economic Policy not merely to be accepted but also extended into other areas of the economy.

The Central Committee, which had sanctioned this initiative, could not be accused of cowardice. A highly unpopular agrarian reform was not to be compromised; instead it would be reinforced. The decision had been taken that the Conference would be confronted with the full range of the party leadership's thought. Five lengthy lectures had come from Lenin, Milyutin, Khinchuk, Sviderski and Preobrazhenski. The time had come for the audience to announce its response.

The first speaker from the floor was I. M. Vareikis, who headed the Vitebsk Provincial Committee and had criticised the Central Committee in the Civil War.[132] Vareikis talked of the hostility to the New Economic Policy in the party.[133] He himself did not object to the abolition of grain requisitioning, and everyone else who mentioned it at the Conference agreed – however reluctantly – that the decision had been 'correct'. But the extension of the New Economic Policy was another matter altogether for them. Vareikis, like speakers after him, attacked Lenin. However cleverly Lenin had positioned himself under the shelter of the Central Committee, he failed to dispel the perception that he was the architect of the reform. Vareikis, a Bolshevik sophisticated in the party's doctrines, challenged the Marxist validity of Lenin's attitude to the peasantry. Lenin in previous works had described the peasantry as a feudal class in an advanced stage of disintegration, under the impact of capitalist economic development, into two antagonistic new classes: the proletariat and the bourgeoisie; he had also stressed in the Party Programme that the party should enhance the interests of the poorer and middling segments of the peasantry. To Vareikis's mind, the New Economic Policy abandoned this approach.[134] Not troubling to fire a shot over the bows, he had blasted a hole in the contents of *On the Food Tax*.

The next speaker was Yuri Larin. He scrutinised Lenin's pamphlet with acidic wit. Larin had not forgotten Lenin's description of his proposal for a 'single economic plan' as 'the most boring scholasticism'.[135] Now that Lenin's own proposed ideas, theses and booklet were being savaged, Larin remarked: 'At this moment, comrades, I would remind comrade Lenin that writing theses is a rotten job!'[136] His substantive contention was that the New Economic Policy should give greater attention to large-scale industry and the plight of the urban working class. He had the Conference's sympathy, being granted permission to speak for three times the prescribed length of time.[137]

There was no respite next morning on 27 May. Lenin had touched a raw nerve in his opening report by demanding that the local party committees should exercise greater initiative in fulfilling the Tenth Congress's resolutions. N. L. Meshcheryakov, from the *Pravda* editorial board, retorted that the People's Commissariat of Food Supplies would not tolerate the slightest deviation from highly centralist forms of management. He added that Lenin and the Central Committee should take the blame for the low level of understanding about the New Economic Policy in the provinces.[138] Central Committee member V. Y. Chubar added to Lenin's woes. Chubar reasserted that kulaks had a greater part in agriculture in Ukraine than in Russia. Like Vareikis, he called for a policy which discriminated more strictly between the rich and the poor of the village; and he suggested that Lenin should offer 'not *belles lettres* but something definite' about the attitude to be taken to rural capitalism.[139] The subsequent three speakers spoke with similar antagonism. Always the target was Lenin. Some relief was offered when Osinski spoke; but even Osinski averred that the central party leaders should be more specific about the time-scale for the New Economic Policy.[140] But then the assault started again. A. S. Kiselev, a Workers' Oppositionist, attacked what he and others treated as the neglect of large-scale industry.[141] Not a single delegate rose in Lenin's defence. There had been no such Congress or Conference in the history of the Bolshevik party, not even in the Brest-Litovsk dispute.

Khinchuk, Preobrazhenski and Sviderski returned to the platform towards the end of the session. Their words were supportive of Lenin; this was important since by then it was clear that he was being held individually culpable. Even so, Khinchuk blurted out that Lenin's report had veered in the direction of 'fantasy'. He asserted in particular that large-scale factories had already succumbed to disintegration. The real industrial intiative in the country was already in the hands of small enterprises. In short, Lenin's report had been out of touch with the real situation.[142] With supporters like this, Lenin needed no opponents. The strains showed in Lenin's concluding statement. He mistakenly assumed that his critic Vareikis was representing the opinions of 'Petrograd comrades' (whereas Vareikis had spoken explicitly about non-metropolitan cities).[143] Such blundering led into over-aggressiveness: 'What was said by Vareikis was essentially uncommunistic and was reminiscent of Martov in content.' To Vareikis's enquiry whether the peasantry constituted a class, Lenin gave a positive but curt answer: he refused to open a dialogue over this important aspect of Marxist theory.[144]

The pressure on the central party leadership remained. Delegates had already insisted that a report on the Fourth Congress of Trade Unions be put on the agenda.[145] The brouhaha had been too noisy for the Party Conference to ignore. Molotov was given the job of reporting on the item in the fourth session in the evening. He enlivened his story by accusing both the Workers' Opposition and the supporters of Trotski in the 'trade union controversy' as having deviated from Bolshevism.[146] Molotov made no secret about the resentful relations in the Central Committee. The atmosphere in the Sverdlov Hall grew heavier. Tension increased, but nobody was prepared for what happened next. Molotov had given information about everything except the Central Committee's comportment towards the Congress of Trade Unions. Lenin had been absent for most of the report. But catching the end of it as he returned to the hall, he could contain himself no longer. There was nothing he objected to in Molotov's presentation. Rather it was that he suddenly felt that the difficulties which he had experienced in the Central Committee should be made public. This was a completely uncharacteristic step: he never asked others to pity him.[147] But the bruising he had suffered at the Conference had wounded him deeply. Without warning he demanded the right to speak after Molotov. The Central Committee's work, and his own in particular, had been criticised by practically everybody. He insisted on a right of reply.

Lenin rasped that in the two months since the Party Congress illnesses had struck the Central Committee. An exhausted Trotski had been given leave of absence. Zinoviev had had two heart attacks. Kamenev's chronic heart condition had not improved. Stalin had been unwell and Bukharin had only just recovered from an unspecified disease: 'Thus the entire Central Committee became ineffectual'.[148] Lenin implied that the work of the Central Committee had fallen entirely upon his shoulders. His account was not without credibility: a Central Committee plenum had taken place on the last day of the Party

Congress in mid-March, and did not meet again until mid-May.[149] Yet Lenin failed to add was that the Politburo had filled the breach. Between the Congress and the Conference it convened a dozen times. Attendance had varied no more than in the Civil War. Kamenev, Zinoviev and Stalin were present at most of them. It had not been a one-man Politburo in spring 1921.[150]

Nonetheless Lenin had indisputably carried a greater load than the rest, and the load involved a concatenation of crises in the economy, administration, politics, security and foreign policy. It was in this situation that Central Committee member Tomski perpetrated his act of disobedience to the Central Committee's policy on the trade unions. Lenin had seen red. This most self-controlled man, whose outbursts were always deliberate, declared: 'Here it was difficult to keep a cool head.' This meiosis, if expressed by anyone else, would have provoked laughter. Coming from Lenin, it sounded utterly serious. His anger persisted, and he told the Conference how he had proceeded to invoke the Party Congress's resolution on party unity and demand the expulsion of Tomski from the Central Committee and from the party.[151] This revelation astonished the Conference; no one had known how abrasive the situation had been among the central party leaders. Lenin, still infuriated, told the Conference that he hoped that this case of insubordination to the Central Committee would be the last. He reverted to his theme of the 'correlation of two class forces', as constituted by the working class and the peasantry. Describing it as the trickiest aspect of the New Economic Policy, he again expressed the fear lest it should find expression in internal party factions. Tomski's pro-worker orientation was, in Lenin's opinion, a sign of such a danger. The solution was greater discipline.[152]

The Conference was shocked into silence. An open vote was called and the decision was taken not to debate his contribution.[153] It was as if everyone understood that the Conference had to apply salve to the central leadership's wounds. The irritation displayed by speakers in the earlier discussion of the New Economic Policy had at any rate been unaccompanied by specific proposals on policy. Vague adjustments alone had been put forward. A climate of disgruntled, even apologetic, acceptance had been formed. Nobody liked the New Economic Policy: not even Lenin exulted in it. He had managed to win over the Conference by staving off the verbal assaults and exhausting and shaming his opponents. More than that: he had re-affirmed that he had done his best in difficult circumstances. Essentially he wanted confirmation that he had done his best and that his measures were approved. No other Bolshevik leader could have saved the foundations of the New Economic Policy at this Conference in quite this way. Lenin sat down, battered but victorious at last.

The Conference then turned to two other political issues. Karl Radek reported on 'the role of the Socialist Revolutionaries and Mensheviks' and suggested that the Bolshevik party was being infiltrated by its enemies. The Socialist Revolutionaries were especially worrisome. Radek noted that Chernov and his friends were expecting an 'SR insurrection' with the participation of the peasantry. He sat down after calling for 'a merciless struggle' against both Socialist Revolutionaries and Mensheviks.[154] After a short break, in the absence of Zinoviev who was ill, Radek gave a second report on the Communist International. He was exercised by the possibilities of socialist revolutions in Europe. Already, as he admitted, there were controversies among Politburo members as to whether the Communist International confronted a period of 'quiescence' when the capitalist economies would stabilise themselves and prevent revolutionary conturbation. Yet Radek also adduced J. M. Keynes's book on the treaty of Versailles, which had cogently interpreted the peace in Europe as dangerously punitive towards the industrial capacity of the vanquished powers.[155] Consequently revolutions might not long be delayed. Radek left it at that, having itemised the current debate and called for further analysis. Then he came to the March Action. Radek placed the blame for the fiasco squarely upon the German communist leadership. Once Clara Zetkin and Paul Levi had stormed out of the German Central Committee, a group of incompetent hotheads had been left in charge.[156] Radek studiously avoided mentioning the encouragement offered to the same hotheads by Zinoviev and Bukharin. In this instance, at least, the Central Committee of the Russian Communist Party succeeded in putting a lid on its past deliberations and mistakes.

The Conference's fifth and last session was held on 28 May. Open-season sniping at the Central Committee was resumed when Molotov reported on party organisation. E. O. Bumazhny attacked Lenin. He repeated the contention that, while Lenin rightly stated that the provincial organisations did not understand the New Economic Policy, the fault lay with the lack of clarification available from the Central Committee. For Bumazhny, Lenin's *On the Food Tax* was aimed at too sophisticated a readership. Lenin had misjudged the needs of situation: the ordinary party members as well as the Bolshevik intellectual élite had to be addressed. A 'short party catechism' should rapidly be composed for dissemination among the rank-and-file membership. But Bumazhny's reprimand was ignored; the Conference's will to end polemics supervened.[157]

The composite resolution on the economy proposed by the Central Committee spokesmen, with a few amendments, was passed.[158] Co-ops, small-scale private industry, monetary stabilisation became integral segments of the New Economic Policy. Trouble looked as if it would arise when a perceptive delegate shouted out that a discrepancy existed between the respective assumptions about the prospects of European socialist revolution displayed by Radek and Lenin. But Lenin replied dismissively. He would only declare broadly: 'Of course, if revolution occurs in Europe, we'll naturally change the policy.'[159] A certain Shatunov raked over the coals by announcing disgust that words such as trade were included in the resolution on the New Economic Policy. This time Lenin reacted more diplomatically. 'The question,' he conceded aimiably, 'is a delicate one, of course.' But he secured the Conference's rejection of the suggested amendment.[160] He also succeeded in repudiating a request for greater emphasis on the consolidation of state-owned collective farms.[161] The only amendment that appealed to him came from Kiselev, who proposed that 'punitive measures' should be taken throughout the economy to eradicate corruption.[162] Lenin assured the Conference that he did not intend the New Economic Policy as a capitalist free-for-all. But his closing speech stressed, too, that the New Economic Policy would be implemented 'seriously and for a long time'. The European revolution was ultimately vital to the October Revolution. But the Russian Communist Party could not guess when it would happen.[163]

For the moment the Bolsheviks had to elaborate their measures on the premise that the October Revolution stood alone. His speech obtained the traditional applause. But it was not ecstatic. The Conference had been gruelling, and had put Lenin on his mettle. The job of selling the New Economic Policy to the party was far from over. But nobody could any longer state that the reform had been slipped into the Bolshevik official projections without sustained consultation and ratification. However reluctantly, the delegates had accorded sanction to the resolutions of the Party Congress. The audience was not happy with itself; but it had been given the chance to express its mind and then voted with the Central Committee. It was perhaps fitting that the Conference was brought abruptly to a closure without the usual collective rendition of the *Internationale*.[164]

DIVIDED RETREAT

The Conference had barely finished when, supplied with suitable drafts
from the Central Committee, Sovnarkom embarked on a legislative
campaign to extend the New Economic Policy. The lines sketched by
Lenin, Milyutin, Khinchuk, Sviderski, and Preobrazhenski were
pursued with panache. In June 1921 Sovnarkom announced its
intention to achieve 'a healthy monetary circulation'.[165] Official
indifference to inflation disappeared. In July, a licensing system for
private traders was introduced.[166] In August, the large nationalised
factories were put under obligation to balance their books. The profit
incentive returned, and the Party Conference's priority for the recovery
of small and medium-sized industrial enterprises led to the leasing of
most of them to private businessmen.[167] In September, the government
insisted that no attempt should be made to narrow wage differentials.
Nor should factories be expected to give social-security support to their
workers; and collective wage bargaining through the trade unions was
re-established in November[168] Furthermore, the quest for foreign
concessionaires able and willing to assist the country's economic
reconstruction, especially in the timber and oil industries, continued.
Salvation, having failed to be secured by the export of revolution,
was sought through the import of capital.[169] The party and state
authorities could not be accused of inactivity: instructions, decrees and
laws issued like a flood through a broken dam in the second half of
1921.

Lenin had been the only Politburo member to speak at the
Conference; but thereafter he said even less about the New Economic
Policy than in the months of spring. This engendered stories which
made the conflict between Vareikis and Lenin still more colourful than
in reality. Nikolai Valentinov, an ex-Bolshevik who had many contacts
with the Bolshevik leadership in Moscow, recorded having heard that
Vareikis shouted that Lenin had lopped off 'whole chapters of
Marxism'. Lenin is said to have retorted: 'Please don't try giving me
training as to what to take and what to leave out of Marxism: hens
aren't taught by their eggs.'[170]

The widespread gossip about the Tenth Party Conference showed
that antagonism to the New Economic Policy, while being too
ineffectual to change it, remained strong. It was not until October
that Lenin recommenced his public defence of reform. Commemorating the fourth anniversary of the Bolshevik party's seizure of power, he
wrote in *Pravda*: 'Would that such a global affair could be begun

without failures and without mistakes! But begun it we have. We are carrying it through. It is precisely now with our "new economic policy" that we're correcting a whole series of mistakes, that we're learning how to construct a socialist building in a petty-bourgeois country without mistakes.'[171] His only other major statements came in two speeches: the first to the régime's educational officials, the speech to the Moscow Bolshevik Party Provincial Conference in late October.[172] The Moscow activists gave him a hard time. I. N. Stukov and V. G. Sorin harangued him over his contempt for War Communism. The re-inception of legal private commerce was another bone of contention. S. M. Semkov shouted at him: 'They didn't teach us how to trade when we were in prison!'[173] The Eleventh Party Conference returned to such matters in December 1921. Illness prevented Lenin's attendance and Kamenev deputised for him. Passionate criticisms of major aspects of the New Economic Policy were made. Yuri Larin drew attention to the inadequacy of food supplies to workers.[174] M. P. Zhakov complained about the vagueness of the party's intentions as explained by its central leaders.[175] A. Z. Goltsman asserted that, in the race to meet the demands of peasant consumers, the interests of large-scale industry had been neglected.[176]

Perhaps the most acute comments at the Eleventh Conference came from Evgeni Preobrazhenski, who drew attention to rural social developments. His main point – an ominous one for all Conference participants – was that the New Economic Policy offered little to the poor peasants. As Preobrazhenski demonstrated, they lacked the equipment to cultivate their allotted land. This would compel them to rent it out to richer peasants. Soviet laws would be broken, and the main beneficiaries would be the kulaks.[177]

Lenin's health improved sufficiently on 23 December for him to address the Ninth Congress of Soviets; and, although the old fire was evident, he offered no promise of immediate economic betterment. He turned rousingly to the international political situation: 'In conclusion I must state, comrades, that the problem which we are resolving this year and which we have as yet resolved so badly – the unifying of the workers and peasants in a solid economic union even in circumstances of the greatest poverty and devastation – has now been correctly posed by us; it is a correct line that we have taken, and there can be no doubts on that score. And this problem is not only Russian one but also global.'[178] He did not hasten to try to rebut Preobrazhenski's commentary. Indeed cognoscenti of Lenin's agrarian analysis in 1917 would have noticed how closely Preobrazhenski followed it;[179] Lenin could not dismiss his critic out of hand. But Preobrazhenski, who until then had worked harmoniously with Lenin, irritated him more than any other leading Bolshevik opponent at the time. In March 1922 Preobrazhenski summarised his objections in a set of theses which indicated 'a tendency towards collapse' in the economy of the poor sections of the peasantry. Lenin castigated the 'empty' phrases and 'boring' expressions of intent. He regarded the theses as basically 'unsuitable'.[180] And yet his own proposed changes were rather limited in scope. The collapse of poor-peasant agriculture, he suggested, should instead be described as a hold-up of development; and the anti-kulak passages should be softened so as to commit the party only to a '*limitation* of the exploitative aspirations' of the kulaks.[181]

Lenin was vague about his general vision of the New Economic Policy in the medium-term future. His recurrent talk of retreat invited the question as to where it should be halted. On 29 October 1921 he replied as follows: 'This question is incorrectly posed because only the further implementation of our turnabout can give material for an answer to it. We shall retreat until we have learned for ourselves, until we have prepared ourselves to go over into a solid attack.'[182]

This was the sort of rhetorical soufflé which, if cooked by a Provisional Government minister in 1917 or a Bolshevik opositionist in 1918–1920, Lenin would have relished puncturing. For the moment he busied himself with practical modifications of the New Economic Policy and, as with Preobrazhenski, discouraged theoretical dispute. In this he had the advantage that, at least by midsummer, no central or local Bolshevik leader seriously proposed that the Politburo should re-introduce food-supplies requisitioning. This was the crucial ingredient of the New Economic Policy, and the Kaganoviches and Tsyurupas ceased to call for its removal. Nevertheless there remained much to argue about. Even if the food tax and the retail trade in grain was no longer controversial, questions persisted as to how far the New Economic Policy should be extended. Lenin, despite a certain success in inhibiting the growth of a highly abstract discussion of Marxist theory, could not reasonably abort deliberations on particular issues. It was predictable that not all his fellow Bolsheviks were reconciled to the further measures on trade, finance and industry. The condition of the entire urban sector of the economy was a source of widespread concern. The Russian Communist Party especially prided itself as being a party for the workers. Its objectives for the future economy began from the premise that cities, factories and large-scale social units were the crucible of the development of communism.

Yet it became impossible to avoid discussion when, on 7 August 1921, none other than Politburo colleague Trotski wrote to the Central Committee calling for a revision of official measures on industry. He asked for the State Planning Commission to be charged with 'the elaboration, supervision and regulation of the implementation of an economic plan on a daily and hourly basis'. The existing muddle in the large nationalised factories would thereby be eradicated. Essentially Trotski called for the State Planning Commission (or Gosplan) to be accorded legislative authority.[183]

In fact all Bolshevik leaders were committed to the reinforcement of central state planning sooner or later; and Lenin was no exception either in 1921 or thereafter. Furthermore, he was determined that any discussion about the New Economic Policy should involve only Bolsheviks. He could not stress too heavily that Bolshevik hegemony over contemporary issues of politics, economics and culture should be maintained,[184] and he kept a weather eye open for those anti-Bolsheviks seeking to take advantage of the reforms introduced by the Politburo. He spotted such attempts especially quickly when they appeared in the form of the printed word. One of his angriest missives was to the People's Commissariat of Agriculture on 27 August 1921. The reason for his intemperance was the permission being given to S. Maslov, no less a figure than the last Minister of Agriculture in Kerenski's Provisional Government, to publish his book entitled *The Peasant Economy*. Bolsheviks arguing among themselves were one thing; Bolsheviks indulging their enemies by allowing them access to the printing press was entirely another. Lenin reviewed the Maslov book in a few brief words worthy less of the *Times Literary Supplement* than of the polemical tracts of John Calvin or Huldreich Zwingli: 'From a glance it is evident that this is a disgusting little bourgeois book through and through, conning the peasant with its exhibitionistic bourgeois "scientific" falsehood'.[185]

But he could not be so scathing about Trotski: cordial relations among Politburo colleagues had to be maintained.[186] A further reason lay in the origins of the New Economic Policy. Even as Lenin had been initiating discussions on agrarian reform in February 1921, he was chairing Sovnarkom sessions which required Gosplan to draw up a single comprehensive plan for all sectors of the economy.[187] The implication of this is that Trotski was not challenging the validity of New Economic Policy but asserting a desire for the party leaders to abide by the original common assumption that central state planning would accompany the abandonment of grain requisitioning.[188]

If Trotski's proposal in August 1921 was that the Politburo's February 1921 assumption should be honoured and given additional practical force, it was Lenin's thinking that had changed. The New Economic Policy, as it had evolved after the Tenth Party Congress, had involved the abolition of important aspects of the state's authority to intervene in the operation of industry, agriculture and trade. The scale of Soviet state intervention remained massive, but legislation had indubitably reduced it considerably by midsummer. Lenin promoted the change and disliked Trotski's proposal on the grounds that it would lead to bureaucratic meddling. The Central Committee, while not denying the need for a central state economic plan, sided with Lenin in refusing to provide Gosplan with the more ambitious rights requested for it by Trotski.[189] A battle lay ahead. Scarcely had the ashes of the 'trade union discussion' been raked into the earth than Trotski and Lenin were lighting a touch-paper for yet another inflammation of the party. Nevertheless even Trotski had learned a lesson from the winter of 1920-1921. Another such controversy, fought tooth and nail ideologically, was not to his liking. It may also be that he understood that, if he bided his time, such was the antagonism to the current particular development of the New Economic Policy that the majority of party leaders might come over to his opinions. No wonder that Lenin had been acting cautiously with his day-to-day tactics since the Tenth Party Conference. Not for the first time he must have mused whether those calling themselves Leninists were really on his side.

8 Against the Wall

Official party rules are not the most accurate guide to the reality of party life. The quest for unity is honoured in the breach. Few political parties can afford to alienate existing or potential members by too severe an insistence on compliance with centrally-imposed decisions. Even the single party in a one-party state can encounter difficulty in eliminating factionalism from its affairs; indeed, as in Kenya in the 1970s and Zimbabwe in the 1980s, the indulgence of factions can act as a safety-valve for the maintenance of the régime. But other one-party states, especially those whose rulers feel internationally isolated and grossly unpopular in their own society, dispense altogether with this mechanism. For Saddam Hussein in Iraq, nothing but utter obedience to his command sufficed from the start of his dictatorship.

Such obedience is obtainable only through the application of terror to the party. The Bolsheviks declared adherence to the strictest centralism and discipline in successive versions of their rule-book; but factions, organised or semi-organised, continued to exist despite the resolution banning them at the Tenth Party Congress. The proclaimed goal of a party sculpted from a monolithic block was not achieved. Naturally this was not how Bolsheviks critical of Lenin saw matters. For them, his power had reached not far short of the dictatorial. Lenin saw things differently, to the point of outright exasperation. When Adolf Ioffe had written to him in this vein, he responded on 17 March 1921 with text and verse on the difficulties he perennially faced in getting his way: 'The old Central Committee (1919–1920) beat me down on one of the most gigantically important questions, as you know from the discussion [about the conflict between the Water-workers Union and Tsektran in the early stage of the "trade union controversy"]. On questions of organisation and personnel there is verily no end to the occasions when I have been in the minority. You yourself saw examples of this many times when you were a Central Committee member.'[1] Thus Lenin refuted the claim that he had established a dictatorship over the party; but his own words, with their condescending implication that Ioffe was overwrought because of an excessive workload, was evidence of a confident dominance bordering

219

on arrogance. His was indisputably the most influential voice in the Politburo. And the Politburo ruled the country in the interstices of the Central Committee meetings.

The other central public institutions were subordinate to the party apparatus. A Politburo member ran each of them. Lenin chaired Sovnarkom and the Council of Labour and Defence; Kamenev the Moscow City Soviet and the Moscow City Party Organisation; Trotski the People's Commissariat of Military Affairs; Stalin the People's Commissariat of Nationality Affairs and the Workers' and Peasants' Inspectorate; and Zinoviev the Executive Committee of the Communist International and the Petrograd City Party Organisation. Candidate members of the Politburo also had crucial posts. Bukharin edited *Pravda*; Kalinin was the chairman of the Central Executive Committee of the Congress of Soviets; and Molotov was the senior member of the Secretariat. The powers of these institutions interlocked with and overlapped each other. Each major issue had an impact on all the institutions. But just as the People's Commissar of Military Affairs had the right to poke his nose into economic strategy, so Lenin interfered in innumerable corners, large and small, of public life.[2] As Sovnarkom chairman, he had even more natural reason than other Politburo members to get involved. The minutiae of governmental affairs were grist to his mill. While he was fit, he had no thought of changing his routine. Never having been good at delegating responsibility, he felt no impulse to change his habits while the Soviet state attempted to implement the contentious New Economic Policy.

The one central institution which, in his estimation, needed an overhaul was that same central apparatus of the party. Like other Bolshevik leaders, he had heard and ignored critics like the Democratic Centralists who said – among other things – that the party ought to re-organise its bodies in Moscow in pursuit of greater efficiency. So long as dominant and reliable figures such as Sverdlov and Stasova were in charge, Lenin had not cared a fig. He had agreed that systematisation was required in 1919 when Krestinski, Preobrazhenski and Serebryakov took over; but, when illness affected them in turn, he made no effort to seek replacements.

His attitude had begun to shift in 1921. On the quiet, he wanted the Orgburo and Secretariat to destroy the threat from the respective sympathisers of Shlyapnikov and Trotski. Moreover, the New Economic Policy required more flexible processes of deliberation than in the Civil War. The supervision of an emergent mixed economy demanded that the central party organs should effect a masive increase in their control of the party in the provinces. The situation necessitated a larger staff in the centre and a set of Departments within the Secretariat, and Molotov was given the job of bringing this about. Lenin treated him brusquely. Once he even wrote: 'This is a scandal, an incredible delay. I shall raise the question of the C[entral] C[ommittee] apparatus at the Politburo. Eh, eh! *It mustn't go on like this.*[3] Even the new Registration and Distribution Department was unsatisfactorily organised.[4] Molotov was blamed. Whether the charge was fair is open to doubt (even though everyone from Trotski to the most unsocialist historians have assumed so!). Let us look at the facts of Molotov's career. Later, despite his notoriety as an arch-Stalinist, he was universally recognised as an excellent office manager. Trotski, in a typical bit of double thinking, characterised him as a typically unimaginative but methodical bureaucrat.[5] Lenin's letter was really an instance of the party's supreme leader driving a subordinate to higher levels of industriousness. Molotov had only to show a degree lower than total assiduity, and Lenin would pounce on him. He was a demanding boss. His personal assistants in Sovnarkom had witnessed this already. First with him had been Vladimir Bonch-Bruevich. Then came Nikolai Gorbunov. By 1921, his secretaries Lidiya Fotieva and Mariya Volodicheva were fulfilling such a function: he wore them all out by his exigent political style.[6]

He had no complaints about Molotov's ability to tighten party discipline. A purge was announced in June 1921.[7] Drunkenness, careerism, religious belief, idleness and corruption were the basic categories for expulsion. But there was also a stated goal of removing Bolsheviks who had failed to carry out party instructions: this was clearly aimed at activists who, despite the ban on factions at the Tenth Party Congress, campaigned overtly for their views. Not only Trotski's supporters but also the Democratic Centralists kept clear of any such potential accusation. But the Workers' Opposition were not so inhibited. Around a quarter of the entire membership of the Russian Communist Party was expelled by the end of the year.[8]

How many lost their party cards through membership of the Workers' Opposition is not yet known. Shlyapnikov and his friends insisted that expulsions of this kind were many in places like Nizhni Novgorod, and they successfully demanded that a commission of enquiry should be established. The fact that three commissions were sent there before the purgers were given a formally clean bill of health suggests that the Workers' Opposition truly suffered as it claimed.[9] Yet the mud did not stick to Lenin (in contrast to the way it caked him in relation to his economic retreat of 1921). After the Tenth Party Congress he avoided harassing any of his critics, from Shlyapnikov to Trotski, in public; and his comments on Preobrazhenski were known only to fellow central colleagues. He left the dirty business to the Orgburo and the Secretariat. Lenin acknowledged to Stalin that he was not quite *au fait* with the scale of the Orgburo's activity in re-assigning party officials to jobs across the country.[10] This did not demonstrate that Orgburo member Stalin was bamboozling Lenin. Nothing of the sort! Lenin and Stalin were allies. Molotov's difficulties in reforming the Secretariat had led to Stalin's being asked to help with the recently-inaugurated Agitation-Propaganda Department.[11] It was not as if Lenin himself was uninvolved in assignments of personnel at the very highest level. The Politburo continued to have ultimate control.[12] There is no sign that Lenin was unhappy about the policy on assignments pursued by Stalin and Molotov. Lenin, as his reprimand to Molotov about technical matters of organisation demonstrates, was not slow to complain whenever he was annoyed – and everyone knew he had the authority to get the results he desired.[13]

His distance from the implementation of intra-party discipline permitted him to take a paternal attitude to dissentient Bolsheviks. On 5 August 1921 he wrote to G. I. Myasnikov, who inspired several activists who proceeded to form the small anti-Bolshevik socialist parties, such as Workers' Truth and Workers' Group, after the Tenth Party Congress. Another socialist who had influenced them was none other than Lenin's inveterate adversary Aleksandr Bogdanov. A favourite slogan among them was that the initials of the New Economic Policy, the NEP,, stood for the New Exploitation of the Proletariat.[14]

Myasnikov wished 'freedom of the press for everyone from the monarchists to the anarchists inclusively', arguing that their news-papers would expose the abuses of official power.[15] Lenin responded severely: 'Why insist on this mistake of yours, this clear mistake, on this non-party, *anti-party* slogan: "freedom of the press"?'[16] Like Ioffe, Myasnikov was said to be suffering psychologically. His 'nerves' required settling down![17] But Lenin was also comradely: 'We'll get together and we'll work amicably in the same party. The benefit will be immense, but it will come *not immediately* but *very* slowly.'[18] Most Bolsheviks, however critical they were of Lenin, assumed that in some recess of his mind he meant well. Lenin seemed to many as a one-man court of appeal when Bolsheviks felt that the party's principles were at stake. Myasnikov, however, was an exception: he refused to behave in the expected quasi-filial fashion and persisted in factional activity. On 20 February 1922, the Politburo expelled him from the party.[19] Shlyapnikov, while having no connection with the emergent political parties, became equally recalcitrant. The Orgburo sought to limit his impact by transferring him to food-supply jobs in the provinces. Workers' Opposition leader Shlyapnikov refused to accept any appointment outside the capital. On 14 October 1921 Lenin submitted a draft instruction to be issued by the Politburo, reaffirming the validity of the Orgburo's decision about Shlyapnikov.[20]

Behind the scenes Lenin was therefore as firm as the rest of the Politburo in tightening the disciplinary screws. And yet, for the first time since the failed assassination attempt in August 1918, he was often absent when the decisions were taken. Insomnia and severe headaches plagued him.[21] On 4 June 1921 the Politburo at Molotov's prompting required him to take a break from work until the following month.[22] He ignored this altogether. But on 8 July he relented: his condition left him far from well. He wrote to Molotov requesting permission to ease his working load for a month. With his doctor's agreement, he would come to his office only twice or three times a week – and then only for two to three hours – so as to be able to attend the Politburo and Sovnarkom.[23] Yet his condition did not much improve, and the Politburo on 9 August insisted on his taking a more extensive rest. This time he was co-operative, writing bluntly to the Politburo a couple of days later: 'I can't work.'[24]

In fact he still intervened frequently in Politburo and Sovnarkom business by letter,[25] and on 13 September he resumed his normal workload duties. [26] Indomitable though he was, he found he could not fully carry out his duties. On 28 November, wishing to make an organisational re-arrangement for the duration of his incapacitation, he wrote to Aleksandr Tsyurupa proposing to introduce and regularise a system for running Sovnarkom in his own absence. Aleksei Rykov and Aleksandr Tsyurupa, his deputies in Sovnarkom, would divide areas of competence between them. In justifying his proposal, he oddly made scant reference to his illness. Instead he simply stated that a formal two-deputy system would facilitate tighter supervision of the New Economic Policy.[27] Equally odd was his favouring of Tsyurupa after the trouble between them when the the tax in kind was first being discussed and implemented; but Tsyurupa had come to recognise that the New Economic Policy was a fact of political life and was probably flattered that Lenin thought highly of his technical competence. In any case, Lenin had made his overtures rather late. Before a definitive official decision could be taken, he had to apply for extended sickness leave on 6 December: 'Comrade Molotov, I'm leaving today. Despite my reduction of the portion of work and increase in the portions of rest over recent days, my insomnia has increased like the devil.'[28] The Politburo gave permission for him to move out to the elegant country mansion commandeered by the party at the village of Gorki and turned into a sanatorium.

Still he was a reluctant patient. Not only did he write articles as well as memos but also he made working trips to Moscow: he was determined to keep himself involved in the politics of the central party leadership. The Politburo, with or without him, was the country's basic governing organ. But Sovnarkom was a lesser body needing someone to look after it while he was away. The proposal for a formally-demarcated system of deputies remained on his mind as a contingency plan as he prepared for the Eleventh Party Congress.[29]

In the Politburo there was little enthusiasm for Lenin's suggestion. Below the Politburo, Sovnarkom was the most influential institution in the Soviet state. No doubt Lenin had thought he had squared all the available circles by including Tsyurupa, a doubter about the New Economic Policy, in his thinking. But he had reckoned without the calculations of most of his Politburo colleagues. If Lenin was not going to hold the Sovnarkom chairmanship actively, then his immediate colleagues – Kamenev, Stalin, Trotski and Zinoviev – needed time for discussion and compromise before agreeing as to who should become his temporary deputies.[30] It deserves emphasis that they were not (as is often supposed in East and West) unreasonable in their reluctance to accede to Lenin's proposal. Why should he dominate them in his absence? Each Politburo member had confidence in his individual achievements and potentiality; none were shrinking violets when the distribution of power among them was an issue. Furthermore, the seriousness of Lenin's physical debility was as yet unperceived. Not only did Lenin play down his worries but also his doctors were generally encouraging. A hurried decision on the management of Sovnarkom was not to the Politburo's liking; in those winter months when party and government were hard pressed by questions of economics, internal security and foreign policy had their attention.

A further factor was the wariness of each central Bolshevik leader about his colleagues after the disputes among them in 1920–1921. The 'trade union discussion' and the Tomski affair were in their minds, and the Tenth Party Conference had left them edgy about the situation in the party as a whole. Lenin's proposal, mild and merely technical though it seemed, could easily have re-opened controversy. Lenin the anti-factionalist, moreover, was a factionalist himself when his interests were in danger. Trotski and Bukharin knew this from recent direct experience. Lenin's motives could not always be assumed to be of the purest type. The party's patriarch was admired by his close associates, but not to the point of uncritical devotion.

It is possible that Lenin continued to grind his factional axe even in the winter of 1921–1922. At New Year he no longer had much to fear from Shlyapnikov, who had long since left Moscow as demanded by the Politburo.[31] But the suspicions about Trotski persisted. Lenin took trips to Moscow which allowed him to participate in intra-party discussions. Anastas Mikoyan, admittedly not the most reliable memoirist, purportedly was summoned to the Kremlin from Nizhni Novgorod for a meeting in Stalin's flat. They talked first about the threat from the Workers' Opposition; but both agreed that Trotski was more menacing. According to Mikoyan, Stalin told him that Lenin had empowered him to prevent Trotski's provincial supporters from being elected as delegates to the next Party Congress. Mikoyan was asked to travel to Siberia to meet M. M. Lashevich and pass on the scheme in the name of Stalin and Lenin.[32] Stalin asked Mikoyan to tell only Lashevich about this, and to pretend that he was travelling to Siberia on family business. Stalin and Mikoyan had just completed their conversation when the door handle turned and in walked Lenin in his familiar cap and black overcoat. Lenin jokily remarked: 'Are you discussing your Caucasian disagreements?'[33] Stalin was a Georgian, Mikoyan an Armenian. Lenin supposedly said no more, save for asking Stalin whether he had passed on what had earlier been agreed between himself and Stalin; but this, in Mikoyan's account, was proof enough for him that the covert plan against Trotski enjoyed the collusion of Lenin.[34]

Perhaps the meeting was a fiction of Mikoyan's imagination. Perhaps it took place, but Stalin misled Mikoyan about Lenin's being involved in the conspiracy. Perhaps Mikoyan told the truth and had been told the truth by Stalin. Whatever may be the accuracy of the memoir, the supporters of the Platform of Ten may indeed have decided to restrict the support for Trotski at forthcoming party gatherings in Moscow; and, even if Lenin was not involved in such schemes, he would have been a beneficiary of them. The Central Committee knew that he urgently wished his and not Trotski's interpretation of the New Economic Policy to be accepted in the party. At Lenin's instigation, Trotski had been rebuffed when demanding greater emphasis on central state planning, and was predictably unwilling to grant automatic sanction to Lenin's proposal for a formal system of deputies in Sovnarkom.

THE THIRD CONGRESS OF THE COMMUNIST INTERNATIONAL

Lenin's troubles with non-Bolsheviks were considerably fewer than with the party. To be sure, he was not universally approved. Far from it: memories of the Civil War died hard, and even many workers detested him.[35] And yet, despite his reluctance to speak often in favour of the New Economic Policy, he was identified as its main promoter, and this led to an increase in his popularity. He was credited with whatever easement in material conditions resulted from the reforms of 1921.[36] Just as the Decree on Land in October 1917 had become known as 'Lenin's Decree', so the abolition of War Communism was counted unto him for virtue. This growing reputation had its irony. The man who sent out Tukhachevski to suppress the Volga peasants was becoming beloved of the peasantry. Nor did anti-Bolshevik professional cadres employed by the Soviet state withhold admiration even though he was still capable of letting the Cheka loose upon individuals among them.[37] Of all Politburo members, undoubtedly he was the most popular.

His prestige was equally high among foreign communists; for the New Economic Policy had not caused a rift within the Communist International, only some misgivings. Kronstadt, too, was passed over in virtual silence. While Lenin attentively watched over his Russian Communist party in the changing conditions of 1921, he took his eye off his leading comrades in Germany, Italy, Britain and France. The March Action in Berlin had been attempted with barely any consultation with him, and he did not immediately become involved in the resultant discussions in the Executive Committee of the Communist International.[38] But a debate could not indefinitely be postponed: a questionnaire was issued to fraternal communist parties about the prospects of revolution in the rest of Europe.[39] Quietly Lenin had decided what kind of answer he would accept. Clara Zetkin, a German opponent of the March Action before it occurred, wrote to Lenin complaining of the wild incompetence of Béla Kun.[40] This was in April 1921. A response came forth from Kun and the German communist leader August Thalheimer in their 'Theses on the Tactics of the Komintern'.[41] Karl Radek then entered the reckoning. The Executive Committee of the Communist International, led by Kun's patron Zinoviev, appointed Radek to draft its own theses on the topic for submission to the International's Third Congress in late June.[42] Radek's wording dwelt dutifully on the need for German communists to win the support of more workers than those who were already communist party members; but he avoided demanding a working-class majority: instead he called for 'the decisive strata' of the proletariat to be pro-communist before revolution should be attempted.[43]

When Kun found this too weak, Radek re-phrased it as 'the socially-decisive parts of the working class'.[44] The significance of the textual difference is opaque; but the purpose was unmistakable: Radek and Kun agreed that the acquisition of support from a majority of German workers should not be a prerequisite for insurrection. Whereas in autumn 1917 Lenin would have had no objection to such thinking, in 1921 he thought it to be 'the cretinism of the "leftists"'. Calling for a clearer formulation of the theses, he urged that there should be 'no opportunity for anyone to discover in them whatever he wants'.[45] He feared lest Kun and Thalheimer, who had instigated the March Action, would repeat the shambles on other occasions. On a point of party discipline, Lenin abandoned his original wish to reverse Paul Levi's expulsion from the Communist Party of Germany; but he conceded privately that Levi's warnings against the Action had been proved right in the event.[46]

Lenin, burdened by the Soviet domestic political agenda, took three months after the Tenth Party Congress before inserting himself into the affairs of European communism. Trotski was doing the same; he exclaimed to Radek that the March Action had been botched from the start. But Lenin and Trotski did not conspire with each other.[47] Mutual distrust harmed their relationship after their battles over the trade unions. Lenin all the same impressed his unflattering opinion of Kun upon Zinoviev, who was responsible for letting Kun loose in Berlin;[48] and Zinoviev obediently drew Radek, Bukharin and others together in a working group to produce yet another draft version of the theses. At Lenin's insistence, they included a phrase about the need to get the support of 'the majority of the working class' before power should be seized. In return they demanded that discussion of the March Action should be avoided.[49] Even so, the leaders of the Communist Party of Germany felt betrayed by this compromise, and wrote to Lenin defending their past actions. On 15 June they met and pressurised him. He responded with a heated rejection of their case.

Next day they wrote to the Central Committee of the Russian Communist Party, still unapologetically describing the Action as a step forward for the communist movement.[50] Lenin stated that he was sorry for showing his anger at his meeting with them.[51] But he made no retraction on matters of substance. On 17 June he resumed his attack at the Executive Committee of the Communist International; probably it was then that he denounced 'les bêtises de Béla Kun: not the most conciliatory comment.[52] He declared, too, that Kun was not 'a real Marxist'.[53]

By then Lenin, Trotski and Kamenev were working closely to thwart Zinoviev, Bukharin and their supporters in the Communist International.[54] Several days before the Congress opened in the Bolshoi Theatre on 22 June 1921 it was obvious that Kun and Thalheimer had lost the struggle, and that Zinoviev's remaining aim was to disguise his own incompetence and to pretend that he was near to the subsequently-established position of Lenin. The scene of decisive strife had already occurred in the Executive Committee of the Communist International. The Congress followed the pre-ordained line. The Russian Communist Party's mastery of the international communist movement was consolidated.

On 23 June the Congress convened for its debates in the Kremlin's Andreevski Hall. A slight change was made to the Politburo's planned agenda when it was decided to take Trotski's report on the 'World Economic Crisis and the New Tasks of the Communist International' as the first item.[55] Doctrinal legitimacy was to be obtained before practical measures would be discussed. Lenin, at least on this matter, felt he could trust Trotski. His health was unsettling him, and he went off to Gorki late on 25 June. He did not return to the Congress until midday on 27 June. A few hours later he returned to Gorki in his chauffeured limousine.[56] At last on 28 June, at session eight, he spoke for the first time at the Congress.[57] While his ideas dominated the proceedings, his physical presence did not. There had been no Congress like it; not even at the Tenth Party Congress had he been absent so persistently. His contribution came in remarks on the factory occupations in northern Italian cities in 1920. Erroneously he claimed that no Italian communist had participated in them.[58] This unwarranted disparagement passed without serious riposte; Lenin was tolerated more generously than he deserved even among admirers. His ambition was evident: he wished to prevent, by fair means or foul, the repetition of Kun's adventurism (or indeed of his own ultra-optimistic revolutionary strategy in the Polish–Soviet war of summer

1920 if he had thought about it). On 30 June Lenin turned up again to the debates, listening attentively to Radek's frequently-amended report on the 'Tactics of Komintern'.[59] He had assumed that the decisions of the Executive Committee would be obeyed; but passions ran high about the March Action and this was the point in the Congress where, unless care was taken, things might go awry. Lenin kept Radek under appropriate surveillance.

The report and debate on tactics were crucial. As Lenin had anticipated, the German participants expressed their opposition to the Executive Committee's line; and Lenin felt it necessary to respond in the eleventh session on 1 July. He first admitted that the officially-proposed theses on Comintern tactics were 'a compromise'. Then he nailed his own colours to the mast. To the Congress's surprise, he proceeded to justify the open letter written by Paul Levi calling for a political alliance of all the parties of German socialism in January 1921 (even though Lenin still refrained from seeking Levi's re-instatement in the Communist Party of Germany). He also demanded the retention of the phrase about 'the majority of the working class' in the theses. Lenin told the Congress that the German communists should adopt the Russian Bolshevik strategy of 1917. Supposedly the October Revolution in Petrograd was attempted only after the party had secured 'the majority of soviets of workers' and peasants' deputies' on its side.[60] This was falsehood. The Bolsheviks acquired a neat majority even in the urban soviets only after the Petrograd seizure of power, and Socialist Revolutionaries of various types were favoured by most peasants.[61] A myth was propagated in the pursuit of political acquiescence.

Nevertheless Lenin did not want totally to humiliate Thalheimer, and was willing to refer paradoxically to the March Action as 'a big step forward'.[62] In sessions thirteen and fourteen, on 2 July, the overtly comradely ambience among the leaders of the Russian Communist Party was destroyed. The culprit was Kun. In a speech of self-defence, he claimed to agree with Zinoviev and Lenin but not with Trotski; his ploy was to imply that Lenin and Trotski disagreed about the March Action. Zinoviev thereupon affected to believe that the original theses of Radek had not been substantially altered by the several amendments. This was too much much for Trotski, and he subjected Kun to ridicule. Kun, a resilient soul, requested to make a further contribution. But Zinoviev, despite being furious with Trotski, terminated the debate; the theses of Radek were passed quickly and unanimously by Congress.[63] Lenin had missed the proceedings. He presumably calculated that, as long as his principal aims were not challenged, he should let the other Bolshevik leaders deal with the problems; his health, too, was bothering him. Nevertheless Trotski, noting his non-attendance, asked him for help in repelling the attacks on him.[64] But Lenin declined their request. On 4 July the Congress accepted theses on 'The World Situation and the Tasks of the Communist International' in Lenin's absence.[65] It is hard to reject the hypothesis that, while revolutionary prospects remained dim, he did not want to waste time with the Communist International. He put more effort into the Politburo and into discussions about a concessional agreement being negotiated with the British firm of Urquharts.[66]

Lenin tacitly recognised this by opting to present a report on Russia rather than on Europe.[67] This came in session seventeen on 5 July with the debate on 'The Tactics of the Russian Communist Party'. His arguments for the New Economic Policy as delivered to the Tenth Party Conference in May 1921 were replicated with confidence. Bolsheviks had heard it all before. For the delegates to the Congress of the Communist International it was the earliest available chance to listen to Lenin himself explaining the measures of reform. The Congress had already gone as the Politburo had expected, and Lenin's status as the leader of the October Revolution made it unlikely that his report would attract much criticism. Lenin spoke for one hour and ten minutes. Only a speaker from the Communist Workers' Party of Germany objected, announcing that 'the clear demarcation line dividing us from the Hilferdings is entirely erased; the whole internal link with contemporary class struggle is completely missing'.[68] His comment was ignored: Lenin's theses were adopted by acclaim.[69] But his was an organisation which had split from the official Communist Party of Germany. It had been invited to the Congress against Thalheimer's wishes and was disowned by the Communist International shortly afterwards.

The Congress resumed its vital deliberations on the theses on 'The Tactics of the Komintern'. Lenin wrote emolliently to the commission working on the final draft, explaining his criticism of Kun. He regretted having given offence to the Hungarian communists, but stuck to his basic analysis: 'Therefore I hasten to communicate in writing: When I myself was an émigré (for more than 15 years), I several times took "too left" a position (as I now can see). In August 1917 I too was an émigré and made too "leftist" a proposal to the Central Committee which fortunately was utterly rejected.'[70] He also met up with the

German delegation and, while using tactful words, insisted that their party show complete obedience to the directives of the Congress of the Communist International.[71] He spoke in similar fashion to a joint meeting of German, Polish, Czechoslovak, Hungarian and Italian delegations on 11 July. Lenin repeated that lessons had to be learned from Bolshevik history. He told his audience how the slogan of European civil war, which he had approved in emigration in 1915, had had to be shelved in order that the party might win popular support in 1917;[72] and this time his historical accuracy was unchallengeable. Acknowledgement of personal error was Lenin's most obvious characteristic. His frankness is yet another indication of his zeal to hold foreign communist parties to a cautious standpoint. If he had applied himself with such energy at the beginning of the Congress, this frantic activity might not have been necessary.

But on the whole he could be pleased. The German leader Robert Koenen was entrusted with the report on 'Organisational Structure'.[73] Lenin and his Bolshevik associates, having dominated the Congress, had an incentive to give the impression that the Communist International provided its member parties with equal rights. In reality the Politburo had ruled the Congress from beginning to end. The thrust for a less risky revolutionary strategy around the world had been imposed. The Indian delegate Roy repeated his criticism from the Second Congress; in particular, he exclaimed, with reason, that the Soviet *rapprochement* with the major capitalist powers damaged the campaign for revolution in the colonial countries. This struck a chord with the Congress. Roy successfully proposed an amendment to the theses on 'The World Situation and the Tasks of the Communist International' expressing hostility to the rising bourgeoisies of the colonies.[74] The Turkish delegates were on his side, and informed the Congress about their political difficulties since the signature of a treaty between Soviet Russia and Turkey.[75] Lenin could tolerate the complaint. Europe had worried the Politburo before the Congress, and the proceedings had passed satisfactorily. On 12 July, as the Congress drew to a close, he absented himself and left the final ceremonies to Zinoviev.

THE ARTS, SCIENCES AND SCHOLARSHIP UNDER LENIN

The changes in Bolshevik foreign policy, now ratified by the Communist International, preceded the agrarian reform discussed from February 1921 and embodied in law in April. Not everything about the party's orientation was altered by the New Economic Policy, and many groups in society waited to see whether their own treatment by the authorities would be modified. Among these was the artistic intelligentsia. By the end of the Civil War there were writers and painters who expected an end to strict state control. Measures to supervise the country's arts had begun with the Bolshevik seizure of power in Petrograd. The Decree on the Press on 28 October 1917 severely restricted freedom of expression in general.[76] Not only active politicians but also novelists and poets with strongly anti-Bolshevik opinions were put on guard that Sovnarkom would retaliate against strong criticism by barring their access to printing facilities. Dozens of newspapers were closed in 1917–1918.[77] The Cheka's importance increased in artistic matters and authors who offended the régime lived in fear of arrest. It is true that the poet Nikolai Gumilev, who was shot in 1921 on a false charge of complicity in a 'White Guard' plot, was the only major writer to suffer this fate. But the milieu was generally intimidatory to those who disliked Bolshevism. The earning of a daily crust supervened over other interests in the Civil War, and the state took advantage of indirect modes of control. Lenin had given approval in November 1917 to the introduction of a state monopoly in the reprinting of the Russian classics.[78] In 1919 a huge publishing house, Gosizdat, was established. The nationalisation of existing printing presses supplied Gosizdat with massive influence over which new books should appear. Analogous state institutions were set up for other areas of the arts.

Lenin's pre-occupations were understandably with the Whites, the foreign interventionist forces, the party, food supplies to the cities, the Comintern. The arts impinged little on either his political activity or his intellectual concerns in the early years of 'Soviet power'. His initiatives were few, and even his involvement in deliberations on artistic matters was exceptional. On 17 July 1918 he had chaired Sovnarkom when fifty monuments to heroic rebels of the past were commissioned. First in the list came Spartacus, the instigator of the greatest slave revolt in antiquity; Marx and Engels were fifth and sixth. The Roman tribune Tiberius Gracchus and Brutus, Julius Caesar's slayer, came second and third.[79] The choice of subjects can hardly have been Lenin's. He would surely have placed Marx and Engels more prominently, and his classical studies as a youth would surely have reminded him that neither Tiberius Gracchus nor Brutus were liberators of the people.

Lenin proceeded to give a speech at the unveiling of the monument to Marx and Engels on the first anniversary of the October Revolution.[80] But subsequently his interventions in 'high culture' tailed off. In 1918–1919 they were virtually non-existent. In January 1920 he wrote to Anatoli Lunacharski, People's Commissar of Enlightenment, requesting an academic group to be set up to compile a new modern Russian dictionary incorporating the linguistic developments between Aleksandr Pushkin and Maksim Gorki.[81] In February he requested the People's Commissariat of Posts and Telegraphs to support the radio laboratory in Nizhni Novgorod; and in June he put his weight behind a project to create an observatory at Pulkovo. At the end of the year he talked to all and sundry about the need to for electric power throughout the economy.[82] Fitfully and in vain he enquired about progress with the dictionary.[83] In addition, he kept an eye on Zinoviev's project for a modern Russian atlas – and he pointed out the several mistakes in it.[84] But his caustic scorn was reserved for sloppy proof-reading. A book on Russo-French relations between 1910 and 1914 was castigated for 'the shameless, truly Soviet slovenliness for which the punishment should be prison'.[85] These wild words were not, in this instance, meant to be taken literally. The book's author remained free. Indeed there were occasions when Lenin protected leading figures from the arts. Beseeched by Gorki, he ordered the release of prose writer Ivan Volny from a Cheka jail in April 1919;[86] and Gorki again bent Lenin's ear in 1921 to get medical and financial care for the dying Aleksandr Blok, one of the greatest Russian poets of the century.[87]

Lunacharski, with Lenin's contented acquiescence, was empowered to instigate and co-ordinate artistic policy. The Politburo knew that most creative artists opposed Bolshevism mentally and that several, even if they were unwilling to join the White armies, wanted to leave the country. The right to emigrate was frequently withheld in case the individuals should propagate anti-Soviet ideas abroad.[88] Yet maltreatment of writers and artists at home could be equally damaging, and the Politburo made arrangements, on Lunacharski's proposal, for major poets to be supported materially at public expense. This did not constitute a long-term policy for attracting artists of high quality to the side of the régime. Lenin dimly perceived this. In private he conceded that nearly all existing writers (and he was always more sensitive to literary than to other artistic developments) hated the Bolsheviks: 'New writers must be created from the workers, from the peasants.'[89]

This was a common party aspiration. Lunacharski and Bukharin gave speeches encouraging the working class to supply pieces for newspapers.[90] Lenin followed their line. But within the consensus there were tensions which grew stronger at the end of the Civil War. Lenin's taste in literature had been formed in the nineteenth century; and he knew what he liked and expected others to agree. As a youngster he had warmed to the novelist Ivan Turgenev. He had grown to love the novels of Lev Tolstoi and the short stories of Anton Chekhov, and never stinted in his admiration for the revolutionary writer Nikolai Chernyshevski whose novel *What Is To Be Done?* had been used by Lenin as the title of his own 1902 pamphlet on party organisation. He never ceased quoting the poet and critic of tsarism, Nekrasov.[91] Lenin was primarily a man of the word, and wrote nothing about music, painting, sculpture or dance in his long career. Not that his spirit was closed to the other arts. He had attended light operas in his émigré years. He also was mightily attracted to Beethoven.[92] But it was words on the printed page that evoked the supreme enthusiasms of the Bolshevik leader. Not only did he profess a very reasonable preference for schools to receive scarce resources in preference to ballet troupes, but also he was not unduly worried that the Bolshoi Theatre might be closed for a while in 1922.[93] He would not have been similarly apathetic about a proposal to shut down printing presses.

Meanwhile Maksim Gorki, while attenuating his objections to the Lenin's revolutionary project, failed to produce works of artistic merit;[94] and among other outstanding writers who sided with the Bolsheviks there were none who adhered to the 'natural realism' of Lenin's favourite classics.[95] Vladimir Mayakovski was a case in point. Lenin declared: 'I don't belong to the admirers of his poetic talent, even though I entirely confess my lack of competence in this area.' Mayakovski's merit in his eyes lay only in satirising the endless meetings characteristic of governmental and party activity.[96] Otherwise Lenin found him and the self-styled 'Futurists' uncongenial. He urged that the state's near-monopoly of printing presses should be used to prevent publication of Mayakovski's lengthy poem '150,000'; he also proposed to limit Futurist publications to no more than twice-yearly print-runs of 1,500.[97] Similarly permission for Aleksandr Bogdanov, who continued to write on social and political theory, to publish and lecture was within the gift of the Politburo: Lenin kept his ex-Bolshevik adversary on a tight rein.[98]

Censorship held no horrors for Lenin. His past experience of it had convinced him of its efficaciousness rather than of its undesirability.

This was not said openly by him or any other Bolshevik leader. His main pronouncements had been made while Nikolai II was on the throne. They came in two articles: 'Lev Tolstoi as the Mirror of the Russian Revolution' and 'Party Organisation and Party Literature'. The article on Tolstoi was written in 1908. It was an interesting piece of journalism, dedicated to the novelist's widely-celebrated eightieth birthday and focussed on the political ramifications of his oeuvre. In Lenin's view, Tolstoi represented the 'contradictions' of contemporary peasant life. Thus the Russian peasantry was anarchistic, obscurantist and backward-looking while also reaching forward to new forms of society. Lenin claimed that Tolstoi inadvertently summarised this vision and failed to draw the necessary political conclusion: namely that only class struggle, and not pacifism or a sentimental ruralism, would transform the life of the people.[99] This incisive, if controversial, thesis was not untypical of the approach to literature taken by most socialist writers in Russia. Aesthetic merit was recognised and admired; but the political message, whether expressed or merely implicit, was taken as all-important. Lenin was no better and no worse than nearly all his comrades in boiling down works of art to their contribution to politics. In government he behaved accordingly.

Indeed, writing 'Party Organisation and Party Literature' in 1905, Lenin had called for party-mindedness to be embodied in works of art: 'What does this principle of party literature consist of? Not only in the fact that, for the socialist proletariat, literary matters cannot be an instrument of pressure by individuals or particular groups and cannot be in general matters for individuals independent of the general proletarian cause. Down with non-party *littérateurs*! Down with supermen-*littérateurs*! Literary matters must become a part of the general proletarian cause, must become "a cog-wheel and screw" of a single, monolithic, great social-democratic mechanism brought into motion by the entire conscious vanguard of the entire working class.'[100]

Naturally we have to remember that Lenin wrote these words about a party which did not yet have power and, furthermore, a party which had exiguous finances and limited access to printing facilities. Lenin's purpose at the time was to advise how to organise the party's newspapers (and to commission and control literary contributions to them) while being under threat from the Romanov monarchy.[101] This was not a blueprint for literary policy in all times and under all conditions. Rather it was designed to secure the party's interests in competition with other parties and under harassment by the Ministry of the Interior. The boundary between what was pro-party and what was anti-party was definable by reference to the party programme. Writers who did not like the political control over the contents of publication were free to join another party. Lenin added: 'Freedom of speech and press must be complete.'[102] He denied that workers would by a show of hands vote to decide 'questions of science, philosophy, aesthetics'.[103] A distinct autonomy seemed to be offered by Lenin to literature. Albeit in stilted style, he conceded: 'It is beyond dispute that in this matter there is an absolute necessity to guarantee a larger space for personal initiative, individual inclinations – a space for thought and fantasy, form and content. All this is indisputable; but all this only goes towards demonstrating that the literary section of the party affairs of the proletariat cannot be identified through a pre-fixed pattern with the other sections of the party affairs of the proletariat.'[104]

And yet, for all his apparent sensitivity to the needs of the artistic intelligentsia, Lenin repudiated any concept of freedom. Financial and political constraints bore down upon everyone, including writers: 'It is impossible to live in society and be free from society.'[105] This, in a narrowly philosophical sense, is a defensible proposition. Coming from Lenin, however, it was freighted with menace for freedom of the arts under socialism. It would prove easy for his supporters to argue that 'Party Organisation and Party Literature' recommended that littérateurs be forced to conform directly to the party's requirements under the dictatorship of the proletariat.[106]

The article had not been so specific; and, while he interfered in the lives and working conditions of writers after the October Revolution, he did not instal a comprehensive, detailed direction of literature. Nor did he produce a theoretical article to underpin his various measures. Despite acquiring a posthumous reputation as the founder of Soviet artistic policy, he was not at the centre of discussions when the Bolshevik central leadership at last confronted the problem that the party had not acquired a phalanx of party *littérateurs*. As the New Economic Policy got under away, most persons active in the arts did not welcome Bolshevism. Zinoviev presented the leadership's conclusions to the Twelfth Party Conference in August 1922 (while Lenin was recuperating from a stroke).[107] He emphasised that the New Economic Policy would not involve 'freedom of the press for the bourgeoisie', and attacked the 'counterrevolutionary ideas' still appearing in print.[108] But unconditional repression would not work to the party's benefit either. The resultant resolution conceded that Bolsheviks, since they did not have many *littérateurs*, would have to find tolerable allies among literary groups which at least did not oppose them.[109] Trotski in 1923 went still further, stressing that literature needed a certain autonomy of expression if it was to produce works of beauty. This was not far from the principle enunciated by Lenin in 1905.[110] It was a great pity, for the fate of Soviet literature in the 1930s, that he was too ill to re-affirm such a commitment in 1922. His silence would eventually allow Stalin to pluck out all the most authoritarian aspects of Lenin's pre-revolutionary writings and deploy them for the total subjugation of literature to the state.[111]

AWAY FROM GENOA

Overlordship of the arts, sciences and scholarship was left by Lenin to trusted subordinates. Not so international relations. The foreign policy of Soviet Russia was held tightly in Lenin's grasp. He and Chicherin, People's Commissar for External Affairs, were in regular communication. Chicherin was bright, inquisitive and creative. But he was a former Menshevik; he was well-known for his comfortable gentry background. He had been invited to assume his post, when it was laid down by Trotski after the signature of the Brest-Litovsk treaty, as a sympathiser of the party who had diplomatic experience. Unlike other holders of important jobs in Soviet politics, consequently, he needed patronage in order to make his way. Chicherin needed Lenin whereas Lenin merely found Chicherin a useful expert.

International relations were highly contentious among leading Bolsheviks; but Lenin and Chicherin agreed on most matters and priorities. And Chicherin, from his side, admired Lenin's intuitive understanding of the skills of diplomacy. Like a traditional foreign minister bargaining on behalf of a weak state, Lenin wanted to manoeuvre between various capitalist powers; he wanted to play them off against each other. He was bracingly free, especially after military defeat at the hands of the Poles, from excesses of revolutionary rhetoric. Lenin's objective was the securing of further economic and political agreements with the advanced industrial countries. The Anglo-Soviet treaty confined him and the Soviet government, but not the Communist International, in their propaganda offensive on colonialism; but he was unrestrained in his comments on the Treaty of Versailles, on the inequities of capitalism and on the inevitability of communism's triumph. He was adamant that the Soviet state's policies, customs and laws were not up for barter. If capitalist countries, individually or collectively, wanted to deal with the Bolsheviks on this basis, well and good. If not, the Bolsheviks could and should bide their time. He counted on nothing happening very quickly; but he would work with Chicherin towards that end. His New Economic Policy, at least as he initially perceived it, demanded the cementing of further ties with the advanced capitalist countries.

Nevertheless he had no great hopes of the victorious Allied powers. French ministers could not ignore the huge losses sustained by French private investors when Lenin's government had unilaterally renounced Russian state debts. Even Lloyd George was treated with low expectancy. In London the coalition cabinet under his leadership sought a revision of international relations in Europe which would facilitate a more rapid economic reconstruction and would inhibit the re-emergence of political tensions. This would include an admittance of both the Soviet and German governments to all-European official discussions. On pragmatic grounds Lloyd George believed that French severity towards Germany since the treaty of Versailles ought to be moderated. Nor had he ever accepted Winston Churchill's arguments for an Allied crusade against Bolshevik Russia; on the contrary, he had maintained that the communist experiment would be terminated most effectively by the restoration of trade links which sooner or later would undermine Lenin's régime.

Lloyd George, while succeeding temporarily in London, predictably had difficulties in Paris. Both the French prime minister Aristide Briand and, more particularly, his president Alexandre Millerand were mindful of the French assets recently expropriated by Sovnarkom. The willingness of British political and business interests to bargain with Lenin was not shared in France, and it took months of persuasion for Lloyd George in the Allied Supreme Council to secure assent to an international conference to seek a resolution of Europe's problems. His cause was not eased by the insistence of the Soviet People's Commissariat of External Affairs that, if ever Sovnarkom were to recognise debts contracted by Nicholas II and the Provisional Government, the Allies would have to accept Soviet counter-claims for damage inflicted as the result of British and French intervention in the Civil War.[112] But Lloyd George did not relent. For him, the Anglo-Soviet trade agreement of March 1921 was but a springboard into the pool of a continental settlement grander even than the Versailles treaty. He urged that an international business consortium be formed, including the Germans, for promotion of economic recovery in eastern Europe and Russia (as well as for the promotion of recovery at home), and that a meeting should be held to discuss the terms whereunder this might be done.[113]

Chicherin and the People's Commissariat of External Affairs looked on Lloyd George rather favourably, and differences with Lenin began to gain in significance. The Politburo scarcely took cognisance of Lloyd George's intensive activity. Throughout his years in power Lenin had acted as if an orientation towards the German government might be more useful, if only in the short term, than the quest for a pan-European settlement. From Brest-Litovsk in 1918 through to his occasional remarks in 1920,[114] he had dropped hints about this. By 1921 the arrangements with Germany for increased trade and for joint military training were already working well. Lenin's instinct led him increasingly to scorn the British initiative. Karl Radek, presumably with Lenin's knowledge, published an article in *Pravda* on 4 December 1921 urging German politicians and businessmen to recognise their opportunities in Soviet Russia.[115] In reply to Chicherin, Lenin called for Lloyd George to be faced down. On 3 January 1922 he proposed that the Soviet authorities should reject the Allied terms as totally unacceptable.[116]

Lloyd George and Briand met next day in Cannes. They agreed that the Soviet government, if it wanted to receive Western economic assistance, would have to recognise state debts and establish a legal framework for private enterprise as well as suspend communist propaganda abroad. A conference would be held in Genoa and the Bolsheviks would be invited to attend.[117] Even this set of terms caused ructions in Paris. Briand was compelled to resign and his place as prime minister was taken by his critic Raymond Poincaré. Lenin became even more pessimistic about the proposed international conference. Furthermore, he was warned by Krasin not to travel to Genoa. The dangers of assassination were judged excessive. London would have been a venue where surer precautions might be taken against Russian monarchists and Socialist Revolutionary terrorists.[118] But Lenin thought himself indispensable to the Revolution, and on 12 January wrote to the Politburo declaring that not only he but also Trotski and Zinoviev should be prohibited from travelling abroad at all. Not even London was safe.[119] The disappointment affected not only Lloyd George but also the Western public. Everyone wanted to see what Lenin looked like. Did he really have the appearance of the Devil? Were the rumours true that he wore a suit? Did he look Jewish? Did he behave respectfully or was he a brawling Russian worker? Appetites had been whetted by lurid reportage, and the prospect of the Soviet leader's appearing in the streets and on newsreels had been attractive. The welcome which awaited Chicherin in Genoa would have been dwarfed if Lenin had journeyed westwards. But Lenin was immovable. On 16 January he wrote again to the Politburo suggesting that the Italian government should be asked for assurances that, even without him, the Soviet delegates would not be attacked by fascists. He maintained, too, that Chicherin should reinforce the current negotiations with the Germans in advance of the Genoa conference.[120]

The technical preparations continued to worry Lenin. He demanded that radio communications be made available, and a Soviet warship be moored off the Italian riviera.[121] He was even more concerned that Chicherin wished to deal positively with Lloyd George. Chicherin's latest papers were described by Lenin as evidence of illness:[122] this was Lenin's typical reaction to differences with colleagues. If they disagreed with him, he would initially try to assume the best of them: namely that some disease had temporarily affected their brains. And so, on 22 January, he impressed on the Politburo by letter that the delegation should agree to recognise debts only if they were to be covered in their entirety by Soviet counter-claims in relation to Allied military intervention in 1918–1919. Chicherin should also be instructed, according to Lenin, to make a demonstrative defence of Germany as the victim of the Versailles treaty and to try to split off the USA diplomatically from Britain and France.[123] Lenin continued to rail against Chicherin's willingness to concede to Lloyd George. He should immediately be sent off to a sanatorium to recuperate![124] Lenin's toughly anti-British and pro-German orientation was now fixed in his mind. He was sending Chicherin to Genoa (albeit not to a sanatorium) without expectation of a comprehensive settlement in Europe.[125]

For a while the impression was maintained that Lenin would head the delegation, with Chicherin as his deputy. But the Central Committee, no less than Lenin, did not want Lenin to leave Moscow – and in any case his health still gave grounds for worry.[126] Lenin continued to harass the People's Commissariat of External Affairs. Chicherin's own Deputy Commissar, Maksim Litvinov, argued in favour of acceptance of the Cannes terms before the Politburo on 3 February.[127] Lenin was having none of it. He also introduced an unexpected irritation. Unlike Chicherin, he had low hopes of the Conference, and therefore could indulge his favourite foreign-policy ploy of trying to divide the capitalist powers. Lenin successfully recommended that the Soviet delegation should make its proposals in a 'bourgeois-pacifist' spirit.[128] Chicherin objected. All his life, even when he had been a Menshevik, Chicherin had opposed pacifism. Now he resolutely opposed Lenin's attempt to play on what both of them regarded as pacifist illusions.[129] But Lenin insisted, reassuring Chicherin that the party leadership's commitment to communism and non-pacifism was undiminished.[130] On 16 February, Lenin repeated to Chicherin that the Soviet delegates should not panic. Sovnarkom had never acceded to the Cannes terms, but had nevertheless received an invitation.[131] If the French were to exert further pressure, then Lenin demanded that Chicherin should propose a formula drawn up by Krasin: 'All countries recognise their state debts and are obliged to compensate the damages and losses caused by the action of their governments.'[132] So-called petit-bourgeois and bourgeois-pacifist support should be sought. Divisions among capitalist powers should be encouraged; and under no circumstances, Lenin demanded, should Chicherin sign anything without consultations with Moscow.[133]

The Politburo was approached by Lenin, who was spending much time at the Gorki mansion, for plenipotentiary authority to write his own directives to Chicherin in Italy.[134] This bossy initiative was rejected, and Chicherin departed in peace to Berlin before going on to Genoa. He remained unconvinced that the Germans wanted to draw closer to Sovnarkom.[135] Nor was he sure that too obvious a reconciliation with Berlin would not harm the Soviet republic's relations with the victorious Versailles powers. Lenin's recklessness alarmed him.

And yet the Genoa proceedings, which began on 10 April, tended to validate Lenin's inclination. The French reined in the British, and the British were increasingly themselves divided: Conservative ministers in London were restive with Lloyd George. Chicherin for his part was restricted by the Politburo's adhesion to the viewpoint of Lenin. He wriggled out of his chains to affirm his readiness to accept 'just' requests in respect of expropriated foreign assets.[136] Fellow delegate Jan Rudzutak informed Moscow about him. Lenin persuaded the Politburo that a telegram be sent instructing Chicherin to correct this derogation from official party policy.[137] Meanwhile Chicherin himself had been surprised by the German resolve to settle separately with the Bolsheviks. No serious relief from the severity of the Versailles treaty had been offered to Berlin by the British and French. A bargain with Moscow became more tempting. Based at their hotel in Santa Margherita near Rapallo, Chicherin and his fellow delegates consolidated the agreements of the previous year. The 'Russians' and the Germans renounced all claims against each other about war losses and damage as well as about nationalised property. Full diplomatic relations would be resumed. Commercial ties were to be based on the principle of most favoured nation.[138] The general consequence was a breach in the front of European capitalism. Germany was a loser power at Versailles but still a major power, and had decided to treat with the land of the October Revolution on equal terms. Lenin could have been forgiven for believing that his judgement had been justified. He entirely abandoned interest in the Genoa negotiations. The point was, Lenin urged, to base future international planning upon the Rapallo paradigm. The Central Committee agreed and, at its plenum on 16 April, firmly resolved to reject British and French pressure to sign no separate treaties.[139]

At the same session Lenin accused the Soviet delegation of having been too soft in negotiations. The Central Committee repudiated his case and ruled that Chicherin had comported himself correctly.[140] But Lenin would not let the matter drop. He wrote fiercely to the Politburo about 'the unprecedented, disgraceful and *dangerous* [sic] vacillations of Chicherin and *Litvinov*.' The Politburo agreed, but – on Stalin's proposal – refused Lenin's request that Chicherin be officially disowned.[141] Lenin was undeterred. He also urged that the Soviet representatives should immediately break off discussions at the Genoa Conference.[142] Again he was turned down: the Politburo did not wish to annoy the British and French unnecessarily. On 9 May 1922 he chided Chicherin for 'flirting' with Rome rather than cajoling Italy to follow the example of Germany.[143] But there the matter rested, and Lenin calmed down and started to enjoy his achievements of the past months. Enforced convalescence had not prevented him from getting his way over the main questions in foreign policy. He was not disappointed with the Genoa Conference; no, he was thrilled that Genoa had given the opportunity for Rapallo. He looked forward to future Rapallos.

SHOW TRIALS AND REPRESSION

There were other topics that kept him agitated. He had declared to the Ninth Congress of Soviets, in the last week of 1921, that the terror had been crucial to victory in the Civil War.[144] The Cheka had been the sword of the October Revolution; its murderous activities has been purposefully arbitrary. Entire social groups had been pre-emptively attacked through the system of the arrest and execution of hostages. Jails had been packed with victims. A system of concentration camps had been established, and the Cheka had been the most feared organ of state power. From 1921, however, the régime wished to calm the apprehensions of society. The New Economic Policy's success would depend, as he quickly foresaw, on the establishment of much greater legal predictability. This did not mean that a law-based order was the party's objective; on the contrary, the Bolsheviks remained legal nihilists – and Lenin in this respect was their principal theorist.[145]

But a concordat was tacitly provided whereby citizens could sleep easily abed if they did not engage in activity deemed inimical to the régime. Discussions on a Civil Code began in higher party circles in the winter of 1921–1922. Lenin stipulated that the Bolsheviks should reserve the option of terrorist methods. In May 1921 the Cheka had been allowed to apply the death penalty, without reference to other security organs, for thefts of state property.[146] Lenin supported Dzierzynski despite objections from N. V. Krylenko. But Krylenko kept to his campaign for greater judicial formality.[147] By 1 December 1921, Lenin had been won over, and he helped draft a Politburo minute for the narrowing of the Cheka's powers of arrest and for the reinforcement of the revolutionary tribunals as the source of judgement and sentencing.[148] This had been Kamenev's plea in the Civil War, and a commission including Dzierzynski, Kurski and him was to produce a draft.[149] Kamenev lobbied for the Cheka's disbandment. Incommoded by ill-health, Lenin left the business to his associates.[150] By 23 January 1922 the commission was ready to report. Its main recommendation was for the Cheka to be disbanded, being replaced by a Main Political Administration (GPU) attached to the People's Commissariat of Internal Affairs (and chaired by the Internal Affairs Commissar). The turning over of the sentencing of offenders to the revolutionary tribunals was confirmed.[151] Predictably the Cheka's leaders objected. But Kamenev had not done as well as appeared. Lenin made plain, in a letter to the veteran Cheka leader Unszlicht, that the reform's effects were to be restricted. He urged Unszlicht to take Cheka staff with him into the Main Political Administration. In other words, the Cheka's abolition would be a cosmetic operation; and Lenin required an increase in the 'speed and *force* of the repressions' by the Cheka officers. 'Banditism' (or armed opposition to the régime) should be met with 'shootings on the spot'.[152]

Unszlicht, who became the deputy chairman of the Main Political Administration, was encouraged by Lenin to use him as an intermediary in the Politburo on behalf of repressive agencies.[153] Lenin stressed that the Bolsheviks refused to 'recognise courts that were above classes'.[154] He also toughened up Kurski's drafts of the Civil Code. On 15 May 1922 he insisted that 'all aspects of activity of Mensheviks, S[ocialist] R[evolutionaries], etc.' should come within the scope of crimes punishable by death. Lenin, ex-lawyer from the Volga, was unfussed by legal niceties; he called for the Civil Code to have a propagandistic passage linking such activities to '*the international bourgeoisie* and its struggle against us'.[155] Two days later he had another thought. Kurski ought to avow 'the *essence* and *justification of terror*' in the forthcoming Code.[156]

Lenin in his last period was not a proponent of legal reform and universal civic rights. He had not stopped being a legal nihilist.[157] This was true notwithstanding his occasional interventions to save individuals from perdition.[158] Such a custom was reminiscent of the Romanov emperors. Lenin's apparent humanitarianism was displayed only fitfully. His intention remained to root out opposition to Bolshevism before it could constitute itself as an opposition. Unszlicht was warned 'not to be caught napping by a second Kronstadt'.[159] Lenin worried especially about the anti-Bolshevik parties. The Mensheviks and Socialist Revolutionaries were primary targets since the liberal and conservative political groups had been crushed in the Civil War. Exemplary punishment, in Lenin's opinion, was necessary. Dzierzynski had reported to the Central Committee on the Mensheviks and Socialist Revolutionaries on 28 December 1921, and a secret decision had been taken 'to predetermine the question of handing over the Central Comittee of the Socialist Revolutionaries to the court of the Supreme Tribunal'. Kamenev, Dzierzynski and Stalin were charged with oversight over the management of official publicity.[160] A decision on the Mensheviks was held in abeyance.[161] Lenin supported Dzierzynski, and on 22 February 1922 wrote to Kurski urging the 'putting on of a series of *model* trials in Moscow, Piter [Petrograd: R. S.], Kharkov and several other most important centres'. Not justice but popular propaganda should be the objective. Lenin told Kurski to compel the judges to strengthen repression in line with central party policy, not stopping short of executing the defendants.[162]

This was no passing fancy. On 27 March 1922 he answered criticism by the Mensheviks and Socialist Revolutionaries with the threat: 'Kindly let us stand you against the wall for this!'[163] An international meeting of socialists was taking place in Berlin with Bolshevik participation. Radek and Bukharin led the delegation from Moscow.

These two discovered that European socialist concern about the Red terror might jeopardise Soviet interests at the forthcoming Genoa Conference. Radek promised that the trial of the Socialist Revolutionaries in Moscow would not be followed by executions.[164] Lenin was angered. *Pravda* on 11 April 1922 carried his piece 'We Have Paid Too Dear', castigating Radek and Bukharin for having made undue concessions to the Kautskyites and their sympathisers.[165] Meanwhile Dzierzynski had been instructed to re-examine the amnesty granted to the Socialist Revolutionaries in February 1919.[166] The menace to defendants in the Moscow trial was clear.

Despite abiding by Radek's assurances in Berlin,[167] he pressed for severe punishment for political resistance. The repression of the Mensheviks and Socialist Revolutionaries, according to Lenin, was only half of the business. They had also to be vilified. He wanted the Soviet press to conduct a campaign linking anti-Bolshevik socialists in Russia with 'the international bourgeoisie'.[168] They ought to be rubbished as unpatriotic to the point of serving as agents of foreign states. Popular opinion needed to be rallied to the Bolsheviks. Not confining this repression to politics, Lenin aimed to retaliate against hostile opinion in culture. The Politburo accompanied its day-to-day general control over the arts, science and scholarship[169] with a sharp exemplary campaign of violence. Lenin wrote a memo to his personal assistant N. P. Gorbunov, who had received a request for the release of the distinguished chemistry professor M. M. Tikhvinski from a Cheka prison: 'Chemistry and counter-revolution are not mutually exclusive.'[170] The logic here is impeccable. But Lenin's sentiment was a sign of his extreme worries about groups who might influence public opinion against Bolshevism. His supervision of repression was close. In June 1921, for example, he scrutinised a list of professors – whose specialisms included civil engineering, zoology and music – arrested recently in Petrograd. His comments and recommendations about individuals were extraordinarily detailed.[171]

In this instance he leaned towards gentleness.[172] Usually he was less merciful; a book edited by the philosophers Nikolai Berdyaev and S. L. Frank on the ideas of the German writer Oswald Spengler induced Lenin to announce to Josef Unszlicht: 'In my opinion, this is like "a literary front" for a White Guard organisation.'[173] There was nothing in fact openly hostile to the Soviet government. Yet Berdyaev, an ex-Marxist who had converted to Christianity while remaining committed to socialism and philosophical individualism, was compelled to go into emigration. The insulation of Soviet readers from thinkers who might deflect them from Bolshevism was an explicit aim. Dozens of intellectuals were expelled in 1922. Lenin worried only about the detailed practical results. More 'communist-*littérateurs*' should be drawn into checking whether decisions to close particular cultural and economic journals were appropriate. Lenin claimed that there had been recent cases of both premature and tardy closures.[174]

Writers who displeased him attracted his anathema. 'These,' he declared, 'are all open counter-revolutionaries, clients of the Entente, an organisation of its servants and spies and corrupters of student youth.'[175] Nor did he forget about that other traditional bogey of Bolshevism, the Russian Orthodox Church. Violence against priests had been relaxed under the New Economic Policy.[176] The emphasis of state policy, with Lenin's encouragement, lay upon vigorous atheistic propaganda. But the itch to repress the Orthodox Church had not faded. On 19 March 1922 Lenin wrote to the Politburo that the ecclesiastical authorities in the town of Shuya had organised a demonstration against the government's decree on the compulsory sale abroad of ecclesiastical treasures to raise funds to relieve the famine by the Volga. Central party leaders wanted to take advantage of the Church's hostility to the decree. Events in Shuya, in Lenin's opinion, offered a chance to return to direct repression. Trials should be held of Church leaders not only in Shuya but also in Moscow and other cities. Patriarch Tikhon should not be touched for fear of provoking demonstrations against the Bolsheviks. But open season was announced on the rest of the Church hierarchy: 'The greater the number of representatives of the reactionary clergy and reactionary bourgeoisie we manage to shoot on this basis, the better. It is precisely now that we should deliver a lesson to this public so that they dare not even think about resistance for several decades.'[177]

The Politburo met next day in Lenin's absence through illness.[178] Out of the full members who were present, only Stalin had been baptised as a baby in the Orthodox Church; but they decided that the lapsed Orthodox Church member Vladimir Ilich Ulyanov-Lenin had strayed beyond the boundaries of pragmatism. The offenders in Shuya should certainly be arrested; but warnings should be given to priests not to allow a demonstration to recur; trials should be initiated only in instances of active resistance to the confiscation of Church treasures.[179] This was a severe decision even if it lacked Lenin's thirst for bloodletting. The trial of the Shuya clergy and their friends ended with the death sentence being passed on the defendants on 8 May 1922. Trotski agreed with the convalescent Lenin's demand for execution.

Five were then shot, and only Kamenev's intervention saved the lives of the rest of them.[180]

Lenin, who was known for melding ideological inclination with *Realpolitik*, had for the moment lost his touch. Possibly his illness and irregular attendance at the Politburo from late 1921 left him adrift. The disease itself perhaps induced the intermittent rages which expressed themselves politically in his demands for a series of executions of Socialist Revolutionaries and bishops.[181] In his favour it may be added that he retreated before the Politburo's advice.[182] He yielded to Trotski on religious questions. Trotski, who was as impassive as Lenin in ordering executions, was among the first to discern that the Orthodox Church could be neutered politically if the clerical faction of the 'Living Church' were helped to prominence. Supporters of this faction included Bishop Antonin; they called for a massive renovation of the Church's internal and external policies and were willing to effect an accommodation with the Soviet government.[183] The need to give covert assistance to the likes of Bishop Antonin had already been recognised in Trotski's draft motion for the Politburo on 20 March 1922.[184] On 15 May, Trotski criticised *Pravda*'s failure to play up the factional divisions in the Church to the party's advantage. According to Trotski, such propaganda would be useful in 'raking the ground for the seeds of atheism and materialism'. Lenin's reaction was ecstatic: 'True. 1000 times true!'[185]

Illness, too, prevented him from day-to-day involvement in the long-heralded trial of leading Socialist Revolutionaries beginning on 8 June 1922. The question whether to subject the Mensheviks to the same treatment had been discussed again in the Bolshevik Central Committee.[186] But the focus was retained on the Socialist Revolutionaries. It had been fear of the peasants that had induced Lenin to introduce the New Economic Policy, and it was logical for him to terrorise the party which was most popular among them. The charge sheet sought to implicate their Socialist-Revolutionary Central Committee, not excluding those such as Viktor Chernov who was then in emigration, with direct responsibility for the attempt on Lenin's life in August 1918, for political and military support for the White armies and for post-war links with the Allied governments.[187]

This was a fabrication. The Party of Socialist Revolutionaries was indeed involved in the episode at the former Mikhelson factory, and many of its members fought for Komuch against the Reds. Yet few had sided with the Whites. The claim was outrageous that, from start to finish, the Socialist-Revolutionary Central Committee had participated actively in the counsels of Kolchak, Denikin and Yudenich. Socialist Revolutionaries in a large number joined the Reds in the Civil War, and the Bolsheviks had recognised this by the amnesty granted to them in 1919. The defendants in the House of Trade Unions near the Kremlin were victims in what became known in the 1930s as a 'show trial'. Little pretence at impartiality was made; the chairman of proceedings was Yuri Pyatakov, Bolshevik Central Committee member. Speeches on the iniquity of the Socialist-Revolutionary leadership were made by supposedly soft-hearted Bolsheviks such as Nikolai Bukharin and Anatoli Lunacharski.[188] Sentences of death were passed on 7 August on the most unbending among the defendants. The death sentences were suspended by the Presidium of the All-Russian Central Executive Committee of the Congress of Soviets on the following day according to the assurances given in Berlin in April by Radek and Bukharin. Trotski was annoyed, arguing that lives should be spared only if the defendants forswore hostile activity against the Bolshevik party and the Soviet government.[189] This was tantamount to re-imposing the death sentences. Great courage had been displayed throughout the trial by most of the accused, and they were as unlikely to abase themselves before the Bolsheviks as the Bolsheviks would have bowed the knee to Aleksandr Kerenski.

It was as well for the Socialist Revolutionaries that, while Trotski was challenging the commutation of the death sentences, the architect of the Cheka and Red Terror was out of political action; for he was convalescing in a sanatorium on the outskirts of Moscow.[190] Sentences on bishops and priests of the Orthodox Church were lightened and the Menshevik trial, after continued discussion in the Central Committee, was thought inappropriate. The Bolshevik party had shown its teeth and cowed its enemies. Dictatorship had been shown to mean dictatorship; and, while the Politburo debated practicalities of implementation, there was no division on principle.

THE ELEVENTH PARTY CONGRESS

Politburo members and the rest of the Central Committee wanted no interference and no upsets. The party was to be presented with decisions and consulted only minimally; the first year of the New Economic Policy, coming after the disputes of 1920–1921, had been a battering experience. Lenin considered it vital that a united front should be formed by the Central Committee, and had exerted himself to this end despite ill-health as preparations were made for the opening of the Eleventh Party Congress in Moscow on 27 March 1922. Although he did not say so, what he wanted above all was a quiet Congress, a Congress without vituperative polemics and ideological controversy.

He and his colleagues carefully vetted the agenda in advance; their wish for a peaceful Congress caused them to avoid a fundamental debate on the New Economic Policy, on foreign trade, on agrarian measures, on the Civil Code, on Genoa.[191] The controversies were to be dampened down. Party unity and loyalty to the line of the Central Committee were the objective. The main obstacle was not the Workers' Opposition, which had recently sent an open letter of complaint about its treatment to the parties of the Communist International.[192] Nor were the trade unions any longer regarded as a very contentious topic.[193] Shlyapnikov and Tomski had ceased to be vital threats to Lenin's version of the New Economic Policy. But Lenin had reason to feel anxious about Preobrazhenski and his theses on the agrarian question. Lenin and Preobrazhenski had exchanged fierce criticisms about the impact of governmental measures upon various strata of the peasantry. The row had continued through the winter of 1921–1922, and Preobrazhenski wished to have the topic debated at the Party Congress[194] Lenin needed to stop this at all costs; for Preobrazhenski, arguing before a Bolshevik party audience about the bias of such measures in favour of the kulak, might well meet with a favourable response. On Lenin's instigation, the Politburo on 20 March 1922 rejected Preobrazhenski's theses, removed them from the Congress agenda and permitted Preobrazhenski only to address an unofficial side-gathering during the Congress proceedings.[195] Two days later the Central Committee confirmed this. The Politburo obtained compliance from it even though most Central Committee members had yet to scrutinise copies of Preobrazhenski's theses and Lenin's critique of them.[196]

The tranquillising of the Congress was also ensured by Lenin's willingness to deliver the Central Committee political report. His shaky physical condition bothered him enough to ask that a supplementary report should be got ready, and Kamenev was allotted this task.[197] Minor disagreements ensued. At the same meeting of the Central Committee, Tomski unsuccessfully demanded the abandonment of an enquiry into the composition of the Soviet trade union leadership.[198] Moreover, disquiet was expressed about the Secretariat. One of its members, Emelyan Yaroslavski, proposed that each Department of the

Secretariat should be headed by a Central Committee member.[199] But these were secondary matters. Harmony was restored by the end of this lengthy meeting. With its achievement Lenin looked forward to a Congress which would sanction the kind of New Economic Policy he had put in place.[200]

Proceedings began with a brief and well-received welcome from Lenin.[201] Evgeni Preobrazhenski tried to disturb things by calling for a debate on party policy in the countryside; but his plea was repudiated. Central and local leaders had been primed to intervene against him.[202] Lenin returned to the lectern to deliver the Central Committee's political report. The Genoa Conference was still in process, and he limited himself to a few curt remarks on it and explicitly ruled out the certainty of success.[203] His report was mainly taken up with a defence of the New Economic Policy. The restoration of the 'link' with the peasantry, he asserted, was the paramount immediate aim of the party. Bolsheviks needed to learn how to facilitate a resurgence of trade. Lenin unashamedly repeated that the stage of economic development reached by the country was not socialist. Soviet Russia was characterised rather by 'state capitalism'. Lenin lamented Bukharin's absence from the Congress as depriving him of the opportunity to debate the matter definitively.[204] But he insisted that, even though the proletariat had supposedly become the ruling class, the economy remained essentially capitalistic; and he stressed the need to keep capitalism within acceptable bounds.[205] Exactly where those bounds lay were not explained by him in theoretical terms. But on practical measures he was forthcoming. The party had expanded the New Economic Policy to its furthest necessary extent: 'We have spent a year retreating. Now we must say in the name of the party: enough!' Turning to the Workers' Opposition, he accused them of infantile behaviour since the Third Congress of the Communist International. They had acted impermissibly in appealing above the head of the Russian Communist Party to the other communist parties.[206] This was schoolmasterly admonition. Towards the Mensheviks and other non-Bolshevik parties he was much less restrained. Public activity would be answered with revolutionary courts and firing squads.[207]

The New Economic Policy as it stood, Lenin urged, could and should be made to work. Lenin emphasised that the party already had sufficient political and economic power in its hands. The chief impediment to the advance towards communism was the country's low general level of culture. The Bolsheviks, constituting a small percentage of the population, were dependent on a large and ideologically alien state bureaucracy. Only when the masses had acquired the necessary skills in literacy and administration could the advance be resumed, and Lenin made clear that the tiny communist minority itself could not really claim competence that made it the equal of, far less the victor over, the bourgeoisie.[208] A serious shift in emphasis was visible. In 1921 he had argued that the peasantry (or rather petit-bourgeois elementalism!) had been the basic threat to the régime. Not only rural revolts but also small-scale agricultural units had scared him. Now he gave priority to cultural development. This had been among his concerns for years, but never as the prime domestic issue.[209]

He dripped this message into the party's ear without many delegates noticing. If he had put 'culture' at the top of the Congress agenda, the reaction might have been different. Softly, softly! A good deal of his speech, indeed, was given over to banter. He was at the peak of his confidence. In the evening Vyacheslav Molotov delivered the Central Committee's organisational report. It rivalled Krestinski's in the previous year for mind-numbing detail, but was also decidedly less apologetic.[210] Yet Nogin on behalf of the Revisory Commission spared little in criticism.[211] The Central Committee was not given an easy time. Lenin was exempted from maltreatment; practically everyone who castigated official practices and attitudes managed somehow to cloak themselves with the legitimacy of the leader's past words. Mykola Skrypnik acclaimed Lenin's reference to the Ukraine's status as an independent republic.[212] Preobrazhenski, however, was one of the exceptions. He derided the Politburo's interference even in questions about the price of individual food items, and expressed doubt that Politburo members such as Stalin could reasonably be entrusted with simultaneous tenure of several governmental and party posts.[213] Preobrazhenski nevertheless had no cogent answer to the problems he identified. His recommendation for the formation of an Econburo to accompany the Politburo, as Lenin commented, would not have been easy to demarcate.[214] Nikolai Osinski tried to keep the central party leaders under attack. He explained that he had tried in vain to get a debate on the agrarian question in the Politburo, the Central Committee or the recent Party Conferences.[215] Lenin's unwillingness to discuss the agrarian underpinnings of the New Economic Policy was highlighted. But to no effect. The Congress held stoutly to its agreed agenda.

Next day, at session three, Lenin was attacked by Workers' Opposition leader Aleksandr Shlyapnikov (who nevertheless referred to him as Vladimir Ilich).[216] An internal party grouping that should have been ended its life in the previous year was far from being moribund. There were also criticisms of Lenin which were non-factional in origin. Dmitri Manuilski, a Bolshevik leader in Kiev, objected to his talking of Ukraine as an independent republic. Lenin's will to maintain the public fiction of several independent republics attracted the Skrypniks and repelled the Manuilskis, and laid a basis for a roaring controversy later in 1922.[217] Noticeable, too, was Manuilski's statement that Lenin was out of touch with developments in Ukraine.[218] Manuilski claimed to have put Lenin right in private conversation. Such condescension to him was an early sign that the next political generation was ready to prove its virility. Trotski rallied to Lenin. In a wide-ranging contribution he defended the New Economic Policy, the 'link' with the peasants, the campaign against factions, the use of specialists.[219]

Lenin was pleased that no one had called for the New Economic Policy's abandonment; and, in mock self-disdain, he turned to critics such as Yuri Larin and noted that the 'terroristic power' that had vanquished the world's armies and installed a dictatorship of the proletariat had yet to win victory over 'Larin's army': 'Here we have a total defeat!.'[220] Contentedly he returned to his convalescence and to the wires from Genoa. The Congress could proceed without him. At session four, Molotov was given a further grilling. Lenin declined to assist: it was enough for Lenin that the political and organisational reports of the Central Committee were passed by a huge majority.[221] Discussion was resumed on the Workers' Opposition. Aaron Solts from the Central Control Commission accused Shlyapnikov of gross misbehaviour. Shlyapnikov responded in kind. At the fifth session, on 29 March, S. P. Medvedev and Aleksandra Kollontai took Shlyapnikov's side.[222] Predictably, Solts's motion was accepted and the Congress transferred its attention to Zinoviev's report on the Communist International. Mikhail Tomski, rehabilitated after his extraordinary dispute with Lenin in April 1921, followed with a report on the trade unions, which urged that strikes should be permitted in state enterprises as well as in the private sector.[223] Surprisingly Trotski yet again spoke in support. At session six, he explained that his arguments for the strict subordination of the trade unions to the state in the controversy before the Tenth Party Congress was a corollary to his failure to persuade the Central Committee to drop grain requisitioning in February 1920. If a degree of private profit could not be allowed in trade, an even heavier emphasis on state control would be needed to restore production.[224]

Trotski's rationalisation of his earlier case was incredible to those delegates who could remember that he had continued to call for the militarisation of the trade unions even after the Politburo, with his approval, had opted to introduce a graduated tax in kind in February 1921; but, in tactical terms, his words had an emollient effect upon the Congress. They offered the chance for Trotski and Lenin to bury their differences. As in the Civil War, they agreed about most aspects of Bolshevik party policy.

This display of amity among the central party leaders was ruined when speakers took exception to the apparently uncontroversial assertion by Trotski that 'specialists' and not workers should influence industrial decisions. Trotski wanted managers to be allowed to manage. Lenin's stress upon the tasks of cultural and technical development were not much at variance with Trotski's ideas. But Lenin wanted a quiet Congress, not a dispute on authority inside factories – and anyway he probably did not want to put things as unreservedly as Trotski. Tomski bridled at Trotski's remark, and a short' but bitter clash followed between Tomski and Trotski. Tomski made a forceful case that trade unions should retain a place at the table of management in each factory.[225] But the storm blew over. The Congress delegates, like Lenin, desired to avoid serious upset. As for Trotski, he proceeded to deliver a report on the Red Army.[226] The organisation of the armed forces had again become contentious in recent months. Mikhail Frunze, presently Ukrainian government deputy premier, called for the acceptance of a 'uniform military doctrine' which in Trotski's opinion was full of abstract theorising. Trotski stressed competence, qualifications, professional training. Congress listened to him respectfully and moved on to other business.[227]

Further debates followed on 30 March. Grigori Sokolnikov reported on the financial situation, frequently invoking the authority of his absent comrade Lenin.[228] His optimism was challenged by Preobrazhenski (who, interestingly for someone who was later charged with having an anti-peasant attitude, suggested that state was imposing too high an interest rate in its loans to the peasantry).[229] G. I. Lomov asserted that Sokolnikov as People's Commissar for Finances had turned state industrial trusts into nests of speculative activity.[230] 'Speculation' was a dirty word in the Bolshevik lexicon. Pyatakov joined in the assault on him. Sokolnikov, he declared, had deprived

vital state industries of investment. Pyatakov and his supporters on the
left of the party did not urge a return to War Communism, but their
vision of the New Economic Policy included a continued commitment
to the priority of state-owned, large-scale industry.[231]

Consequently the fact that no one challenged the desirability of the
New Economic Policy did not preclude the potential for dispute about
what should be its limits. Lenin had stated that there should be no
further retreat; but Preobrazhenski and Pyatakov at the Congress –
and they had Trotski's tacit sympathy – felt that the retreat on central
state investment and planning was already excessive. The Bolshevik
'leftists', as they were soon to be described, were a bomb waiting to
explode. They had detonated themselves in a fairly controlled fashion
at the Party Conferences in 1921, and it was only a stroke of luck that
discouraged them from going further at the Eleventh Congress. If
Trotski had placed himself at their head, much more destruction would
have been wreaked. Perhaps the memory of the 'trade union discussion'
discouraged him. Moreover, he was reluctant to make too bold a
rupture with his Politburo colleagues at a time of Lenin's illness. For
once, he saw sense. Sokolnikov took his castigation like a man, merely
grumbling that Pyatakov seemed to have forgotten that the Congress
had already sanctioned the year's activities of the Central Committee.[232] The wish to heal Bolshevism's rifts took over again. At the ninth
session on 31 March, Zinoviev reported on party recruitment measures.
Deferential remarks abounded. Zinoviev opined in carefree manner:
'The dictatorship of the proletariat, as comrade Lenin says, is a very
cruel thing.' Such sententiousness was used to justify the closure of
further recruitment to the party on the grounds that far too many
careerists and non-Bolshevik socialists had infiltrated the ranks.[233] His
ideas were discussed at session ten; and Mikhail Kalinin, welcoming
the consensual climate of debate, asserted with pleasure that opponents
of the Central Committee – Larin as well as Osinski and
Preobrazhenski – had been directly responsible for one fifth of its
decisions.[234]

The resolutions on trade unions and on finance were passed by vast
majorities at session eleven on 2 April.[235] The sole disturbance came
from disagreements on the agrarian question. Under pressure from
delegates, the party leadership had relented its ban on discussing it at
the Congress. A Congress section had been set up to formulate a
resolution 'work in the countryside'. Osinski was chosen to report on
its behalf. Lenin was unhappy with the change of plan and moved to
prevent any full-scale attack on the party's agrarian reforms. He had

written to Osinski urging that the draft resolution should be phrased so as not to tie the Central Committee's hands in future. A verbal fudge, he maintained, was desirable. If there was to be a formal resolution, moreover, Lenin wanted to include clauses on permission for the hiring of labour and the renting of land. Osinski concurred, and – with only slight modifications – Lenin's proposed clauses were accepted by the section.[236]

Ukrainian Bolshevik leader V. Y. Chubar made an attempt on the Congress floor to have them excised. Not for the last time, a leading Ukrainian Bolshevik sought a hardening of the official line on agriculture.[237] Osinski personalised his retort: 'Comrade Lenin clearly tried to fix this in place, and comrade Chubar is coming out precisely against it.' This did the trick. Osinski's presentation became official party policy.[238] A final session was held that evening. Lenin, the ghost at the feast for most of the Congress, returned to hear Kamenev announce the results of the elections to the Central Committee. There were, this time, few surprises. Some newcomers grabbed places. Both Frunze and Chubar were rewarded for their outspokenness, and even Anastas Mikoyan's criticism of Zinoviev did not prevent him from being made a candidate member. The door remained closed to most past supporters of Trotski. Preobrazhenski, Serebryakov and Krestinski were kept out; only A. A. Andreev and Christian Rakovsky, who had been less strident in Trotski's cause in 1920–1921, made a successful return. But effort was made to inhibit overt dissension: the normal announcement of the order of popularity in the elections was omitted.[239] Lenin closed the proceeding with a brief address. His last words were more a warning than a confident statement of fact: 'Should there be voices is our party speaking against this ultra-slow and ultra-cautious movement, they will be isolated. The party as a whole has grasped this and now will show by its deeds that it has comprehended the need at the present moment to construct its work precisely in this fashion and only in this fashion. And once we have understood this, we will succeed in achieving our objective!'[240]

9 Testament to a Revolution

ILLNESS AND PRECAUTIONS

Dispute is basic to politics. But discussions among ambitious and even vengeful leaders are often softened by the knowledge that a common will needs to be displayed to society. This is especially necessary for a dictatorial élite. The risk of opposition increases if the general public perceives that the leaders are divided. Prominent Bolsheviks were not unusual in trying to hide away the altercations among themselves. By and large they had succeeded since the Tenth Party Congress. Most people knew next to nothing about the Bolshevik wrangling about the New Economic Policy; and the rumours about dissension in the party, which had came to the ears of those observers with friends in the party's higher échelons, were dying down. The display of unity at the Eleventh Party Congress reinforced the image of a unified central leadership.

Reality was different. And it was Lenin, despite his recurrent calls to his leading comrades to stick together and avoid dispute, who instigated the greatest controversies in the second half of 1922. He turned angrily upon most of his colleagues, one by one, over several evolving policies. There were rows about foreign trade, about state bureaucracy, about the Soviet constitution, about party administration and even about the division of responsibilities among these same colleagues. Feelings about the New Economic Policy still ran high. Bolshevik leaders, including Lenin, were irked that a retreat from supposedly socialist policies had been forced upon them. Their awareness of the country's political and economic weaknesses served to make them edgier still. Not only Lenin and Trotski but also the rest of the Politburo peppered their public statements with references to the French Revolution and its eventual retreat from ideological radicalism. The possibility that the New Economic Policy might initiate a counter-revolution from within was in their thoughts and was sustained by the stridency of attacks made by non-Bolshevik Russians in emigration who predicted this very dénouement. N. Ustryalov, a Kadet, urged his friends to return to Russia to help rebuild Russia and ready themselves for the attrition of Bolshevism; and Mensheviks and Socialist-Revolutionaries constantly declared that the economic retreat would have to be followed by political concessions. Would the glory of the October Revolution be buried in the mud of a capitalist restoration?

Lenin's illness reduced the chances for differences of opinion remaining amicable in the Politburo. He had always had a tendency towards intemperance if he was not in control of a situation. He hated his enforced convalescence at the Gorki mansion-cum-sanatorium, and did everything possible to keep in touch with Moscow. A direct telephone line was installed, which saved him from having to route his calls via Podolsk.[1] He had a library of four hundred volumes and cinema facilities were also installed, and a Rolls-Royce bought in London in 1921 by Foreign Trade Commissar Lev Krasin was kept for him in the garage.[2] But he still resented the slackening of his grasp on decisions made in party and government. Furthermore, his choleric propensities were aggravated by a medical condition which involved sharp swings between elation and depression. Through the early months of 1922 his irascibility had worsened as the problems with his health recurred and his authority became harder for him to impose.

On 25 May 1922 his difficulties almost became terminal when he suffered a major stroke at Gorki.[3] Colleagues had become accustomed to his determination to participate in politics from a distance, and the failure of the doctors to predict the event lulled them into assuming that he might soon recover completely. His headaches and insomnia in 1921 had been seriously debilitating, but no permanent disablement seemed in prospect. The stroke was a shock for everyone. He had kept his worst symptoms a secret from all around him. There were only three exceptions to this: his personal doctor F. A. Gete and his personal bodyguard Petr Pakaln;[4] and another doctor, L. O. Darkevich, who examined him as recently as 4 March. With Darkevich his mood was especially gloomy: 'Could it not be, of course, that this carries the threat of madness?' But Darkevich tried to reassure him that no such diagnosis was plausible.[5] Even so, Lenin kept his own pessimistic counsel.[6] At the news of his major stroke, he could no longer sieve out what he wanted the doctors to know. A group of them were sent out from Moscow to attend him, and were shocked by his condition. His whole right side was affected. The arm and leg were immobilised, and he lost the capacity of speech. Professors Förster and Klemperer from Germany were among the distinguished specialists who attended him. The Gorki sanatorium by early June had more doctors than patients and administrative staff.[7]

The central party leaders surveyed these developments carefully, deciding to make no public announcement. It was four weeks after the stroke before *Pravda* carried a medical bulletin. By then the Politburo was facing difficulty in explaining Lenin's protracted absence from Moscow. Even so, the bulletin made light of the illness and emphasised that a rapid recuperation was anticipated. No reference to a stroke was made.[8] Lenin was later to joke bitterly about such evasiveness: 'I used to think that the best diplomats were in The Hague, but it turns out that they're in Moscow: they're the doctors who composed bulletins about my illness.'[9]

He had coped with bouts of ill-health for many years. As a youth he had been as strong as an ox, but an ox who had been looked after well by his mother and their servants. Both a steady life-style and regular meals were difficult to guarantee once he left home for St Petersburg in autumn 1893. Certainly he had enough money for decent lodgings. And yet the circumstances of a clandestine revolutionary, even after he departed for the emigration in 1900, were disruptive. The constant demands of being a writer as well as an organiser took their toll on him, and the nervous strain of his polemics aggravated his malaise. He suffered an ulcer in 1893, a bout of pneumonia in 1895, insomnia in 1899. Both the ulcer and the insomnia were recurrent problems.[10] Lenin had always been attentive about his health. His warders in prison in 1895 were impressed by his daily routine of press-ups and trunk-rolls, and Nikolai Valentinov recalled how unusual he was among fellow revolutionaries in his determination to stay fit.[11] Yet there was no relief from political irritations. His 'nerves' were a topic of complaint by him, especially during and immediately after disputes with party opponents.[12] He often wrote to his relatives about his need to get back on an even physical keel. Exhaustion caused by his ulcer and the sleeplessness was made worse by severe headaches. The loss of his youthful rude health agitated him. Krupskaya recorded the change: 'He was not weak, but he was also not particularly strong.'[13] Doctors were often consulted by him. In Switzerland, at some unspecified time after 1900, he had visited a prominent medical specialist. The verdict was blunt: 'C'est le cerveau.'[14]

Lenin was alarmed. His father had died of cerebral atherosclerosis in 1886, and he must have surmised that the same fate might await him. Problems continued in the ensuing years. Even before the assassination attempt in August 1918, his insomnia, nerves and headaches had discomfited him badly.[15] The symptoms persisted in the Civil War. Maksim Gorki heard from Lenin about the pains in his head; his sister

Mariya remarked how savage they had become by the winter of 1920–1921. Professor Osipov, one of Lenin's doctors, was later to discover about incidents involving more than headaches. When out hunting in the woods, the Soviet leader had slumped down on a tree stump, clutching and rubbing his right leg. On that occasion Lenin had tried to make little of his difficulty: 'My leg's tired, I've got pins and needles.'[16] These were to be hints for Osipov that Lenin had almost certainly suffered a series of mild strokes. Indeed there had been a number of 'partial attacks' which involved a temporary loss of consciousness lasting from between twenty minutes and two hours.[17]

Professor Klemperer in early 1922 had not implausibly proposed that his troubles might stem from lead-poisoning brought about by the two bullets still trapped in his head after the assassination attempt. One of these was removed by surgery on 23 April 1922 in the Soldatenkovski Hospital in Moscow.[18] In advance of the operation, Lenin had yielded a little to his doctors' recommendations by agreeing to reduce his workload.[19] On 11 April he had returned to his project for the re-organisation of Sovnarkom in his temporary absence. As previously, he wanted to divide the various People's Commissariats into two groups and to allot one group to Rykov and the other to Tsyurupa. The novelty was that Lenin now urged that Rykov and Tsyurupa should use the Workers' and Peasants' Inspectorate (or Rabkrin) as their main administrative apparatus of supervision.[20] Trotski gave a scathing response. He despised Rabkrin as well as its chairman Stalin; he also reasoned against Lenin that the proposal in general depended excessively on amicable relations existing between Rykov and Tsyurupa. Lenin was simply juggling with personalities and inter-institutional rules whereas, according to Trotski, the solution to the chaos in economic policy and its implementation was to elevate the State Planning Commission to the position of supreme control over industrial investment and production.[21]

The sole full member of the Politburo to approve Lenin's scheme was Kamenev.[22] Lenin irritatedly replied on 5 May, defending Rabkrin and rejecting Trotski's demands about the State Planning Commission.[23] It was a complicated disagreement. If Trotski had a correct perception of the weakness of the scheme Lenin advocated, Lenin was right to speculate that Trotski was using the occasion to trundle out old hobby-horses from their stables.

Trotski and Lenin argued as if it could be taken for granted that Lenin would shortly return to his political jobs. The scheme proposed by him was carefully limited to the matter of his Sovnarkom deputies and their functions. He thereby implied that he would always be in ultimate command and that his incapacity would be temporary. Not even his stroke on 25 May 1922 changed his attitude, and Lenin was determined to resume his full duties with all speed. His doctors did not discourage him in his ultimate aim; none seems to have appreciated the gravity of his condition.[24] They insisted, however, that he should not return to work until such time as his health had drastically improved. This was evidently going to involve many weeks. He remained at Gorki the entire summer, and this time there were to be no trips to Moscow and to his office in the Kremlin; he had to content himself with being visited by friends and associates and being tended by his wife Krupskaya and his sister Mariya.[25] His recuperative capacity surprised the medical staff. By 13 July he was writing to his secretary Lidiya Fotieva: 'You can congratulate me on my recovery. The proof: my handwriting, which is *beginning* to become human.'[26] He hustled his doctors into letting him read newspapers again. He even began to hold forth to his colleagues about their own medical problems. In late August he instructed A. I. Sviderski not to return to Moscow political life until after mastering the use of his new false teeth and becoming fully fit again. The Russian Socialist Federal Soviet Republic's most reluctant patient advised other patients to take their own convalescence seriously.[27]

Lenin, his bossy exuberance and his eye for detail restored to him, planned to re-enter political activity and its intensity. His hopes were misplaced. The stroke of 25 May had been of major dimensions and, as Professor Osipov indicated, had probably occurred at the end of a sequence of several lighter strokes. Each of them stemmed from a sudden inadequate supply of blood, known as ischaemia, to the brain.[28] His symptoms, as manifested in mid-1922, seemed to Osipov to constitute a classic case of atherosclerosis: the clogging up of the arteries with a fatty material which has a fibrous covering and forms a sort of plaque within the arteries.

Other hypotheses were confidentially canvassed within the medical fraternity. The most extraordinary was the possibility that the bullets from the August 1918 attempt on his life had been tipped with poison. This made good copy for *Pravda*, but the doctors no sooner had debated it than they rejected it. Whereas a South American Indian who smears his arrow with curare can shoot a deadly substance into the body of his intended victim, a Russian Socialist Revolutionary would have burned off the toxin simply by firing the gun.[29] Even so, it cannot be wholly discounted that the attempted assassination had caused lasting serious damage. The black-outs he had suffered in the Civil War, for example, may have been signs of an epilepsy induced by the bullets. It remains possible, too, that Klemperer's removal of the bullet disturbed the brain again and brought about the major stroke a few weeks later. Another hypothesis was that Lenin was suffering merely from massive over-work. No doubt his workload reinforced the symptoms; but the majority opinion among Lenin's doctors was surely right to reject the idea that therein lay the basic cause of the disease (even though this did not prevent Politburo from touting it in the press in order to reinforce the Bolshevik leader's image as a self-sacrificing benefactor of Soviet society).[30]

There was another potential diagnosis which the Politburo withheld from public deliberations: namely that Lenin had syphilis. Rumours to this effect were already doing the rounds in Moscow, and continued in subsequent years.[31] It cannot be ruled out that a sexual liaison before the Revolution infected him or that he inherited syphilis from his father. The questions asked of him by the specialists show that the same thought had occurred to them.[32] Nevertheless Lenin also impressed them with his naïveté about such a possibility even though he made an effort to consult lots of medical textbooks so as to diagnose himself.[33] Many symptoms indeed point away from syphilis as the principal cause. Lenin had had problems since he had been a young man; and yet the onset of strokes to sufferers of syphilis usually occurs within fifteen years of the original infection. Furthermore, periods of remission from the progressive paralysis are typically few whereas Lenin had led a normal life for most of his career.[34] Professor Averbakh inspected him in 1922 and found no significant defect in his eyes[35] In addition, Lenin experienced hallucinations in the later stages of his disease.[36] Such phenomena are hard to reconcile with a diagnosis of syphilis. On the other hand, it may be that Lenin had had some extra-marital liaison more recently, perhaps even since the October Revolution, and that Averbakh's test was unable to detect a syphilitic condition in its early stages. As yet we cannot say beyond peradventure that Lenin was not suffering from it.

No wonder his doctors were perplexed. He could easily have been the victim of more than one illness; and not all his medical difficulties were necessarily linked to the disease which eventually killed. Even now the identity of this disease cannot be stated with certainty. Nevertheless, while several hypotheses cannot be definitively repudiated, the evidence on balance suggests that his principal affliction in mid-1922 is likely to have been an hereditary weakness resulting in atherosclerosis.

Atherosclerosis, which is one of the forms of what is still commonly referred to as arteriosclerosis or 'hardening of the arteries', is often associated with hypertension. This occurs when there is persistent high pressure of blood against the arterial walls. Research has linked hypertension, moreover, to various types of person. He or she may be obese or eat too much salt or smoke nicotine. It is true that Vladmir Ilich Lenin was stocky rather than fat and that he was militantly anti-smoking. Admittedly, too, we have no information about how much salt went into his diet). But other characteristics fit him closely. Hypertension is strongly associated with heredity – and Lenin's father had died of a brain haemorrhage; and his siblings died from analogous conditions. Hypertension also tends to affect both those with an aggressive, hyperactive temperament and those working in a stressful environment.[37] This perfectly characterised Lenin's circumstances. He had had various medicaments for his symptoms, but the worsening symptoms before 1921 had not been treated with the principal measures that might have prevented a stroke: a protracted rest and a permanent withdrawal from activities involving stress. Nothing short of his retirement from politics would have sufficed, and even then there would have been no assurance of effective prevention. There was no known cure for atherosclerosis – and none exists today. After Lenin's major stroke had taken place, furthermore, the chances of recovery had greatly narrowed; and they were rendered exiguous in the extreme by his resolve to resume his duties just as soon as the initial debilitation had disappeared. His thinking was medically disastrous. Lenin's affected arteries were linked to the brain, and the major stroke was a sign that a worse one might yet occur.

Yet Lenin simply could not understand a life outside politics. Even if he had retired and taken up study and writing, political questions would have dominated his mind. One of his exasperated doctors exclaimed: 'Just you try and stop a silkworm weaving his thread.'[38] Nor would his thinking on politics have been more measured and restrained. Strokes paralysing the right side of the body may simultaneously produce uncontrollable violent alternations of mood. Elation can give way to depression, and depression back to elation. The patient may laugh or sob for no explicable reason.[39] Lenin's policies of spring 1922 were savage even by his standards. Bishops and priests should be killed, Socialist Revolutionaries and Mensheviks killed, fraudulent bureaucrats killed. It was as if he could not control himself; and perhaps this was instinctively felt by those colleagues who moderated the measures he demanded at the time.[40]

The nature of this medico-political linkage resists conclusive analysis. In particular, the hundreds of pages of accounts kept by his doctors after his stroke contain information written within the framework of assumptions superseded by decades of clinical science's development. Nevertheless one salient fact requires consideration. This is that the violent changes of mood did not develop for the first time in the last years of his life. Nikolai Valentinov, who had known the Bolshevik leader in Switzerland, was impressed by the similarity between his own memory of the Lenin at the turn of the century and the memoirs by Bolshevik leaders about the Lenin who had suffered a major stroke. Valentinov also noted that, in the pre-revolutionary years, it was usually a crisis in politics which precipitated the elation or the depression in Lenin.[41] The contemporary intra-party situation seemed to influence his physical condition. This by no stretch of the imagination means that the disease originated in politics. The interpretation is rather that his symptoms were aggravated by his public concerns, and that the chemistry of his condition would have existed regardless of his political involvement. As his health worsened, furthermore, the vehemence of his political declarations increased. In mid-1922 he was consequently in no mood to be crossed by friend or foe about the slightest aspect of his version of the New Economic Policy.

THE FOREIGN TRADE CONTROVERSY

The first object of his wrath was the proposal, first made by Vladimir Milyutin who until then had been close to Lenin in his thinking, to repeal the state monopoly on foreign trade which had been introduced on 22 April 1918. Lenin had always thought that the New Economic Policy would involve severe restrictions upon the influence of capitalists.[42] But industrial recovery was slow. The flow of capital into the country through the signature of concessionary agreements was negligible. The various trade treaties obtained by the Russian Socialist Federal Soviet Republic were encouraging; but the unilateral abrogation of the debts contracted by Nikolai II and the Provisional Government had inhibited potential investment.

Several leading Bolsheviks began to argue that the business of imports and exports therefore be partially denationalised. Milyutin, as Soviet representative at the Baltic economic talks in the Latvian capital of Riga in late October 1921, learned how reluctant were foreign entrepreneurs to do their deals only with the Soviet government; and he found support from Kamenev for the idea that, if imports of private foreign capital were to be allowed through the projected concessions, there were no ideological or practical reasons for prohibiting private import and export of goods. The People's Commissariat of Foreign Trade was criticised for its inefficiencies. If a repeal was not allowed, Milyutin asserted, smuggling on a massive scale would occur.[43] Lenin, while not denying that the Commissariat was highly bureaucratic, was appalled by talk of denationalisation. With the support of Leonid Krasin, People's Commissar for Foreign Trade, he had secured the rejection of Milyutin's proposal by the Politburo on 10 November 1921.[44] Other figures in the party leadership rallied to Milyutin. For instance, Finance Commissar G. Y. Sokolnikov argued that private exports should be permitted so long as they involved payment in the form of foodstuffs which would be brought back into the country. Lenin objected in writing to Kamenev that there was nothing wrong with the monopoly if only adequate 'terror' were to be applied to those foreigners who were 'buying up our officials with bribes'.[45]

By early March 1922 he had appeared to have won;[46] but already on 15 May he was worried enough to write to Stalin as General Secretary of the Central Committee requesting the Politburo's approval for a directive confirming the monopoly.[47] The rumblings inside the party leadership in favour of repeal were said by N. N. Krestinski, the Soviet diplomatic plenipotentiary in Berlin, to be inducing businessmen to delay making potential deals with the Soviet government. The Politburo accepted Lenin's request on 22 May – only three days before his major stroke.[48]

Yet Kamenev and Bukharin were unpersuaded by his arguments; and even Stalin, who agreed to the issuance of the directive, had come to believe that 'a *weakening* of the monopoly would become inevitable' (as he remarked on his copy of Lenin's letter).[49] Lenin's summer convalescence gave the proponents of denationalisation their chance. On 8 August, in his absence, the People's Commissariat of Foreign Trade was discussed by the Central Committee. Trotski, like Lenin, was hostile to the repeal of the state monopoly. He favoured the making of a public announcement that the monopoly would stay in force; but, after much debate, he was defeated.[50] If Lenin and Trotski had trusted each other better, things might have been different. But the central party leaders in any case needed to determine policy one way or the other. At Kamenev's instigation, foreign trade came before the Politburo yet again on 7 September.[51] Sensitivity, perhaps even dread, about Lenin's opinions persisted, and the Politburo decided a week later to keep Lenin closely informed about the latest shifts in its policy.[52] Possibly Kamenev had sensed the possibility that Lenin might be about to abandon his own position. Negotiations between Krasin and the British metallurgical firm of Urquhart had led to a draft contract. On 12 September, Lenin wrote to the Politburo brusquely urging that the People's Commissariat of Foreign Trade should be ignored. Krasin, he declared, had envisaged a concession which was 'a cabal and a daylight robbery'.[53]

Presumably Kamenev concluded that the draft contract demonstrated that the People's Commissariat would always be less competent than the private sector. Lenin, however, did not make this inference. For him, the episode confirmed the desirability of applying greater control over the activities and personnel of the People's Commissariat of Foreign Trade. The controversy was bound to erupt as soon as he succeeded in participating more closely in the deliberations of the central party leadership. The advocates of the repeal of the state monopoly ignored his wishes at their peril. On 6 October the Central Committee plenum again considered the topic of imports and exports.[54]

There the People's Commissar of Finances, G. Y. Sokolnikov, made a subtle proposal by demanding only a partial repeal. He cautiously limited himself to calling for 'temporary permission for imports and exports in particular categories of goods or with application to particular frontiers'.[55] Lenin could not attend the plenum, but contacted participants including Stalin and Trotski. He wrote, too, to the Central Committee on 13 October, repeating his critical innuendoes about Sokolnikov (who was said to be a 'lover of paradox') and claiming that the decision had been imposed on a tired Central Committee which was ill-informed and would have 'voted for anything after a few minutes *e basta*'. Lenin argued that to open the ports of Petrograd and Novorossiisk would immediately lead to the country being devoid of flax, which was worth three times as much abroad, and would deprive the existing inflow of gold bullion to the Commissariat of Finances through sales of Russian raw materials. Excise duties would not bring in the amount of revenues expected by Sokolnikov. But the major reason for keeping the monopoly, according to Lenin, would be the likelihood that the peasantry would otherwise defy the government. Since its inception, he had stressed that the New Economic Policy should involve the maintenance of state control over trade; and he saw terrible dangers in any lessening of control: 'A specialist-smuggler at the frontier is one thing; but it is entirely another matter to have the *entire* peasantry which will defend itself *as a whole* and fight against any authority trying to deprive it of its "own" profit'.[56]

Lenin, sensing that he could not quickly overturn Sokolnikov's proposal, called for a postponement of implementation for two whole months.[57] Stalin was by then entirely on the side of Milyutin and Sokolnikov; and not only Kamenev but also Zinoviev and Bukharin were firmly convinced that 'the Old Man' had got it wrong and that the economy's desperate condition necessitated the repeal.[58] But Stalin led the way by telling the Central Committee, as its General Secretary, that he was willing to retreat in the face of Lenin's 'insistent proposal'. After consulting the other members, he announced the postponement requested by Lenin.[59]

Active supporters of Lenin in the party leadership's front rank were few. Only Krasin, whose objections were now circulated to all Central Committee members with Stalin's consent, backed him.[60] In normal health, Lenin could have managed in this situation; and indeed he was sufficiently recovered to take the chair at meetings again. On 12 October 1922 he had participated directly in a Politburo session. Next day he led the discussions at the Council of Labour and Defence. On 17 October he took his place in Sovnarkom.[61] The old routines were being resumed. In deference to medical advice he intercalated extra 'rest days' into his working week; but even this particular self-restraint ceased in the following month.[62] He was so resilient that on 15 November he insisted on receiving seven separate visitors. One of them, the Italian communist Amadeo Bordiga, discussed European politics with him for an hour and forty minutes.[63] Lenin also made public appearances, most notably at the Fourth Congress of the Communist International on 13 November when he gave a lengthy address.[64] A week later he spoke to the Moscow Soviet.[65] His spirits rose; his recovery seemed at least a possibility despite all his gloominess in the summer. Delegates to the Communist International Congress who had not seen him before were surprised by his vigour on the platform. As the Congress drew to its close, Lenin began to contemplate the debate on foreign trade postponed until the forthcoming Central Committee plenum

Nevertheless signs had been visible in previous weeks that he was not as well as he seemed. At Sovnarkom on 24 October, as Kamenev noticed, Lenin had criticised a draft law without realising that he had lost his place in his notes; he had even read aloud the same passage twice. Kamenev, Stalin and Zinoviev met to discuss his condition and concluded, understatedly, that 'Vladimir Ilich easily gets tired and obviously gets over-tired'.[66] A month later their concerns were proved realistic. The severe aches and pains returned on 25 November, and Lenin was incapacitated. The duty secretary's report was clipped and to the point: 'Vladimir Ilich is ill, he was in the office for only five minutes, dictated three letters by telephone, to which he wanted to have replies at a later date. Mariya Ilinichna [Lenin's sister] said not to bother him with anything – and that, if he himself enquires after the answers, to ask whomever is appropriate. No receptions, no errands in the mean while.'[67] The doctors this time were successful in their insistence: Lenin was to stop work absolutely for a whole week.[68]

He did not comply at all. He still used the phone, and there were few days when he did not come into the office.[69] Reviewing their patient's condition on Sunday, 2 December 1922, again the doctors insisted: he was to ease down his rota of duties. He was forbidden to chair the Politburo on Tuesday and was allowed to do so only briefly on Thursday; and it was stated that he should go off to Gorki for a few days' rest immediately afterwards.[70] Lenin was a tough old bird and in fact kept on working; but on 13 December, at eleven o'clock in the morning, his doctors advised that he would be seriously at risk if his disobedience continued. Total rest was prescribed.[71] Lenin obeyed, but only after arranging contingency measures for the Central Committee plenum. His contacts over the previous six weeks, when he had seen and written to every Politburo member, indicated that he could not count on victory in the controversy over the state foreign-trade monopoly. Krasin would not suffice as an ally. By midday on 12 December Lenin had made up his mind to ask Trotski for support.[72] First he sent a brief note.[73] To Lenin's delight, Trotski replied positively the same day.[74] The old difficulties remained. Trotski argued that all foreign trade should be placed under the authority of the State Planning Commission so that the revenues from import and exports could be channelled directly into industrial capital investment.[75] For Lenin, this was too reminiscent of War Communism for comfort; and, on 13 December, he persuaded Trotski that they could lay this particular issue aside while campaigning in common for the retention and strengthening of the state foreign-trade monopoly.[76]

By 15 December he rejoiced: 'I consider that we have reached total agreement. I ask you to announce our solidarity at the plenum.'[77] The reactions of the other Politburo members can well be imagined. Their relief that they would not have to face him in the Central Committee was lessened by the discovery that the proxy defender of the monopoly would be not Krasin, whose People's Commissariat of Foreign Trade was acknowledged even by Lenin to have its faults, but by Trotski. Lenin had turned the tables on them.

The Central Committee was to consider the premises of foreign trade on 18 December. Lenin sent it a letter rejecting the criticisms of Krasin made by Bukharin, who had emerged as the theorist among those calling for the abolition of the state monopoly. It is striking how similar were Lenin's arguments to those he had used in inaugurating the New Economic Policy. He continued to believe that the maintenance of the government's economic control was vital. If private trade abroad were to be allowed, he asserted, the exporter would 'mobilise around himself the entire peasantry in the fastest, surest and unequivocal fashion'. Only the interests of 'the speculator, the petit bourgeois and the higher sections of the peasantry' would be served; and, when flax sold for fourteen roubles in Russia and for only four and a half roubles in Britain, it was easy to predict an outflow of crucially-needed raw materials from the country. Control, control, control![78] On 15 December Lenin, pleased with his work, wrote to Stalin and emphasised that his own absence should not be allowed to deflect the Central Committee from a final decision on foreign trade: 'I have now completed the winding up of my affairs and can calmly depart.' Zinoviev and Stalin had already indicated that they would not oppose Lenin's standpoint on foreign trade, and Lenin had heard that Kamenev was rumoured to feel likewise. The Central Committee duly confirmed a dutiful proposal by Zinoviev for the retention of the state monopoly.[79] From the sanatorium a message was sent to Trotski on 21 December: 'It is as if we've succeeded by a simple movement of manoeuvre in capturing a position without having to fire a shot.'[80]

FRIENDS AND COMRADES

The formation of the Lenin–Trotski alliance confounded the hopes of Stalin and Zinoviev of excising Trotski from the core of the central party leadership. Nothing had seemed so unlikely earlier in the year. Trotski had been highly suspect to Lenin since the 'trade union controversy', and Stalin had been among Lenin's most valuable supporters in limiting the influence of the party's left wing.[81]

Lenin's health problems in the winter of 1921–1922 had pushed him closer and closer to Stalin. Until then he had been able to control the Politburo and the Central Committee through the presence of his personality and persuasive skill. But an adjutant was required to run the party machinery in the provinces. Vyacheslav Molotov was politically more reliable for Lenin than his trio of predecessors: Krestinski, Serebryakov and Preobrazhenski. But Molotov did not enjoy the local party respect crucial for keeping the party together.[82] Lenin needed a new Sverdlov, and he thought Stalin would fit the bill despite the unsettled relations between them in the past. Before the February Revolution Lenin, despite describing him as 'the wonderful Georgian',[83] had conflicted with him over the State Duma, over the party's agrarian policy, over relations with the Mensheviks; and in 1917 Stalin had not initially welcomed *The April Theses* or the call by Lenin, after the 'July Days', to drop the slogan of 'All Power to the Soviets'.[84] After the October Revolution there continued to be friction between them. Lenin and Stalin differed about the prospects of European socialist revolution, about the employment of Imperial officers in the Red Army and about the 'national question'. In 1920, moreover, Lenin had objected to the maverick behaviour of Stalin in the Red Army's invasion of Poland.[85]

Consequently it is erroneous to suppose that Lenin was entirely ignorant about the kind of politician whose candidacy for appointment as General Secretary of the Central Committee he accepted after the Eleventh Party Congress.[86] In any case, bad blood had not come between Lenin and Stalin; as yet their disputes had been kept within the bounds of a party which thrived on polemics. Stalin had never been a yes-man; he had always been prickly, volatile and rumbustious; he had the reputation of an administrator who could impose his will upon any recalcitrant organisation. Just such a colleague – a colleague who had appeared to concur with Lenin on most fundamental current issues – was to Lenin's liking as he himself made arrangements for his convalescence.

The purpose of the General Secretaryship, a newly-invented post, was to supply its holder with the full authority of the Central Committee in overseeing the implementation of central party directives and co-ordinating the central party apparatus. It was a substantial job for a substantial politician. Naturally it was not meant to accord plenipotentiary power. On the contrary, the rule that the Central Committee had no permanent chairman remained in place.[87] Molotov after the Tenth Party Congress had been designated as 'the responsible secretary' of the Central Committee, and the title set him clearly apart and a little above the other secretaries. Stalin as General Secretary stood high above them. He was already a Politburo member (whereas

Molotov had only even become a candidate member when selected as 'responsible secretary'). Nevertheless the very authoritarian qualities which commended Stalin to his allies were uncongenial to others. At the Eleventh Party Congress there were several delegates who, when filling in their ballot papers for the election to the next Central Committee, had specified a wish that Stalin, Molotov and Valeryan Kuibyshev should become Central Committee secretaries.[88] How many delegates did this is unclear, but there were enough of them for their unprecedented – and probably not spontaneous – action to be discussed at the first plenum of the Central Committee after the Congress. Kamenev kept to proprieties by explaining both to the Congress and the Central Committee that the Central Committee plenum did not have to comply with the wishes of 'a certain section of delegates' by appointing Stalin. But he obviously wanted this result, and the Central Committee indeed duly appointed him.[89]

There was also concern lest Stalin's multiple tenure of posts in party and government should impede his ability to handle any one of them. Preobrazhenski had said as much at the Eleventh Party Congress.[90] At the plenum of the Central Committee it was Lenin who intervened to put minds at rest. On Lenin's initiative, Stalin was asked to find himself competent deputies for his jobs in government.[91] This was not the suggestion of someone who opposed Stalin's appointment. Nor did it indicate an underestimation of the potential power of the post. Quite the reverse: Lenin thought the General Secretaryship so important that its first holder was asked to liberate himself from governmental posts in order to discharge his duties. Lenin urged that the time had come for the entire Secretariat to be overhauled. Not only Stalin but also the other secretaries should devote themselves to internal party affairs, and the schedule of the Secretariat's opening hours should be fixed and advertised.[92]

At first Lenin and Stalin worked enjoyably together. Despite yearning to get back to the Kremlin and resume participation in Politburo and Sovnarkom meetings, Lenin kept his frustrations in check most of the time. An exception occurred in July, when he wrote to Kamenev suggesting that the Central Committee should be cut back to a membership of three: Molotov, Rykov and Kuibyshev. None of these had voting rights in the Politburo. Cheekily Lenin added that the Central Committee should have only three candidate members, Kamenev, Zinoviev and Tomski.[93] Kamenev and Zinoviev, of course, were already Politburo members. What he was trying to suggest, not too sophisticatedly, was that he did not trust the Politburo to run the party in his absence; he was willing to exclude most full members of the Central Committee from its ranks – or else, in the case of Kamenev, Zinoviev and Tomski, to reduce their status humiliatingly. His pretext was that central party leaders in general were so overworked as to endanger their health. Consequently a lengthy period of leisure was in order. So, too, was a deceleration of the rate of decision-taking. His outward appearance of care masked a determination that, in his absence, nobody should enact measures he disliked. It was almost as if he had decided that, if he was going to be ill, practically all of his colleagues should willy nilly have medical ailments diagnosed on their behalf.

It was a dotty scheme. If anyone else had made such a proposal, especially if it had involved a loss of operational control by Lenin, he would have judged the man insane.[94] Lenin on this occasion was ignored by his colleagues. His behaviour was reported to the rest of the Politburo, and the matter was dropped. If they had been feeling uncharitable, they, might have concluded that their leader was behaving rather like a spoiled child accustomed to getting his way. Instead they assumed that this was quirkiness induced by illness; and Lenin, for his part, came to recognise that he would not succeed by ranting. He had to win colleagues over to his viewpoint. A degree of self-restraint was therefore crucial.

In particular, his aim was to avoid offending Stalin, whom he had left off his proposed list of members for the diminished Central Committee:[95] tantrums could not be afforded. Lenin liaised by phone and letter with Stalin. For his part, Stalin saw the sense in travelling out to Gorki for direct consultations. He wished to allay any suspicion harboured by Lenin that the Politburo was doing things which, if he had been fit, would have incurred Lenin's displeasure. No Bolshevik leader saw Lenin in summer 1922 more than did Stalin. Between July and September the two met nine times.[96] Bukharin and Kamenev were also visitors but, strangely in view of their past collaboration,[97] Zinoviev appeared only once: possibly his Petrograd responsibilities limited his ability to do more than pay fleeting visits to Moscow.[98] Stalin cut a jovial figure with Lenin out at Gorki; he was an excellent mimic and raconteur when the mood was upon him, and cracked jokes while they discussed politics.[99] Lenin put Stalin at his ease. When knowing that the General Secretary was about to arrive, he would quietly request his sister Mariya to place a bottle of wine at Stalin's disposal. The two of them got on famously. When Lenin suggested that police surveillance should be instituted on his doctors, Stalin took this as the sign of a return to health.[100] There was no Politburo member more vigilant for conspiracy and sabotage than Stalin, who was delighted to find a congenial spirit in Lenin.

The only notable discomfiture in the conversations between Lenin and Stalin was not of Stalin's making. Lenin, frequently despairing of making a full recovery, asked Stalin for poison. Ever since Marx's son-in-law Paul Lafargue had committed suicide in 1911, the Bolshevik leader had been determined that he would do likewise if ever his health became similarly beyond hope of repair. Krupskaya and Lenin had talked about this at the time.[101]

In May and June 1922 he was intermittently convinced that his recovery would either not occur or would not last if it did. But he did not turn for a cyanide capsule, his preferred mode of self-extinction, to his wife or to his sister. Instead he turned to Stalin.[102] Stalin agreed to do his bidding. Why had Lenin chosen his political colleague for this mission? According to Mariya Ulyanova, it was because he had no rival as 'a person who was as hard as steel and devoid of any sentimentality'.[103] So much for the idea that the scales tumbled from Lenin's eyes as regards Stalin's personality only at the very end of 1922! Another conversation proved how hard the Georgian Bolshevik really was. In one of his several reminiscences about old adversaries, Lenin spoke fondly about Yuli Martov. Lenin and Martov had belonged to the same St Petersburg Marxist organisation in the 1890s; they had founded the newspaper *Iskra* together in the emigration in 1900. Subsequently they had fallen out: Lenin the Bolshevik struggled against Martov the Menshevik. Now Lenin heard that his former comrade was ill and destitute in Berlin, and asked Stalin as General Secretary to see that financial assistance was dispatched to him. Stalin immediately retorted: 'What, start wasting money on an enemy of the working class! Find yourself another secretary for that.' Lenin was both distraught and angry at such an attitude; but it was this attitude that made Stalin the man who would be most likely to indulge the request for the capsule of cyanide.[104]

And yet even Stalin was unsure of himself. The conversation had lasted only five minutes, and was the second time when Lenin had extracted the promise.[105] As he left Lenin's bedside and went into the small ante-room, he accosted Mariya Ulyanova and Nikolai Bukharin. Revealing what had passed between him and Lenin, he asked them what he should do. Their firm response was that Stalin should retract his promise. Stalin agreed, and he returned to Lenin and fibbed that he had consulted the doctors again and had been told that 'all was not lost'. Lenin perked up a little at this and asked: 'Are you up to some cunning?'. Stalin answered with a question of his own: 'When have you seen me being cunning?'[106]

Naturally Lenin had seen many displays of cunning from Stalin over the years; their joint machinations in the Bolshevik faction before 1917 and in the Soviet government after the October Revolution can have left him with few illusions. They continued to get on well. Stalin and he talked often about the political threat posed by Trotski.[107] It is hard to resist the conclusion that Lenin still believed that he could use Stalin as his trusty adjutant. Privately he was condescending about his Georgian colleague; and, when Mariya Ulyanova drew attention to Stalin's cleverness, Lenin the ex-émigré writer and theorist stupidly replied: 'He is far from being intelligent.'[108] Such a misperception of Stalin's mental capacities was common enough to the intellectuals of Bolshevism. The humiliation felt by Stalin reinforced his determination to wreak a terrible revenge on them when the opportunity came. He himself had always had ambitions as a theorist as well as an administrator, and evidently thought his writings on the national question to be a substantial contribution to a growing revolutionary corpus; and, while Stalin could not match the flashes of inspiration in the humanities and the social sciences displayed by Trotski and Bukharin, there is little in the work of Zinoviev, Kamenev, Pyatakov or any other outstanding Bolshevik politician which put them out of his intellectual class. And, quite apart from Stalin's qualities as a theorist, it was fatuous for Lenin to refer to him so casually as unintelligent.

Lenin's overt friendliness to Stalin was anyway predicated upon need. Without Stalin, he could not control Trotski. But the disputes with Stalin over policies on foreign trade and on other matters reversed the situation: Trotski was needed in order to control the ever more rampant Stalin. Zinoviev had long since ceased being a close adjutant.[109] The foreign-trade controversy, moreover, had shown Zinoviev and Kamenev to have come close to Stalin politically.[110]

Kamenev's refusal to pick up the anti-Stalin banner was the final inducement for Lenin to turn towards Trotski. Mariya Ulyanova watched the situation closely, knowing that the switch in her brother's affections characteristically resulted from what she tactfully called 'diplomacy'.[111] He had never liked Trotski, but pragmatic calculation overruled his emotions. Their past disagreements had once provoked Trotski to shout at Lenin that he was a 'hooligan' at a Politburo meeting. Lenin had turned 'white as chalk' but only muttered that 'someone's nerves seem to be playing them up'.[112] This self-restraint might now pay dividends. Lenin was acquainted with Trotski's vanity. His insistence on writing about himself in the third person in his memoirs on 1917 fooled no one: Trotski's self-abasement was a method for attracting public admiration.[113] It was the general experience that Trotski was a poor member of any collective. Lenin was choosing him in the absence of a sensible and reliable alternative and was giving no guarantee that, should his own health be restored to him, he would not revert to a more cautious relationship. He also knew that Trotski was not as confident as he appeared. Trotski had even refused to lead the People's Commissariat of Internal Affairs in 1917 on the grounds that a Jew could not hold such a post in a country notorious for antisemitism.[114] No doubt he used this as a pretext for avoiding jobs he simply did not fancy. But the very fact that Trotski talked in this fashion was probably a sign that strong traces of diffidence were detectable in his arrogant character. He had his greatest impact when working with the approval of Lenin. The October Revolution and the Civil War had brought them together, and Lenin was inviting Trotski to resume close collaboration.

THE GEORGIAN AFFAIR

Lenin's rumblings in the dispute over foreign trade were a pallid rehearsal of his volcanic eruption about the new Constitution. A Congress of Soviets was due to be held in late December, and its proceedings were expected to define the relations between Russia and the other Bolshevik-led republics of the former Russian empire. The Politburo's need in 1921 had been to implement the New Economic Policy and to secure political control, but the inter-republican constitutional problem could not be permanently ignored; and Lenin and Stalin remained as divided as in 1920 about the shape of the future links among all the Soviet republics from the Arctic to the Black Sea. Lenin still desired a multi-republican federation wherein the Russian Socialist Federal Soviet Republic was a constituent republic alongside the other Soviet republics; Stalin continued to call for the other Soviet republics simply to be pulled into the Russian Socialist Federal Soviet Republic with rights of regional autonomy.[115] Nothing had happened in the interim to change the mind of either protagonist. Tensions between Moscow and the non-Russian republics increased in 1921–1922, with Ukraine and Georgia being especially annoyed by the provisions of the treaties they had signed with the RSFSR. To Lenin, this showed the correctness of his project for a multirepublican federation; to Stalin, it demonstrated the opposite: namely that Soviet rule would be in danger unless the various republics were pulled directly into the RSFSR and subjected to tighter control.

Temporarily, however, there was little conflict between them. In particular, they concurred about Georgia. The Georgian Bolsheviks strenuously objected to Stalin's proposal that the Georgian republic should be incorporated in a Transcaucasian Federation (which in turn would enter the RSFSR). Remembering Lenin's call for sensitivity to be shown by the party and the armed forces after Georgia's conquest, they wrote to him in supplication. If Stalin was impervious to their pleas, then surely Lenin would help them.

But Lenin proved, to their astonishment, to be as unsympathetic; the person who in 1921 had intimated a willingness for a rapprochement between Bolshevism and Menshevism in Georgia turned a deaf ear to them.[116] Both Lenin and Stalin were suspicious of Azeri, Armenian and Georgian nationalism. The Armenian-Azerbaidzhani dispute had reinforced the notion that, if left to themselves, the republics of the Transcaucasus would each succumb to the chauvinistic bacillus.[117] A regional federal authority should be able to forestall inter-republican strife; and, much as the Georgian Bolshevik leaders felt done down by this, they had not always shown attitudes typical of socialist internationalism. They had exploited the logistical position of Tbilisi in the region's transport system to the obvious detriment of the two other Transcaucasian republics. Their insistence on keeping a separate republican currency had incurred further suspicion; and their direct diplomatic relations with Turkey, involving sensitive aspects of foreign trade, alarmed Moscow further. The Georgian Bolsheviks had even wished to introduce a law on citizenship which would discriminate heavily against the several non-Georgian minorities in the republic.[118] Not even Lenin was yet disposed to take much notice of Budu Mdivani's accusations of Muscovite persecution when Sergo Orzhoni-kidze and Stalin came forward with a proposal for a Transcaucasian federation.[119]

Where the Georgian Bolsheviks failed, however, the party leadership in Ukraine had some success. Mikhail Frunze, deputy chairman of the Ukrainian government, chafed against the limitations on his powers because of the Russo-Ukrainian treaty worked out in December 1920, and demanded a review of the treaty and its implementation at the Politburo meeting of 4 May 1922.[120] A week later the Politburo established a commission to investigate the issues; its chairman was to be Frunze.[121] But the Ukrainian party leaders in Kiev refused to wait on events. On 16 May, they voted to bypass Moscow and contact all the other republics about relations with the RSFSR.[122] Frunze, too, was coming to the conclusion that his commission's terms of reference, being limited to problems between RSFSR and Ukraine, were intolerably restrictive.[123]

The urgency of the need for a general constitutional settlement at last become obvious to every Politburo member; and, from Lenin's viewpoint, the timing could not have been worse. The trouble caused by Frunze and his associates happened barely a week before Lenin's stroke. If Lenin was to affect the outcome of discussions, he had to act at long range as well as to combat the debilitating effects of his illness. Worse still, he was not immediately aware that Stalin was sticking militantly to his own proposals. Lenin's guard was lowered by a number of factors. His information about Moscow politicking came to him to a considerable extent through Stalin. Furthermore, Stalin initially did not seem as uncompromising as he later appeared. The appointment of Frunze to head the Politburo commission in May displayed *prima facie* evidence that indulgence was being shown to the case of the non-Russians. For his part, Stalin avoided controversy for as long as possible. There is no sign that Stalin's 'autonomisation' project was discussed by Lenin and Stalin at the Gorki sanatorium in the summer. The result was that, despite their vehement disagreement in 1920, Lenin remained confident that Stalin would yield to him: only gradually did he conclude that the General Secretary was not only intransigent but even devious on the matter.

After the Russo-Ukrainian flurry and Lenin's stroke the question was again pushed into the background. Only on 10 August, weeks before Lenin returned to work in the Kremlin, did the Politburo instruct the Orgburo to 'prepare the question of the interrelationships between the RSFSR and the independent republics'.[124] Stalin was the Orgburo's most influential figure, and the decision to leave the composition of a drafting commission in the hands of the Orgburo was almost certainly a device to secrete the decisions away from Lenin. Normally the choice of such an important commission would be made by the Central Committee or the Politburo.[125]

The Orgburo met on 11 August and set up a commission consisting of a representative from each of the republics as well as the following centrally-based leaders: Stalin, V. V. Kuibyshev, G. Y Sokolnikov, S. Ordzhonikidze and C. G. Rakovsky.[126] Stalin was deputed to write a project for its perusal.[127] This he did, and the commission accepted and transmitted it to the central party bodies of the various republics for consideration. Stalin's project was briskly to the point: he judged it 'sensible' for the so-called independent republics to be subsumed within the existing Russian Socialist Federal Soviet Republic. Republican commissariats of justice, education, agriculture, workers' and peasants' control, health and social insurance would continue to be regarded as 'independent'. Even the commissariats of the interior were added to the list.[128] The proviso was that the Cheka could override all decisions about security. In addition, all matters of finance, trade, industry, security, transport, communications, food supplies and military organisation would be handled directly by the Russian Socialist Federal Soviet Republic; and no national appellation other than the word 'Russian' was to appear in the union's title.[129]

The decks were cleared for a struggle between Lenin and Stalin; and Stalin, quite apart from having the advantage of being fit and active, felt that he had reason on his side and that the party would support him. The memory of Lenin's difficulties on the 'national question' in 1917–1919,[130] when Stalin had been mainly on his side, reinforced Stalin's intuition that Lenin would lose this time. Stalin had always been a centraliser and a politician who had regarded the concessions to nationalism in the Civil War as an involuntary indulgence, or, as he put it, mere 'liberalism'.[131] A single governmental centre in Moscow was his aim. He was in a hurry: he did not even specify the rights to be enjoyed in the expanded Russian Socialist Federal Soviet Republic by the various republics about to enter it.[132]

All seemed to go well for Stalin at first. The Azerbaidzhan Central Committee, led by Stalin's ally Sergei Kirov, approved the scheme in general on 11 September.[133] The Armenian Central Committee took the same line five days later; and on 16 September the party's Transcaucasian Regional Committee confirmed this on behalf of Bolsheviks in Armenia, Azerbaidzhan and Georgia.[134] But things were already unravelling for Stalin. The Georgian Central Committee had riled the Transcaucasian Regional Committee and its leader Ordzho-nikidze by rejecting Stalin's scheme on 15 September.[135] This was blatant opposition, and it followed the Georgians' campaign against their inclusion in the Transcaucasian Federation earlier in the year.[136] Even the Armenian party was less than ecstatic about Stalin's proposals, asking that the republics should explicitly be accorded 'broad autonomy' within the Russian Socialist Federal Soviet Republic and that time should be set aside to prepare the population for what was to happen.[137] Meanwhile the Belorussian Central Committee evasively called for a constitutional settlement on the basis 'analogous to the relations established between the RSFSR and the Ukraine'.[138] This was not the open support expected by Stalin. The Ukrainian Central Committee, moreover, curiously failed to discuss his scheme.[139] There was a tacit reluctance among local Bolsheviks to accept the status of mere 'autonomous republics' for their territories. They did not want to ape the model of the Bashkir Republic within the Russian Socialist Federal Soviet Republic. Nor were they re-assured by private contacts with Stalin, who denied the need for a code of political rights for the republics.[140]

Stalin's troubles worsened as Lenin intervened on the side of the objectors. Quite when he asked for the materials to be dispatched to the Gorki sanatorium is unknown; but probably it was after the middle of the month. Stalin was worried enough to write to him in self-justification on 22 September, explaining that the existing system of governance was really in 'sheer chaos'. The various republican administrations frequently ignored each other; and, in a nudge at Lenin's sentiments about the country's foreign trade, he remonstrated that Turkish bankers already had influenced decisions about the Georgian economy. Warming to his theme, Stalin asserted that nationalism in the peripheral areas would become a threat to the régime unless stern measures were quickly taken. He spelled out, as he had failed to do in his draft resolution, that he favoured 'autonomisation' as the solution.[141]

Lenin had apparently been left little time to influence matters. The Orgburo commission meanwhile met on 23 September and accepted Stalin's project as a basis for further discussion; the dissentient voices from the non-Russian republics were cowed into silence. Only the Georgian representative Kote Tsintsadze, who deputised for the ill Mdivani, dared even to abstain.[142] Mdivani returned next day, objecting to the unseemly haste of the decisions already taken. Petrovski from the Ukraine was similarly unhappy, and Armenia's representative Lukashin was disconcerted by Stalin's brusqueness about the rights of the republics in the future federal order.[143] It was at this point that Lenin came back into the reckoning. He talked with Sokolnikov on 25 September and with Stalin himself for over two hours the next day. On both occasions the national question was addressed.[144] Stalin was pulled up short. Lenin agreed with the charge that Stalin was pressing the accelerator too hard. He also exacted changes in the commission's draft. The new federation was to be called the Union of Soviet Republics of Europe and Asia and not the Russian

Socialist Federal Soviet Republic. Indeed the Russian Socialist Federal Soviet Republic would join it as one of the several constituent republics, and a set of new supreme organs of power would need to be established. Stalin agreed to drop his plan for autonomisation; he would also slacken the pace of the drafting process so that Lenin could participate.[145]

But Stalin proved to be slippery. He and his supporters in the commission wrote to Central Committee recommending the formation of a Union as demanded by Lenin – and they proposed the Union of Soviet Socialist Republics as the title. But their difficulty with the Georgians rankled with them, and they quietly revived the idea that Armenia, Azerbaidzhan and Georgia should enter the Union as members of a Transcaucasian federation and not as separate republics.[146] This was bound to lead to trouble. Equally disruptive was Stalin's letter to the Politburo on 27 September objecting to the establishment of separate legislative organs for the Union of Soviet Republics and the Russian Socialist Federal Soviet Republic: a clear attempt to re-introduce his old project by the back door.[147]

If Stalin underestimated Lenin's determination, others did not. At the Politburo on 28 September, Kamenev warned Stalin by memo: 'Ilich has girded himself up for war in defence of independence.'[148] Stalin was undismayed: 'What is required, in my view, is firmness against Ilich.' Kamenev commented that resistance would only make things worse in the end. Lenin would see to that! Taken slightly aback, Stalin scribbled: 'I don't know. Let him do as he thinks sensible.'[149] Lenin had got his tail up. He announced to Kamenev: 'I declare war to the very death on Great Russian chauvinism.'[150] By this he meant not only Russians in his party who overlooked the wishes of the non-Russians in the general population but also non-Russian Bolsheviks who were similarly insensitive. This matter cropped up at the Central Committee plenum which began on 6 October. Lenin was well enough to attend, but had to withdraw at midday because of toothache.[151] Mdivani, though disappointed, wrote to Georgia describing how vigorously Lenin had put his arguments.[152] Kamenev and Bukharin took up the torch from Lenin and denounced the seepage of chauvinism into the Soviet state's activities.[153] Nevertheless Stalin had made the necessary modifications to his project, giving ground on the question of separating of Union and Russian administrative organs. The plenum approved of his draft, and set up a further commission to formulate a final project for the Congress of Soviets. The members included Stalin, Kamenev, Pyatakov, Rykov, Chicherin and Kalinin as well as representatives from each of the non-Russian republics.[154]

Stalin in any case saw that Lenin was not properly recovered. When Lenin returned to chair Sovnarkom on 3 October, an agreement held among its members to avoid controversy lest he become agitated. (In fact he became a lot more agitated because of this plot of gentility against him!)[155] Stalin also knew that the Georgian Bolshevik leaders' hostility to being included in a Transcaucasian federation still cut no ice with Lenin. The campaign against them in Tbilisi was maintained. Stalin's ally Beso Lominadze was sent by him from Petrograd to become Georgian Central Committee secretary.[156] Open season was declared on the Mdivani group.[157] At a meeting of the Transcaucasian Regional Committee of the Bolshevik party, Ordzhonikidze referred to them as 'chauvinistic filth'.[158] The Mdivani group's complaint reached Lenin's ears, but he replied that he was amazed at the improper tone of their criticisms of Ordzhonikidze. If there was a problem, he suggested, then the Secretariat should handle it.[159] Stalin enjoyed himself, calling on Ordzhonikidze to 'punish' the Georgian Central Committee by transferring its recalcitrant members to posts outside Georgia. Ordzhonikidze delightedly complied, referring to the Georgian Bolshevik opposition as a 'Menshevik deviation'.[160] The Georgian Central Committee then took a step unprecedented in the party's history: most of its members resigned *en masse* on 22 October.[161]

The collective resignation had little effect at the time. Lenin did not sympathise with them, and Kamenev and Bukharin wrote to them condemning their action.[162] A new Georgian Central Commmittee was appointed from Moscow on 24 October.[163] In vain did the resigners write to Lenin protesting the justice of their cause.[164] As yet Lenin, while not liking Stalin's attitudes, thought that his actions were justified. And Stalin showed his guile by acceding to the demand of the Georgian Bolshevik dissenters for an investigative mission to be sent to Tbilisi.[165] He could not have seemed fairer. But he was stil plotting; the Secretariat, under his guidance, suggested that the mission should be constituted by Felix Dzierzynski, V. S. Kapsukas-Mickiewicius and L. S. Sosnovski. Mdivani was annoyed especially about Sosnovski, and secured his removal.[166] His substitute was D. Z. Manuilski: hardly an improvement since Manuilski had already helped to stiffen Stalin's resolve against making concessions to the so-called nationalists.[167] A whitewashing job was being set up in favour of Stalin and Ordzhonikidze. The dissentient Georgian Bolsheviks nervously awaited their fate. They proclaimed that Stalin was blind to the fact that Bolshevism had only the most slender support among Georgians in general, that Georgia had had to be conquered and that undying national enmity towards Moscow would result from Stalin's constitutional project. No doubt, too, Mdivani and his friends were finding after the establishment of 'soviet power' that their own internationalism was suffused with a national pride. In Tblisi the tension grew.

A small incident in the Georgian capital in late November 1922 changed the balance of political forces. A. I. Rykov, one of Lenin's deputies in Sovnarkom, was convalescing there and had Ordzhonikidze and Kobachidze, a Mdivani supporter, round for the evening as guests. Dispute broke out when Kobachidze accused Ordzhonikidze of riding 'a white horse'.[168] This was a taunt that Stalin's ally was behaving with the arrogance of a satrap. Ordzhonikidze, overwrought with all the enmity towards him in his native land, flew into a rage and fell upon Kobachidze. Kobachidze was no match for him and received a beating.[169]

Lenin in Moscow was beginning anyway to see the need to keep an eye on Stalin. The General Secretary's behaviour in the debate on foreign trade had already irritated him, and Lenin knew about his ruthlessness from a variety of Georgian sources. Lenin asked his secretaries to find out when Rykov and Dzierzynski, who was also already in the Transcaucasus, would return to Moscow.[170] The Dzierzynski mission started its four-day investigation on 5 December.[171] Lenin asked to see Dzierzynski and Rykov, immediately after their return, in Moscow on 12 December. Their conversations were lengthy. Dzierzynski's report left out many details available to him in Tblisi; but the ambience of Lenin's study made him drop his guard and he let slip the information about Ordzhonikidze's physical assault on Kobachidze.[172] Lenin was appalled. Nothing which happened in the ensuing days reassured him. The report of the Dzierzynski mission was accepted by the Orgburo on 21 December, and a decision was taken to recall Mdivani, Kavtaradze and their main adherents from work in Georgia.[173] Lenin's illness prevented his attendance at meetings, but he started to dictate notes.[174] On 28 December he recorded an *aide-mémoire* with a plan to write a piece 'on the national question and on internationalism'.[175] This was initiated on 30 December. The opening words were portentous: 'Evidently I am deeply guilty before the workers of Russia inasmuch as I failed to intervene with sufficient vigour and sufficent sharpness in the notorious question of "autonomisation", officially designated, it seems, as the question of the union of soviet socialist republics.'[176]

But it was too late to stop the formation of a Union (which was now to be called the Union of Soviet Socialist Republics) on the principles established with Lenin's consent before the dispatch of Dzierzynski to Georgia. A Congress of Soviets in the Transcausasus had overruled the objections of the Georgian dissenters; and the Central Committee in Moscow on 18 December, welcoming the report of its constitutional commission under Stalin, set up yet another for the business of final editing.[177] This was ratified at a Congress of Soviets of the Russian Socialist Federal Soviet Republic. Fittingly it was Stalin who presented it for approval to the First All-Union Congress of Soviets on 30 December 1922.[178] The deed was done. The Georgian Bolsheviks had been defeated. Ordzhonikidze had got away with his outrageous behaviour and Stalin had manoeuvred the Central Committee towards a result which, while not giving him exactly what he had originally desired, was satisfactory to him. It was the greatest political setback for Lenin in his party since before the February Revolution of 1917.

'LETTER TO THE CONGRESS'

The abrupt worsening of Lenin's condition on 13 December 1922 quickened his awareness that he might soon die, and unflinchingly he pondered how best to arrange the political succession. The Bolshevik party leadership had been casual in drafting legislation; they were activists and wanted action, not fine laws which could never be broken. They were also collectivists and, although no one doubted that Lenin had enjoyed a predominant political position, he had no formal title to this effect within the party. Consequently no such title could be transferred to a chosen successor. Nor did his colleagues wish to appear disloyal by bringing the question of succession into the open. Any such démarche would have invited charges of overweening personal ambition.

The only leader who could broach the question was Vladimir Ilich Lenin himself, and it was typical of his tough-mindedness that he determined to do so. On 23 December 1922 he called Mariya Volodicheva to him: 'I want to dictate you a letter to the Congress. Take this down!'[179] He had in mind the Twelfth Party Congress, scheduled to convene in spring 1923. His courtesies had stayed with him and he apologised to Volodicheva for keeping her away from public meetings being held in Moscow. He also asked why she looked so pale. But his own physical condition was obviously worse than he would admit. His memory, too, was weak; he could not even remember the date. Exhausted by the first four minutes of dictation, he let Mariya go away and resumed his attempt only next afternoon at six o'clock, stressing to the secretary that his words on the page were to remain '*absolutely* secret'.[180] The urgent task, he wrote to the forthcoming Party Congress, was to raise the authority of the Central Committee. He noted that conflicts were already occurring between 'small bits of the Central Committee', and suggested that these could be prevented from becoming fatal for the party by the simple device of increasing the number of Central Committee members to '50 to 100' and stipulating that they should come from the working class. His main worry was the durability of the party's rule over society in a world of states hostile to the Soviet republic. Why the presence of workers would make a decisive difference was not explained. Nor was it shown how they would acquire the skills to reconcile the clashing 'bits of the Central Committee'. Lenin did not even specify how to ensure that the workers were chosen on an unbiased basis. The entire proposal was the handiwork of unconscious despair.

Nevertheless his pro-worker utopianism of 1917 had not completely left him even after all the disappointments. In the second session of his dictation he evidently retained less faith in his colleagues. Addressing the topic of 'the parts' of the Central Committee, his language became altogether less opaque. Nothing he had written in his career was so blunt about people he worked with. His choice of leaders was no less remarkable. It would have surprised nobody that Trotski, Zinoviev and Kamenev were on his list. Trotski was the renowned co-instigator of the October Revolution, Zinoviev headed the Executive Committee of the Communist International and Kamenev was chairman of the Moscow Soviet. All three were also Politburo members and constantly in the public eye. Bukharin's inclusion, too, was no surprise since, although he was not a Politburo member, he was *Pravda*'s editor and enjoyed broad renown as a theorist and propagandist; he belonged to the younger generation in the highest échelons of the party and might have been expected to play a role in future dispositions of power.[181]

Yet it remains difficult to understand the references to Pyatakov who was only a Central Committee member and deputy chairman of the State Planning Commission and was not peeved by his relatively lowly condition.[182] Lenin's perspicaciousness was dipping here. Or was it? Rykov and Tsyurupa, who had figured in his planning for the re-organisation of the governmental machinery, were rightly excluded from the list even though they were prominent politicians with much current power. Lenin knew that they lacked the weight to affect the balance of authority in political conflicts. More acute still was the importance he attached to the sixth leader on his list: Stalin. Few Bolsheviks outside the Politburo membership would have judged him to be any more worthy of inclusion than Pyatakov. To be sure, he was General Secretary; but this post was not yet seen to be possessed of unchallengeable influence. Stalin, moreover, was thought to lack competence as a theorist – a major failing in a Bolshevik leader of that epoch. Lenin not only included him but also contended that a clash between Stalin and Trotski, 'the two outstanding leaders of the present-day Central Committee', could even 'lead inadvertently to a schism' in the party. It was in order to avoid such an eventuality that he was dictating his thoughts with the intention of purveying them to the Party Congress. A party split, he asserted, was the greatest threat to the survival of the Soviet republic.[183]

None of the six colleagues came out well from Lenin's comments. 'Comrade Stalin, having become General Secretary, has concentrated boundless power in his hands,' he noted, 'and I am not convinced that he will always manage to use this power with sufficient care.' Not a word of praise was uttered about him. Trotski by contrast was described as 'the ablest person' in the Central Committee; but Lenin added that he had an excess of self-confidence and was attracted by 'the purely administrative side of affairs'. Lenin tendentiously recorded, too, that Trotski's behaviour in the trade union controversy of 1920–1921 showed an intolerable inclination towards a defiance of the Central Committee (as if Lenin had never committed the same supposed misdemeanour).[184]

The comments on Zinoviev and Kamenev were similarly negative and thinly-explicated. 'I shall merely recall,' Lenin stated , 'that the episode of Zinoviev and Kamenev in October was, of course, no coincidence.' But he asked that their past should no more be held against them personally than Trotski's pre-revolutionary non-Bolshevism. And yet the implication remained that neither Zinoviev nor Kamenev were fit holders of supreme political office. On Bukharin, Lenin's comments were equally astringent. 'Bukharin,' he declared, 'is not only the party's most valuable and greatest theoretician but also he is rightly considered the entire party's favourite; but his theoretical views can only with considerable doubts be categorised as fully Marxist since there is something scholastic in him.' Lenin was merciless: 'He has never studied and, I think, never fully understood dialectics.' Like Trotski, Bukharin received a plaudit fainter than the accompanying reproach. Pyatakov was treated even less generously. His 'outstanding will-power and outstanding talents' were not such as to make him dependable 'on a serious political question'.[185] The effect of the collective portraiture was devastating. Lenin had concluded that not one of his highly-placed colleagues was worthy to succeed him. The party leadership was filled, it appeared, with a combination of arch-authoritarian and (if his remarks on Zinoviev and Kamenev are at all decodable) vacillatory figures. The negative features constantly outweighed the positive.[186]

Some of this may be attributed to the circumstances of rushed dictation and also, perhaps, to the sadness of an old lion trapped in his lair and knowing that he might not escape. Immodesty, too, was observable. Lenin, despite believing in the popular accessibility of Marx's ideas, was blithely asserting that the party's second greatest theorist had basically misconceived the nature of Marxism. Altogether the portraits were a gallery of pessimism and were intended to be perceived as such.

The unstated message was that no single leader should succeed him. He envisaged a collective leadership, with no individual in sole charge. Lenin did not claim that the plan was a panacea. But the alternative, which was to have Trotski or Stalin alone at the helm, appeared to him even worse. Of the two men, he had come to prefer Trotski despite his reservations. This was obvious in Lenin's recent letters seeking an alliance with him on questions of the day where Stalin stood in his way. In late December, too, Lenin asked Krupskaya to confide the message to Trotski that his feelings towards him since Trotski had escaped from Siberia to London in 1902 had not changed and would not change 'until death itself'.[187] Nevertheless no fragmentation of the existing leading core of the party was envisaged. Trotski was not to be the new Lenin. The dictated words stopped short of such a conclusion; for Lenin found it distasteful to draw attention to himself directly. At any rate, it was ironical that his last messages to the party focussed on the dangers of a party split. He had been the most notorious splitter in European socialist history before he seized governmental power. He had threatened to leave the Central Committee in 1918 over the Brest-Litovsk dispute and was willing to split the party. The tacit judgement he was proposing, then, was boastful in the extreme: that only he knew when and why to threaten the party with a split.

He had deliberately offered only the flimsiest portraits of his colleagues' psychology.[188] He had mentioned Trotski's excessive 'self-confidence' (again without sign of sensing how easily the description fitted him too). But otherwise he had stuck to comments on outward behaviour. And his avoidance of the analysis of character was accompanied by an inclination to trace the potential for a party split to general factors of the environment of politics after the October 1917. 'Our party,' he maintained, 'relies upon the support of two classes and, for this reason, its instability is possible and its fall is inevitable if agreement between the two classes should ever prove to be unobtainable.'[189]

This cumbersome remark was meant to indicate that Trotski and Stalin might eventually find themselves on opposing sides in a dispute about the rival claims on the party's favour on behalf of the working class and the peasants. 'But I hope,' Lenin added, as if chiding himself for his gloomy thoughts, 'that this is an all too distant future and an all too improbable event to talk about.'[190] In fact a conflict between Trotski and Stalin over the pace of industrialisation and over the respective interests of the workers and the peasants broke out quickly after Lenin's death.[191] Lenin got the substance right, but the timing wrong. Yet even this is too kind to him; for it is doubtful whether the main social basis of the party's power was truly constituted by the working class and the peasantry. The alienation of most workers from the party was already a commonplace of Bolshevik thought, and nearly all peasants were either too exhausted or too ignorant to take the Soviet regime seriously. Lenin's bipartite summary of the party's dependence on the two classes, furthermore, omitted to mention its reliance on the sprawling administrative stratum in order to maintain its own 'stability'. Be that as it may, what is striking about Lenin's judgement is his correct perception that a party split could occur even if a policy dispute about the working class and the peasantry did not divide Trotski and Stalin. Lenin foresaw that a schism was possible simply over issues of personal jealousy and ambition.[192]

COVERT OPERATIONS

What Lenin did in his character sketches was odd; but, in strict terms, he had not infringed the prohibition upon his political activity imposed by the Central Committee plenum on 18 December. But his other activities continued to flout the wishes of the Central Committee. Shortly before the plenum, he had asked E. M. Yaroslavski to take notes on the contributions made to the foreign-policy debate by Bukharin and Pyatakov[193] – and he had made this secret request despite his alliance with Trotski; for Yaroslavski was known to dislike Trotski. Evidently Lenin aimed to have an independent source of information: yet another sign that he took nothing and no one, not even his new ally Trotski, for granted. The plenum resolved to remove Lenin from all connection with active politics for the duration of his illness, and devolved upon Stalin an 'individual responsibility for Vladimir Ilich's isolation as regards both personal relations with officials [of the party: R. S.] and correspondence'.[194]

Thus the man designated in the sketches as one of the two leaders most likely to divide his beloved party regulated his contacts with the world. Lenin recked nought of this. On 21 December he asked his wife Nadezhda to take down a short letter by dictation to Trotski, requesting him to represent their viewpoint on foreign trade to the Congress of Soviets.[195] For this he had surreptitiously acquired the permission of Dr Förster without consulting Stalin.[196] Yet Trotski wished to be seen to be a loyal member of the leadership and told Kamenev of the letter's receipt.[197] Stalin urged Kamenev to express gratitude that Trotski refused to contravene the Central Committee's instructions about Lenin's convalescence.[198] But Stalin was mightily displeased in himself and, on 22 December, picked up the phone to Krupskaya. He was known for his insensitive turn of phrase. His wife, Nadezhda Allilueva, had recently been working as one of Lenin's shorthand typists and had asked her colleagues round to the house to see her new-born daughter. The door was left open as Stalin walked in, and Allilueva reminded him that the baby might catch a cold. Stalin retorted that she would die all the sooner.[199] Even so, Krupskaya had never been the butt of his foul tongue; and she was offended by the obscenities he uttered on learning about the infringement of the Central Committee's interdiction on communication between Lenin and other leaders without Stalin's sanction. Krupskaya, usually the epitome of what in Britain would be called Victorian self-control, fell to the floor sobbing in shame and anger.[200]

Next day, she recounted her humiliation to Kamenev, exclaiming: 'In all the past 30 years I have not heard a single obscene word from a single comrade; the interests of the party and of Ilich are no less dear to me than to Stalin.'[201] Krupskaya kept the incident secret from Lenin, however, on the grounds that he might be upset. Everything was geared to getting him better. And, in purely formal terms, she presumably could see that her action had indeed infringed a Central Committee decision putting Stalin in charge of Lenin's isolation and convalescence.

That Stalin could have lost his own self-control to the extent of bad-mouthing his leader's wife and comrade is remarkable. It may be that, as was rumoured about him not long afterwards, he had already concluded that Lenin's life was fast drawing to its close and that he had nothing to lose. Perhaps he judged that 'Lenin is *kaput*'.[202] This would tally with a recollection made four decades later by Lidiya Fotieva, who served as Lenin's chief secretary. She claimed that the aggravation of his medical condition induced him to approach Stalin yet again for a phial of poison.[203] Stalin could have had no more vivid sign that Lenin's energies were fading. But he also knew about Lenin's resilience. The struggle over foreign-trade policy continued to exercise the minds of the Bolshevik leaders. Lenin was still a dangerous and important piece on the chess-board. It could well be that Stalin's growing confidence was matched by a sharpening sense of exasperation, and that the pressures upon him became ungovernable, just for a moment, on 22 December. The message dictated by Lenin to Krupskaya, which was the goad for Stalin's outburst, had been a request to Trotski to act as his ally in the Politburo conflict.[204] Such a coalition, even with Lenin on his sickbed and operating at a small fraction of his normal capacity, was a threat to Stalin's continuing advance on power.

Stalin was put directly on guard on 23 December by a conversation with Mariya Volodicheva. This was Lidiya Fotieva's junior partner as Lenin's secretary, and it was she who took down the first section of his 'Letter to the Congress'. This did not mention Stalin by name; but it counselled structural change in the central party organs as well as recommending that Trotski's ideas on economic planning should be welcomed by the party.[205] Lenin evidently was intent on some political reform, and no one had more to lose from this than Stalin. Volodicheva did not merely discuss Lenin's words with Stalin: she handed him the text.[206]

Volodicheva obviously appreciated the importance of what had been dictated; her immediate reaction had been to ring up Fotieva and ask what to do with the dictated piece.[207] Fotieva, who was an admirer of Stalin, advised her to show it to him. Going round to his flat, she came upon Stalin in conclave with Ordzhonikidze, Bukharin and A. M. Nazaretyan (who worked in the Central Committee Secretariat). Stalin snatched the letter, instructed his wife to look after Volodicheva and adjourned with the men – o tempora, o mores – to discuss the contents. After a few minutes they re-emerged and Stalin, whose hands hung heavy by his side, told her directly: 'Burn it!'[208] She obeyed. But when she saw Fotieva and their colleague Mariya Glyasser next day, these two expressed horror at her action in destroying Lenin's letter. In fact Volodicheva had left four copies of it in the safe in Lenin's Kremlin office. The three women agreed that the best step would be for Volodicheva to type out a fifth copy to replace the one reduced to ashes. This was done.[209] According to Volodicheva, she did not know that Lenin had meant the contents to be guarded from the view of others. She purported to be astonished when told this by him next day; and she deceived him into believing that his wishes had not been infringed.[210] But she lied then and she lied in her memoir. She had consulted Fotieva in the first instance only because it was obvious to her that Lenin was concocting a plot. She revealed it to Stalin precisely on the grounds that a secret anti-Stalin ploy was in hand.

Lenin went on with his dictation; his intransigence was such that Stalin, who was formally in charge of his medical supervision, consulted with Bukharin and Kamenev. The result, on 24 December, was the granting of permission to have a short-hand typist with him for between five and ten minutes daily. This was tied to a general prohibition on any politician, relative or domestic servant passing information to him about current politics.[211] Stalin hoped to cut off his potential for interference at its tap-root.

Volodicheva was summoned again by Lenin the same evening. The Soviet leader, hated by his enemies at home and abroad as the Red dictator, did not take easily to dictation of the literary kind. He liked to see his manuscript, to pace up and down his office, to insert and excise until the last possible moment; and, when once induced to use the services of a short-hand typist in mid-1918, he had given it up as a bad job.[212] But there was no other option in 1922. Volodicheva tactfully put it to him: 'I know that I'm your necessary evil, but only for a short period.'[213] Lenin felt reassured that his words would remain confidential. She had the courage to confess that she had had to take a red pencil to some of his stylistic errors.[214] But this reversal of roles, reminding him of school-days, bound them closely together. He for his part taught her the conventions of copy-editing.[215] It was Volodicheva who took down the six thumbnail sketches of Bolshevik leaders. But her colleagues, Lidiya Fotieva and Mariya Glyasser, also took turns in the busy last week of December 1922 when the Congress of Soviets was in session. All three were friends, and Lenin must surely have trusted them implicitly. He enjoined that no one was to have access to the materials except himself or, in the event of his death, Krupskaya. The intention was that, in due time, he would retrieve it from the safe and pass it on to the Party Congress.[216]

But it is a moot point whether they stayed loyal to his command. They had already run to Stalin, already lied to Lenin, already shown they knew what was at stake. In their later lives they were willing political handmaidens unto Stalin; and there is definite evidence that at least Glyasser took an anti-Trotski position in the controversies of 1923.[217] Indeed Fotieva, not long before she died, admitted to having handed over further items dictated by Lenin before his death.[218] Nothing can yet be proved, but it would not be totally surprising if these young women, squeezed in a vice of contrary loyalties and sensing that Lenin would not last much longer, continued to yield information to Stalin. Not only the first item in Lenin's so-called 'testament' but quite possibly the entire series of items may have been in his hands as quickly as they could be deciphered from the short-hand notes of Lenin's trusted amanuenses.

10 Deaths and Entrances

PROBLEMS OF LENINISM

Hypothetical questions proliferate about all great historical perso-
nages. What religion would have dominated Europe if Saul, the son of
a tent-maker, had not taken the road to Damascus? Or what would
have become of Christanity if Charles Martel had not defeated the
previously invincible Moors at Poitiers? Would a Second World War
have been prevented if Adolf Hitler had been assassinated? A question
of the same order arises in connection with Lenin: would the history of
the USSR have been greatly different if premature illness had not
ended his life?

It is necessary to pause before proceeding to the dramatic last
months of Lenin's career in order to take stock of the issues. Iosif
Stalin remained keen to present himself as a devoted and consistent
Leninist who secured continuity after Lenin's death.[1] This led him to
throw a blanket over the disagreements between them in the winter of
1922–1923. Lenin had objected to several of Stalin's policies, and
demonstrably perceived these disagreements as constituting a basic
divergence over strategy. Generations of Stalin's enemies took this as
proof positive that he indeed betrayed true Leninism. But Lenin's
judgement is not reliable. It was a feature of his career that he inflated
matters of secondary or third-rate importance, consciously or
otherwise, into objects of life-and-death political struggle. There is no
denying that the multifaceted dispute of 1922–1923 was highly
significant; but it did not affect the fundaments of the régime's
principles. These did not figure in the communications between Lenin
and Stalin for the simple reason that they belonged to the zone of their
shared and deeply-felt assumptions. Without using the terminology,
both leaders enthused about dictatorship, the one-party-state, violence
in pursuit of political goals, massive state economic direction, cultural
persecution, militant atheism, ideological monopoly, forcible maintenance of a multinational state. The list, while not being endless,
involved inclinations and aspirations that made blood brothers out of
the Kremlin's premier and the party's General Secretary. Nothing said
or done by the dying Lenin suggested that he had changed his mind on
such fundamental essentials of post-October Leninism.[2]

The fact remains that the USSR suffered unbridled mass terror in the 1930s. The party leaders, with few exceptions, were exterminated. Stalin and his cronies liquidated their rivals and organised a bloodbath which drowned millions before it was blocked up. There is little doubt that the vengeful, unhinged character of Stalin was crucial to this murderous episode. Lenin had a stature among his colleagues and a personal equilibrium that rendered him unlikely to espouse such ghastliness. We cannot be sure; but it is also improbable that the War Communist methods used in the late 1920s to pulverise the peasantry into submission and undertake the collectivisation of agriculture by main force would have occurred to Lenin as a desirable project. But these were excesses of Leninism, albeit excesses unimagined in their proportions and distortions by Lenin, which were practised by Stalin.

And yet, just as the gap between him and Stalin over policies should not be exaggerated, so we must query the supposition that the thought of Lenin underwent massive alteration in the last two or three years of his life. Modifications occurred, large and distinct modifications, but they were not significant enough to merit the conclusion that he had changed the rudiments of his thought. Nobody proclaimed Lenin's constancy more loudly than that other great claimant to his mantle: Lev Trotski. Through the 1920s and 1930s Trotski denied that Lenin had changed his mind at the end; and he added always that Stalin emasculated the basic orientation of Lenin's thought. In this he had to ignore the commonalty of Lenin's and Stalin's ideas in several basic respects. He also tried to indicate that, had he lived, Lenin would have espoused policies identical with Trotski's.[3] There was in fact more in common between Trotski and Lenin. They had a subtler view on the modes and substance of revolutionary strategy than the crude Stalin. Bolsheviks, they implied, had to be sophisticated dictators. Even they still had their differences: Lenin was reluctant to move as quickly as was wanted by Trotski towards a tight system of state economic planning; and Trotski almost certainly was more committed than Lenin to risks in foreign policy if only the cause of a German socialist revolution might be advanced. But that Trotski, no less than Lenin and Stalin, adhered to a common basic set of assumptions is undeniable.

This is true also of Nikolai Bukharin. The story is well-known about Lenin's affection for the man, and Bukharin was to suggest that it was his own strategical ideas as published in the mid-1920s that reflected Lenin's deathbed cogitations and aspirations. Neither Trotski nor Stalin, then, but Bukharin! With Trotski there is the evidence of the letters seeking a coalition in December 1922; with Stalin there are all the instances of mutual hostility between him and Lenin in the same month. With Bukharin the sources are more partial: they are reducible mainly to Bukharin's remembrances about what was said to him by Lenin in the fateful winter of 1922–1923.

Bukharin was to assert that, as they talked in the beautiful gardens and woods at Gorki, Lenin confided a novel idea of the possibilities of a 'transition to socialism'. According to Bukharin, this included an emphasis on evolutionary, peaceful means for achieving socialist objectives.[4] Lenin purportedly had come to believe that the local peasant community could be persuaded eventually to turn itself into a collective farm and that this transformation, be it accomplished only at a snail's pace, would be the decisive factor in the party's revolutionary strategy. Bukharin was destined to fall out politically with Stalin in the late 1920s when Stalin began to oppose the New Economic Policy; and Bukharin naturally did not fail to suggest that Bukharin and Lenin had been at one in contending that a complete absence of force was both desirable and possible. Thus it is proposed that Bukharinism was simply the latest version of Leninism approved by Lenin in his own lifetime. And yet Lenin's plans for the New Economic Policy do not sustain the notion that he had switched to a fully evolutionary prognosis. Quite the contrary: his writings in 1922 include demands for increased state economic intervention and for increased cultural and religious repression; and at no point did he relent his suppression of other political parties. The beatification of Lenin as the putative creator of communism with a human face is moonshine: Lenin lived and died a Leninist.

Not that Bukharin did not have his points of accord with Lenin in this period. He supported Lenin's line on the national question; but he was also opposed to Lenin in the foreign-trade dispute and had been complicit in the deception of Lenin when Mariya Volodicheva handed Lenin's dictated notes to Stalin. Bukharin was his own man, and differed from Lenin on other basic questions of policy. He retained a commitment to Bogdanov's call for a 'proletarian culture'. While Lenin's emphasis lay upon the introduction of literacy and account-keeping, Bukharin looked forward to workers developing their own cultural practices and institutions to replace 'bourgeois' dominion in social thought.[5] Nor must it be accepted that Bukharin himself was a saintly humanitarian. He did not aim to repeal the party's monopoly of power or the instrumentalities of repression.[6]

Bolshevik leaders shared in politics more than they individually held apart. Their disagreements lay within the definable range of Bolshevik ideas. Elastic as it was, Bolshevism was not infinitely stretchable; and its political assumptions, after the experience of the October Revolution and the Civil War, no longer had the capacity to reach the nearest points of Western social-democracy. The party leadership had brought this about. Even the 'soft' leaders had hardened their attitude since 1917. It is not inconceivable that Bolshevik policies might have been diverted on to a more peaceful, evolutionary path if the party had been less centralised, if ordinary party members had had a greater impact and if the brutalisation of politics in Russia had not gone to extraordinary lengths in the years immediately after the seizure of power in Petrograd. Yet these possibilities were not realised. So that, whatever compromises Lenin might have made if he had lived longer, the régime would have remained a dictatorship with massive state intervention in economic and social affairs. In addition, Lenin was an impulsive creature. To be sure, he had confided in his own notebooks in November 1922 that he expected the revolutionary advance of the second half-decade of Soviet power to be 'slower' than in the first half-decade.[7] His concern about the peasantry's well-being, moreover, was accompanied by continued public assertions that peasant influence over governmental measures should be strictly limited. But privately he put it more starkly; for Lenin, the question was: 'Who leads? The peasantry (bourgeoisie) or the proletariat?'[8] Lenin the class warrior was not politically defunct. There was no guarantee that the itch to take on the peasantry, when fears about its rising affluence and influence arose in the mid-1920s, would not have driven him to desperate measures.

FLIES IN THE MILK

Lenin had resumed the secretarial sessions, this time with Lidiya Fotieva on 26 December 1922. He argued that the new working-class members of the Central Committee, after its proposed increase in size, would acquire an administrative training of benefit to the entire Soviet state. The personnel and institutions of this state, he repeated, constituted a problem inasmuch as they had largely been inherited 'from the tsar and from the bourgeoisie'. The Workers' and Peasants' Inspectorate had not satisfactorily discharged the task of supervising and controlling its operations, and Lenin emphasised that the introduction of workers to the Central Committee would improve the situation.[9] This argument, flimsy as it was, posed yet another threat to Stalin's position since he was the Inspectorate's chairman. Trotski had persistently derided the Inspectorate.[10] Lenin's similar criticism indicated that Trotski and he were drawing together. This impression was reinforced on 27 December when Mariya Volodicheva took over as short-hand copyist from her colleague Fotieva. Lenin declared a change of mind on the State Planning Commission, pronouncing in favour of expanding its areas of competence. He did not wish these to include legislative authority, but he came closer to Trotski by suggesting that the State Planning Commission should make submissions to soviet legislative organs.[11] Lenin specifically defended the two current leaders of the State Planning Commission, G. M. Krzhizhanovski and Y. L. Pyatakov, against attacks on them; he liked the balance between the cautious Krzhizhanovski and the assertive Pyatakov. Next day, when Fotieva resumed secretarial repsonsibilities, he explained that their joint appointment was a means of avoiding the administrative peremptoriness which he had levelled against Pyatakov earlier in his notes.[12]

The State Planning Commission remained on his mind on 29 December, as Volodicheva made notes for him. He demanded that the Commission's communist functionaries should check on the loyalty of the 'bourgeois' experts.[13] Repetitiousness was affecting his day-to-day commentary. He also returned fitfully to the question of increasing the Central Committee's size and proposed that the new working-class members should have 400 to 500 members of the Workers' and Peasants' Inspectorate at their disposal so as to supervise the state administration in general.[14] Lenin's wording had a rambling quality: he did not explain how Central Committee members laden with these extraordinary duties would simultaneously discharge the task of keeping the Politburo and Orgburo leaders from each other's throats. The 'Letter to the Congress' lacked analytical thoroughness.

Yet his mental powers had not entirely left him. On 30 December he had recorded, by dictation, his feelings of guilt about the Georgian affair and the new federal constitution.[15] He doubted that the single state apparatus linking and dominating all existing republics, as set out in the Central Committee draft presented to the Congress of Soviets, would differ substantially from the old Russian Imperial apparatus. Lenin argued that 'the infinitesimal percentage of soviet and sovietised workers would drown in that sea of chauvinistic Great Russian rubbish like a fly in some milk'; and he momentarily queried the immediate desirability of forming the Union of Soviet Socialist Republics: 'There is no doubt that it would be appropriate to delay with this measure until such time as we can swear by this apparatus as being truly our own.'[16] He even complained that, in the light of incidents such as Ordzhonikidze's physical assault on Kobachidze, the right of secession would remain 'an empty piece of paper'.[17] The non-Russians needed protection against Russian thuggery, and Lenin picked out Stalin's 'hastiness and administrative pre-occupation' for censure.[18] The General Secretary's cunning in sending a non-Russian, Dzierzynski, to investigate the Georgian Bolshevik Central Committee's grievances did not escape his notice. According to Lenin, the Pole had displayed 'a truly Russian attitude'. Dzierzynski's self-identification with the Russian cause was allegedly typical over-reaction by a non-Russian official who sided with Moscow.[19]

On New Year's Eve Lenin summarised his position by saying that genuine internationalism involves the largest nation behaving with scrupulous sensitivity towards the smaller nations within the same state. He recalled the nasty epithets used by Russians about Tartars, Ukrainians and Poles in the days of his Volga childhood. A Georgian acting oppressively in relation to Georgia was objectively 'a crude Great Russian thug'. Failure to handle the national question carefully inflamed passions , diverted political attention and damaged 'the basic interest of proletarian solidarity'.[20]

His recommendations meandered somewhat. His first was highly general: Lenin emphasised a commitment to 'retaining and reinforcing the union of socialist republics'. He sensed that his words might otherwise be interpreted out of context by non-Russian nationalists. Lenin had also asserted that only the People's Commissariat of External Affairs was reliably devoid of influential figures from the old régime; and yet he failed to prescribe a remedy. Possibly he was already agitated by yet another matter: namely what to do about the persecutors of the Georgian Bolshevik leadership. He demanded the exemplary punishment of Ordzhonikidze, the reconsideration of the materials in the Dzierzynski report and the holding of Stalin and Dzierzynski as 'politically responsible for this entire truly Great Russian nationalistic campaign'.[21] Stalin had already been singled out for concern in the earliest sections of the 'Letter to the Congress', but the nature of the menace to him remained unclear. For Lenin briskly moved on to a last recommendation. This was that Bolsheviks, while keeping the USSR in existence, should accept that the plans for constitutional integration might have to be dropped. Only the People's Commissariats of External Affairs and of Military Affairs should immediately be unified in Moscow; the other governmental institutions should fall under the authority of the various 'independent' republics.[22] This was in direct contrast with the decisions taken at the All-Union Congress of Soviets. He was at pains to affirm that he did not contemplate the USSR's disintegration. He mentioned that the Bolshevik-led republics would stay under general party discipline, and that any breakdown in co-ordination 'between Moscow and the other centres can be paralysed by party authority'.[23]

This was proof that, despite his renewed talk about the right of secession, he had no intention of honouring it. Even so, he wanted to avoid openly offending the non-Russians and to promote the example of inter-ethnic co-operation as a beacon of hope to 'the hundreds of millions amongst the peoples of the East'. He reposed faith in the anti-imperial movements in China and India, stressing their crucial role in the downfall of global capitalist imperialism.[24] Lenin's passion was distinct in every line, and this final political campaign was being mounted by a very determined 'Old Man'.

In the following days he dictated a number of *Pravda* articles on several subjects. These were published either straightaway or within a few months.[25] It was the national question and the position of Stalin which most perturbed him.[26] His family and medical staff observed how the two topics gnawed at him until, on 4 January 1923, he made up his mind. Lenin called in Lidiya Fotieva and asked her to retrieve from the safe the notes he had dictated about his leading colleagues on 23 and 24 December. She listened in awe as he added a codicil: 'Stalin is too crude, and this inadequacy, which is wholly acceptable in our milieu and in exchanges among us communists, becomes intolerable in the post of General Secretary. I therefore urge comrades to think of a method for transferring Stalin from this position and to appoint another person to this position who in all other respects differs from comrade Stalin through the one advantage [i.e. over Stalin: RS] of being more tolerant, more loyal, more polite and more attentive to comrades, less capricious and so on.'[27] Fotieva dutifully inscribed these sentences in her notebook and, unlike her friend Volodicheva, chose to leave them in their original disjointed language. Lenin guessed that he might not have put a fully cogent case, and added: 'This circumstance may appear an irrelevant triviality. But I think that from the viewpoint of preventing a split and from the viewpoint, as previously described by me, of the interrelationship of Stalin and Trotski, it is not a triviality – or else it's a triviality which is capable of acquiring decisive significance.'[28]

LAST ARTICLES

Precisely how Lenin would try to deal with Stalin was not intimated.[29] That he wanted him removed from the Secretariat is evident; but beyond that nothing is clear. There is no suggestion that Stalin's political career would be completely finished if Lenin were to get his way; it is not certain that his removal from the Central Committee was Lenin's objective (and indeed, after the fracas with Tomski in 1921, Lenin knew what limits existed to his own authority).[30] All that is certain is that Lenin wanted to prevent Stalin from realising his potential to become the dominant Bolshevik leader; it is not even clear that Stalin in Lenin's intention would be excluded from the Central Committee.

With remarkable tenacity the sick Lenin meanwhile produced articles in abundance for *Pravda*. It cannot be demonstrated that Fotieva conveyed the latest pieces from his 'Letter to the Congress' to Stalin; it is also conceivable that Stalin did not importune her for further reports on the direction of Lenin's thought: both of these are possibilities.[31] But Stalin's agility in protecting himself makes them not entirely plausible. In any case Stalin must have gauged the hostility of Lenin towards him from the first section of the 'Letter' as revealed to him by Volodicheva, and the contents of the *Pravda* articles can have left no doubt in Stalin's mind. The first article, written on 2 January and published two days later, was fairly innocuous. It centred on a 1920 survey of literacy in Russia. The fact that less than a third of the adult population were classifiable as literate induced him to scoff at all the proposals for a specifically proletarian culture. The fundamentals of 'bourgeois culture', Lenin declared, had yet to be established (and here he was implicitly criticising not Stalin but Bukharin). The cultural imperatives of the party were enormous.[32] The budget of the People's Commissariat of Enlightenment ought therefore to be iron-clad. Lenin, under his wife's influence, acknowledged that 'a new posing of questions of pedagogy' was desirable; but apparently this would mainly involve a reconsideration of the treatment of religion in the schools; and he urged that propagandists should emphasise the allegation that Jesus Christ had never lived. The political underpinnings of tuition were important. The emphasis was laid by him both upon the right of the state to prescribe the contents of all education and upon its obligation to regard the raising of the technical accomplishments of society as its cultural priority.[33]

Nothing in these considerations was at variance with Lenin's previous writings. The notion that he came over, in his last months, to a different standpoint on culture has no scrap of justification. No hint that he wanted to revoke the policy of sending artists and philosophers into emigration, no hint of relenting in his militant atheism, no hint of support for opening Bolshevism to a polyphony of cultural voices. As earlier, he wanted literacy, punctiliousness, account-keeping.

Nor was there much new in his article 'On Co-operation', which was dictated and written up between 4 and 6 January 1923. Not enough attention, he stated, was being paid to co-operatives.[34] He had long since abandoned his own opposition, before 1917, to the co-operative movement on the grounds that it served capitalist interests. The difference now, he declared, was that the state was not bourgeois but socialist. He stood by his contention that the establishment of co-operatives would not be equivalent to 'the construction of a socialist society'.[35] He picked up again the question of culture. Compulsory universal participation, on an active basis, would make the population 'civilised'.[36] Inverted commas embraced the adjective: Lenin sensed that its usage bore a resemblance to the kind of remark made by Victorian capitalist philanthropists. But he brought his own touch to the theme by insisting that participation should be ubiquitously implemented with sanctions of state coercion. He reckoned it might take a decade or two before success was achieved. At the moment, according to Lenin, the trading methods of the peasant were 'Asiatic' and 'non-European' and the peasantry was 'uncultured'. The aim should be a society of 'civilised co-operative members'.[37] The seizure and securing of political power were essential to socialist strategy, and nineteenth-century advocates of co-operatives such as the Welshman Robert Owen were utopian in not recognising this. But cultural development, insofar as international political and military factors allowed, should now become the 'centre of gravity' of the party's activity.[38]

Not a word signified a change of heart on dictatorship, terror or repression of free artistic thought. Lenin's article called only for a shift in the emphasis of policies; it did not include a recognition that it had been wrong to make the October Revolution 'in an inadequately cultured country'.[39] This idea was resumed in his review of Nikolai Sukhanov's multi-volume history of the two Revolutions of 1917. Sukhanov was a left-wing Menshevik. His history was a brilliant eyewitness account and was enhanced by the author's acquaintance with a wide circle of leaders in all the political parties. After all, his wife

Galina had put their flat at the disposal of the Bolshevik Central Committee on 10 October 1917 when the decision to seize power had been taken.[40] Menshevism had traditionally adhered to the principle that, until capitalism had reached economic and cultural maturity in a given country, it would be dangerous and futile to inaugurate 'the transition to communism'; and this continued to be Sukhanov's objection to Bolshevik strategy.

Lenin postulated that Sukhanov displayed 'the pedantry of all our petit-bourgeois democrats'. His major point was that Marxism demanded eternal 'flexibility'.[41] This meant that the peculiarities of Russia, situated between East and West and between advanced industrialism and the pre-industrial condition, had to be taken into account. There were bound to be 'several partial novelties' in the establishment of socialism under the Bolsheviks. The notion that a general pattern existed to be followed by each country was ludicrous. Lenin freely conceded that, in Marxist terminology, the level of 'development of the productive forces' was too low for the immediate inception of socialism in Russia.[42] But he appended a question: 'If the creation of socialism demands a definite level of culture (although nobody can say precisely what is constituted by this definite "level of culture" since it is different in each of the West European states), why can't we make our beginning by using revolutionary means for the conquest of the prerequisites for this definite level and only *subsequently*, on the basis of worker-and-peasant power and the soviet order, move onwards to catch up other peoples.'[43] No question mark appeared at the end of the sentence, indicating that Lenin assumed that its contents were sufficiently self-evident to provoke no contradiction. Even so, he had never previously framed his arguments in this way. Before 1917 he, too, had assumed that socialism could not be introduced before social and cultural prerequisites were satisfied; and between the February and October Revolutions he had avoided the topic. What his article 'On Our Revolution' did was to give a retrospective legitimation to his strategy of October 1917.[44]

Napoleon Bonaparte's dictum was recalled by Lenin: 'On s'engage et puis. . . . . on voit.' The textbooks, he suggested, could be thrown away. Kautsky's work had been useful in its time; but it did not prescribe strategy for all places and all times.[45] He had spoken like this in the heat of the October Revolution, but it was unusual for him to invoke the authority of a figure such as Napoleon who did not stand in the socialist pantheon: his self-revelation as a political gambler and improviser was unprecedentedly frank.[46]

Without directly saying so, he stressed the importance of luck and contingency in giving the Bolsheviks their chance. It had been the 'first imperialist war' which had brought about 'the complete inescapability of the condition' of the workers and peasants and had pushed them towards taking 'any chances' of a solution through a socialist seizure of power.[47] But Lenin felt fully confident intellectually only when his opinions were supportable by classic Marxist texts; and his usual method was to dredge up references to Marx and Engels or to his own earlier work. But his current emphasis on cultural backwardness, international political vulnerability and the Russian peasantry made it inappropriate to rehearse the citations in *The State and Revolution*.[48] Instead Lenin adduced Marx's hope (as expressed in a letter of 1856) that a dual revolt of workers and peasants might overthrow German capitalism.[49] The Bolsheviks in Lenin's view followed this tradition. To his dying breath, he avoided recourse to Marx's favourable comments on the Russian populists, who wanted to base a socialist society upon what they took to be the egalitarian practices and potential of the peasant village commune; he opposed agrarian socialism: his Marxism continued to hymn the virtues of workers, towns and large-scale organisation. Lenin remained true to himself to the end, and the equivocations of Marx himself in the last years of his life were ignored.[50]

'On Co-operation' and 'On Our Revolution' were not published in *Pravda* until May 1923. But another article, 'How We Should Reorganise Rabkrin', was quickly put into the press despite touching Stalin's vital interests. The Workers' and Peasants' Inspectorate, still had him as its People's Commissar; and Lenin had complained about its efficiency. Now he suggested that its staff should be reduced to between 300–400 employees and should consist almost entirely of professionally qualified persons. They should work, furthermore, on behalf of the party's Central Control Commission. The supervisory tasks of party and government should be united. The Central Control Commission, staffed by workers and peasants, would learn to run the state and improve its work; it would also, by delegating members to participate in Politburo sessions, supervise what went on in the central party apparatus. Lenin specified that not even the authority of the General Secretary ought to get in the way of the Central Control Commission's interventions.[51]

Pravda published 'How We Should Reorganise Rabkrin' on 25 January. The first draft had been even more pointedly hostile to Stalin. Lenin had originally called upon the Secretariat to be more efficient in its preparation of materials for Politburo sessions.[52] He had also wanted to claim that the increase in the number of Central Committee members would bring about 'a diminution of the personal, accidental element in its decisions'.[53] This was close to revealing that political disputes and personal rivalries existed at the apex of the party, and it would have rightly been taken to be an attack on Stalin. Lenin acceded to editorial alteration; perhaps he anyway judged it inappropriate to give Stalin an early warning of his intentions about him (even though Stalin may well have already known through his secretarial helpers!).[54] And so he limited the references to 'high politics' and personalities in his public utterances. Through February 1923 he pondered the issues raised in his various recent pieces and finished a 5,000-word dissertation on 2 March: 'Better Fewer, But Better'. His cultural pre-occupations were to the fore. Much as had been done to promote working-class people to administrative position in the Soviet state, he declared for the first time that such workers were 'insufficently enlightened'.[55] Further training was needed for them. This was true even for those exemplary labourers chosen to fill the Central Control Commission: 'It is necesary to work on them for a lengthy period.'[56] A transformation in culture at every level of politics and in every social group was crucial. There was 'bureaucracy' even in the party.[57]

But his scheme would not have eradicated it. He had criticised the Civil War against the excessive interference of party bodies in state administrative matters as being productive of bureaucratic confusions. And yet here he was recommending a fusion of Central Control Commission and Rabkrin. The propriety of the matter did not concern him morally or politically.[58] Nor did he worry that the same Central Control Commission members who were meant to have the will and sophistication to hold the Politburo to heel were themselves to operate as mere administrative apprentices to Workers' and Peasants' Inspectorate specialists. He mentioned the paradox only to brush it aside.[59] His proposals for institutional change were light-headed, querky and desperate; they came from a man who approved the basic structures of the party and state he had helped to create: they were a thinking conservative's charter.

And finally – for these were the last pages ever to be dictated by Vladimir Ilich Lenin – he turned to Russia's situation in world politics. The pressures of the great capitalist states could be expected to persist. The victorious powers in the Great War had enslaved Germany. There were also signs of changes in social policy in the West which, by bettering material conditions, might serve to postpone the revolutionary explosion predicted by Lenin since mid-1914.[60] But the Great War had also shaken the East 'out of its rut'. Global capitalism, together with the colonial system, approached the ultimate crisis. The problem for the Bolsheviks and the Soviet state was to hold on long enough, and he definitively rejected the assumption that the transition to socialism in the USSR would be fast. Problems of cultural and economic backwardness were a constant impediment.[61] Foreign policy ought to be oriented upon staying out of international conflicts. Capitalism (as he had long ago indicated in his booklet on *Imperialism*),[62] could not exist without economic rivalries which spilled over into wars. Perhaps the Soviet Union might be protected from invasion by conflicts between the great capitalist states. But more likely the entire political camp of capitalism would be distracted from an anti-Bolshevik crusade by struggles by their respective colonies for national liberation.[63]

The Bolshevik party, hoping for this favourable outcome, should concentrate on the maintenance of the supposed leadership by the workers over the peasantry. It should also seek to keep the trust of the peasants and reduce financial waste, administrative inefficiency and political unreliability in the state. The New Economic Policy had the potential not only for industrial reconstruction but also for further industrial advance. Electrification of the country should be a goal. Thus would the Soviet Union endure until the times became propitious for the worldwide socialist revolution.[64] Lenin the visionary and the inspirer of his party declared that 'these are the great tasks I am dreaming about'.[65] His career ended fittingly with a perspective which, while he freely anticipated a troubled future, precluded the probability of ultimate defeat. Waiting for the times to change had become, in his formulation, a rousing revolutionary summons. *Pravda* printed his piece on 4 March 1923.[66]

BREAKING WITH STALIN

Stalin was troubled by what he knew of Lenin's intentions, and the latest articles alarmed him. Early in 1923 he begged Mariya Ulyanova to intercede with him: 'I love him with all my soul. Tell him this in some way.' But Lenin scoffed at Stalin's words as relayed by his sister, and only at her insistence did he coolly consent to return Stalin's greeting.[67] Ill as he was, he was gradually recovering. In January the entire right side of his body was paralysed, but he could speak fluently.[68] He was annoyed at his lost powers: 'Look what a memory I've got! I completely forgot what I wanted to say! What the hell! Astonishing forgetfulness!'[69] He was forbidden to read intensively or to discuss current politics with those around him. But he ordered a load of books, old and new, on themes as various as economics, religion and administration; and Mariya and his wife Nadezhda were among those who read aloud to him at his bedside.[70] By February he looked fitter and had recovered a degree of flexibility in his right hand, arm and leg.[71] His ability to dictate articles gave him an influence on the situation in the Politburo. Stalin saw the need for a certain compromise. While detesting Trotski, he recognised the danger that the alliance between Lenin and Trotski might constitute. Of all people it was Stalin who on 6 January 1923 proposed that Trotski should be appointed as Lenin's deputy in Sovnarkom with special reponsibility for the Supreme Council of the National Economy (and that Pyatakov, whose attitude to the New Economic Policy was not unlike Trotski's, should head the State Planning Commission).[72] Trotski yet again refused. On 17 January Stalin suggested that Trotski could combine the Sovnarkom deputy chairmanship with the leadership of the State Planning Commission; but Trotski was unpersuadable.[73]

Stalin may even have anticipated this and wanted to have ammunition to fire at Trotski as being very arrogant.[74] Trotski justifiably maintained that his duties in military administration precluded simultaneous attention to the economy. If his Jewish ancestry really did inhibit him (and there must be a suspicion that he exaggerated his feelings),[75] he behaved with an almost total lack of circumspection in not making this more widely clear. He also did himself no favours by remaining scrupulously silent about the surreptitious misbehaviour of Stalin and other Central Committee members. He was too loyal for his own good. Unlike Lenin, he did not take seriously the threat from Stalin.[76]

Lenin had to act fast. Stalin's determination to have his way in the Georgian affair was undiminished. Dzierzynski's report on his visit to Tbilisi in the previous December was approved by the Orgburo on 13 January 1923 and passed on to the Politburo. A few days were allowed for Mdivani and other dissentient Georgian Bolshevik leaders to raise objections, but this was a mere display of courtesy. On 25 January, the Politburo confirmed the obfuscatory report of Felix Dzierzynski.[77] Lenin had meanwhile begun to move. Two days before, he had completed the final draft of 'How We Should Reorganise Rabkrin' and insisted on its acceptance by the *Pravda* editors. Bukharin, unhappy about Lenin's jibes at 'proletarian culture' (which was dear to Bukharin's heart) and unwilling anyway to publish so controversial a piece, asked the Politburo to give a ruling. Krupskaya abetted her husband by phoning Trotski and invoking his help.[78] The Politburo members met on 24 January. The problem for them was that Lenin was well enough to check whether his article was printed. Stalin's colleague in the Secretariat, Valeryan Kuibyshev, suggested a plan to deceive the 'Old Man'. A single copy of the newspaper including the article should be printed for Lenin's benefit on 25 January. He would not be told that no other copies on that day carried his piece. Trotski opposed Kuibyshev and demanded normal publication. At first only Kamenev supported Trotski, but eventually it was decided to accede to Lenin's request. To have refused him would have required a unanimity in the Politburo which did not exist.[79]

Lenin's authority as party leader had not vanished; and, while being worried by questions of state administration, he was pre-occupied by the political business in Georgia. Also on 24 January he took the initiative by setting up his personal group to monitor events. This consisted of Lidiya Fotieva, Mariya Glyasser and N. P. Gorbunov.[80] Fotieva was asked to request permission for the relevant documents on Georgia to be released for the group's inspection – Lenin knew that neither Stalin nor the doctors would allow him to examine them directly himself. The choice was not happy. Fotieva and Glyasser were as thick as thieves and devoted to Stalin. Glyasser, moreover, was demonstrably hostile to Lenin's potential helpmate Trotski.[81] Only Gorbunov was unlinked to Stalin. But Lenin's advantage lay in his will to win, his prestige with Fotieva and Glyasser (who admired him as well as Stalin) and the very uncertainty about his health: no one could yet be sure that he was doomed. The file compiled by the group could not have been more thorough.[82]

Having sanctioned *Pravda*'s publication of 'How We Should Reorganise Rabkrin', the ascendant leaders in the Politburo panicked. They deplored the suggestion by Lenin that, if preventive measures were not taken, a split in the central party leadership was a distinct possibility.[83] On 27 January 1923, consequently, a circular letter was sent to the party's province-level committees to indicate that the central leadership was not in fact divided. A strong hint was dropped that Lenin, divorced from participation in Politburo discussions, was not really *au fait* with current issues. It was signed not only by Stalin and Kamenev but also by Trotski.[84] The Politburo continued to insist that he should not take part in current political business, and Lenin's three-person team were not allowed to ignore their prior responsibilities. Thus, although permission was given on 1 February for them to inspect the official materials at the basis of Dzierzynski's report, Lenin had to accept that several weeks would be required for them to assess them properly.[85] Lenin remonstrated with Volodicheva: 'If I had my freedom, I could easily do all this for myself.' He then laughed as he savoured the implications of the word 'freedom'.[86] Meanwhile he put regular pressure on Lidiya Fotieva to do a quick and efficient job and to keep to her schedule.[87] It is difficult to believe that she entirely complied. Not until 3 March did Fotieva, Glyasser and Gorbunov present their report to him on the vexed questions of the party's politics in Georgia. At last he was ready to go to war on Stalin.[88]

His resolution was stiffened by a conversation with his wife. Krupskaya accidentally blurted out the details of Stalin's behaviour on the night of 22 December 1922. Exactly when it was that Lenin found out is not known. But his reaction, on 5 March, is well-documented. He wrote to Stalin as follows: 'You had the rudeness to call my wife to the telephone and use foul language on her. Although she told you that she agreed to forget what was said, nevertheless this fact became known through her to Zinoviev and Kamenev. I do not intend to forget so easily what has been done against me, and it goes without saying that I consider anything done against my wife to have been done also against me. Therefore I ask you to decide whether you agree to take back what you said and apologise or you prefer to break relations between the two of us.'[89]

On the same day he asked Trotski to take up the Georgian Bolsheviks' case on his behalf.[90] Trotski was urged, too, to contact Kamenev, who was not at one with Stalin in the matter and was about to depart for the Georgian Communist Party Congress.[91] Trotski complied, but without the maximum of dynamism – perhaps a sign that he was cagey about appearing to make a bid for the supreme leadership. Simultaneously Lenin was developing tactics with ever greater confidence (even though his physical condition was worsening as a result of his mental agitation).[92] He had told Mariya Volodicheva to hold on to the letter until 6 March. Consultations took place among Volodicheva, Krupskaya and Mariya Ulyanova, and Krupskaya forbade the letter's dispatch.[93] All this was kept from Lenin as he dictated a note to Mdivani and Makharadze: 'With all my heart I am following your cause. I'm upset at the crudity of Ordzhonikidze and the connivances of Stalin and Dzierzynski. I'll prepare some notes and a speech for you.'[94] Lenin's condition worsened in the night of 6–7 March. But Krupskaya and Mariya Ulyanova felt unable to delay his letter any longer. Volodicheva went out on her errand to Stalin's office. He stood up as he read it, hardly able to believe his eyes: 'This isn't Lenin who's talking, it's his illness.'[95] At first he tried to stand on his dignity in replying: 'If my wife were to behave incorrectly and you had had to punish her, I should not have regarded it as my right to intervene. But inasmuch as you insist, I am willing to apologise to Nadezhda Konstantinovna.'[96] Subsequent reflection made him just a little less truculent. His note as deposited in Lenin's office referred to the duty laid upon him to see that no political information reached Lenin as he convalesced and to Krupskaya's infringements. He admitted to having upbraided her five weeks previously (whereas the fateful incident had occurred eleven weeks ago) but claimed there had been no rudeness, adding almost casually: 'If you consider, however, that the maintenance of "relations" requires me "to take back" the above-mentioned words, I can take them back, while refusing, however, to understand what is the matter here, where my "guilt" lies and what in particular is being asked of me.'[97]

Kamenev, who was consulted by Stalin, was appalled by the 'acid' quality of his formulations and was convinced that the apology would not satisfy Lenin.[98] A struggle between Lenin and Stalin on the personal and political front was virtually inevitable. How Stalin must have regretted that he had not handed the 'Old Man' the cyanide phial! But cringe before Lenin he would not. He and Mariya Ulyanova had a blazing row by phone: Stalin was adding to the hurts to Lenin's pride which would have cost Stalin dearly in due time.[99] His own Georgian self-esteem and his exasperation after months of frustration and over-work were bursting the bonds of his self-restraint. What saved him from a goring by the bullish Lenin was nothing he did in his own defence but the rapid decline in Lenin's health. The letter was never read out to him. On 8 and 9 March he deteriorated further. Next day he suffered a massive spasm. He was paralysed all down his right side; he all but lost the capacity of speech. His left hand, too, was rendered immobile. His participation in the politics of his country was terminated.[100]

MAN IN THE BATH-CHAIR

The physical deterioration continued. No attempt was at first made to move him from the Kremlin, where he had lived over the winter. But a

mild, temporary improvement in May 1923 induced the doctors to
state that, so long as a specially-upholstered vehicle could be provided
and driven at a slow pace, the patient should be transferred again to
Gorki.[101] The symptoms were recurrent. Apart from the pain
associated with the paralysis, he had insomnia and suffered perpetual
headaches. His appetite faded. He was easily made nervous and
agitated.[102] In mid-July there were further problems. His temperature
rose steeply, and he had a stomach illness. It looked as if his final crisis
was at hand. But remission followed within days. He began to sleep
normally and sometimes to sit up in bed. He could also hobble around
on the arm of one of his devoted male nurses. Eventually he could
move independently with the aid of a walking stick.[103] Nadezhda
Krupskaya and Mariya Ulyanova were in more or less constant
attendance, and Krupskaya took lessons so as to be able to teach Lenin
to speak. It was a long job, but he made progress. He tried singing the
'Internationale'. His will to survive was strong: he even began to write
with his left hand.[104] On 1 August he was re-learning how to recite the
alphabet. A week later he demanded that his doctors should allow him
to read newspapers again. His spirit seemed indomitable.[105]

But frequently he became depressed. He hated the doctors. On 31
July he had exploded in rage about them and drove them from his
bedside. For a lengthy period they were constrained to 'observe' from
the safe distance of the doorway of the next room. Only Professor
Osipov was allowed near, and he on pain of dismissal if he should
broach the matter of illness.[106] Lenin sometimes fell into despair. When
Krupskaya told him how well he was doing, he retorted: 'It won't
last.'[107] She herself had worries, ceasing to believe anything told her: 'I
now understand that the doctors know nothing.'[108] Once she broke
down into tears, and Lenin gave her a handkerchief to comfort her.[109]
The strain on her was terrible, and was increased on those days when
without warning he subjected her to a verbal lashing. And, despite his
enormous will-power, Lenin also wept profusely. Usually it happened
when he supposed that no one could notice him.[110]

Lenin was embarrassed at appearing weak and helpless (and this
embarrassment was subsequently felt by the builders of his cult – it was
not until the late 1980s that the intimate details of the progress of his
illness were pulled out of the archives). Lenin's sudden collapses into
tearfulness would now be considered a normal aspect of his medical
condition.[111] Alternating periods of deterioration and improvement are
also characteristic. The doctors treating Lenin were doing their best at
a time when the understanding of the brain was at a much lower level

than today. Krupskaya had every right to be sceptical about the doctors; and Lenin, remembering that his father had died of the same illness in his early fifties, had cause for his underlying pessimism. Not that he gave up. Not at all: his capacity for human fellowship was not exhausted when he shooed away his doctors. He took well to his nurses. One of them, Ekaterina Fomina, had been with him since the attempt on his life in 1918. Others he loved were the young medical students who worked on shifts as nurses, especially Nikolai Popov and Vladimir Rukavishnikov. Petr Pakaln, his bodyguard, was the person he especially liked to push him around the ground in the bath-chair purchased for him from J. A. Carter and Co, London WC1.[112] In addition, he discovered that he was not the sole patient under treatment in the sanatorium. None other than Aleksandr Preobraz-henski, a comrade from his days in Samara in the early 1890s and currently an agricultural functionary, was convalescing in another wing of the building. They spotted each other by chance, and embraced – and Lenin decamped for three days to the wing of the mansion where Preobrazhenski had a room.[113]

He did not take kindly to articifial efforts to 'entertain' him.[114] He knew what he liked and would not be imposed upon. Visits by his brother Dmitri's son Viktor, a lively six year old, were especially pleasant for him. At Christmas, celebrated according to the Russian Orthodox calendar on 7 January 1924, he greeted the children of the nearby countryside and passed on a pair of slippers (which he had received as a gift) to a little girl who caught his eye. He was far from being miserable all the time.[115] But his happiness, such as it was in the circumstances, came mostly from what little hope he kept of returning to a normal life. He relished, for example, the chance to look after his own nurse Popov when he arrived at the sanatorium and was not given a meal before his shift began.[116]

The slim prospect of returning to politics kept him going. Krupskaya saw this and told him to think of Gorki as his prison. This remark horrified nurse Ekaterina Fomina, but his wife knew him well: she was reminding him how much intellectual work he had done when held captive in the House of Detention in St Petersburg. An appeal based on the opportunity for work was the likeliest to get through to Lenin.[117] On 10 August he insisted on receiving *Pravda* and other newspapers.[118] He had recovered enough to be able to glance through them and pick the passages he wanted Krupskaya to read out to him. Any effort by her to censor the material, for fear of agitating him, was in vain. He knew when she was tricking him. This touched him particularly when he asked about associates from earlier periods in his career. Many had become his political enemies: Pavel Akselrod, Aleksandr Bogdanov, Yuli Martov and Aleksandr Potresov. Krupskaya tried to ignore his questions about Martov, who had died in 1923. But she reckoned without Lenin's physical recuperation. By autumn he could get up and down the stairs by himself, and entered the library to check up on his wife's equivocation. He found the relevant copy of the previous year's newspaper and discovered for himself the obituary notice.[119] He also took an interest in longer pieces of work. He listened as Krupskaya read Trotski's recently-published *Questions of Everyday Life* and Maksim Gorki's autobiography *My Universities*. He managed to read some tales by Jack London, chuckling with his wife about his supposed 'bourgeois moralism'.[120] A few of his fellow Bolshevik leaders came out to see him. Nikolai Bukharin was the only one of the first rank; but he also saw Evgeni Preobrazhenski, I. I. Skvortsov-Stepanov, Nikolai Krestinski, Osip Pyatnitski and others. Both Bukharin and Preobrazhenski recorded that, inching his way back towards semi-recuperation, he did not delude himself about his ultimate chances.[121]

He was the despair of his handlers. On 18 October 1923 he looked out of the window and saw a car. Downstairs he went, sat inside it and demanded to be taken to Moscow.[122] Consultations among Krupskaya, Mariya Ulyanova, Professor Förster and Petr Pakaln hurriedly took place. Dissuasion did not work on Lenin. Perhaps he was in one of his temporary moods of elation; or perhaps this was just typical of his lifelong will-power. The car set off at the slowest of paces. Lenin was beside himself with delight. By chance the passengers discerned Professor V. Rozanov on the road and picked him up. They all arrived at the gates of the Kremlin towards dusk. Lenin went up to his old office and to the meeting room of Sovnarkom. Next day, being a bibliophile to the last, he went through his book-cases and retrieved three volumes of Hegel. He also perused his own notebooks. Refreshed and encouraged, he got back into the car in the early evening and returned to the Gorki sanatorium.[123]

In the remaining months of 1923 Lenin went out riding in the car in the vicinity. Sometimes he was taken to the woods, where he watched the hunters going after foxes and hares.[124] In his bath-chair, he was pushed around the gardens next to the house. The doctors were impressed at his gusto. He was able, with difficulty, to speak with his familiar intonations and to read aloud a little.[125] But worrying symptoms still occurred. From mid-October, for example, he experienced black-outs lasting 15–20 seconds. At first they happened once every three of four weeks, but they became more frequent. Lenin's bursts of irritation also returned.[126] The significance of the black-outs was at that time little understood. The doctors anyway wanted to encourage positive thinking. Professor Feldberg, who had been invited to join the medical team, suggested that a complete recovery was possible by summer 1924.[127] Förster and others remained more cautious. The finest available Russian and German medical expertise was evidently in a quandary – except for the eccentric judgements of the newly-arrived Feldberg. None of them were Bolsheviks: Lenin had a highly-developed contempt for those among his comrades who had qualified as doctors. But all those physicians at the sanatorium, who greatly outnumbered the patients by the end of 1923, were conscientious and skilled practitioners of their craft. Not even Lenin's hostility to them dispirited them. Whatever their opinions about the politics of the leader of world-wide communism, they did what they could to secure his recovery.

THE POLITICS OF MORTALITY

Lenin's incapacitation over these several months worked to Stalin's favour. If the stroke of March 1923 had killed him immediately, then a question would have simultaneously arisen about what should be done with his 'Letter to the Congress' and his recommendation that Stalin should be dismissed from the General Secretaryship. The Thirteenth Party Congress had been scheduled for April. Lenin's evident intention had been to present his thoughts as dictated to Fotieva and Volodicheva in the preceding winter to the assembled delegates (even if someone else would have had to read them out aloud). He had added the stipulation that, if he were to die, his wife was to have the exclusive duty to open the sealed envelopes and reveal them to the party. He had been afraid that he might not last out until the Congress. But he had not allowed for what actually happened: that he would be alive at the time of the Congress but unable to communicate his political wishes to those around him. A stay of his proposed punishment of Stalin was the result. Stalin meanwhile had a wonderful opportunity to prepare his defence. This involved an attack on the one leader, apart from Lenin, who was clearly hostile to him: Trotski. It also called for a mending of fences in relations with Kamenev and Zinoviev. Kamenev in particular had withheld support from Stalin in the Georgian affair. A tripartite coalition of Stalin, Kamenev and Zinoviev was vital to Stalin's retention in the core of the central party leadership; and he had to be willing even to let Zinoviev enjoy greater prominence than he would otherwise have obtained.

Initially all went well for him. Trotski, having received Lenin's materials on the national question (including the draft article where Stalin, Dzierzynski and Ordzhonikidze were specifically criticised),[128] refrained from an unconditional assault on Stalin. In line with Lenin's wishes, he spoke with Kamenev about his worries about developments in Georgia before Kamenev met the Georgian Bolshevik leaders in Tbilisi. Trotski showed solidarity with Lenin's policies but, according to his later account, did not seek punishment for Stalin, Dzierzynski and Ordzhonikidze.[129] In addition, Stalin had been alerted to the need for wariness. Lenin's note demanding an apology to Krupskaya had put him on guard; and Trotski, following up the points made by Lenin in his article, wrote to Stalin asking him to incorporate several amendments in the theses prepared by Stalin for the forthcoming Party Congress.[130]

Stalin played cautiously at first. He sent a telegram to Ordzhonikidze warning him not to be abrasive towards their Georgian Bolshevik opponents in the next few days.[131] Trotski's criticisms of his theses were accepted word for word. Stalin even incorporated the point that the danger posed to the party by the nationalism of non-Russian Bolsheviks was a reaction to Great Russian chauvinist behaviour; and the amended version was supplied to *Pravda* on 24 March.[132] This, however, was the 'phoney war' period. At the next meeting of the Politburo, on 26 March, Stalin clashed with Trotski. Kamenev, who had acted honourably in giving everybody a free voice at the Georgian Party Congress, returned from Tbilisi with proposals including the transfer of dissentients like Budu Mdivani from Georgia.[133] Trotski demanded that Mdivani's group should be relieved of the charge of constituting a 'deviation' from Bolshevism; that the 'excessive centralism' of the Transcaucasian Federation should be resisted; and that Ordzhonikidze should be transferred from work in the region. But these requests were turned down.[134] On 31 March the Central Committee plenum supported the Politburo's position. Trotski had made only the barest dent in Stalin's armour. Stalin enhanced his position at the same plenum when he was seen to support Lenin's proposal for an increase in the number of Central Committee members whereas Trotski argued against it.[135] Nothing could better illustrate Trotski's lack of political nous: the premium on being perceived as

Lenin's faithful follower had never been higher. Trotski was true to his principles at his own cost.

Then something happened which destroyed Stalin's equanimity. On 16 April, Lidiya Fotieva returned to her duties after an absence over nearly three weeks and informed Stalin, Kamenev and Trotski that Lenin had told her, shortly before his last attack, that he intended soon to publish the article on Georgia and the national question which he had dictated on 31 December 1922.[136] Both Kamenev and Trotski had discussed its contents. The danger for Stalin was that Lenin had not only called for a re-orientation of policy on Georgia but also picked out Stalin for specific censure.[137]

Trotski and, at first, Kamenev favoured publication in accordance with Lenin's newly-reported wishes.[138] Stalin hit back by telling the Central Committee that Trotski had misled the party by failing to reveal Lenin's article to the party in due time.[139] Trotski retorted that he had had no knowledge that Lenin had wanted immediate publication, and Stalin backed down in conversation with him. But no written retraction followed, to Trotski's annoyance.[140] Stalin was going to brazen it out. He was assisted by the feeling of several party leaders, including Kamenev and Zinoviev, that Stalin's humiliation would serve to elevate their dreaded rival Trotski to supreme power. Mariya Ulyanova took a similar approach.[141] Further consultations led to a decision on 18 April to divulge Lenin's article not to the party at large nor even to the Twelfth Congress as a whole but instead only to the heads of provincial delegations to the Congress.[142] This was not a mere slap on the wrist for Stalin; but it was short of being a body-blow. Stalin also knew that, in Bolshevik debates on the national question in the past, he himself had been closer to the core of his party's opinion than had Lenin; and he continued to benefit from the fact that Lenin's recommendation for the sacking of Stalin from the General Secretary-ship was unknown to the rest of the Politburo.[143] He could therefore weather the crisis. Shamelessly he advocated that Trotski should deliver the Central Committee's political report to the Twelfth Party Congress.[144] No one could charge Stalin with gratuitous hostility to Trotski. Trotski was being wrongfooted at every turn.

Zinoviev, who was certainly keen to remove the mantle from Lenin's back, gave the political report instead;[145] and Trotski did nothing to indicate that the Politburo was riven by rivalries. Stalin's speech on the national question contained no apology for past misdeeds. On the contrary, he laid emphasis on his contention that the Georgian Bolshevik opposition to the formation of the Transcaucasian

Federation in 1922 showed that nationalism had taken the offensive.[146] In reality he knew that not even Lenin had urged the dissolution of the Trancaucasian Federation. Thus, in the eyes of most delegates, Lenin was made to appear closer to Stalin's position than was the case. Stalin's bid to seem the loyal and trusted adjutant of Lenin continued as he presented Lenin's proposals for internal party re-organisation to the Congress. He conspicuously lauded the plan to expand the Central Committee and to merge the Central Control Commission and the Workers' and Peasants' Inspectorate.[147] At the same time Trotski was lulled into complacency by the wording of decisions on economic policy. Kamenev, Stalin and Zinoviev made no objection to the calls for a greater emphasis on central state planning in industrial development.[148]

'Lenin' and 'Leninism' had, for the first time, become entirely the playthings of Bolsheviks other than Lenin. Speech after speech professed loyalty to him and the hope that he would soon return. *Pravda* printed a supplement: 'Comrade Lenin on Holiday'.[149] The truth about his medical condition, even if allowance is made for the optimism of his doctors, was kept from the Congress. Stalin took the lead in distorting Lenin's intentions as indicated in his last notes and articles. He had already defused the bomb laid for him in relation to the Georgian affair. He now removed the detonator placed by Lenin in his proposals for the re-organisation of the central party apparatus. The expanded Central Committee was filled with opponents of Trotski; the Central Committee was neither able nor wanted to impede the actions of Stalin, Kamenev and Zinoviev; and the combined organs of the Central Control Commission and the Workers' and Peasants' Inspectorate were instruments for Stalin's future assaults on Trotski.[150] Stalin's increased power began to concern Kamenev and Zinoviev. Kamenev had kept a certain distance from him until the Twelfth Party Congress; but it was Zinoviev who took the initiative in trying to restrain Stalin. In the course of summer 1923 he held a meeting with Bukharin and others in a cave near the spa resort of Kislovodsk. It was hardly a conspiratorial affair since Kliment Voroshilov, closely linked with Stalin, was present. Agreement was reached that Stalin's power over the Secretariat should be reduced by introducing others to its membership. Even Trotski's name was mentioned in this connection. But Stalin reacted subtly. As guarantee that he meant none of his colleagues any harm, he acceded to Zinoviev, Trotski and Bukharin being invited to attend the Orgburo. He no doubt calculated that their other responsibilities would limit their ability to participate. His position in the Secretariat, whence Lenin had secretly planned to sack him, was secure.[151]

The official campaign to exalt 'Leninism' was intensified. It was a term ostensibly resisted by Lenin in his active life since he claimed only to conserve, replicate and develop the ideas of Marx and Engels.[152] But it was Lenin's 'teaching' that was stated by Kamenev to be the 'touchstone' of the Politburo's discussions in Lenin's absence.[153] Even more effusively, Zinoviev declared that the party yearned for guidance from Lenin like 'a thirsty man who on a hot summer's day comes upon a deep, clear spring to drink his fill'.[154] Kamenev founded a Lenin Institute in Moscow to co-ordinate the research on Lenin and the publication of his works. An appeal was issued by Kamenev and Stalin for items of Leniniana to be released by their holders. A museum was established in Lenin's honour.[155] The veneration of Lenin burst previous limits: he was seer without equal; he was doughty national hero; he was unblemished saint; he was the light of the world.

The purpose of the reverential excess was plain: Lenin was to be used as a means of gathering support for the central party leaders within the party and for the party in society as a whole. The all-purpose cultic symbolism was flagrantly instrumental to this end. Stalin was already elaborating extravagant projects. According to stories circulating in Moscow in the mid-1920s, he called together Politburo colleagues in autumn and argued that a plan ought to be made for the contingency that Lenin might soon die.[156] Those present would seem to have included Stalin, Trotski, Kamenev, Bukharin, Kalinin and Rykov. Kalinin insisted that, if Lenin were suddenly to pass away, his funeral should be a magnificent state occasion. But what next? Stalin suggested that cremation would offend the sensibilities of most Russians. But he was not in favour of ordinary burial either. Instead he intimated that 'contemporary science' made it possible to embalm his body and preserve it for a considerable period. Stalin put this in such a way as to imply that he was only relaying a proposal coming from provincial party leaders. But he nevertheless outraged Trotski, Kamenev and Bukharin. They abhorred the wish to treat Lenin's corpse, whensoever it became available as such, as if it were the reliquium of an Orthodox Church saint; their Marxist world-view was offended. Only Rykov and Kalinin did not directly oppose Stalin, but even they failed to endorse his plan unambiguously.[157]

The question was anyway hypothetical. But Stalin's insistence on addressing it showed that he was thinking in greater detail than was any rival about the scenario after Lenin's death.[158] The lessening of the threat from Lenin, however, brought the danger of Trotski and his supporters more prominently in view. Trotski had missed chances to do down Stalin which were not passed up by Stalin in his moves against Trotski. Stalin envied his popularity in the country, feared the resonance of his ideas among hundreds of party activists and opposed – at least at that time – his suggestion that the state should quickly intensify its intervention in industry, commerce and agriculture. The frail stability of politics under the New Economic Policy appeared to be under threat from Trotski.

Trotski gave him his opportunity in October 1923. Forty six of his sympathisers, including E. A. Preobrazhenski, signed a public letter criticising the shambles of economic administration in previous months. A crisis in food supplies had resulted from peasant resentment at the rise in the cost of industrial goods to thrice the level of agricultural goods in real terms as compared with 1913. A more vigorous policy of industrial development was demanded. Preobrazhenski also criticised the clampdown on criticism within the party. He wanted a return to earlier traditions of debate and decision. Trotski belatedly declared his support for the Declaration of the Forty Six. He was immediately accused of disloyalty to the principle of collective leadership enunciated by Zinoviev at the Twelfth party Congress in April. His anti-Bolshevik past was held against him. At the Central Committee plenum in October 1923, he stood up to defend himself and denied any intention of breaking with the Politburo and planning a Bonapartist coup. But he was clear that economic and political measures in earlier months had annoyed him. In December 1923 he published *The New Course* articulating these opinions. Dogged by ill-health and laden with the image of a disturber of the Leninist party leadership, he was tactically outplayed. His support in provincial party committees was whittled down by the double barrage of Zinoviev's arguments and Stalin's organisational manipulations. The scene was set for a show-down dreaded by Lenin since 1922. At the Thirteenth Party Conference in January 1924 his chances of breaking up the alliance of Stalin, Kamenev and Zinoviev were blown to the winds. A split in the party, with Stalin and Trotski on opposing sides, was in the making; and Stalin consolidated his grasp on the Secretariat of the Central Committee. The speed of Trotski's humiliation astounded even Stalin's adherents. Only if Lenin were to recuperate and quickly return to public office would Stalin's advance on power be reversed.[159]

Epilogue

THE ICON DIES

The man in the bath-chair at the Gorki sanatorium waited eagerly for news about the Party Conference. Nadezhda Krupskaya trembled about his potential reaction and fed him as little information as she could. She reassured him by saying that the Conference's final resolution had been passed by an overwhelming majority.[1] This was true, but deliberately misleading since it concealed the savagery of the debates. Furthermore, a veil was drawn over the beginning of a contest among the Politburo members which had been feared by Lenin since December 1922. Krupskaya's deceit stemmed from humane motives: the full truth would undoubtedly have upset him deeply.

Lenin's physical decline allowed her to get away with this. He had complained to the duty-nurse Nikolai Popov on 19 January that his eyes were giving him trouble. Popov, still trusted by Lenin more than the professorial doctors, had enough training to diagnose the symptoms of conjunctivitis. Lenin was given dark glasses to ease the problem temporarily;[2] and Professor Averbakh, a leading ophthalmologist from Petrograd, was asked to inspect the patient next day. Averbakh was given a gentle reception by his prospective patient at 9 p.m. But it was also noted that a certain apathy had begun to characterise Lenin's mood. He told the doctor that he felt very poorly and that his eyes still hurt, but Averbakh could discover no specific treatable condition. Lenin's appetite was weakening and he went to sleep at 11 p.m.[3] By then it was clear to Krupskaya and all the watchers at his bedside that he was deteriorating quickly. No one expected much improvement in him on 21 January. Krupskaya sprang out of bed in the adjacent room at 7 a.m. Going through to him, she was at first reassured. He seemed to be sleeping restfully, and she left him undisturbed. He woke up at 10 a.m. By then it was apparent that he had weakened again since the previous day. He would only take a cup of black coffee for breakfast. Professor Förster, standing by the door because of Lenin's imprecations against his regular doctors, was seriously concerned and watched him carefully.[4] Lenin went back to sleep until 2.30 p.m. By then Professor Osipov had taken over from Förster and allowed Mariya Ulyanova to give him a weak bouillon. The afternoon was spent in tense expectation.[5] A spasm occurred around six o'clock. Lenin lost consciousness, sweating prodigiously and stretching his legs out rigid. Osipov and Förster worked in union. Not only Nadezhda but also his sister Mariya, bodyguard Petr Pakaln and nurse Vladimir Rukavishnikov stayed to help. Taking his pulse, the doctors found that his heart rate had risen to 130 beats per minute. His lungs were breathing irregularly and too fast, in a Cheyne-Stokes syndrome. His chest was giving out croaking sounds. After some minutes there seemed grounds for hope as his heart pulse rate fell back to 90.[6] But the improvement was temporary. The fever resumed and the patient moaned endlessly. Krupskaya grasped his hand. He opened his eyes, but she noticed that they seemed to show less and less sign of consciousness.[7] A compress was applied to his head, more in desperation than hope. The final crisis was at hand. A check was taken of his temperature by Rukavishnikov. It was worryingly high.[8] Krupskaya held his 'hot, wet hand' tighter. The blood rushed to his face.

At 6.50 p.m. he suddenly let out a great sigh and became motionless: his life was over. Everyone knew it, but still worked in a hopeless endeavour to restore his consciousness. Professor Förster called for some camphor and applied it to the dead man's nose. Artificial respiration was also attempted for twenty five minutes. But all to no avail. The bright ruby flush on his cheeks had disappeared. Krupskaya looked at him and 'only saw how the bandage was coloured with blood and how the mark of death lay upon his mortally pale face'.[9] In subsequent years all manner of myths arose about these last moments. Prisoners in Stalin's labour camps in the 1930s heard a legend that, knowing his end had come, Lenin called upon the ministrations of a Russian Orthodox priest. Another story, which was nourished by Trotski's hints in exile about Lenin's requests for poison, was that Stalin had killed him. But no such sensationalism is based on the available evidence. Lenin had died because the sclerosis affecting the blood vessels supplying his brain had reached an ultimate stage. Lenin died of natural causes, genetically conditioned. He died politically unrepentant and religiously indifferent. The news of his decease was relayed immediately to Moscow. In the mansion on the Gorki estate everyone was in a condition of shock. Nadezhda Krupskaya and Mariya Ulyanova, after the years of caring for him, were utterly distraught and worn out.

While he was alive, his wife and sister had had some influence on the treatment of him. His death changed this. The news was quickly relayed to the Kremlin and the long-laid plans of his Politburo colleagues, especially Stalin, were put into effect. The corpse of Lenin became a primary object of policy. No announcement was yet made. The press for months had avoided any worrying reportage on Lenin's condition (and the doctors themselves had been trying to stay optimistic).[10] At first only Lenin's immediate family was told what had happened. In the night of 21–22 January the central party leaders assembled in Zinoviev's flat in the Kremlin. Also present were Stalin, Kamenev, Kalinin and Dzierzynski. Kamenev was deputed to ring V.D.Bonch-Bruevich, Lenin's personal assistant after the October Revolution, to arrange for the disposal of the corpse while they took the more 'political' decisions.[11] A request was made to Professor A.I.Abrikosov to conduct an autopsy, and Bonch-Bruevich got ready to take a train to Gorki in the morning. He travelled in the company of Lenin's sister Anna and brother Dmitri.

Abrikosov arrived on the same day and carried out the autopsy. His four-hour investigation, which involved opening Lenin's brain, confirmed that a chronic sclerosis of arteries and a massive stroke had resulted in a fatal haemorrhage of the cerebral area.[12] On 23 January the body was carried down in sombre procession to the little railway station at Gerasimovka and transported to Moscow. The coffin was placed at Trade Union House. In the Russian tradition, it was lidless while the lying-in-state took place. A guard stood permanently to attention and Krupskaya spent whole days seated by the body. Hundreds of thousands of visitors waited in bitterly cold temperatures to pay their last respects to Lenin.[13] Posters, booklets, obituaries were appearing everywhere; telegrams came in from every city.[14] Meetings of mourning were held at factory gates. Vows to remain true to Lenin's memory were common.[15] On 26 January a special session of the Second All-Union Congress of Soviets was held. The major party leaders were present and spoke. Zinoviev, in a powerful oration, declared that the response to Lenin's death demonstrated the abiding faith of the Russian people in his ideas. As if speaking to Lenin directly, he stated: 'To our father. Our dear father! You have left your children forever; but your voice, your words will never die in our proletarian hearts.'[16] Then Stalin, using similarly religious imagery, gave his funeral oration. His words include an invocation to the persona of the deceased leader: 'We swear to you, comrade Lenin, that we will not spare our lives in order to strengthen the union of the working people of the whole world – the Communist International!'[17] Bukharin's speech was also uplifting: Lenin was 'a herald, a prophet, a leader'.[18]

There was a notable absentee: Trotski. His health had troubled him during his controversy with the rest of the Politburo, and he was on his way by train to the Abkhazian resort of Sukhumi by the Black Sea. On learning by telegram that Lenin had died, he asked Stalin whether he should return to Moscow. Stalin told him that he need not bother.[19] Foolishly Trotski accepted Stalin's advice. He left Stalin and others to enhance their public standing. When the day of the funeral arrived, 27 January, the pall-bearers did not include the October Revolution's most famous surviving leader.

At 9 o'clock in the morning, the coffin was carried forth from Trade Union House by Stalin, Zinoviev and six workers. Then Kamenev and Kalinin replaced Stalin and Zinoviev.[20] The coffin was borne to Red Square. A funeral oration was read by Grigori Evdokimov, Zinoviev's associate in Petrograd and the possessor of a mighty bass voice. Then the *Internationale* was played. It was foggy, and the thousands of mourners, ordinary men and women from Moscow as well as party officials, sombrely filed past the bier in homage to his memory. The central party leaders returned in the afternoon. Zinoviev, Kamenev, Stalin, Bukharin, Molotov, Tomski, Rudzutak and Dzierzynski stepped forward to lift the coffin and, at 4 o'clock, lowered it gently into the vault prepared below the Kremlin wall. The event was marked by a barrage of noise lasting three minutes. Factory hooters were sounded, cannons and rifles were fired. Life in Moscow and other cities came to a standstill. The crowds on Red Square bowed their heads, and then sang a socialist funeral hymn.[21] It was an occasion of brief ceremony and great dignity; and the signs of grief among the population, while they were not universal, demonstrated that the continued honouring of Lenin would not be entirely artificial. He had become a hero to millions, a controversial but yet a national hero.

Already the telegraph offices indicated that the memory was to be kept eternal: 'Lenin has died, but Leninism lives!'; and placards posted up in central Moscow declared that 'the grave of Lenin is the cradle of Mankind'.[22] Suitable rituals were being discussed within the Politburo. Nadezhda Krupskaya and Lenin's blood relatives were horrified by the proposal that her late husband should be embalmed and, even worse, put on public view.[23] By then Stalin had enough votes on his side, and the known opposition of Trotski, Kamenev and Bukharin was of no avail.[24]

Stalin's motivations are not wholly clear. But he had attended an Orthodox seminary as a lad and must have known about the tradition among Russian Christians that incorruptible human remains were proof of sainthood. Since 1922, furthermore, newspapers had carried reports on the discovery of the well-preserved sarcophagus of the Pharaoh Tutenkhamen in the sands near Luxor. There has even been outlandish speculation that Stalin's thought displayed the imprint of the notion developed by the philosopher N. F. Fedorov that the resurrection of the dead would shortly become a scientific possibility and would bring about mankind's salvation.[25] And yet, while the motives for the mummification of Vladimir Ilich have yet to be disclosed in detail, the general impetus is not obscure. Stalin had an intuitive understanding of the power of political symbolism. Mass mobilisation, as he perceived, required the utilisation of traditional images and new techniques. Ceremonies could therefore not simply replicate the past; they had to be inventive. Traditions were being manipulated everywhere. Not only Benito Mussolini but also the British royal family were proving adept at constructing fresh and self-serving versions of their relationship with their societies. Stalin was efficient at this task. What appeared to contemporary intellectuals as outrageous and grotesque soon became acceptable to Soviet society in general.

The coarse treatment of the feelings of Lenin's relatives continued. The technical aspects of embalming were overseen by the People's Commissar of Foreign Trade and ex-engineer Leonid Krasin.[26] Experiments were carried out on corpses in Moscow's morgues. An autopsy was published in newspapers, mentioning virtually every organ of his body. The medical specification, accompanied by mawkish editorials, was much denser than the typical post mortems on Russian emperors. Very probably the Politburo wished to counteract the rumours in Moscow that Lenin had been poisoned or that he had died of syphilis.[27] The public had to be reassured that the evidence of his corpse concorded with the assertion that his blocked and rigidified cerebral arteries had burst, flooded his cranium and brought a sudden but natural end to a disease which had afflicted him for years.[28]

A wooden mausoleum was constructed over the vault holding his coffin. An armed guard was placed on permanent duty and visitors were allowed to pay their respects in daily lines on Red Square. The party proclaimed the eternal verities of Leninism. Soon it became known as Marxism-Leninism, a hyphenation signalling that Lenin's contributions to the canon of Marxism were regarded as deep and original as those of Marx and Engels. Each major contender in the political struggle to succeed Lenin produced their summaries of his work and represented himself as his most loyal follower. Kamenev, Trotski, Bukharin, Stalin and Zinoviev contrived to justify their principal propositions in theory and in policy by reference to Lenin's writings. Busts of Lenin appeared in the shops. Posters, articles, books were mass-produced. In the party it became almost impossible to propose a policy without claiming its derivation from his wishes and commands; and the plan to recruit hundreds of thousands of workers to the ranks of Bolshevism was designated as the Lenin Levy. He had been turned into an icon, beatified by his founding of the Bolshevik party and his leadership of the October Revolution. Yet the Politburo was insistent that this was a living icon. The poet Vladimir Mayakovski – who had never been Vladimir Ilich's favourite writer – wrote exultantly: 'Lenin lived, Lenin lives, Lenin will live!'

The pathos of his last months was played down, if not forgotten. The uncertainties he had had at various moments in his career were ironed out of all accounts. The mistakes that even Lenin had admitted were brushed under the carpet. The notion was reinforced, too, that great men make history and 'the masses' follow them. As the party's ultra-centralisation continued, so the historical Lenin receded into the background and the image of a veritable demiurge of world politics was propagated in the films, plays and textbooks of the Soviet authorities. Lenin had scoffed in his lifetime at his idealisation. He had done this weakly, and never stopped it happening. But his embarrassment was real. He would have been as ashamed as was Krupskaya at the ludicrous uses made of his name, ideas and activities. Krupskaya resolutely and demonstratively refused to visit the Mausoleum. But even she participated in the fashioning of the cult around his memory. Her memoirs were wistful, sharp but always completely devoted. The irony was that the man who, more than any other, presided over the prettification and exaggeration of his role in the socialist movements worldwide was none other than he whom Lenin had sought to discharge from the seat of power in the Bolshevik party. Thus Lenin underwent posthumous humiliation at the hands of his latter-day enemy.

Pity for Lenin the politician is hardly in order. He was a merciless polemicist, a ruthless terrorist and an unrepentant defender of practically everything done by him and his party. On his death-bed he did not envisage a strategy of liquidating millions of innocent and hard-working peasants. Nor did he aim to exterminate his enemies, real and imagined, in the party. But he did not fundamentally revise his attitude to horrors which he had perpetrated between 1917 and 1922. Nevertheless he was also a secular 'believer'. His vision of a future for mankind when all exploitation and oppression would disappear was sincere. This surely is the central point about his life. The danger posed by the Lenins is not that they are simply power-crazed. It is that they combine a thirst for power with an ideological intolerance that casts down all in their path. Lenin was dignified and thoughtful, a decent man in his personal relations. But his willingness to carry through his ideas against all the evidence that they did not work as he had expected is an object lesson of twentieth-century politics. Lenin at least had the excuse, if this is what it is, that he and the Bolsheviks were trying out something for the first time. They were bound to commit blunders. Again and again their apologists have depicted them as worthy triers who had no chance to anticipate that the results of their handiwork would confound their dreams. This is wishful nonsense. The political parties which resisted the Bolsheviks, particularly the socialists among these opponents, warned with exactitude in 1917 what would happen. Those who followed Lenin and Marxism-Leninism outside Russia were taking the line of a political movement that, by its actions, had already conclusively failed to demonstrate the practicability of its ideals. They were deceived by the apparent 'success' of the Soviet republic in simply surviving in a capitalist-dominated world; and they too readily accepted the claims of Bolshevik party propaganda.

But they also were responding to the conditions of distress, social and political, in their own countries. In most societies these conditions have not been improved in the years after Lenin's death. Only a minority of the globe's national economies have provided prosperity for most of their people. To that extent it would be foolhardy to predict, even after the spectacular demise of communism in Eastern Europe, that all-or-nothing politics of the left as well as the right will not recur in the world. But about one thing we can be certain: there will never be the like of Lenin again.

Notes

As in Volumes One and Two, the system of transliteration used in the chapters is modified in the endnotes to conform with the conventions of the SEER in respect of authors' names and the titles of their works in Russian. The abbreviations used in the endnotes are as follows:

BK	Vladimir Il'ich Lenin. *Biograficheskaya khronika* (Moscow, 1970–1982), vols 1–12.
Comintern II	*Workers of the World and Oppressed Peoples Unite! Proceedings and Documents of the Second Congress of Comintern, 1920* (edited and translated by J. Riddell: New York, 1991).
DSV	*Dekrety Sovetskoi Vlasti* (Moscow, 1957–), vol. 1 ff.
GARF	*Gosudarstvennyi arkhiv Rossiiskoi Federatsii.*
ITsKKPSS	*Izvestiya Tsentral'nogo Komiteta Kommunisticheskoi Partii Sovetskogo Soyuza* (1989–1991).
KVIII	*Vos'maya konferentsiya RKP(b). Dekabr' 1919 goda. Protokoly* (Moscow, 1961).
KIX	*Devyataya konferenstiya RKP(b). Sentyabr' 1920 goda. Protokoly* (Moscow, 1972).
KX	*Protokoly Desyatoi Vserossiiskoi konferentsii RKP(b). Mai 1921 g.* (Moscow, 1933).
KXI	*Vserossiiskaya konferentsiya RKP (bol'shevikov). Byulleteni, 19–29 dekabrya 1921 goda* (Moscow, 1921–1922), nos 1–5.
LS	*Leninskii sbornik* (Moscow, 1924–1985), vols 1–50.
PSS	*Polnoe sobranie sochinenii V. I. Lenina* (Moscow, 1958–1965), vols 1–55.
RTsKhIDNI	*Rossiiskii tsentr dlya khraneniya i issledovaniya dokumentov noveishei istorii.*
SIX	*Devyatyi s"ezd RKP(b). Mart-aprel' 1920. Protokoly* (Moscow, 1960)
Stalin, *Sochineniya*	*Sochineniya* (Moscow, 1946–1951), vols 1–12.
SVII	*Sed'moi ekstrennii s"ezd RKP(b). Mart 1918. Stenograficheskii otchet* (Moscow, 1962).
SVIII	*Vos'moi s"ezd RKP(b). Mart 1919. Protokoly* (Moscow, 1959).
SX	*Desyatyi s"ezd RKP(b). Mart 1921 g. Stenograficheskii otchet* (Moscow, 1963).
SXI	*Odinnatsatyi s"ezd RKP(b). Mart–aprel' 1922 g. Stenograficheskii otchet (Moscow, 1961).*
SXII	*Dvenadtsatyi s"ezd RKP(b). 17–25 aprelya 1923 g. Stenograficheski otchet* (Moscow, 1968).
TKK	*Tretii kongress Kominterna. Razvitie kongressom politicheskoi linii kommunisticheskogo dvizheniya. Kommunisty i massy* (edited by F. I. Firsov: Moscow, 1975).

TP	*The Trotsky Papers, 1917–1922* (edited by J. Meijer: The Hague, 1964, 1971), vols 1–2.
Trotski, *Sochineniya*	*Sochineniya* (Moscow, 1925–1927), vols 1–21.
TVK	*Tretii Vsemirnyi kongress Kommunisticheskogo Internatsionala. Stenograficheski otchet* (Petrograd, 1922).
VIKPSS	*Voprosy Istorii Kommunisticheskoi Partii Sovetskogo Soyuza* (1962–1991).
VL	N. K. Krupskaya, *Vospominaniya o Lenine* (Moscow, 1968).
VVIL	*Vospominaniya o V. I. Lenine* (Moscow, 1968–1969), vols 1–5.

The Moscow archives used in this volume include mainly the following:

The Russian Centre for the Conservation and Study of Documents of Contemporary History (*RTsKhIDNI*):

fond 5, opis' 2:	Party Congress delegates' questions to Lenin; sundry party discussions from 1919; Georgian Affair file.
fond 17, opis' 2:	Party Central Committee plenums.
fond 17, opis' 3:	Politburo of the Party Central Committee.
fond 44, opis' 1:	Ninth Conference of the Party.
fond 46, opis' 1:	Tenth Conference of the Party.

The State Archive of the Russian Federation (*GARF*):

fond 1318, opis' 1:	People's Commissariat of Nationality Affairs
fond 6980, opis' 1:	Drafting Commission of the RSFSR Constitution
fond R-130, opisi 2–5:	Sovnarkom
fond R-130, opis' 6:	Governmental commissions, 1922

CHAPTER 1: MERCILESS RETREAT

1. *PSS*, vol. 36, p. 207.
2. Idem, p. 172.
3. Idem, p. 195.
4. Idem, pp. 196–7.
5. Idem, pp. 175, 182 and 196.
6. Idem, pp. 174, 175 and 201–2.
7. Idem, p. 189.
8. Ibid.
9. Idem, p. 179.
10. Idem, p. 183.
11. Idem, p. 179 and 183.
12. Idem, pp. 191–2.
13. Idem, p. 197.
14. Idem, pp. 200 and 206.
15. See below, pp. 10 and 12.
16. L. D. Trotskii, *O Lenine. Materialy dlya biografa* (Moscow, 1924), p. 111.
17. See idem, p. 112.
18. *Pravda*, 3 January 1924.

19. See R. Service, *The Bolshevik Party in Revolution. A Study in Organisational Change* (London, 1979), p. 80.
20. See idem, pp. 82–3.
21. See idem, pp. 104–5.
22. *RTsKhIDNI*, f.17, op. 2, ed.khr.1, p. 5
23. *Programma kommunistov (bol'shevikov)* (Petrograd, 1918), passim.
24. See Volume Two, pp. 323–6.
25. *GARF*, f.130, op. 2, ed. khr.1, pt. 3: 8 May 1918, item 2.
26. Ibid.
27. Ibid.
28. Idem, 9 May 1918: item 1.
29. *DSV*, vol. 2 (1959), pp. 264–5.
30. *PSS*, vol. 36, p. 374.
31. *DSV*, vol. 2 pp. 416–9.
32. See V. Brovkin, *The Mensheviks after October. Socialist Opposition and the Rise of the Bolshevik Dictatorship* (Cornell, 1987), pp. 177–8.
33. See idem, pp. 227–8
34. *PSS*, vol. 36, pp. 327–45
35. See Brovkin, *The Mensheviks*, pp. 227–8
36. See above, p. 4.
37. See V. M. Fić, *The Bolsheviks and the Czechoslovak Legion. The Origin of their Armed Conflict, March to May 1918* (New Delhi, 1978), pp. 20–1, 26–7 and 80–91.
It has been suggested that Trotski, still not being reconciled to the Brest-Litovsk treaty, hoped to deploy the Legion if ever the struggle against the Germans on the Eastern front might be resumed. But this would not explain why Trotski so stupidly alienated the feelings of the Czech and Slovak troops.
38. See Fić, op. cit., p. 262.
39. See idem, pp. 284–5
40. See above, p. 8.
41. See Fić, op. cit, pp. 291–3
42. See idem, pp. 307–8, 313, 336–7
43. See Yu. G. Fel'shtinskii, *Bol'sheviki i levye esery, oktyabr' 1917 – iyul' 1918. Na puti k odnopartiinoi diktature* (Paris, 1985), pp. 127–8.
44. *Krasnaya kniga VChK*, vol. 1 (2nd corrected edition: Moscow, 1989), pp. 185–6.
45. Idem, p. 252–6. See also Fel'shtinskii, *Bol'sheviki i levye esery*, pp. 145–59.
46. Ibid.
47. See idem, pp. 164–73.
48. G. A. Solomon, *Sredi krasnykh vozhdei* (Paris, 1930), p. 83.
49. See below, pp. 37–42 and 242–7.
50. V. D. Bonch-Bruevich, *Vospominaniya o Lenine* (2nd edition: Moscow, 1969), p. 309.
51. L. D. Trotskii, *O Lenine* p. 118.
52. Idem, pp. 118–9.
53. G. Hilger and A. G. Meyer, *The Incompatible Allies. A Memoir-History of Soviet-German Relations, 1918–1941* (New York, 1953), p. 7.

54. See Fel'shtinskii, *Bol'sheviki i levye esery*, pp. 214–5.
55. This suggestion is cautiously made by Yu.G. Fel'shtinskii, ibid.
56. *Krasnaya kniga*, vol. 1, pp. 252–61.
57. *Pamyat'*, no.2, p. 27.
58. See Volume One, p. 139.
59. See below, p. 74–5.
60. *Proletarskaya revolyutsiya*, 1927, no.4(63), p. 128.
61. *Krasnaya kniga*, vol. 1, p. 299.
62. See Volume Two, pp. 326–7 for examples of Lenin's dismissiveness of the Left Communists.
63. *PSS*, vol. 36, especially p. 324.
64. Idem, p. 105.
65. Idem, p. 250.
66. See his hurt comment in idem, p. 253.
67. Idem, p. 323.
68. Idem, p. 324.
69. Not that he was averse to essaying this practice: see below, pp. 237–41.
70. *PSS*, vol. 36, p. 324.
71. Idem, p. 324.
72. See B. Pearce, *How Haig Saved Lenin* (London, 1987), chap. 1.
73. See idem, pp. 15 and 16.
74. See idem, p. 33.
75. See idem, p. 32
76. *ITsKKPSS*, 1989, no.4, p. 143.
77. Idem, pp. 143–4.
78. *ITsKKPSS*, 1989, no.4, p. 144.
79. Ibid.; and see Pearce, *How Haig Saved Lenin*, p. 46.
80. See idem, pp. 16–17 and 23.
81. See idem, p. 23.
82. See idem, pp. 68–9.
83. See idem, pp. 45–6.
84. *PSS*, vol. 50, p. 117.
85. See Pearce, op. cit., p. 65.
86. See the document quoted in D. Volkogonov, 'Leninskaya krepost' v moei dushe pala poslednei', *Moskovskie novosti*, no.29, 19 July 1992, p. 20.
87. See Pearce, op. cit., chap. 12.
88. *PSS*, vol. 35, pp. 56–7.
89. *RTsKhIDNI*, f.17, op. 2, d.1, p. 3.
90. *GARF*, f.6980, op. 1, ed.khr.3, p. 1 and 7–8. See also Kh. Libman, 'O pervoi Sovetskoi konstitutsii' in A. Alymov *et al.* (eds), *Ob izmeneniyakh sovetskoi konstitutsii. Sbornik statei* (Moskva, 1935), p. 52; V.P. Portnov and M.M. Slavin, *Stanovlenie i razvitie konstitutsionnogo zakondatel'stva Sovetskogo Rossii, 1917–1920 gg.* (Moscow, 1987), p. 161.
91. *PSS*, vol. 35, p. 286; *DSV* vol. 1, p. 350.
92. See Volume Two, p. 287.
93. *Pravda*, 9 April 1918.
94. Ibid.
95. Ibid.
96. Ibid.

97. See Volume Two, pp. 285–6.
98. See idem, p. 286. Reading Stalin's article, Lenin may well also have been disconcerted by the apparent neglect of the requirement to avoid giving unnecessary provocation to the German government after the treaty of Brest-Litovsk.
99. See below, p. 23.
100. Commission meetings, 5 and 10 April 1918: *GARF*, f.6980, op. 1, ed.khr.3 (pp. 12 and 15) and 4 (pp. 6–7, 9, 17–18 and 79–80).
101. Idem, ed. khr.5, p. 22.
102. Idem, ed. khr.6, p. 1.
103. Idem, p. 10.
104. Idem, pp. 4 and 13.
105. Trotskii, *O Lenine*, pp. 113–4. See also Volume Two, p. 287.
106. *GARF*, f.6980, op. 1, ed.khr.9, p. 1.
107. See the evidence in idem, ed.khr.11, p. 1.
108. Ibid.
109. Idem, p. 2.
110. L. D. Trotskii, *O Lenine.*, pp. 113–4; *BK*, vol. 5, p. 600.
111. Indeed Steklov had been a leading political figure after the February Revolution, serving in March 1917 as editor of *Izvestiya*.
112. *BK*, vol. 5, pp. 623–4.
113. *Izvestiya*, 19 July 1918.
114. *DSV*, vol. 2, p. 552.
115. See Volume Two, pp. 216–23.
116. *DSV*, vol. 2, p. 553.
117. Idem, p. 554.
118. Idem, p. 561–2.
119. Idem, p. 553.
120. Idem, p. 559.
121. Idem, p. 555–6.
122. See below, pp. 274–81.
123. *DSV*, vol. 2, p. 554.
124. See V. Fić, *The Bolsheviks and the Czechoslovak Legion*, pp. 116–26.
125. See idem, p. 116.
126. See R. Service. *The Bolshevik Party in Revolution*, p. 82.
127. See E. Mawdsley, *The Russian Civil War* (London, 1987), p. 61.
128. *PSS*, vol. 50, pp. 370 and 378.
129. Idem, p. 178.
130. Ibid.
131. *TP*, vol. 1, p. 154.
132. *PSS*, vol. 50, p. 179.

CHAPTER 2: CLOSING THE CIRCLE

1. *PSS*, vol. 37, p. 82. I have inserted the exclamation marks in this and the quotation in the following note; obviously Lenin in such circumstances must have been exclaiming at the time.
2. Idem, p. 83.

3. Ibid.
4. Idem, p. 84.
5. Idem, p. 85.
6. *Pravda*, 31 August 1918.
7. See the medical testimony published years later: 'U rannego Il'icha. Po vospominaniyam vrachei-kommunistov Obukha Veisbroda', *Pravda*, 30 August 1923.
8. 'K istorii pokusheniya na Lenina (neopublikovannye materialy', ed. I. Volkovicher (*PR*, 1923,nos 6–7, dopros 2, p. 282; dopros 4, p. 284.
9. Idem, p. 279.
10. For a particularly exigent examination of the evidence, see Semion Lyandres, 'The 1918 Attempt on the Life of Lenin: a New Look at the Evidence', *Slavic Review*, 1989, no.3, pp. 437–41.
11. See idem, p. 441.
12. *Bednota*, 1 September 1918, p. 1.
13. 'K istorii pokusheniya na Lenina (neopublikovannye materialy', loc. cit., p. 279.
14. *Pravda*, 31 August 1918.
15. V. D. Bonch-Bruevich, *Vospominaniya o Lenine, 1917–1924* (Moscow, 1963), p. 293.
16. See S. Lyandres, 'The 1918 Attempt', p. 442 for an analysis of Sverdlov's behaviour.
17. See the argument of Lyandres, op.cit..
18. See idem, p. 434.
19. ibid.
20. See below, p. 244.
21. See idem, p. 435.
22. P. Mal'kov, 'Zapiski Komendanta Kremlya', *Moskva*, no.11, 1958, p. 137.
23. Semion Lyandres argues (op. cit., pp. 441–2) that the motivation was to clear up the case before Lenin's return to work. While this may have been a factor, I feel that the larger political agenda of Sverdlov may have been more significant.
24. See ibid.
25. M. Gor'kii, 'V. I. Lenin', *VVIL*, vol. 2, p. 255.
26. See the memoir of M.I. Ulyanova, ITsKKPSS, 1991, no.6, pp. 193–4.
27. See Volume Two, pp. 218–22, 223 and 224.
28. *PSS*, vol. 37, p. 290.
29. See Volume Two, p. 221.
30. *PSS*, vol. 37, pp. 244–5.
31. Idem, p. 245.
32. See Volume Two, p. 219–20.
33. See idem, p. 221.
34. *PSS*, vol. 37, p. 248.
35. This sentence, incidentally, was quoted by Lenin from his pamphlet co-written with G. E. Zinoviev, *Socialism and the War* (Geneva, 1915). What is remarkable by comparison is the lack of gradual build-up to violent invective in *Proletarian Revolution and Kautsky the Renegade*.
36. Idem, pp. 253–4 and 256.
37. See R. Geary, *Karl Kautsky* (Manchester, 1987) pp. 73–8.

38. *PSS*, vol. 37, p. 257.
39. See Volume Two, p. 222.
40. *PSS*, vol. 37, pp. 265–6.
41. Idem, pp. 259–60.
42. Idem, pp. 300 and 301.
43. Idem, p. 299.
44. Idem, pp. 275–6
45. Idem, passim.
46. Idem, p. 292.
47. Idem, pp. 321–2
48. Idem, p. 308.
49. See Volume Two, p. 223.
50. L. D. Trotskii, *Terrorizm i kommunizm* (Petersburg, 1920).
51. See below, pp. 291 ff.
52. *Izvestiya*, 17 September: report on the second half of a Central Committee meeting.
53. See G. Leggett, *Lenin's Political Police. The All-Russian Extraordinary Commission for Combatting Counter-Revolution and Sabotage (December 1917–February 1922)* (Oxford, 1981), pp. 113–4 pp. 113–4.
54. *GARF* f.R-130, op.2, d.1(2) and 1(3): SNK, 29 January 1918 and 2 May 1918.
55. L. D. Trotskii, *Trotsky's Diary in Exile* (London 1959), p. 80.
56. *RTsKhIDNI*, f. 17, op.2, d.1, item 5.
57. See below for the communications between Moscow and Ekaterinburg prior to the killing of the Romanovs. For a denial that Lenin had nothing to do with the order to kill, see V.M. Molotov in F. Chuev (ed.), *140 razgovorov s V.M.Molotovym* (Moscow, 1992), p. 77.
58. See Yu. Buranov ans V. Khrustalev, *Gibel' imperatskogo doma, 1917–1919 gg.* (Moscow, 1992), p. 261.
59. *GARF*, f.R-130, op.2, dd.1(3), item 4.
60. Not that Kolchak and Denikin were known as pre-eminent monarchists.
61. See the telegram quoted in Buranov and Khrustalev Gibel', p. 261.
62. See ibid.
63. *GARF*, f.R-130, op.2, d.2 (2): SNK, 17 August 1918, item 3.
64. M. Cherniavsky, *Tsar and People: Studies in Russian Myths* (New Haven, 1961).
   Lenin declined to answer a query at the Eighth Party Congress why a trial of Nikolai II had not been organised: *RTsKhIDNI*, f.5, op.2, d.2, p. 5.
65. See Volume One, pp. 99 and 135 and Volume Two, p. 226–7.
66. *GARF*, f.R-130, op.2, d.2(3).
67. See Leggett, *Lenin's Political Police*, p. 102.
68. See idem, p. 111.
69. See idem, p. 114.
70. Ibid.
71. *ITsKKPSS*, 1989, no.6, p. 163.
72. Ibid.
73. *Izvestiya*, 3 September 1918.
74. Idem, no. 244, 9 November 1918.

75. *PSS*, vol. 50, p. 106.
76. Ibid.
77. See his demands at the Central Committee, *ITsKKPSS*, 1989, no.12, p. 150.
78. See R. Medvedev, *Let History Judge: The Origins and Consequences of Stalinism* (London, 1971), p. 13.
79. See I. Deutscher, *Trotsky: The Prophet Armed* (Oxford, 1954) vol. 1, chap.12.
80. See for example PSS, vol. 51, pp. 85–6.
81. On Bukharin see Leggett, *Lenin's Political Police*, pp. 136–7 and pp. 162–3.
82. See, for example, *ITsKKPSS*, 1989, no.6, pp. 146, 160 and 163; no.8, p. 159; no.12, p. 139, 169–70 and 174; 1990, no.2, p. 165.
83. Idem, 1989, no.6, p. 160.
84. *ITsKKPSS*, 1989, no.6, p. 146.
85. See Leggett, op. cit., pp. 162–3.
86. ITsKKPSS, 1989, no.12, p, 169.
87. Idem, pp. 169–70.
88. Idem, 1990, no.2, p. 165.
89. Ibid.
90. *TP*, vol. 2, p. 278.
91. See Leggett, op. cit., pp. 464–7.
92. See the documents quoted in 'Ubit pri popytke k begstvu', *Moskovskie novosti*, no.24, 14 June 1992, p. 24.
93. See the document quoted by P. Voshchanov in 'Moral' v politike net', Komsomol' skaya pravda, 12 February 1992.
94. Ibid.
95. See Volume Two, p. 101.
96. *PSS*, vol. 37, p. 64.
97. For an account of the German military collapse in the West as well as its relation to the Eastern front, see B. Pearce, *How Haig Saved Lenin*, pp. 55–78.
98. See the minutes in *ITsKKPSS*, 1989, no.6, pp. 154–5 (16 September 1918); p. 158 (2 October 1918), when Lenin was empowered to proceed to report on the international situation to the All-Russian Central Executive Committee); p. 161 (22 October 1918); p. 162 (25 October 1918); p. 167 (17 December 1918); p. 169 (19 December 1918).
99. *RTsKhIDNI*, f.17, op.2, d.1, p. 7.
100. *PSS*, vol. 50, p. 135.
101. M. Drachkovitch and B. Lazitch, *Lenin and the Comintern*, vol. 1, pp. 40-1.
102. *PSS*, vol. 50, p. 183.
103. Idem, p. 185.
104. Idem, pp. 183, 194 and 201.
105. Idem, p. 194.
106. Idem, p. 186.
107. Ibid.
108. Ibid.
109. *GARF*, f.130, op. 2, d.2: Sovnarkom meeting, 5 October 1918.

110. *PSS*, vol. 37, p. 120: speech of 22 October 1918.
111. *GARF*, f.130, op. 2, d.2: Sovnarkom meeting of 16 November 1918.
112. See below, pp. 62–6.
113. See his statements in November and December 1918: *PSS*, vol. 37, pp. 212 and 375.
114. Idem, vol. 50, p. 227.
115. See Volume One, p. 167 and Volume Two, pp. 225 and 226.
116. See J. P. Nettl, *Rosa Luxemburg* (Oxford,1960), vol. 2, p. 696.
117. See idem, p. 700–1.
118. See idem, p. 699.
119. See idem, p. 752.
120. See A. Lindemann, *The 'Red Years'. European Socialism Versus Bolshevism, 1919–1921* (London, 1974), pp. 50–1.
121. *PSS*, vol. 50, p. 258.
122. See below, pp. 67–72.
123. *PSS*, vol. 50, p. 221.
124. See J. Channon, 'Siberia in Revolution and Civil War', in A. Wood (ed.), *The History of Siberia from Russian Conquest to Revolution* (London, 1991), pp. 172–3.
125. See E. Mawdsley, *The Russian Civil War*, pp. 85–111.
126. *PSS*, vol. 50, p. 220.
127. See *PSS*, vol. 37, *passim*: this covers the period July 1918 to March 1919. It is true that Kolchak's name comes up in Lenin's project resolution of the Central Executive Committee of the Congress of Soviets. But the following points are noteworthy: first, the project was for an institution not led by Lenin; two; the project was not subsequently identifiable by the general public as having been written by Lenin; three, the project was dedicated to the banning of a Menshevik newspaper and not to the military threat posed by Kolchak.
128. See Volume Two, pp. 211–3.
129. See A. Ulam, *Expansion and Coexistence,* (2nd edition: London, 1973) pp. 96–7.
130. See E. H. Carr, *The Bolshevik Revolution*, vol. 3 (London, 1953), pp.112–3 and 115–6.
131. See R. McNeal, *Bride of the Revolution. Krupskaya and Lenin* (Ann Arbor, 1972) p. 190–1.
132. E. V. Gimpel'son, *Voennyi Kommunizm. Politika, praktika, ideologiya* (Moscow, 1973), gives a sophisticated version of this canard.
133. I. Mints, *God 1918* (Moscow, 1982) pp. 362–3.
134. *PSS*, vol. 36, p. 359
135. Ibid.
136. Idem, p. 393.
137. Idem, pp. 409–11.
138. Idem, p. 433 .
139. See E. H. Carr, *The Bolshevik Revolution*, vol. 2 (London, 1952) p. 152.
140. Idem, p. 491.
141. See T. V. Osipova, 'Razvitie sotsialisticheskoi revolyutsii v derevene v pervyi god dikatury proletariata', in M. Volkov et al. (eds), *Oktyabr' i sovetskoe krest'yanstvo, 1917–1922* (Moscow, 1977) pp. 88.

142. See A. Nove, *Economic History of the USSR* (London, 1969), p. 61.
143. See Volume Two, p. 314.
144. *PSS*, vol. 37, p. 207.
145. Idem, p. 413.
146. See the interesting dissection of rhetoric in L.Lih, *Bread and Authority* (Berkeley, 1990), chap.6.
147. *PSS*, vol. 37, p. 41.
148. Ibid.
149. *Izvestiya*, 18 August 1918.
150. *DSV*, vol. 2, pp. 413–6.
151. See E. H. Carr, *The Bolshevik Revolution*, vol. 2, pp. 158–9.
152. See idem, pp. 52–3.
153. *SVIII*, p. 21.
154. *GARF*, f.R-130, op.3, d.3, p. 3
155. This calculation is based on the table of data provided in Strizhkov in Volkov et al. (eds), *Oktyabr' i sovetskoe krest'yanstvo*, p. 140.
156. See idem, p. 141.
157. *PSS*, vol. 37, p. 522.
158. See E. H. Carr, *The Bolshevik Revolution*, vol. 2, pp. 154–5.
159. *PSS*, vol. 37, pp. 1–20.
160. For a typical example where all rural problems for the Bolsheviks are blamed upon kulaks, see *PSS*, vol. 37, p. 360.
161. See Volume Two, p. 270.
162. *RTsKhIDNI*, f.17 op.2, d.1-2: the exceptions were a brief discussion of 'specialists' on 7 April 1918 (idem, d.1, item 1) and another on bank workers on 16 September 1918 (d.2, item 1).
163. See, for example, *PSS*, vol. 37, pp. 397–401.
164. *GARF*, f.130, op. 2, d.1(5), item 6.
165. Idem, d.2(2), it.9.
166. See below, p. 159.
167. See E. H. Carr, *The Bolshevik Revolution*, vol. 2, p. 198.
168. See R. Service, *The Bolshevik Party*, p. 110–1.
169. For the classic account of this change see L. Kritsman, *Geroicheskii period velikoi russkoi revolyutsii. (Opyt analiza tak nazyvaemogo 'voennogo kommunizma')*, (2nd edition: Moscow, 1926).
170. See S. N. Prokopovich, *Narodnoe khozyaistro SSSR* (New York, 1952), vol. 1, p. 329.
171. See L. S. Gaponenko, *Sovetskii rabochii klass, 1918–1920 gg. Sotsial' no-politicheskie izmeneniya* (Moscow, 1974), p. 341.
172. *GARF*, f.130, op. 2, d.2(2): Sovnarkom, 5 October 1918.
173. Idem, d.2(2): Sovnarkom, 29 July 1918, item 9.
174. Idem, d.2(2): Sovnarkom, 3 August 1918, item 9.

CHAPTER 3: ONLY ONE YEAR

1. See R. Service, *The Bolshevik Party in Revolution*, chaps 3–4.
2. *SVII*, pp. 170–1.
3. See Service, *op.cit.*, pp. 101–2 and 105–6.

4. See Volume Two, pp. 289–90.
5. See, for example, *GARF*, f.R-130, op.2, d.1(2), item 5: 31 January 1918.
6. For example, *PSS*, vol. 37, p. 397.
7. N. Osinskii, *SVIII*, pp. 164–5.
8. See R. Service, *The Bolshevik Party*, pp. 102 and 109.
9. E. B. Genkina, *Lenin – Predsedatel' Sovnarkoma i STO* (Moscow, 1960), chap.1.
10. See R. Service, 'From Polyarchy to Hegemony: the Party's Role in the Construction of the Central Institutions of the Soviet State, 1917–1919', *Sbornik*, no.10, 1984, pp. 77–90.
11. *SVII*, p. 171.
12. See R. Service, *The Bolshevik Party*, p. 102.
13. See idem, pp.106–9; and Service, 'From Polyarchy to Hegemony', loc. cit.
14. Stalin, *Sochineniya*, vol. 4, pp. 197–224.
15. *TP*, vol. 1, p. 228.
16. See above, note 2.
17. *SVII*, p. 171.
18. See R. Service, *The Bolshevik Party*, p. 105.
19. See idem, p. 106.
20. See idem, p. 58.
21. Not that this stopped Stalin in later years from exaggerating the Politburo's significance in an effort to establish his own credentials as one of the architects of the October Revolution: see R.Slusser, *Stalin in October: The Man Who Missed the Revolution* (Baltimore, 1987), pp. 246–8.
22. *ITsKKPSS*, 1989, no.6, pp. 160; see also meetings recorded in idem, pp. 167–9.
23. Idem, p. 175. N. A. Petrovichev in the official *Partiinoe stroitel'stvo: uchebnoe posobie* (Moscow, 1970), p. 141 suggests that a Political Bureau, too, was set up at this time. The above-cited section of Central Committee minutes do not refer to a Political Bureau; but perhaps the 'Bureau' of mid-December 1918 is what is being mentioned.
24. Idem, pp. 175–9.
25. *ITsKKPSS*, 1989, no.7, 147; I. V.Stalin, *Sochineniya*, vol. 4, p. 197 ff.
26. *ITsKKPSS*, 1989, no.7, 147.
27. I. V. Stalin, *Sochineniya*, vol. 4, p. 121.
28. See R. Tucker, *Stalin as Revolutionary, 1879–1929. A Study in History and Personality* (London, 1974), pp. 192–3
29. *TP*, vol. 1, p. 134.
30. Idem, p. 140.
31. Idem, pp. 158 and 160.
32. Idem, p. 158.
33. Idem, p. 160.
34. For examples of Lenin getting only the second copy see idem, pp. 114, 134, 140, 146.
35. *ITsKKPSS*, 1989, no.6, p. 164.
36. L. D. Trotskii, *Moya zhizn'. Opyt avtobiografii* (Berlin, 1930), vol. 2, chap.26. Admittedly, the sole extant record of this exchange comes from one side in the dispute.

37. *ITsKKPSS*, 1989, no.6, pp. 163–4.
38. See F. Benvenuti, *The Bolsheviks and the Red Army* (Cambridge, 1988), p.49; and *ITsKKPSS*, 1989, no.6, p. 164.
39. *TP*, vol. 1, p. 164.
40. *LS*, vol. 37, p. 106.
41. See Benvenuti, *The Bolsheviks*, p. 92.
42. See, for example, Stalin, *Sochineniya*, vol. 4, pp. 118–21.
43. L. D. Trotskii, *Moya zhizn'*, vol. 2, pp. 422–3. Trotski is the only source for this so that a degree of scepticism may be in order. Nevertheless the contents are clearly in line with the rest of the available information about Lenin's attitude.
44. See an eloquent statement of this case in Benvenuti, op.cit., pp. 313–18.
45. See below, pp. 256 ff.
46. The notion, however, that Stalin would never have headed the central party leadership if Sverdlov had not died is altogether too contingential: Stalin's victory over his opponents did not derive predominantly from his accession to the Secretariat in 1922.
47. See R. Service, *The Bolshevik Party in Revolution*, pp. 102–3 and 109.
48. This is recorded in the agenda of the Central Committee for 16 March 1919: *ITsKKPSS*, 1989, no.8, p. 165.
49. See above, pp. 63–4.
50. The Central Committee's compliance with the Eighth Party Congress's instructions on the Politburo, Orgburo and Secretariat was made at the 25 March 1919 plenum: *ITsKPSS*, 1989, no.12, p. 133.
51. R. N. Hunt, *German Social Democracy, 1918–1933* (New Haven, 1964), p. 112.
52. *PSS*, vol. 37, p. 486.
53. See Volume Two, p. 72.
54. *PSS*, vol. 50, pp. 227–30.
55. See Volume Two, pp. 60–66 and 97–118.
56. In comparison with the scale of its consequences for the history of Europe, the documentary base for the Comintern's formation is paltry since so many decisions were made orally. See *PSS*, vol. 37, pp. 489–90 for Lenin's speech to the Comintern's opening session.
57. *Der I under II. Kongress der Kommunistischen Internationale. Dokumente der Kongresse under Reden W. I. Lenins* (Dietz Verlag Berlin, 1959), pp. 45–50.
58. See B. Lazitch and M. M. Drachkovitch, *Lenin and the Comintern*, vol. 1, p. 56.
59. *PSS*, vol. 50, p. 229.
60. Idem, vol. 37, p. 489.
61. See A. S. Lindemann, *'The Red Years'. European Socialism versus Bolshevism, 1919–1921* (Berkeley, 1974), pp. 49–50.
62. See idem, pp. 50–1.
63. *PSS*, vol. 37, p. 490.
64. *SVIII*, pp. 501– 4.
65. See Lazitch and Drachkovitch, op.cit., vol. 1, p. 67.
66. See idem, pp. 80–3.
67. *PSS*, vol. 37, pp. 492–3.

68. Idem, pp. 494–5, 497 and 499.
69. Idem, pp. 503–4.
70. This is stated explicitly in a private comment on Zinoviev's draft theses on 'The Foundations of the III International': idem, vol. 54, p. 502.
71. *The Communist International, 1919–1943. Documents* (Ed. J. Degras: London, 1971), vol. 1, pp. 17–24.
72. Idem, pp. 26–8.
73. Idem, pp. 32–5.
74. Idem, p. 44.
75. Idem, p. 38.
76. *PSS*, vol. 37, p. 511.
77. See Benvenuti, *The Bolsheviks and the Red Army*, pp. 92–6.
78. *Pravda*, no.49, 4 March 1919. See also *Stenograficheskii otchet pyatoi nizhegorodskoi gubernskoi konferentsii RKP (bol'shevikov)* (Nizhni Novgorod, 1918), p. 67; *Nizhegorodskaya kommuna*, no.27, 6 February 1919 and no.32, 12 February 1919.
79. See below, pp. 80–1.
80. *Pravda*, no.49, 4 March 1919.
81. *Proletarii* (Simbirsk), no.51, 2 March 1919.
82. *Pravda*, no.155, 12 March 1919.
83. See Service, *The Bolshevik Party in Revolution*, p. 103.
84. *PSS*, vol. 50, p. 183.
85. See Volume Two, p. 318.
86. *ITsKKPSS*, 1989, no.9, pp. 135 ff.
87. See below, pp. 173–6.
88. *ITsKKPSS*, 1989, no.9, p. 189.
89. Idem, p.157.
90. See, for example, *PSS*, vol. 37, pp. 99 and 156.
91. *Trotsky's Diary in Exile, 1935* (London, 1959), p. 80.
92. Idem, vol. 38, p. 53. For an account of the lukewarm open support by Lenin see Benvenuti, *The Bolsheviks*, pp. 92–3.
93. *ITsKKPSS*, 1989, no.9, pp. 175–81; *Izvestiya*, 25 February 1919.
94. Idem, 1989, no.8, p. 157.
95. Idem, p. 158.
96. Idem, p. 164.
97. Idem, pp. 161–2.
98. See below, pp. 79–80.
99. Idem, 1989, no.8, p. 164.
100. *SVIII*, p. 4.
101. Idem, p. 5.
102. Idem, p. 6.
103. Idem, p. 8.
104. Idem, p. 11.
105. Ibid.
106. Idem, p. 12.
107. Idem, p. 16.
108. Idem, p. 20.
109. Idem, p. 21–2.

110. Idem, p. 24.
111. Idem, pp. 27–8.
112. On the commission's establishment at the Seventh Party Congress in March 1918, see Volume Two, p. 332.
113. Idem, p. 47.
114. Idem, p. 48.
115. Idem, pp. 49–50.
116. Idem, p. 52.
117. Idem, p. 53.
118. Idem, p. 55.
119. Idem, p. 78.
120. Idem, pp. 79 and 80.
121. Idem, p. 87.
122. Idem, p. 90.
123. Idem, p. 92.
124. Idem, p. 94.
125. Idem, p. 106.
126. Idem, p. 115.
127. Idem, p. 129–31.
128. Idem, p. 136 and 143. The Russian phrase is *ideinoe rukovodstvo*, which strictly speaking is translatable as 'leadership in the sphere of ideas'.
129. Idem, pp. 146 and 150.
130. *ITsKKPSS*, 1989, no.9, pp. 175–81
131. Idem, pp.181–4; *SVIII*, pp. 153–8.
132. For examples, see *ITsKKPSS*, 1989, no.9, pp. 139 (A. F. Myasnikov), 141 (E. M. Yaroslavski), 144 (F. I. Goloshchekin), 149 (Abramov), 153 (S. K. Minin).,
133. Idem, p. 171.
134. *ITsKKPSS*, 1989, no.11, p. 151.
135. This fifth session was withheld from all editions of the Congress proceedings; it was first published in *ITsKKPSS*, 1989, no.11, pp. 144–76.
136. Idem, p. 144–51.
137. Idem, p. 152.
138. Idem, p. 157.
139. Idem, pp. 161–2.
140. Idem, p. 163.
141. Idem, pp. 167–8.
142. Idem, p. 169.
143. Idem, p. 168.
144. Idem, p. 172: the Russian word *nevinnost'* implies both ignorance and naïveté.
145. Idem, pp. 173 and 175.
146. Idem, p. 176.
147. *SVIII*, p. 273.
148. Idem, pp. 164–5.
149. Idem, p. 170.
150. Idem, p. 178.

151. Idem, pp. 186 and 190–3.
152. Idem, pp. 202–3.
153. Idem, p. 214.
154. Idem, p. 322.
155. *PSS*, vol. 38, p. 95; *SVIII*, p. 53.
156. Idem, p. 398.
157. Idem, p. 337.
158. See below, pp. 191–4 and 274–82.
159. *SVIII*, p. 340.
160. Idem, p. 340.
161. *ITsKKPSS*, 1989, no.9, p. 179.
162. Idem, p. 181; *SVIII*, pp. 421–2.
163. See Benvenuti, *The Bolsheviks and the Red Army*, pp. 125–6.
164. See above, p. 80.
165. *SVIII*, p. 347.
166. Idem, p. 354.
167. Idem, p. 362.
168. Idem, pp. 229, 231 and 241 (V. V. Kuraev, who nevertheless urged that the process would take 'whole decades': idem, p. 234); p. 244 (I.N. Gorshkov); p. 248 (P. L. Pakhomov); p. 264 (A.S. Savelev).
169. See for example idem, p. 246 (V. P. Milyutin).
170. Idem, p. 271.
171. Idem, p. 362.
172. Idem, p. 364.
173. Idem, p. 366.
174. *ITsKKPSS*, 1990, no.1, pp. 135–55 but especially 135 and 136.
175. Compare the drafts with the final version in *PSS*, vol. 38, pp. 81–124 and 417–446.
176. Idem, p. 417.
177. See Volume Two, p. 000.
178. *PSS*, vol. 38, pp. 421–2 and 425.
179. See P.G.Smidovich's objection that Lenin's draft included the assumption that further 'imperialist wars', like the Great War, were to be expected: *ITsKKPSS*, 1990, no.1, p. 137.
180. Idem, p. 424.
181. Idem, p. 426.
182. *ITsKKPSS*, 1990, no.1, pp. 138–9 and 140.
183. *PSS*, vol. 38., p. 427.
184. Ibid.
185. See above, p. 78.
186. *PSS*, vol. 38, p. 428.
187. Ibid.
188. Idem, p. 83 ff.
189. *PSS*, vol. 38, pp. 429–30.
190. Idem, pp. 430–1.
191. Idem, p. 432.
192. Idem, p. 433.
193. Idem, pp. 434–5.
194. Idem, p. 437.

195. Idem, p. 439.
196. Idem, p. 440–2.
197. Idem, pp. 443–5.

CHAPTER 4: AND OURS SHALL BE THE VICTORY

1. *TP*, vol. 2, p. 30.
2. This is only a guess; and I have to admit that Lenin would have been stupid to assume that his fate would have been different if his direct complicity stayed secret.
3. This is Evan Mawdsley's idea: *The Russian Civil War* (London, 1987), p. 232.
4. On the primarily non-Russian regions, see pp. 92–7.
5. *PSS*, vol. 50, p. 328.
6. Idem, vol. 51, p. 56.
7. See Volume Two, p. 247.
8. L. D. Trotskii, *Moya zhizn'*, vol. 2, p. 404; *TP*, vol. 1, pp. 712 and 716.
9. See E. Mawdsley, op.cit., pp. 196–9.
10. *ITsKKPSS*, 1989, no.12, p. 139.
11. *RTsKhIDNI*, f.17, op.3, d.1.
12. *PSS*, vol. 50, p. 328.
13. *ITsKKPSS*, 1989, no.12, p. 139; *PSS*, vol. 50, p. 328; *TP*, vol. 1, p. 578. See also the account in F. Benvenuti, *The Bolsheviks and the Red Army*, pp. 134–5.
14. *PSS*, vol. 39, p. 480: excerpt from Stalin's note quoted in footnote 15.
15. Ibid.; and *PSS*, vol. 39, pp. 57–8.
16. See Benvenuti, op.cit., pp. 139–41.
17. L. D.Trotski, *Stalinskaya shkola istoricheskoi faltsifikatsii*, pp. 54–5.
18. See Mawdsley, *The Russian Civil War*, pp. 195–6.
19. It may be added here, perhaps, that he commented on the reasons for the successful October seizure of power only many months later when he had a political axe to grind: see Volume Two, pp. 326–7.
20. See Mawdsley, op.cit., pp. 281–2.
21. *TP*, vol. 1, p. 688.
22. See above, pp. 77–8.
23. *PSS*, vol. 38, p. 234.
24. *GARF*, f.R–130, op.2, d.2(5): Sovnarkom, 7 December 1918 (item 8) and 21 December 1918 (item 7).
25. See M. S. Kulichenko, *Bor'ba kommunisticheskoi partii za reshenie natsional'nogo voprosa v 1918–1920 gg.* (Kharkov, 1963), pp.54 and 250.
26. See the excellent account by F.Selnicki, *Natsional'naya politika KPSS v period s 1917 po 1922 god* (2nd edition: Sucasnist, 1981), p. 187.
27. See idem, pp. 132–3.
28. *GARF*, f.R–130, op.3, d.3, item 3: 11 January 1919.
29. *SVIII*, p. 425.
30. See M. Kulichenko, *Bor'ba kommunisticheskoi partii*, p. 249.
31. *RTsKhIDNI*, f.17, op.3, d.3, item 2(3).

32. See above, pp. 274–82.
33. *RTsKhIDNI*, f.17, op.3, d.7, item 2(2).
34. Idem, d.9.
35. Idem, d.10.
36. Idem, d.20.
37. *PSS*, vol. 40, p. 42.
38. *ITsKKPSS*, 1990, no.7, p. 163 (which gives the minutes of a December 1919 discussion of past difficulties).
39. Idem, 1990, no.2, p. 164.
40. Idem, 1990, no.7, p. 163.
41. *RTsKhIDNI*, f.17, op.3, d.108, item 1.
42. Idem, d.115.
43. See R.Pipes, *The Formation of the Soviet Union* (Harvard, 1964), pp. 169–70.
44. *RTsKhIDNI*, f.17, op.3, d.105.
45. Idem, d.108.
46. See below, p. 176.
47. See below, pp. 275–82.
48. See below, p. 125.
49. See Volume Two, p. 74.
50. *BK*, vol. 8, p. 1.
51. See Volume Two, p. 139.
52. See idem, pp. 187–8 on his attempt to make his political image more popular.
53. M.I. Ul'yanova, 'Napadenie banditov', *Pravda*, no.21, 21 January 1930, p. 4.
54. Ibid.
55. Ibid.
56. Ibid.
57. *PSS*, vol. 50, p. 317.
58. Idem, p. 324.
59. Idem, p. 329.
60. See R. Service, *The Bolshevik Party*, pp. 123–30.
61. See idem, p. 124.
62. See T.H. Rigby, *Lenin's Government. Sovnarkom, 1917–1922* (Cambridge, 1979), chap.9.
63. *RTsKhIDNI*, f.17, op.3, d.6, item 7.
64. Idem, op.2, d.43, item 8: Central Committee plenum, 8 December 1920.
65. Idem, op.3, d.14, item 1: Politburo, 10 July 1919.
66. See the quotations given in V.M. Kholodkhovskii, 'V.I. Lenin i mezhdunarodnye otnosheniya novogo tipa', in M.A. Kharlamov et al. (eds), *Leninskaya vneshnaya politika Sovetskoi strany* (Moscow, 1969), p. 88.
67. *PSS*, vol. 50, pp. 285–6.
68. Idem, p. 310.
69. Idem, vol. 38, p. 258.
70. Idem, vol. 38, p. 217.
71. See Kholodkhovskii, 'V.I. Lenin i mezhdunarodnye otnosheniya', p. 93.
72. Ibid.; and *PSS*, vol. 50, p. 310.

73. *PSS*, vol. 50, p. 310.
74. Idem, vol. 51, pp. 27–8.
75. *ITsKKPSS*, 1990, no.2, p. 158.
76. *TP*, vol. 1, p. 696.
77. Idem, p. 726.
78. Idem, p. 741.
79. *PSS*, vol. 51, p. 80.
80. See Idem, vols 38 and 39.
81. See Volume Two, p. 246.
82. See E. H. Carr, *The Bolshevik Revolution*, vol. 3, pp. 155–7.
83. *PSS*, vol. 39, p. 197.
84. Ibid.
85. V. A. Shishkin, 'Lenin i mezhdunarodnye ekonomicheskie svyazi' in M. A. Kharlamov *et al.* (eds), *Leninskaya vneshnaya politika Sovetskoi strany*, pp. 198–9.
86. *LS*, vol. 24, pp. 36–7.
87. He got round to such a commentary only in 1920: see, for example, *PSS*, vol. 41, pp. 219–24. Possibly it was a combination of his Civil War workload and even a wish to avoid overt offence to the Allies which made him disinclined to write a pamphlet on the subject in 1919. In 1920, at the time of the Polish-Soviet war, things looked differently to him: see below, p. 118 ff.
88. See above, pp. 17–20; and below, pp. 238–42.
89. *PSS*, vol. 40, pp. 164 and 186.
90. See idem, vols 39, pp. 123, 154, 167–8, 357–8 and 408; vol. 40, 89, 105 and 120.
91. See R. Service, *The Russian Revolution, 1900–1927* (London, 1986), p. 60.
92. *RTsKhIDNI*, f.17, op.3, ed.12, item 2: 10 August 1919.
93. See above, p. 100.
94. See S. N. Prokopovich, *Narodnoe Khozyaistro SSSR*, vol. 1, p. 329.
95. See idem, p. 52.
96. See *PSS*, vol. 39, *passim*; vol. 40, pp. 1–232
97. See E. H. Carr, *The Bolshevik Revolution*, vol. 2, p. 212.
98. This was a sign of Stalin's propinquity to Trotski on the question of 'militarisation' which Stalin chose to overlook in the later 1920s.
99. *LS*, vol. 38, p. 298.
100. Idem, p. 300.
101. L. D. Trotskii, *Sochineniya*, vol. 17, pp. 543–4.
102. Ibid.. See the articles by Francesco Benvenuti, 'Il dibattito sui sindacati', in F. Gori (ed.), *Pensiero e Azione di Lev Trockij* (Florence, 1982), especially pp. 262–3.; and John Channon, 'Trotsky, the peasants and economic policy: a comment', *Economy and Society*, 1985, no.4, pp. 513–23. Nevertheless Trotski had a point in claiming that the earliest variant of the New Economic Policy – introduced in 1921 – owed much to his agrarian project of February 1920: see below, p. 181.
103. *SX*, pp. 349–50.
104. Ibid.
105. See below, p. 114, for the results at the Ninth Party Congress.
106. See Volume Two, p. 314.

107. 'Utro novoi epokhi', *VIKPSS*, 1988, no.2, p. 60; and *DSV*, vol. 1, pp. 237–9.
108. See Volume One, p. 71.
109. See D. Pospielovsky, *The Russian Orthodox Church under the Soviet Régime, 1917–1982*, vol. 1 (New York, 1984), p. 38.
110. Idem, pp. 31–2.
111. Idem, p. 39.
112. *PSS*, vol. 37, p. 186.
113. Idem, vol. 38, pp. 95 and 118.
114. See N. Timasheff, *Religion in Russia* (New York, 1944), p. 54.
115. On later changes, see below, pp. 246–7.
116. *PSS*, vol. 50, p. 143–4.
117. See also below, p. 246.
118. See the account by B.R. Bociurkiw, 'Lenin and Religion' in L.B. Schapiro and P. Reddaway, *Lenin: The Man, the Theorist, the Leader. A Reappraisal* (London, 1967), pp. 112–5.
119. *PSS*, vol. 38, p. 242.
120. Indeed this particular recording was not included with the others made at the same session when an official disc was issued in the 1960s: an indication of covert official anti–semitism – or at least an official unwillingness to identify the régime with sympathy for the Jews.
121. See the discussion in Bociurkiw, op.cit., p. 133.
122. *SVIII*, p. 53.
123. *PSS*, vol. 39, pp. 318–33.
124. See P. Kenez, 'The Ideology of the White Movement', *Soviet Studies*, vol. 32, pp. 58–83
125. See above, pp. 38–43.
126. See Bociurkiw, op.cit., p. 125.
127. See above, p. 85.
128. *PSS*, vol. 12, pp. 142–3.
129. Idem, vol. 17, p. 416.
130. See below, pp. 149–51.
131. *PSS*, vol. 41, p. 309.
132. *SIX*, p. 4.
133. Idem, p. 9.
134. Idem, p. 13.
135. Idem, p. 19.
136. Idem, pp. 21, 22 and 24.
137. Idem, pp. 27–44; and p. 45 (Yurenev), p. 48 (Maksimovski), p. 53 (Lutovinov), p. 56 (Yakovlev), p. 60 (Kiselev).
138. Idem, p. 52.
139. Idem, p. 51.
140. Idem, p. 53.
141. Idem, pp. 62–3.
142. Idem, p. 63 (Volin), p. 66 (Preobrazhenski), p. 69 (Kamenev).
143. Idem, p. 77.
144. Idem, pp. 79–83.
145. Idem, p. 83.
146. Idem, p. 90.

147. Idem, pp. 91, 94 and 107.
148. Idem, p. 115–32.
149. Idem, p. 109.
150. Idem, p. 142.
151. Idem, pp. 142–3.
152. Idem, pp. 150–1 and 152–3.
153. Idem, p. 199.
154. Idem, p. 157.
155. Idem, p. 159–88.
156. Idem, pp. 190 and 195.
157. Idem, p. 210.
158. Idem, pp. 216–7.
159. Idem, pp. 219–20.
160. Idem, pp. 239–41 (Lutovinov) and 247–8.
161. Idem, p. 261.
162. Idem, p. 262.
163. Idem, p. 360.
164. Idem, p. 361.
165. Idem, p. 367.
166. Idem, pp. 377–8.
167. Idem, p. 379.
168. Idem, p. 396.
169. Idem, p. 398.
170. Idem, p. 403.

CHAPTER 5: THE TAR IN THE HONEY

1. See the excellent account of N. Davies, *White Eagle, Red Star. The Polish–Soviet War, 1919–1920* (London, 1972), chapter 2.
2. See idem, p. 107.
3. *PSS*, vol. 40, p. 330.
4. See Volume Two, p. 322.
5. *ITsKKPSS*, 1991, no.1, pp. 113 and 115.
6. See Davies, *White Eagle, Red Star*, pp. 146–8.
7. See idem, pp. 169–70.
8. *ITsKKPSS*, 1991, no.1, pp. 119–22.
9. See Davies, *op. cit.*, p. 148.
10. See idem, pp. 152–3.
11. See idem, p. 140–1.
12. *Ibid.*
13. See Volume Two, pp. 175–6.
14. For a hint see *PSS*, vol. 41, p. 177.
15. See also above, p. 42–3.
16. *PSS*, vol. 51, p. 264.
17. See above, p. 121.
18. *PSS*, vol. 41, p. 4.
19. Idem, pp. 6–7.

20. Idem, p. 8.
21. Idem, pp. 18–19.
22. Idem, p. 22.
23. Ibid.
24. Idem, pp. 23.
25. Idem, pp. 29–31.
26. Idem, p. 33.
27. Idem, p. 39.
28. Idem, pp. 45–6.
29. Idem, pp. 54–5 and 58.
30. Idem, pp. 58–9. He also wanted, but did not say so in his pamphlet, to effect a re-unification of the German Communist Party and the German Workers' Communist Party.
31. This is not to say that this was the view of all Bolsheviks: see Volume Two, pp. 328–32.
32. *PSS*, vol. 41, p. 61.
33. Idem, pp. 63–4.
34. Idem, pp. 71–3.
35. See Volume One, p. 154.
36. *PSS*, vol. 41, p. 70.
37. Idem, p. 71–2.
38. Idem, pp. 88–9.
39. Idem, pp. 93–4 and 98–9.
40. *Comintern II*, p. 98.
41. Idem, pp. 102–3.
42. *PSS*, vol. 41, pp. 217–8.
43. Idem, p. 223.
44. Idem, p. 222.
45. Idem, p. 230.
46. Idem, pp. 231–2.
47. Idem, pp. 232–3.
48. *Comintern II*, p. 128.
49. Idem, p. 130.
50. Idem, p. 134.
51. See A.Rosmer, *Lenin's Moscow* (London, 1971), pp. 66–7.
52. *Comintern II*, pp. 150–6.
53. Idem, p. 159.
54. *PSS*, vol. 41, p. 236–7.
55. *Comintern II*, p. 174.
56. Idem, pp. 202–10.
57. See above, pp. 77–8.
58. *Comintern II*, pp. 218–24.
59. *PSS*, vol. 41, p. 246.
60. Ibid.
61. See Volume One, pp. 40–1.
62. See above, pp. 77–8.
63. See below, pp. 300–1.
64. See Volume Two, p. 156.
65. See Volume One, pp. 37–8.

66. See Volume One, pp. 37–8.
67. On the rough and ready distinction between the two questions see Volume Two, p. 348 (note 114). The traditional contours of the 'national question' were not entirely ignored at the Second Comintern Congress: see the discussion of Otto Bauer and Karl Renner, *Komintern II*, pp. 266–72.
68. Idem, p. 277.
69. Idem, p. 278.
70. Idem, p. 290.
71. Idem, p. 313.
72. Idem, p. 352.
73. Idem, pp. 357–8.
74. *PSS*, vol. 41, p. 249–51.
75. *Comintern II*, p. 418.
76. See Volume Two, pp. 111–2 and 141.
77. *Comintern II*, p. 433.
78. *PSS*, vol. 41, pp. 255–6
79. *Comintern II*, p. 469.
80. Idem, p. 625.
81. Idem, p. 635.
82. See J. Riddell's editorial reconstruction in idem, p. 54. For Marchlewski's critique see the translation in idem, pp. 949–59; for Lenin's revised draft theses, see *PSS*, vol. 41, pp. 169–82.
83. *Comintern II*, p. 654.
84. Idem, p. 660.
85. Idem, p. 671.
86. Idem, p. 681.
87. Idem, p. 682.
88. Idem, p. 686.
89. Idem, p. 699.
90. Idem, p. 706.
91. Idem, pp. 733–5.
92. *PSS*, vol. 41, pp. 260–6.
93. *Comintern II*, p. 744.
94. Idem, p. 721.
95. On the pre-October attitude to Lenin as the pre-eminent figure of Bolshevism see Volume Two, pp. 183–90.
96. I mentioned this as a possibility in Volume One, p. 12. It has now gained confirmation in the letter written by Anna Ulyanova to Stalin in December 1932 and reproduced in *Rossiiskaya gazeta*, 27 February 1992, p. 4.
97. Ibid.
98. See R. Stites, *Revolutionary Dreams: Utopian Visions and Experimental Life in the Russian Revolution* (Oxford, 1989), pp. 65–6.
99. See Volume One, p. 89.
100. See Volume Two, p. 185; and N. Tumarkin, *Lenin Lives! The Lenin Cult in Soviet Russia* (Harvard, 1983), pp. 87–8.
101. *Pravda*, 29 October 1917.
102. See Volume Two, p. 188.

103. *D. Bednyi. Bibliotechka izbrannoi liriki* (Moscow, 1967), pp. 11–12.
104. G. Zinov'ev, *Vladimir Il'ich Lenin* (Petrograd, 1918).
105. See the information given in N. Tumarkin, *Lenin Lives!*, p. 84.
106. *Perepiska*, vol. 4, doc.267.
107. *PSS*, vol. 50, p. 267; *LS*, vol. 24, p. 172.
108. *PSS*, vol. 45, pp. 1–16. Admittedly, this comment was not directed at the particular poem but refers generally to the works of Mayakovski.
109. See R. C. Tucker, *Stalin as Revolutionary*, pp. 465–6 (where a contrast is made with Stalin's later cult).
110. *PSS*, vol. 52, p. 100.
111. See N. Tumarkin, *Lenin Lives!*, p. 105.
112. *Izvestiya*, 2 May 1919.
113. See Volume Two, p. 185.
114. *PSS*, vol. 38, p. 185.
115. See R. Taylor, *The Politics of the Soviet Cinema, 1917–1929* (Cambridge, 1979), pp. 87–8.
116. See above, p. 98.
117. See Tumarkin, op. cit., pp. 107–9.
118. See below, pp. 185 ff.
119. See *PSS*, vol. 41, p. 458.
120. Ibid.; and Lenin's account in his political report to the Ninth Party Conference: *RTsKhIDNI*, f.44, op. 1, d.5, pp. 20–1.
121. See *PSS*, vol. 41, p. 458.
122. See Volume Two, pp. 80, 81 and 126.
123. See the document quoted by D. A. Volkogonov, *Izvestiya*, 27 April 1992, p. 3.
124. Ibid.
125. Evidently much work remains to be done on the 'German orientation' in Soviet foreign policy before 1941.
126. Clara Zetkin, *Erinnerungen an Lenin* (Vienna, 1929), pp. 20–1.
127. Stalin, *Sochineniya*, vol. 4, pp. 323–4 and 333.
128. See N. Davies, *White Eagle, Red Star* (London, 1972), pp. 70–3, 95 and 97.
129. C. Zetkin, *Erinnerungen*, p. 20.
130. L. D. Trotskii, *Moya zhizn'*, vol. 2, p. 129.
131. Not that the Brest-Litovsk treaty was a one-man conjuring trick: see Volume Two, pp. 317–33.
132. See E. Mawdsley, *The Russian Civil War*, pp. 254–5.
133. Trotskii, *Moya zhizn'*, vol. 2, p. 292.
134. See E. H. Carr, *The Bolshevik Revolution*, vol. 3, pp. 162–3.
135. *PSS*, vol. 51, p. 238.
136. See N. Davies, *White Eagle*, p. 137.
137. *PSS*, vol. 51, p. 248.
138. See N. Davies, op. cit., pp. 205–7.
139. Idem, p. 260.
140. See E. H. Carr, *The Bolshevik Revolution*, vol. 3, pp. 213–4.
141. *KIX*, p. 122.
142. Idem, pp. 8–9.

143. Lenin's report was so full of items that would have embarrassed him at home and caused problems abroad that it was truncated and distorted in the contemporary *Pravda* report; and enough potential damage to his reputation existed that it was not included in the published protocols of the Conference in *KIX* in 1972. The references in this paragraph come from *RTsKhIDNI*, f.44, op. 1, d.5, pp. 11–18, 20–1, 27 and 28.
144. *Pravda*, no.216, 29 September 1920; compare *RTsKhIDNI*, f.44, op. 1, d. 5, pp. 33, 35 and 36.
145. *Pravda*, 29 September 1920.
146. See the speeches by Trotski (*KIX*, p. 26) and Stalin (p. 82).
147. *KIX*, p. 15.
148. Idem, p. 17.
149. Idem, p. 25.
150. Idem, p. 26.
151. Idem, pp. 30–1.
152. Idem, p. 26.
153. Idem, p. 32.
154. Idem, p. 36. Again the edition of the Conference minutes is faulty: there is said to be a 'gap in the stenogram' at the point where Lenin is criticised: ibid.
155. Idem, p. 38.
156. Idem, pp. 40–1.
157. Idem, p. 44.
158. Idem, pp. 45–6.
159. Idem, pp. 48–9.
160. Idem, p. 53 (G. N. Kaminski); p. 60 (Chernev); p. 62 (Evdokimov)
161. Idem, p. 56.
162. Idem, pp. 58–9.
163. Idem, p. 61.
164. Idem, p. 67.
165. Idem, p. 69.
166. Idem, p. 70.
167. Idem, p. 70. Lenin was equally aghast at such manifestations of Bukharin's jargon: see below, p. 146.
168. *KIX*, p. 76–7.
169. Idem, p. 79. Lenin's speech was excluded from the official publication of the Conference record on the grounds that it was in an 'uncorrected' condition: editorial note, *ibid*. Harumph!
170. Idem, p. 82.
171. Idem, pp. 83–97.
172. Idem, pp. 103–35.
173. Idem, p. 155.
174. Idem, pp. 151–2.
175. Idem, especially, p. 157.
176. See the account in R.Service, *The Bolshevik Party*, pp. 144–5.
177. *KIX*, p. 153.
178. Idem, pp. 188.
179. Idem, p. 192.

180. Idem, pp. 194–5.
181. Idem, p. 200.
182. Idem, pp. 208–9.
183. Idem, p. 214.
184. Idem, pp. 219–20.
185. See Volume Two, pp. 58–60.
186. *KIX*, p. 229.
187. Idem, p. 232.
188. Idem, pp. 233–4.
189. Idem, p. 234.
190. Idem, pp. 236–40.
191. Idem, p. 243.
192. Idem, p. 255.
193. Idem, p. 267.
194. Idem, p. 267.
195. Ibid.
196. Idem, p. 268.
197. It ought to be added that, unlike Kamenev and Zinoviev, Trotski saw no reason to bow the knee intellectually before Lenin. He continued to put his opinions in his own way and on his own terms: see Volume Two, pp 189–190.
198. *PSS*, vol. 45, p. 345.
199. Idem, vol. 29, p. 162. See Volume Two, p. 92.
200. *LS*, vol. 11, pp. 345–403.
201. See Volume One, pp. 178–190.
202. See Volume Two, pp. 94–5.
203. See, for example, *LS*, vol. 11, pp. 356, 361, 363, 387, 400 and 401.
204. See Volume Two, pp. 139–41.
205. See idem, chap. 10.
206. *LS*, vol. 11, p. 355. See also 350, 257 and 375.
207. Idem, p. 363.
208. Idem, p. 368.
209. Idem, pp. 350 and 356.
210. Idem, pp. 356 and 400.
211. *LS*, vol. 11, p. 348.
212. Idem, pp. 385 and 401.
213. Idem, p. 400.
214. Idem, p. 385.
215. Idem, p. 400.
216. Idem, p. 396. I am unconvinced by Stephen Cohen's attempt to demonstrate that, essentially, Lenin liked Bukharin's book. As I have tried to show in Volumes One and Two, Lenin took his philosophy and Marxology very seriously. The points raised by him in 1920 against Bukharin could not, in this context, have been more serious. His sugar-coating of his criticisms (see notes 21, 22 and 24 below) are to be attributed, therefore, to a wish to avoid giving offence to Bukharin, to get him to accept the criticisms and 'mend his ways'. Lenin, moreover, retained his low estimate of Bukharin as a Marxist theorist to his dying breath: see below, pp. 284–5.

217. *LS*, vol. 11, pp. 352 and 364.
218. Idem, pp. 352 and 390.
219. Idem, p. 400.
220. Idem, pp. 401 and 402.
221. See Volume Two, p. 317.
222. See examples in *LS*, vol. 11, pp. 354, 355, 356, 359, 369 and 371.
223. Idem, pp. 357 and 371.
224. See Volume Two, pp. 90–6.
225. *PSS*, vol. 18, p. 12. See also Volume One, pp. 143–4, 179–83 and 185–7.
226. Bogdanov, let it be added, had long since ceased to debate with Lenin on matters philosophical: see Volume One, pp. 181–7. This adds force to the proposition that Bukharin, who was indeed publishing on such matters, was a major target.
227. See Volume One, pp. 182–3.
228. *PSS*, vol. 18, p. 12.
229. See Volume Two, p. 223.
230. *LS*, vol. 11, p. 394.
231. *Pravda*, 23 July 1918. Easily the best introduction to this theme is J. D. Biggart, 'Bukharin and the Origins of the "Proletarian Culture" Debate', *Soviet Studies*, no.2, April 1987, pp. 229–46.
232. See Biggart, op. cit., pp. 231–2.
233. *PSS*, vol. 51, p. 291.
234. Idem, p. 456.
235. Speech of 19 May 1919: *idem*, vol. 38, pp. 331–2.
236. V. V. Gorbunov, 'Kritika V. I. Leninym teorii Proletkul'ta ob otnoshenii k kul'turnomu naslediyu', *VIKPSS*, no.5, 1968, p. 91.
237. *PSS*, vol. 51, p. 299.
238. Idem, vol. 42, p. 12.
239. N. Bukharin, *Istoricheskii materializm* (Moscow, 1921).
240 Idem.

CHAPTER 6: LESS POLITICS!

1. See R. V. Daniels, *Conscience of the Revolution. Communist Opposition in Soviet Russia* (New York, 1960), chap. 5.
2. L. D. Trotskii, *Rol' i zadachi professional'nykh soyuzov. (K 10–mu s"ezdu partii* (Moscow, 1920), pp. 1–32.
3. Ibid.
4. See Volume Two, pp. 1–6; and this Volume, pp. 264–8.
5. See above, p. 141.
6. On Zinoviev's activities in September and October 1920, see F. Benvenuti, 'Dal Comunismo di Guerra alla NEP', pp. 266–7.
7. *SX*, pp. 815–9.
8. *PSS*, vol. 42, p. 235.
9. *SX*, pp. 813–5 and 830–1.
10. Ibid.
11. *SIX*, p. 182.

12. See Lenin's account in *PSS*, vol. 42, p. 236. It comes in his pamphlet *Krizis partii*, which was accepted at the time as being factually accurate even while being provocative to Trotski and Bukharin. It was nevertheless very selective in its factuality: see below, n.18.
13. *SIX*, p. 109.
14. This was especially obvious in his decision, against his inclination, to side with Lenin over Brest-Litovsk: see Volume Two, p. 325.
15. See also below, p. 175.
16. *PSS*, vol. 42, pp. 235–6.
17. *PSS*, vol. 42, p. 236.
18. See F. Benvenuti, 'Dal Comunismo di Guerra', pp. 267–70.
19. See R. Service, *The Bolshevik Party in Revolution*, pp. 143–4 and 146.
20. *PSS*, vol. 42, p. 236.
21. Ibid.
22. Ibid.
23. Ibid.
24. See above, pp. 113–15.
25. *PSS*, vol. 41, pp. 1–278.
26. See E. Genkina, *Lenin, predsedatel' Sovnarkoma i STO. Iz istorii gosudarstvennoi deyatel'nosti V.I.Lenina v 1921–1922 gg.* (Moscow, 1960), pp. 28–54.
27. *RTsKhIDNI*, f.17, op. 3, d.108, item 16.
28. See also below, p. 217.
29. *RTsKhIDNI*, f.17, op. 3, d.108, item 16.
30. *PSS*, vol. 41, p. 362.
31. Idem, p. 364.
32. See idem, p. 362 ff.
33. See above p. 120.
34. Politburo meeting, 1 September 1920: *RTsKhIDNI*, f.17, op.3, d.106, item 10.
35. Politburo meeting, 19 August 1920: idem, d.103, item 8.
36. See Yu. A. Polyakov, *Perekhod k Nepu i sovestkoe krest'yanstvo* (Moscow, 1967), p. 224; and *RTsKhIDNI*, f.17, op.2, d.45, item 3, p. 1.
37. *PSS*, vol. 42, p. 159.
38. Idem, p. 380.
39. Central Committee plenum, 20 December 1920: *RTsKhIDNI*, f.17, op. 2, d.47, item 5, p. 1.
40. Idem, item 3.
41. *PSS*, vol. 42, p. 95.
42. Idem, p. 101.
43. Idem, pp. 107 and 112.
44. Idem, pp. 162–3.
45. *PSS*, vol. 42, pp. 134, 141, 156–7 and 159.
46. *Vos'moi vserossiiskii s''ezd Sovetov rabochikh, krest'yanskikh, krasnoarmeiskikh i kazach'ikh deputatov. Stenograficheskii otchet. (22–29 dekabrya 1920 goda)* (Moscow, 1921), pp. 42, 49, 122 and 201.
47. *PSS*, vol. 42, p. 176.
48. Idem, p. 179.

49. Idem, pp. 180–1.
50. *RTsKhIDNI*, f.17, op. 2, d.49, item 1, pp. 1 and 6. The original phrase was *individual'noe premirovanie staratel'nykh krest'yan*.
51. Ibid.
52. *PSS*, vol. 42, pp. 185–9.
53. Idem, pp. 190–1.
54. Idem, p. 194.
55. See below, pp. 162-6.
56. *RTsKhIDNI*, f.17, op. 3, d.134, p. 1.
57. Idem, f.17, op. 2, d.59, p. 1.
58. A. Balabanova, *Impressions of Lenin* (Ann Arbor, 1964), p. 14.
59. *Svobodnaya mysl'*, 1992, no.3, p. 81.
60. Idem, p. 83
61. Ibid.
62. Ibid.
63. *PSS*, vol. 42, p. 237.
64. Ibid.
65. Idem, p. 205.
66. Idem, p. 207.
67. Idem, p. 221.
68. Idem, p. 208.
69. See Volume Two, p. 225.
70. *PSS*, vol. 42, p. 208.
71. This interpretation is reinforced by his own account of his speech in 'Krizis partii', idem, p. 239.
72. Idem, p. 208.
73. Idem, p. 240.
74. See R. Service, *The Bolshevik Party*, p. 150.
75. See ibid.
76. 'Eshche raz o profsoyuzakh', *PSS*, vol. 42, p. 280.
77. See Service, *The Bolshevik Party*, p. 151.
78. See idem, pp. 150–1.
79. 'Eshche raz o profsoyuzakh', *PSS*, vol. 42, p. 303.
80. Idem, p. 296.
81. Idem, p. 290.
82. *RTsKhIDNI*, f.17, op. 3: PB, d.127: item, 1, 28 January 1921.
83. See above, pp. 159–61.
84. See J. Aves, 'Industrial Unrest in Soviet Russia during War Communism and the Transition to the New Economic Policy, 1918–1922' (London University Ph. D. dissertation, 1989), chap. 4 ff.
85. See I. Getzler, *Kronstadt, 1917–1921. The Fate of a Soviet Democracy* (Cambridge, 1983), chap. 5 ff.
86. See O. H. Radkey, *The Unknown Civil War in Soviet Russia* (Stanford, 1976), chap. 4 ff.; O. Figes, *Peasant Russia, Civil War. The Volga Countryside in Revolution, 1917–1921* (Oxford, 1989), chap. 7.
87. See V. V. Kabanov, *Krest'yanskoe khozyaistvo v usloviyakh 'voennogo kommunizma'* (Moscow, 1988), passim.
88. See Radkey, *The Unknown Civil War*, chap. 4 ff.

89. See M. Perrie on the limits of popular revolt between February and October 1917 in R.Service, *Society and Politics in the Russian Revolution* (London, 1992), pp. 12–34.
90. *RTsKhIDNI*, f.17, op. 3, d.127, item 1a: Politburo, 2 February 1921.
91. Idem, items 3 and 4.
92. Idem, items 1b-f and 2.
93. As late as 19 February 1921 he displayed such unease about the report on the sowing campaign by a central party commission to which he belonged that he was permitted to make 'counter-proposals' if he should 'find it necessary': idem, d.135, item 3: 19 February 1921.
94. Idem, d.127, appendix ('Draft decision of Political Bureau of the CC of the RKP'), item 4: 2 February 1921.
95. Ibid.
96. Idem, d.127, item 2a: Politburo, 2 February 1921. Preobrazhenski was also asked with Bukharin and Kamenev to formulate an address from the All-Russian Central Executive Committee to the Tambov peasantry, an address which was not to be published nationally.
97. Idem, items 1 and 2. On this issue I agree with Yu. A. Polyakov, whose account of the food-supply discussions among Bolsheviks was the first to cast doubt on the notion that Lenin's thought evolved steadily between mid-1920 and February 1921 and therefore did not undergo a drastic change in February 1921: see his *Perekhod k NEPu i sovetskoe krest'yanstvo*, pp. 225–6, where he criticises the earlier account by E. Genkina, *Perekhod Sovetskogo gosudarstva k novoi ekonomicheskoi politike (1921–1922)* (Moscow, 1954), especially p. 71.
98. *PSS*, vol. 42, pp. 173–4 and 382–6.
99. *BK*, vol. 9, pp. 468 and 565.
100. See Yu. Polyakov, *Perekhod k Nepu*, p. 238.
101. *PSS*, vol. 42, pp. 382–6.
102. *Vos'moi s"ezd sovetov* offers what is a highly abridged version of the proceedings.
103. V. N. Sokolov, *Staryi bol'shevik*, 1930, no.1, p. 130.
104. *PSS*, vol. 42, p. 308.
105. Idem, p. 309.
106. Idem, p. 308.
107. *RTsKhIDNI*, f.17, op. 3, d.131, p. 1. A.Solts from the Central Control Commission as well as Shorokhov and Kuchmenko were also present.
108. *PSS*, vol. 42, p. 333.
109. Ibid.
110. *RTsKhIDNI*, f.17, op. 3, d.131, item 1.
111. See, for example, *RTsKhIDNI*, f.17, op. 3, d.128, items 1b and 1c(2 February); d.131, item 10 (8 February 1921, when Sklyanski was upbraided for insufficient repressive zeal); d.132, item 1(14 February 1921).
112. On 18 February 1921 the commission of Kamenev, Osinski and Tsyurupa suggested immediate publication: *LS*, vol. 20, p. 59. But Lenin advised against, idem, p. 60.
113. *PSS*, vol. 42, p. 333.
114. *RTsKhIDNI*, f.17, op. 3, d.134, p. 2.

115. 'Razverstka ili nalog', *Pravda*, 17 February 1921. A second part of the article appeared on 26 February 1921.
116. Idem, 5, 6, 11 March 1921.
117. *LS*, vol. 20, pp. 58–9.
118. Idem, p. 58.
119. *RTsKhIDNI*, f.17, op. 3, d.135, item 3.
120. *LS*, vol. 20, p. 57.
121. See *GARF*, f.R-130, op. 5, d.5, 6, 7 and 8.
122. *LS*, vol. 20, p. 59.
123. *GARF*, F.R-130, op. 5, d.8, item 10.
124. *RTsKhIDNI*, f.17, op. 3: Politburo, d.136, item 2a.
125. Idem, item 2b.
126. Idem, items 2d, 2e and 2f.
127. *BK*, vol. 10, p. 191.
128. *LS*, vol. 20, p. 66. The date of this 'session of members of the Central Committee' is given as 'the beginning of March 1921'. It is as yet unclear whether this session was the Central Committee plenum of 7 March.
129. Idem, p. 67.
130. *TP*, vol. 2, pp. 388 and 390: two telegrams of 2 March 1921 from M.V. Vladimirov, People's Commissar for Food Supplies for the Ukrainian republic.
131. *LS*, vol. 20, p. 63.
132. *TP*, vol. 2, p. 388.
133. *LS*, vol. 20, p. 57 (editorial note).
134. Idem, pp. 62–3.
135. I have this from an elderly stranger on the Moscow metro: December 1987.
136. See Volume Two, pp. 332–3.
137. See illustration in this volume.
138. See above, pp. 64 ff.
139. This was told to me by Professor V.S. Lelchuk, who heard it from his father.
140. I. Deutscher, *Trotsky: The Prophet Unarmed* (London, 1959) remains the best psychological portrait of the man.
141. See E.H. Carr, *The Interregnum, 1923–1924* (London, 1954), p. 777.
142. See idem, p. 888.
143. On the resentments felt toward Trotski see below, p. 304.
144. I am grateful to R.W. Davies for alerting me to the need to question the face value of Trotski's references to his Jewish background.
145. *Kommuna* (Samara) contains the fullest local record of Trotski's declarations.
146. See Deutscher, *Trotsky. The Prophet Armed*, pp. 94–5 and 161.
147. *SX*, p. 71.
148. See, for example, *SX*, p. 71.
149. *Petrogradskaya pravda*, 5 January 1921.
150. Idem, 6 January 1921.
151. See R. Service, *The Bolshevik Party*, p. 149.
152. A. Mikoyan, *Mysli i vospominaniya o Lenine* (Moscow, 1970), p. 124.
153. See the remarks of N. Kuzmin, *Petrogradskaya Pravda*, 18 January 1921.

154. See idem, 12 December 1920; 28 December 1920; and no.4, 6 January 1921. See also Service, *The Bolshevik Party*, pp. 149–51.
155. *PSS*, vol. 40, pp. 221–4.
156. See Service, *op. cit.*, pp. 151–2.
157. Mikoyan, *Mysli i vospominaniya o Lenine*, pp. 136–7.
158. Idem, pp. 137 and 141.
159. See below, p. 159.
160. See Mikoyan, p. 139.
161. *SX*, pp. 15–18.
162. Idem, p. 24.
163. Idem, p. 25.
164. Idem, pp. 25–6.
165. Idem, p. 28.
166. Ibid.
167. Idem, p. 34.
168. Idem, pp. 31–2.
169. Idem, p. 36.
170. Idem, p. 37.
171. Idem, pp. 40–57.
172. Idem, pp. 57–66.
173. Idem, p. 67.
174. Idem, p. 71.
175. Idem, p. 77.
176. Idem, pp. 78–9.
177. Idem, pp. 82–3.
178. Idem, p. 89.
179. Idem, p. 98.
180. Idem, p. 123.
181. Idem, p. 137.
182. Idem, p. 378.
183. Idem, p. 167.
184. Idem, p. 186.
185. See above, p. 84.
186. See below, pp. 274 ff for the dispute between Lenin and Stalin on the national question in 1922.
187. *SX*, pp. 195
188. Idem, pp. 203 and 205.
189. Idem, pp. 206–7 and 210.
190. See below, pp. 274–5.
191. Idem, pp. 213–14.
192. Idem, p. 214.
193. Idem, pp. 217–92.
194. *BK*, vol. 10, pp. 203 and 204; *SX*, p. 310 (on Dzierzysnki).
195. *SX*, pp. 334 and 335.
196. *PSS*, vol. 43, p. 374–5.
197. *SX*, p. 294.
198. Idem, p. 300.
199. Idem, p. 334.
200. Idem, pp. 349–50.

201. Idem, p. 354.
202. Idem, pp. 378–81.
203. Idem, pp. 391 and 393.
204. Idem, p. 399.
205. Idem, p. 402.
206. Idem, p. 403.
207. Idem, p. 404.
208. Idem, p. 406 and 408.
209. Idem, p. 405.
210. Idem, p. 412.
211. Idem, p. 415.
212. Idem, p. 416 and 418.
213. Idem, p. 421.
214. See especially idem, p. 424.
215. Idem, pp. 432–3.
216. Idem, p. 443.
217. Idem, p. 445.
218. Idem, p. 446.
219. Idem, p. 453.
220. Idem, p. 457.
221. Idem, p. 463.
222. Idem, p. 473.
223. Idem, p. 491.
224. Idem, pp. 518–24.
225. Idem, p. 533.
226. Idem, pp. 539 and 542.
227. Idem, p. 555.

CHAPTER 7: THE RIFLE AND THE SICKLE

1. This occurred in his pamphlet *On The Food Tax*: see below, p. 202.
2. *RTsKhIDNI*, f.5, op.2, d.7, pp. 1–88.
3. Idem, f.17, op.2, d.62, item 1.
4. *KX*, p.103 (editorial footnote 8)
5. *RTsKhIDNI*, f.17, op.3, d.138, item 3b.
6. This is almost certain. He was present, and is named first in the list of participants; and generally, whenever he was not convalescent, he took the Politburo chair.
7. *RTsKhIDNI*, f.17, op.3, d.138, item 3b. The meeting also demanded the insertion of a clause announcing official favour of co-ops.
8. *RTsKhIDNI*, f.17, op.3, d.139, item 2.
9. See Polyakov, *Perekhod k Nepu*, p. 243.
10. On this plan, see *RTsKhIDNI*, f.17, op.3, d.138, item 3b.
11. Idem, f.17, op.3, d.141, item 2.
12. Idem, f.17, op.3, d.144, appendix on commission session of 27 March 1921.
13. Ibid.

14. See above, p. 183.
15. On Ukrainian exceptionalism, see J. D. Channon, 'Peasants and Land Reform in the Ukraine in the Early 1920s' (unpublished paper delivered to the Study Group on the Russian Revolution Conference: Oxford, 1987). I am grateful to John Channon for sharing his thoughts on this matter.
16. See the account by V. P. Milyutin, a commission member: *KX*, p.16. Milyutin has this as a Central Comittee decision; but it was not unusual for Politburo meetings to be described as if they were those of the Central Committee. For the Politburo minutes discussing the commission report in two stages of its formulation see *TsPA*, f.17, op.3, d.142, item 9 (Politburo meeting of 28 March 1921); and idem, d.144 (Politburo meeting of 30 March, which appended the commission's recommendations to its own official minutes).
17. Idem, p. 17.
18. *RTsKhIDNI*, f.17, op.3, d.142, item 9.
19. *Pravda*, 27 March 1921.
20. This was 'On The Food Tax', published in May 1921 as a pamphlet: see below, pp. 201–5.
21. *KX*, p. 92.
22. See below, p. 190.
23. *GARF*, f.R130, op.5, d.10.
24. *Krasnyi kavelerist*, for instance, campaigned for mounted units to accept a delay in their demobilisation so that they might be deployed to coerce the peasantry into increasing their sown acreage.
25. See *TP*, vol. 2, p. 566.
26. Idem, p. 492.
27. See above, p. 167.
28. *PSS*, vol. 43, p. 152.
29. See A. Nove, *Economic History of the USSR*, p. 94.
30. *PSS*, vol. 43, p. 371. I am grateful to Israel Getzler for his advice on the importance of this plan written by Lenin for a speech at the Tenth Party Congress.
31. Ibid.
32. *RTsKhIDNI*, f.17, op.3, d.128, appendix item.
33. Idem, f.17, op.3, d.131, agenda item 10.
34. Idem, d.136, agenda item 2(iv).
35. Idem, f.17, op.3, d.155, agenda item 11.
36. Idem, d.128, agenda item 4(a).
37. See the account by R. Pipes, *The Formation of the Soviet Union* (Cambridge, 1964), pp. 221–41 and 256–60.
38. See idem, pp. 253–5.
39. *RTsKhIDNI*, f.17, op.2, 48, item 3. See the treaty in appendix, p.3.
40. *ITsKKPSS*, 1991, no.4, p. 171.
41. Ibid.
42. Ibid.
43. *RTsKhIDNI*, f.17, op.3, d.234, agenda item 10.
44. See above, p. 78.
45. See above, p. 180.

46. *PSS*, vol. 42, p. 367.
47. Idem, vol. 44, pp. 198–9.
48. See S. V. Kharmandaryan, *Lenin i stanovlenie Zakavkazskoi federatsii, 1921–1923* (Erevan, 1969), p. 104.
49. *RTsKhIDNI*, f.17, op.3, d.145: telephonic consultation.
50. See Kharmandaryan, *Lenin i stanovlenie Zakavkazskoi federatsii*, pp.198–200.
51. See the excerpts quoted in D. A.Chugaev *et al.*, *Natsional'no-gosudarstvennoe stroitel'stvo v SSSR v perioda perekhoda ot kapitalizma k sotsializmu. 1917–1936 gg.* (Moscow, 1972), vol. 1, p. 364.
52. *RTsKhIDNI*, f.17, op.3, d.237.
53. Myasnikov continued to be useful to Stalin's position in the constitutional debate in the following year.
54. See the excerpts quoted in idem, p. 338.
55. See the document quoted in M. S.Kulichenko, *Bor'ba kommunisticheskoi partii za reshenie natsional'nogo voprosa, 1918–1920* (Kharkov, 1963), p. 440.
56. *PSS*, vol. 54, p. 157.
57. See Chugaev, *Natsional'no-gosudarstvennoe stroitel'stvo*, p. 368.
58. See Kharmandaryan, *Lenin i stanovlenie Zakavkazskoi federatsii*, p. 338.
59. See the documents in G. A. Galoyan and K. S. Khudaverdyan (eds), *Nagornyi Karabakh. Istoricheskaya spravka* (Erevan, 1988), pp. 27–33. Naturally these documents were part of a diplomatic polemic between the Armenian and Azerbaidzhani political authorities at the time. My reason for accepting their veracity, even though they come from only one side in the controversy, is that they would be unlikely to have been forged at a time when Armenian officials were still to some extent subject to the scrutiny and discipline of Moscow.
60. See his speeches at the Tenth Party Congress, *SX*, pp. 181–7 and at the Twelfth Party Congress, *SXII*, pp. 481–6.
61. See the interesting explanation of this situation at the nationalities section of the Twelfth Party Congress: *ITsKKPSS*, 1991, no.5, p. 159.
62. See Volume Two, pp. 41–6 and 228–31, and above, pp. 117 ff.
63. *RTsKhIDNI*, 1990, no.9, p. 212.
64. The delegates from the Transcaucasus to the Tenth Party Congress, led by Anastas Mikoyan (an Armenian who had worked in Azerbaidzhan), were not unnaturally very hostile to the policy on concessions: see above, p. 184.
65. See E. H. Carr, *The Bolshevik Revolution*, vol. 3, pp. 282–3.
66. A study of Kamenev and other leaders of the Bolshevik Right is much needed.
67. See above, p. 184.
68. *Sochineniya*, vol. 42, p. 69.
69. See Volume One, pp. 66–7.
70. *PSS*, vol. 43, p. 128 ff.
71. See below for Lenin's opinions on the March Action as expressed at the Third Congress of the Communist International, pp. 226 and 227.
72. See A. S. Lindemann, *The 'Red Years'* (Berkeley, 1974), pp. 283–6.

73. See E. H. Carr, *The Bolshevik Revolution*, vol. 3, pp. 288, 293, 298 and 303.
74. *TP*, vol. 2, p. 434.
75. See Carr, idem, p. 284.
76. *PSS*, vol. 45, p. 287.
77. *TP*, vol. 2, p. 602.
78. See John Erickson, *The Soviet High Command. A Military-Political History* (London, 1962), pp. 128–31 and 150–1.
79. *KXI*, bulletin 5, 29 December 1921, p. 28.
80. See above, pp. 201–5.
81. See above, pp. 145 ff.
82. *KXI*, bulletin 5, 29 December 1921, pp. 10–16.
83. Idem, p. 38.
84. Idem, p. 25.
85. Idem, p. 33.
86. Idem, p. 41.
87. *PSS*, vol. 44, pp. 300–2.
88. *Pis'ma V. I. Lenina iz-za rubezha* (Moscow, 1966), pp.404–5. See the otherwise useful account of M. I. Trush, 'Sovetskaya vneshnyaya politika v sochineniyakh Lenina' in M. A. Kharlamov (ed.), *Leninskaya vneshnyaya politika Sovetskoi strany* (Moscow, 1969), p.48.
89. *PSS*, vol. 43, p.199.
90. Idem, vol. 44, p. 300.
91. See M. I. Trush, 'Sovetskaya vneshnyaya politika', loc. cit., p. 52.
92. *PSS*, vol. 54, p. 136.
93. Idem, vol. 44, p. 301.
94. See the archives quoted by Galoyan and Khudaverdyan, *Nagornyi Karabakh*, pp. 24 and 32–3.
95. See S. White, *Empire and Revolution* (London, 1979), pp. 24–5.
96. This title is sometimes rendered as 'The Tax in Kind'. The Russian original is *O prodovol'stvennom naloge*. It was in this article that Lenin first openly used the term 'War Communism'. On the term's origins see V. P. Buldakov and V. V. Kabanov, ' "Voennyi kommunizm": ideologiya, i obshchestvennoe razvitie', *Voprosy istorii*, 1990, no.3, p. 41.
97. *PSS*, vol. 43, pp. 206–17.
98. Idem, p. 210.
99. Idem, pp. 222–3.
100. Idem, p. 224.
101. See Volume Two, pp. 298–9.
102. See Buldakov and Kabanov, ' "Voennyi kommunizm" ', pp. 42–3.
103. *PSS*, vol. 43, p. 219.
104. Idem, pp. 207 and 228.
105. Idem, p. 231.
106. Idem, p. 234.
107. Idem, p. 235.
108. Idem, p. 237.
109. Idem, p. 238.
110. Idem, p. 241.
111. Idem, pp. 230 and 234.

112. Idem, p. 236.
113. Idem, p. 233.
114. Idem, p. 232.
115. Idem, p. 218.
116. Idem, p. 224.
117. Idem, pp. 225–7.
118. Idem, p. 229.
119. Idem, p. 243.
120. This information came to me from Gennadi Bordyugov, whose work on the Moscow party archives is forthcoming. I am grateful to him for sharing his thoughts and discoveries with me.
121. See E. H. Carr, *The Bolshevik Revolution*, vol. 2, p. 324.
122. Ibid.
123. *RTsKhIDNI*, f.46, op.1, d.3, p. 18.
124. Idem, pp. 18 and 19.
125. *KXI*, p. 96.
126. See *KX*, pp. 1–91; this publication appeared only in 1933: yet another sign that Lenin's Politburo was deeply embarrassed by the nature of the proceedings. The claim that the minutes had been lost was spurious. They are now available in the archives of *RTsKhIDNI* in Moscow.
127. *RTsKhIDNI*, f.46, op.1, d.2, p. 120: mandate commission report.
128. Idem, pp. 61–91.
129. Nevertheless, for those with ears to hear, Preobrazhenski was very emphatic that the central party leadership ought to take up the cause of a centrally-planned economy: idem, p. 91.
130. *KXI*, pp. 18–21.
131. Idem, pp. 51–3.
132. See above, p. 73.
133. *RTsKhIDNI*, f.46, op.1, d.2, p. 112.
134. Idem, pp. 116–7.
135. *Pravda*, no.39, 22 February 1921.
136. *RTsKhIDNI*, f.46, op.1, d.3, pp. 128–9.
137. Idem, pp. 132 and 138.
138. Idem, pp. 140 and 145.
139. Idem, p. 158.
140. Idem, pp. 177–8.
141. Idem, pp. 138 (Larin), 174 (Pintsov) and (Kiselev).
142. Idem, p. 197.
143. Idem, p. 200. This slip was excluded from the officially-approved version of his speech in *PSS*, vol. 43, p. 317.
144. Ibid.
145. *RTsKhIDNI*, f.46, op.1, d.2, p. 2.
146. Idem, d. 3, p. 5.
147. The nearest he had got to self-pity in his political life was in his private *aide mémoire* on his difficulties with Plekhanov in 1900 (see Volume One, pp. 82–3) and in his private letter on his endless polemics to Inessa Armand in 1916 (see Volume Two, p. 127). In 1921, however, he was speaking to a full Party Conference.

148. *RTsKhIDNI*, f.46, op.1, d.3, p. 16. The Russian text runs: 'Takim obrazom ves' TsK okazalsya nerabotosposobnym.'
149. Idem, f.17, op.2, d.62 and 63.
150. Idem, f.17, op.3, d.138–165.
151. Idem, p. 22.
152. Idem, pp. 20 and 22.
153. Idem, p. 31.
154. Idem, pp. 31–46.
155. Idem, pp. 48–58.
156. Idem, pp. 61–2.
157. Idem, p. 94–5.
158. *KXI*, pp. 92–4; *RTsKhIDNI*, f.46, op.1, d.3, p. 132.
159. Idem, p. 125.
160. Idem, p. 127a-b.
     Pages 124–7 are in a somewhat confused state in the archival copy in *RTsKhIDNI*.
161. Idem, p. 124a.
162. Idem, 130.
163. Idem, pp. 133–4.
164. Idem, p. 134.
165. See E. H. Carr, *The Bolshevik Revolution*, vol. 2, p. 345.
166. See idem, p. 336.
167. See idem, p. 303.
168. See idem, pp. 320–1
169. See A.C. Sutton, *Western Technology and Soviet Economic Development, 1917–1930* (Stanford, 1968), chap.2 ff.
170. N. Valentinov, *Novaya ekonomicheskaya politika i krizis partii*, pp. 30–1.
171. *PSS*, vol. 43, pp. 150–1: written 14 October, published in *Pravda*, 18 October 1921.
172. Idem, pp. 155–75 and 191–220. Not until late December 1921 did his pen and voice become as fluent as was customary for him.
173. *KXI*, bulletin 2, p. 35
174. *KXI*, bulletin 2, p. 6.
175. Idem, p. 7.
176. Idem, p. 35.
177. *KXI*, bulletin 3, p. 21.
178. *PSS*, vol. 43, pp. 150–1: written 14 October, published in *Pravda*, 18 October 1921.
179. See Volume Two, p. 235–6 and 237.
180. *PSS*, vol. 45, pp. 44–5.
181. Idem, p. 44.
182. Idem, vol. 44, p. 220. Kamenev's answer to the same question in December 1921 was only a little more substantial: *KXI*, bulletin 2, p. 53.
183. *TP*, vol. 2, pp. 580 and 582. Trotski allowed for matters to be transferred from Gosplan to the Council of Labour and Defence only when Gosplan's own staff could not agree.
184. See below, pp. 242 ff.
185. *PSS*, vol. 53, p. 104.
186. See below, pp. 275–7.

187. See above, p. 171.
188. In other words, the widespread notion that Trotski was raising a fresh issue is erroneous.
189. See E. H. Carr, *The Bolshevik Revolution*, vol. 2, pp. 377–8.

CHAPTER 8: AGAINST THE WALL

1. *PSS*, vol. 52, pp. 99–100.
2. See above, pp. 97–102.
3. *PSS*, vol. 52, pp. 147–8.
4. See R. Service, *The Bolshevik Party*, p. 176.
5. See L. D. Trotskii, *Stalin. An Appraisal of the Man and His Influence* (London, 1947), pp. 146–7, 351 and 373.
6. See below, pp. 288 ff.
7. See Service, *The Bolshevik Party*, p. 163.
8. See idem, p. 164.
9. See idem, p. 165.
10. *PSS*, vol. 53, p. 300.
11. See Service, op. cit., pp. 176–7.
12. See idem, p. 178.
13. See below, pp. 97–102.
14. See Service, op. cit., p. 165.
15. *PSS*, vol. 44, pp. 78 and 80.
16. Idem, p. 82.
17. Ibid.
18. Idem, p. 81.
19. Idem, p. 539 (editorial note 45).
20. Idem, p. 153.
21. On the nature of his illness, see below, pp. 257–62.
22. *RTsKhIDNI*, f.17, op. 17, d.174, item 24.
23. *PSS*, vol. 53, p. 17.
24. Idem, p. 110.
25. *PSS*, vol. 44, pp. 85–118.
26. Idem, p. 119.
27. *PSS*, vol. 45, p. 253.
28. Idem, vol. 54, p. 65.
29. See below, pp. 259–60.
30. Ibid.
31. See R. V. Daniels, *Conscience of the Revolution*, pp. 162–3.
32. A. Mikoyan, *Vospominaniya i mysli o Lenine* (Moscow, 1970), p. 195.
33. Idem, p. 196.
34. Ibid.
35. The forthcoming work of Olga Velikanova will demonstrate this point. In the meantime see her unpublished 1992 article 'Obraz Lenin v obshchestvennom soznanii v SSSR v 20–e gody. Novye materialy'.
36. Ibid.
37. See N. Valentinov, *Novaya ekonomicheskaya politika*, introduction and chap. 1.

38. See above, pp. 197 and 199.
39. See *TKK*, pp. 37–8.
40. See idem, p. 119.
41. See idem, p. 298.
42. See idem, p. 134.
43. See ibid.
44. See idem, p. 135.
45. *PSS*, vol. 52, p. 267.
46. Idem, p. 268; vol. 44, p. 419.
47. *Stalinskaya shkola fal'sifikatsii*, p. 45.
48. *PSS*, vol. 52, p. 273.
49. See *TKK*, p. 137.
50. *TP*, vol. 2, pp. 466 and 468; *PSS*, vol. 44, p. 434.
51. *PSS*, vol. 52, p. 276.
52. See *TKK*, pp. 75 and 443; V. Serge, *Memoirs of a Revolutionary, 1901–1941*, p. 140.
53. *Stalinskaya shkola fal'sifikatsii*, p. 46.
54. Idem, p. 45.
55. See *TVK*, p. 26.
56. *BKh*, vol. 10, pp. 604, 608 and 610.
57. *PSS*, vol. 44, p. 17.
58. Idem, p. 19.
59. Idem, pp. 446–9.
60. Idem, pp. 23, 25 and 26.
61. See Volume Two, p. 263.
62. *PSS*, vol. 44, p. 28.
63. *TP*, vol. 2, p. 472.
64. Idem, p. 474.
65. See *RTsKhIDNI*, pp. 336–9.
66. *RTsKhIDNI*, f.17, op. 3, d.183. See also *BK*, vol. 10, pp. 606, 607 and 641.
67. *PSS*, vol. 44, pp. 34–54.
68. *TVK*, p. 440.
69. *BK*, vol. 10, p. 643–4.
70. *PSS*, vol. 53, p. 14.
71. *LS*, vol. 37, p. 304.
72. *PSS*, vol. 44, pp. 57–8; see also Volume Two, pp. 152, 179 and 180.
73. See *PSS*, vol. 44, p. 56; *TKK*, p. 204.
74. See E. H. Carr, *The Bolshevik Revolution*, vol. 3, pp. 245–7 for an account of Roy's intervention.
75. *TVK*, p. 404.
76. See Volume Two, pp. 270 and 281.
77. See idem, pp. 290–1.
78. V. Polyanskii, 'Nachalo sovetskikh izdatel'stv', *Pechat' i revolyutsiya*, no.7, 1927, p. 233.
79. *Izvestiya*, 2 August 1918.
80. *PSS*, vol. 37, p. 169.
81. Idem, vol. 51, p. 122.
82. Idem, vol. 40, p. 478; vol. 51, pp. 219 and 432.

83. Idem, vol. 52, pp. 179–80.
84. Idem, pp. 163–5.
85. Idem, vol. 54, p. 241.
86. *PSS*, vol. 50, p. 280.
87. *RTsKhIDNI*, f.17, op. 3, d.187, item 2 (12 July 1921); d. 192, item 5 (23 July 1921). See also *V.I. Lenin i A.V. Lunacharskii, Literaturnoe nasledstvo*, vol. 80 (Moscow, 1971), pp. 293–4; *ITsKKPSS*, no.6, 1991, p. 154. See also the concern expressed about Gorki's health in December 1921, *PSS*, vol. 54, pp. 70–1.
88. *RTsKhIDNI*, f.17, op. 3, d.187, item 2 and d.192, item 5. See also *ITsKKPSS*, 1990, no.7, 165.
89. A. Serafimovich, 'Moi vstrechi s Leninym', *Zhivoi Lenin* (Moscow, 1900), p. 230.
90. See S. F. Cohen, *Bukharin and the Bolshevik Revolution*, pp. 207–8.
91. See Volume One, p. 88.
92. *VOVIL*, vol. 2, p. 161.
93. *PSS*, vol. 54, p. 110. On the other hand, he also is solicitous about theatres: see P. N. Lepeshinskii, 'Na povorote', *Lenin, Revolyutsiya. Teatr* (Moscow, 1972), pp. 201–2.
94. This cultural barrenness continued under the rule of Stalin in the 1930s.
95. Not that all the classics of that period adhered to such realism. Gogol and Dostoevski, for example, deliberately distorted and satirised in order to get their desired effects; but neither of them were among Lenin's favourite authors even though he frequently referred to their works and literary characters.
96. *PSS*, vol. 45, p. 13.
97. Idem, vol. 52, pp. 179–80.
98. See Politburo meetings of 6 May 1920, *RTsKhIDNI*, f.17, op. 3, d.75, items 17 and 18 and of 10 October 1921, f.17, op. 3, d.213, item 3.
99. *PSS*, vol. 17, pp. 210–11 and 212.
100. Idem, vol. 12, pp. 100–1.
101. See, for example, idem, p. 102.
102. Idem, p. 102.
103. Ibid.
104. Idem, p. 101.
105. Idem, p. 104.
106. See E. Brown, *Russian Literature Since the Revolution* (London, 1963), chap. 6.
107. On Lenin's illness see below, pp. 256–63.
108. *Vserossiiskaya konferentsiya R.K.P. (bol'shevikov). 4–7 avgusta 1922 g. Byulleten'* (Moscow, 1922), bulletin 3, pp. 80 and 82.
109. This policy continued through the 1920s.
110. See above, p. 235.
111. This is not to say that Lenin's attitude to the arts would have been non-authoritarian if he had lived longer; but the intensity of control would almost certainly have been lower.
112. See S. White, *The Origins of Detente. The Genoa Conference and Soviet–Western Relations, 1921–1922* (Cambridge, 1985), pp. 34–5.
113. See idem, pp. 46–7.

114. See above, pp. 17 ff.
115. *Pravda*, 4 December 1921.
116. *PSS*, vol. 54, pp. 105–6.
117. See White, *The Origins of Detente*, pp. 54–5.
118. *TP*, vol. 2, p. 656.
119. *ITsKKPSS*, 1990, no.4, p. 189.
120. *PSS*, vol. 54, p. 117.
121. *ITsKKPSS*, 1990, no.4, pp. 189–90.
122. *PSS*, vol. 54, p. 118.
123. Idem, p. 134.
124. Idem, p. 136.
125. See for example the instruction to the People's Commissariat of Foreign Trade to sign a business deal quickly with the German firm Krupp: ibid.
126. *ITsKKPSS*, 1990, no.4, p. 189.
127. See Sheinis, 'V Genue i Gaage. Stranichki diplomaticheskoi deyatel'nosti M. M. Litvinova', *Novaya i noveishaya istoriya*, 1968, no.3, p. 57.
128. *PSS*, vol. 44, pp. 382–3.
129. Idem, vol. 54, p. 615.
130. Idem, p. 171.
131. Idem, vol. 44, p. 394.
132. Idem, p. 406.
133. Idem, p. 408.
134. Idem, vol. 54, p. 194.
135. See the excellent account of A. di Biagio, *Le Origini dell'Isolazionismo Sovietico. L'Unione Sovietica e l'Europa dal 1918 al 1928* (Milan, 1990), p. 40.
136. *DVP SSSR*, vol. 5, p. 260.
137. *PSS*, vol. 45, pp. 164 and 171.
138. See E. H. Carr, *The Bolshevik Revolution*, vol. 3, p. 376.
139. *RTsKhIDNI*, f.17, op. 2, d.79, item 1, p. 1.
140. Ibid.
141. *PSS*, vol. 45, p. 172.
142. Idem, p. 183.
143. Idem, p. 185.
144. *PSS*, vol. 44, p. 327.
145. See Volume Two, pp. 221–7; see also above, pp. 38–43 and 242–7.
146. *RTsKhIDNI*, f.17, op. 3, d.164, item 6.
147. Idem, op. 3, d.165, item 4 and d.169.
148. *PSS*, vol. 44, p. 261.
149. *Lenin i VChK* (ed. S. Tsvigun: Moscow, 1975), p. 539.
150. At least this seems to be the case from the presently-available evidence. It is always possible that the selection from the central party archives is misleading in one as yet unrevealed way or another.
151. *Lenin i VChK*, pp. 549–50.
152. *PSS*, vol. 54, p. 144.
153. See, for example, his call to Unszlicht to keep the Central Committee regularly informed about the progress of the repressions deemed

necessary: ibid.. This has the appearance of a tacit alliance to make it difficult for a 'softer' line on terror to be taken in the central party leadership.

154. *SXI*, p. 142: concluding speech on political report.
155. *PSS*, vol. 45, p. 189.
156. Idem, p. 190.
157. See also below, pp. 291 ff.
158. See, for example, *LS*, vol. 37, p. 284 (P.S. Osadchi); *PSS*, vol. 52, p. 101 (G. O. Graftio) and pp. 108–9 (Y. S. Shelekhes), p. 209 (I. R. Klasson).
159. Idem, vol. 54, p. 441.
160. *RTsKhIDNI*, f.17, op. 2, d.75, item 14.
161. *Lenin i VChK*, p. 546.
162. *PSS*, vol. 44, pp. 396–7.
163. *SXI*, p. 25.
164. A. Rosmer, *Moscou sous Lénine*, pp. 218–19.
165. *Pravda*, 11 April 1922.
166. *RTsKhIDNI*, f.17, op. 2, d.78, item 3.
167. *Pravda*, 11 April 1922.
168. *PSS*, vol. 45, p. 145.
169. See above, pp. 231–7.
170. Idem, vol. 53, 169.
171. *Lenin i VChK*, p. 465.
172. Ibid.
173. *PSS*, vol. 54, p. 198: 5 March 1922. The cited remark came in a memo to N. P. Gorbunov.
174. Idem, pp. 265–6.
175. Idem, p. 266.
176. See for example idem, vol. 44, p. 333.
177. *ITsKKPSS*, no.4, 1990, pp. 191–3.
178. *RTsKhIDNI*, f.17, op. 3, d.283, items 5 and 6.
179. *ITsKKPSS*, no.4, 1990, p. 194 (Politburo minute).
180. Idem, p. 195 (excerpt from Politburo minute).
181. See this Volume, pp. 256 ff.
182. Quite how gracefully this was done, however, will only be known when the archives are opened!
183. See D. Pospielovsky, *The Russian Orthodox Church*, vol. 1, pp. 51–5.
184. *ITsKKPSS*, no.4, 1990, p. 194 (Politburo minute).
185. Idem, p. 197.
186. *RTsKhIDNI*, f.17, op. 2, d.75, item 14; op. 3, d.290, 294 and 312 (item 19).
187. See M. Jansen, *A Show Trial Under Lenin. The Trial of the Socialist Revolutionaries. Moscow, 1922* (The Hague, 1982), pp. 50–5.
188. See idem, pp. 67–70 and 75.
189. See idem, p. 135. See *RTsKhIDNI*, f.17, op. 2, d.81, p. 1, it.1.
190. See below, pp. 256–63.
191. *RTsKhIDNI*, f.17, op. 2, d.77, item 1: Central Committee, 25 March 1922.
192. See E. H. Carr, *The Bolshevik Revolution*, vol. 1, p. 209.

193. See above, p. 206.
194. See above, p. 216.
195. *RTsKhIDNI*, f.17, op. 3, d.283.
196. Idem, op. 2, d.77, item 1.
197. Ibid.
198. Ibid.
199. Ibid.
200. See above, pp. 225–6.
201. *SXI*, p. 4.
202. Idem, p. 6.
203. Idem, p. 11.
204. Idem, p. 21.
205. Idem, p. 22.
206. Idem, p. 23.
207. Idem, p. 25.
208. See below, p. 302.
209. See above, p. 300.
210. Idem, pp. 45–59.
211. Idem, pp. 60–72.
212. Idem, p. 73.
213. Idem, p. 84.
214. Idem, p. 85.
215. Idem, p. 87.
216. Idem, p. 102.
217. Idem, p. 117; see also below, pp. 282–4.
218. *SXI*, p. 117.
219. Idem, pp. 128–37.
220. Idem, pp. 140 and 147.
221. Idem, p. 163.
222. Idem, pp. 191–202.
223. Idem, p. 238.
224. Idem, pp. 269–74.
225. Idem, p. 276.
226. Idem, pp. 283–94.
227. Idem, p. 294.
228. Idem, p. 308.
229. Idem, p. 320.
230. Idem, p. 331
231. Idem, p. 339–40.
232. Idem, p. 357.
233. Idem, pp. 391 and 402.
234. Idem, p. 440.
235. Idem, pp. 485 and 491.
236. *PSS*, vol. 45, pp. 133–4; *SXI*, pp. 491–3.
237. Idem, p. 495.
238. *SXI*, p. 495.
239. Idem, pp. 520–1.
240. Idem, p. 522.

CHAPTER 9: TESTAMENT TO A REVOLUTION

1. Information gleaned from trip to Gorki, June 1993.
2. See previous notes.
3. Prof. V. Osipov, 'Bolezn' i smert' V.I.Lenina', *Ogonyok*, no.4, 1990.
4. Ibid.; and M.I. Ul'yanova, 'O Vladimire Il'iche. (Poslednie gody zhizni)', *ITsKKPSS*, 1991, no.3, pp. 183–5.
5. Idem, p. 185.
6. Ibid.
7. Idem, pp. 186 and 191.
8. *Pravda*, 18 June 1922.
9. See M.I. Ul'yanova's memoir in *ITsKKPSS*, 1991, no.4, p. 181.
10. See *idem*, no.1, pp. 128–9.
11. See Volume 1, p. 60.
12. See Volume 2, p. 129.
13. N.K. Krupskaya, 'Iz otvetov na anketu Insituta Mozga v 1935 g.', *Lenin. Chelovek, myslitel', revolyutsioner. Vospominaniya i suzhdeniya sovremennikov. Soratniki, opponenty, deyateli nauki i kul'tury* (Moscow, 1990), p. 98.
14. M.I. Ul'yanova, 'O Vladimire Il'iche', *ITsKKPSS*, 1991, no.1, p. 130.
15. See Volume Two, p. 192.
16. V. Osipov, 'Bolezn' i smert' V.I. Lenina', loc. cit.; and M.I. Ul'yanova, untitled and undated memoir reproduced in *ITsKKPSS*, no.12, 1989, p. 197.
17. V. Osipov, 'Bolezn' i smert' V.I. Lenina', loc. cit.
18. *BK*, vol. 12, p. 295.
19. Idem, p. 296 ff.
20. *PSS*, vol. 45, p. 152-3.
21. *TP*, vol. 2, pp. 716, 718, 720, 722 and 734.
22. Idem, p. 736.
23. *PSS*, vol. 45, pp. 180-2.
24. See below, pp. 308 ff.
25. M.I. Ul'yanova, untitled memoir in *ITsKKPSS*, 1989, no.12, pp. 196–9.
26. *PSS*, vol. 54, p. 273.
27. Idem, p. 275.
28. The information in this paragraph is drawn from B.F. Miller and C.B. Keane, *Encyclopedia and Dictionary of Medicine, Nursing and Allied Health* (Second edition: Philadelphia, 1978), pp. 69–70, 96, 192–3, 196, 491–2. I have also benefited from the advice, always generously given, of those medical professionals mentioned above, p.xx.
29. On the assassination attempt see above, pp. 29–30. See also the searching account of N. Petrenko (B. Ravdin), 'Lenin v Gorkakh. Bolezn' i smert'. (Istochnikovedcheskie zametki)', *Minuvshee. Istoricheskii almanakh*, 1986, no.2, pp. 189–191.
30. See idem, p. 191.
31. See idem, pp. 195–209.
32. See idem, pp. 195–6.

33. M. I. Ul'yanova, 'O Vladimire Il'iche', *ITsKKPSS*, 1991, no.3, pp. 185–6.
34. See note 25.
35. M. I. Ul'yanova, 'O Vladimire Il'iche', *ITsKKPSS*, 1991, no.3, p. 189.
36. Ibid.
37. See note 25.
38. *ITsKKPSS*, 1991, no.5, p. 184
39. See idem, no.3, pp. 192–3.
40. Not that Lenin had not wanted to kill priests before; but this had been expressed at a time of Civil War. Now he issued the call in peacetime.
41. N. Valentinov, *Encounters with Lenin* (Oxford, 1968), p. 147.
42. See above, p. 203.
43. See below, p. 265.
44. *RTsKhIDNI*, f.17, op. 3, d.228, item 2; *PSS*, vol. 44, pp. 562–3 (note 106).
45. Idem, pp. 427–8.
46. *RTsKhIDNI*, f.17, op. 3, d.276, item 1; *Izvestiya*, no.60, 15 March 1922.
47. *PSS*, vol. 45, p. 188.
48. Idem, pp. 548–9.
49. See the quotation in *V. I. Lenin. Biografiya* (Moscow, 1963), pp. 600–1.
50. *RTsKhIDNI*, f.17, op. 2, d.81, item 2; see also idem, p. 6 for Trotski's proposal.
51. Idem, op. 3, d.311, item 24
52. Idem, d.312.
53. *PSS*, vol. 45, p. 220.
54. *RTsKhIDNI*, f.17, op. 2, d.84, item 3.
55. Ibid.
56. *PSS*, vol. 45, pp. 220–1.
57. Idem, p. 222.
58. Ibid.
59. See the documents quoted in idem, pp. 562–3 (note 139).
60. Idem, p. 562 (note 139).
61. *BK*, vol. 12, pp. 411, 413 and 418.
62. *LS*, vol. 39, pp. 430–44: record-book of his secretaries on duty.
63. Idem, p. 440.
64. *PSS*, vol. 45, pp. 278–94.
65. Idem, 300–9.
66. 'Dnevnik dezhurnogo vracha V. I. Lenina v 1922–1923 gg.', *VIKPSS*, 1991, no.9, pp. 41–2.
67. *PSS*, vol. 45, 459–60.
68. *BK*, vol. 12, 502.
69. *PSS*, vol. 45, pp. 460–3.
70. Idem, p. 464.
71. Idem, p. 470.
72. Idem, p. 471; *TP*, vol. 2, p. 774.
73. *PSS*, vol. 54, p. 323.
74. *TP*, vol. 1, p. 778.
75. Ibid.
76. *PSS*, vol. 54, p. 324.
77. Idem, p. 325.

78. Idem, vol. 45., p. 336.
79. *RTsKhIDNI*, f.17, op. 2, d.86, item 1, p. 1.
80. *PSS*, vol. 54, p. 327.
81. See above, p. 225.
82. See above, pp. 220–1, for Lenin's attitude to Molotov.
83. *PSS*, vol. 48, p. 162.
84. See Volume Two, pp. 163 and 203.
85. See above, p. 141.
86. See, for example, M. Lewin, *Lenin's Last Struggle* (London, 1969), pp. 34–5.
87. *RTsKhIDNI*, f.17, op. 2, d.62, item 1, p. 1: Central Committee plenum, 16 March 1921; *idem*, d.78, item 1-i-a, p. 1: Central Committee plenum, 3 April 1922.
88. Idem, d.78, item 1-i-b, p. 1: Central Committee plenum, 3 April 1922.
89. Ibid.
90 *SXI*, p. 84–5.
91. *RTsKhIDNI*, d.78, item 1-ii, p. 1.
92. Ibid.
93. *ITsKKPSS*, 1991, no.4, p. 188.
94. For an example of his willingness to declare a colleague clinically mad, see above 240.
95. *ITsKKPSS*, 1991, no.4, p. 188.
96. This calculation is made by V.V. Startsev, 'Poslednii god', *Moskovskaya Pravda*, 5 February 1990. See *BK*, vol. 12, pp. 357–93.
97. See Volume Two, pp. 106–9.
98. See note 13.
99. Memoir printed as 'M.I. Ul'yanova ob otnoshenii V.I. Lenina i I.V. Stalina', *ITsKPSS*, 1989, no.12, p. 198.
100. *ITsKPSS*, 1991, no.4, pp. 187–8.
101. N.K. Krupskaya, *VL*, p. 182.
102. This, at least, is the recollection of M.I. Ul'yanova in 'M.I. Ul'yanova ob otnoshenii', loc. cit., p. 198.
103. Ibid.
104. Idem, p. 197.
105. Ibid.
106. Ibid.
107. Idem, pp. 197–8.
108. Idem, p. 198.
109. See above, n.15.
110. See above, pp. 264–6.
111. M.I. Ul'yanova, 'M.I. Ul'yanova ob otnoshenii', op. cit., p. 199.
112. Idem, p. 198.
113. See above, p. 173.
114. See the record of a speech by Trotski at October 1923 Central Committee plenum cited and extensively quoted by V.P. Danilov, 'My nachinaem poznavat' Trotskogo', *EKO*, no.1 (187), 1990, p. 57. Professor Danilov interprets Lenin as having wanted to see Trotski as his successor; for a less sanguine approach to the evidence, see below, pp. 283–6.
115. See above, pp. 194–5.

116. See above, p. 192.
117. See above, p. 194.
118. See the account in S. Kharmandaryan, *Lenin i stanovlenie zakavkazskoi-federatsii*, chaps.2–3.
119. *RTsKhIDNI*, f.5, op. 2, d.26, pp. 10–11.
120. *RTsKhIDNI*, f.17, op. 3, d.291, item 2.
121. On Frunze see above, pp. 253 and 255.
122. I. K. Gamburg *et al.*, *M. V. Frunze. Zhizn' i Deyatel'nost'* (Moscow, 1962), p. 292.
123. See idem, p. 294.
124. *RTsKhIDNI*, f.17, op. 3, d.306, item 1, p. 1; *ITsKKPSS*, 1989, no.9, p. 191.
125. An example is the Politburo's appointment of the Frunze commission in May 1922: see above, p. 275.
126. *RTsKhIDNI*, f.17, op. 2, d.78, items 1(i)a-(ii): Central Committee plenum, 3 April 1922.
127. *ITsKKPSS*, 1989, no.9, pp. 192–3.
128. Idem, p. 192.
129. Idem, p. 193.
130. See Volume Two, pp. 175-6; and above, p. 78.
131. *ITsKKPSS*, 1989, no.9, p. 199.
132. Idem, pp. 198-99. See also *RTsKhIDNI*, f.16, op. 2, d.11, p. 6.
133. *ITsKKPSS*, 1989, no.9, p. 195.
134. Idem, p. 197 and 198.
135. Idem, p. 195.
136. See above, pp. 193–4.
137. *ITsKKPSS*, 1989, no.9, p. 195.
138. Idem, p. 197.
139. Idem, p. 203.
140. See S. Lukashin's remark on Stalin's comments, as quoted from archives by S. V. Kharmandaryan, *Lenin i stanovlenie zakavkazskoi federatsii*, p. 343.
141. *ITsKKPSS*, 1989, no.9, pp. 198-9.
142. Idem, p. 200.
143. Idem, pp. 202–3; see also above, note 16.
144. *PSS*, vol. 45, p. 211; *BK*, vol. 12, p. 388.
145. *PSS*, vol. 45, pp. 211–2.
146. *ITsKKPSS*, 1989, no.9, p. 206.
147. Idem, p. 208.
148. Ibid.
149. Idem, p. 209.
150. *PSS*, vol. 45, p. 214.
151. *RTsKhIDNI*, f.17, op. 2, d.84, items 1–3.
152. See the partial quotation in S. Kharmandaryan, *Lenin i stanovlenie zakavkazskoi federatsii*, pp. 347-8.
153. This is implicit in the document quoted in idem, p. 355.
154. *RTsKhIDNI*, f.17, op. 2, d.84, item 1 and appendix 1, pp. 1 and 3.
155. *ITsKKPSS*, 1991, no.5, p. 189.
156. Kharmandaryan, *Lenin i stanovlenie zakavkazskoi federatsii*, p. 347.

157. This is implicit in Stalin's letter to S. M. Kirov, ibid.
158. See the quotation in idem, p. 351.
159. *PSS*, vol. 54, pp. 299–300.
160. Kharmandaryan, op. cit., pp. 351 and 453-4.
161. See idem, pp. 354–5.
162. Ibid.
163. See idem, pp. 355–6.
164. See Kharmandaryan, op. cit., p. 356. This letter also went to Stalin.
165. I am using the term mission so as to distinguish it from the Constitution drafting commissions.
166. See Kharmandaryan, op. cit., p. 369.
167. See his letter of 5 September 1922, *ITsKKPSS*, 1989, no.9, p. 194. For the apppointment of the commission (and Lenin's failure to intervene on its composition) see *ITsKKPSS*, 1989, no.9, p. 148; *PSS*, vol. 45, 459.
168. V. S. Kirillov and A. Ya. Sverdlov, *G. K. Ordzhonikidze (Sergo). Biografiya* (Moscow, 1962), pp. 175–6.
169. Ibid.
170. *PSS*, vol. 45, 465.
171. See Kharmandaryan, *Lenin i stanovlenie zakavkazskoi federatsii*, pp. 370–1.
172. *PSS*, vol. 45, pp. 356 and 470.
173. *ITsKKPSS*, 1989, no.9, p. 148.
174. These notes were to form his 'Letter to the Congress', which are discussed below, pp. 282–6 and 296–7.
175. *PSS*, vol. 45, p. 592.
176. Idem, p. 356.
177. *RTsKhIDNI*, f.17, op. 2, d.87, item 1, p. 1.
178. Kharmandaryan, *op. cit.*, pp. 380–1 and 385; and I. V.Stalin, *Sochineniya*, vol. 5, pp. 156–9.
179. *PSS*, vol. 45, p. 474.
180. Ibid.
181. Idem, p. 344–5.
182. Idem, p. 345.
183. Ibid.
184. Ibid.
185. Ibid.
186. See above, pp. 282–4.
187. L. D. Trotskii, *Moya zhizn'*, vol. 2, chap. 41.
188. *PSS*, vol. 45, p. 345.
189. Idem, p. 344.
190. Ibid.
191. In a way it occurred even before his death, when the 'New Course' controversy broke out in late 1923: see below, p. 316.
192. This seems to be the inference to be made from the comment that 'no measures' would suffice to prevent a party split if a conflict arose over the respective priorities of the workers and peasants.
193. *ITsKKPSS*, 1989, no.12, p. 189.
194. Idem, p. 191.
195. See above, pp. 263–8, for the foreign trade controversy.

196. *ITsKKPSS*, 1989, no.12, p. 191.
197. Ibid.
198. Idem, p. 192.
199. G. Volkov, 'Stenografistka Il'icha', *Sovetskaya kul'tura*, 21 January 1989. Volkov's article was based on conversations with M. A. Volodicheva and written originally in 1963; it includes quotations of Volodicheva's words.
200. M. I. Ul'yanova, undated memoir published in *ITsKKPSS*, 1989, no.12, p. 198.
201. *ITsKPSS*, 1989, no. 12, p. 192.
202. See N. Valentinov, *Novaya ekonomicheskaya politika*, p. 37.
203. See the interview with her conducted by Aleksandr Bek in 1967: 'K istorii poslednikh leninskikh dokumentov', *Moskovskie novosti*, no.17, 23 April 1989, p. 8. This material forms part of a series of interviews with both L. A. Fotieva and M. A. Volodicheva in the same issue (edited after Bek's death by Tatyana Bek).
204. See above, p. 287.
205. *PSS*, vol. 45, p. 343.
206. G. Volkov, 'Stenografistka Il'icha', loc. cit.; A. Bek, 'K istorii poslednikh leninskikh dokumentov', loc. cit., p. 8.
207. Ibid.
208. Ibid.. The phrase comes in Volkov's interview. In Bek's version, Volodicheva said more fully: 'Burn the letter.'
209. Ibid.
210. Ibid.
211. *BK*, vol. 12, p. 547.
212. See Volodicheva's account as reproduced in G. Volkov, op. cit.; see also M. I. Ul'yanova, 'O Vladimire Il'iche', *ITsKPSS*, 1991, no.3, p. 194.
213. Ibid.
214. G. Volkov, 'Stenografistka Il'icha', loc. cit..
215. Ibid.
216. *ITsKKPSS*,
217. A. Bek, 'K istorii poslednikh leninskikh dokumentov', loc. cit., p. 8. See below, p. 305.
218. Bek, op. cit., p. 8.

CHAPTER 10: DEATHS AND ENTRANCES

1. *Ob osnovakh leninizma*, in *Sochineniya*, vol. 6, p. 69 ff.
2. M. S. Gorbachev, *Perestroika: New Thinking* (London, 1987), See also the treatment of Lenin in M. Lewin, *Lenin's Last Struggle*.
3. L. D. Trotskii, *The Revolution Betrayed* (London, 1945). For a similar view see I. Deutscher, *Trotsky: the Prophet Unarmed*.
4. See S. F. Cohen, *Bukharin and the Russian Revolution*.
5. See the excellent analysis of J. D. Biggart, 'Bukharin's Theory of Cultural Revolution', in A. Kemp-Welch (ed.), *The Ideas of Nikolai Bukharin* (Oxford, 1992), pp. 148–58.

6. See his 'Zheleznaya kogorta', *Za pyat' let, 1917–1922. Sbornik* (Moscow, 1922).
7. *PSS*, vol. 45, p. 441.
8. Idem, p. 434.
9. *PSS*, vol. 45, p. 347.
10. *TP*, vol. 2, p. 730.
11. *PSS*, vol. 45, pp. 349–50.
12. Idem, p. 351.
13. Idem, p. 352.
14. Idem, pp. 354–5.
15. Idem, p. 356.
16. Idem, p. 357.
17. Ibid.
18. Ibid. The word used by Lenin for thugs, *derzhimordy*, has no exact equivalent in English: 'snout-holders' would be the literal translation.
19. Idem, p. 358.
20. Idem, p. 360.
21. Idem, p. 361.
22. Idem, pp. 361–2.
23. Ibid.
24. Idem, p. 362.
25. See below, pp. 298 ff.
26. See the memoir of Mariya Ulyanova in *ITsKKPSS*, 1989, no.12, p. 198.
27. *PSS*, vol. 45, p. 346.
28. Ibid.
29. See above, p. 297.
30. See above, p. 206.
31. See above, pp. 288–90.
32. *PSS*, vol. 45, pp. 363–4.
33. Ibid.
34. Idem, p. 369.
35. Idem, p. 370.
36. Idem, p. 372.
37. Idem, p. 373.
38. Idem, pp. 375–6.
39. Idem, pp. 376–7.
40. See Volume Two, p. 251.
41. *PSS*, vol. 45, p. 378.
42. Idem, p. 380.
43. Idem, p. 381.
44. See Volume Two, pp. 223–38.
45. Idem, pp. 381–2.
46. Idem, p. 381.
47. Idem, p. 380.
48. See Volume Two, pp. 216–23.
49. *PSS*, vol. 45, p. 378.
50. See Volume One, pp. 33–7 and 180–1.
51. *PSS*, vol. 45, pp. 384–5 and 387.
52. Idem, p. 449.

53. Ibid.
54. Apart from the evidence of Stalin's foreknowledge in December (see above p. 299), it is also the case that it was his trusted admirer Lidiya Fotieva who took down in short-hand the first draft of this article.
55. *PSS*, vol. 45, 390.
56. Idem, p. 393.
57. Idem, p. 397.
58. Idem, p. 398.
59. Idem, p. 399.
60. Idem, pp. 401–2.
61. Idem, p. 402.
62. See Volume Two, p. 114.
63. *PSS*, vol. 45, p. 404.
64. Idem, p. 405.
65. Idem, p. 406.
66. *Pravda*, 4 March 1923.
67. 'M.I. Ul'yanova ob otnoshenii V.I.Lenina i I.V.Stalina', *ITsKPSS*, no.12, 1989, p. 199.
68. V. Osipov, 'Bolezn' i smert' V.I. Lenina', *Ogonyok*, no.4, 1990.
69. *PSS*, vol. 45, p. 475.
70. *BK*, vol. 12, pp. 557–87.
71. *PSS*, vol. 45, p. 478; Osipov, 'Bolezn' i smert' V.I. Lenina', loc. cit.
72. *ITsKKPSS*, no.10, 1990, pp. 178–9: letter of Trotski to Central Committee and Central Control Commission, 23 October 1923.
73. Idem, p. 179.
74. See also below, p. 313.
75. *ITsKKPSS*, no.10, 1990, p. 179. See also above, p. 000.
76. Extract from his speech on 26 October 1923 to the Central Committee and Central Control Commission, reprinted in *EKO*, no.1 (187), 1990, p. 56.
77. *ITsKKPSS*, no.9, 1990, p. 148.
78. *ITsKKPSS*, no.10, 1990, pp. 172: letter of Trotski to Central Committee and Central Control Commission, 23 October 1923.
79. Idem, p. 172; Kuibyshev's submission to the Khamovniki district party conference commission on 23 February 1924, *ITsKKPSS*, no.11, 1989, 189; Stalin's submission to the same commission on 4 March 1924, Idem, p. 190. Both Kuibyshev and Stalin, ibid., claimed that the deception of Lenin was not proposed at a formal session of the Politburo but in private conversation prior to the given session. Nevertheless it was evidently more than a proposal put forwards as a passing whim; and it was one of the few wrong steps made by Stalin in the first half of 1923.
80. *ITsKKPSS*, no.9, 1990, p. 148.
81. See her letter to Bukharin, 11 January 1924: *Idem*, p. 163. There is no reason to disbelieve that Fotieva felt likewise.
82. See *RTsKhIDNI*, f.5, op. 2, d.33, pp. 1–144.
83. *PSS*, vol. 45, pp. 378–82.
84. *ITsKKPSS*, no.11, 1989, pp. 179–80.
85. *PSS*, vol. 45, p. 480.
86. Idem, p. 478.

87. Idem, p. 479.
88. L. A. Fotieva, *Iz zhizni V. I. Lenina* (Moscow, 1967), p. 315.
89. See Volume One, pp. 33–40.
90. *PSS*, vol. 54, p. 329.
91. *ITsKKPSS*, no.9, 1990, p. 148.
92. *PSS*, vol. 45, pp. 383–8 and 443.
93. *PSS*, vol. 45, p. 486.
94. Idem, vol. 54. p. 330.
95. Bek interview: *Moskovski novosti*, no.17, 23 April 1989, p. 9.
96. Volkov interview, 'Stenografistka Il'icha', *Sovetskaya kul'tura*, 21
    January 1989. Volodicheva claimed to have taken down words such as
    these in her notebooks, which are extant and were consulted by her
    before giving an interview to G. Volkov. A slightly but not substantially
    different form of words was recorded by A. Bek in his interview: see op.
    cit.
        It is unclear whether these notes were meant by Stalin to constitute his
    formal reply to Lenin; but it is not impossible that they were since
    Kamenev is known to have referred to Stalin's 'acid' wording and to the
    unlikelihood that they would satisfy his demand for an apology.
97. *ITsKKPSS*, no.12, 1989, p. 193.
98. *ITsKKPSS*, no.9, 1990, 151.
99. See Volodicheva's account as described to A. Bek, *Moskovski novosti*,
    op. cit., p. 9.
100. N. K. Krupskaya, 'Poslednie polgoda zhizni Vladimira Il'icha',
     ITsKKPSS, no.4, 1989, p. 169.
101. V.Osipov, 'Bolezn' i smert' V. I. Lenina', loc. cit..
102. Ibid.; N. K. Krupskaya, 'Poslednie polgoda zhizni Vladimira Il'icha',
     ITsKKPSS, no.4, 1989, p. 169.
103. Osipov, op. cit.; Krupskaya, op. cit., p. 170.
104. Osipov, op. cit.
105. Ibid.
106. Krupskaya, op. cit., p. 170; see also *ITsKPSS*, 1989. no.4, 170.
107. Osipov, op. cit. Lenin's Russian phrase was: *Eto neprochno*.
108. *ITsKKPSS*, no.4, 1989, p. 183: letter to I.A.Armand, 28 October 1923.
109. N. K. Krupskaya, 'Poslednie polgoda zhizni Vladimira Il'icha', loc. cit.,
     pp. 171–2.
110. *ITsKKPSS*, 1989, no.4, p. 186.
111. Osipov, op. cit.; V. A. Rukavishnikov, 'Poslednii god Il'icha' (text
     prepared by N. Kostin), *Sotsialisticheskaya industriya*, 16 April 1989,
     p. 3.
112. See note 28, p. 367.
113. Krupskaya, 'Poslednie polgoda zhizni Vladimira Il'icha', loc. cit.,
     pp. 171.
114. Idem, p. 170.
115. Idem, p. 172.
116. Ibid.; Osipov, op. cit.
117. Krupskaya, op. cit., p. 172.
118. Idem, pp. 171–2.
119. Idem, p. 172.

120. Idem, p. 173.
121. Idem, pp. 173–4.
122. Idem, p. 174.
123. Ibid.
124. Ibid.; Osipov, op. cit.
125. Krupskaya, op. cit., ibid.
126. Krupskaya, op. cit., p. 172.
127. Osipov, op. cit.
128. Krupskaya, op. cit., p. 172.
129. See above, p. 304.
130. *Moya zhizn'*, vol. 2, pp. 458–62.
131. *ITsKKPSS*, no.9, 1990, p. 158: editorial note based on central party archives.
132. Telegram of 7 March 1923: *ITsKKPSS*, no.9, 1990, p. 152.
133. 'Natsional'nye momenty v partiinom i gosudarstvennom stroitel'stve', *Pravda*, 24 March 1923.
134. *ITsKKPSS*, no.9, 1990, p. 153.
135. Idem, pp. 152–4.
136. See the archival excerpt quoted in D. Volkogonov, *Triumf i tragediya. Politicheskii portret I. V. Stalina*, vol. 1, part 1 (Moscow, 1989), p. 158.
137. *ITsKKPSS*, no. 9, 1990, pp. 155–6.
138. See above, p. 313.
139. *ITsKKPSS*, no.9, 1990, pp. 156–7 and 158. Interestingly Trotski did not phrase this wish entirely unequivocally: he failed to kick Stalin when Stalin was tottering.
140. *ITsKKPSS*, no.9, 1990, p. 159.
141. Idem, pp. 159 and 161.
142. Idem, p. 159.
143. *SXII*, p. 821.
144. The question whether Stalin already knew its full contents is discussed above, pp. 288–90.
145. See R.V. Daniels, *Conscience of the Revolution*, p. 194.
146. *SXII*, pp. 8–53.
147. Idem, pp. 479–95.
148. Idem, pp. 62–3 and 66–7.
149. Idem, pp. 309–52.
150. *Pravda*, 24 September 1923.
151. See Daniels, *Conscience of the Revolution*, pp. 196–9.
152. See E. H. Carr, *The Interregnum, 1923–1924* (London, 1954), pp. 290–1.
153. See Volume One, p. 136.
154. *SXII*, p. 479. The surge of cultic devotion to Lenin is excellently treated in N. Tumarkin, *Lenin Lives! The Lenin Cult in Soviet Russia* (London, 1983), pp. 121–33.
155. *SXII*, p. 6.
156. See Tumarkin, *Lenin Lives!*, pp. 123–6.
157. N. Valentinov, *Novaya ekonomicheskaya politika*, pp. 90–2. Valentinov is often credited with 'total recall' in his memoirs. This is exaggerated. But his recollections are seldom proved to be factually incorrect in general terms. The other problem with his story about the meeting of Politburo

members is that it came to him second-hand or worse. But he is unlikely to have invented the story himself: everyone agrees that he was not a liar. Moreover, his contacts with the élite of the Bolshevik party in the mid-1920s is well-documented. On the whole, considerable tentative credence may therefore reasonably be reposed in his story

158. Ibid.
159. See R. Service, *The Bolshevik Party*, pp. 191–6.

EPILOGUE

1. N. K. Krupskaya, *VOVIL*, vol. 1, pp. 587–8.
2. N. K. Krupskaya, 'Poslednie polgoda zhizni Vladimira Il'icha', *ITsKKPSS*, no.4, 1989, p. 174.
3. V. Osipov, 'Bolezn' i smert' V.I. Lenina', loc. cit.; V. A. Rukavishnikov, 'Poslednii god Il'icha' (text prepared by N. Kostin), *Sotsialisticheskaya industriya*, 16 April 1989, p. 3.
4. Rukavishnikov, ibid.; Krupskaya, op. cit., p. 175.
5. Rukavishnikov, ibid.; Osipov, ibid.
6. See note 5.
7. Krupskaya, op. cit., p. 175.
8. Rukavishnikov, ibid.; Osipov, ibid.
9. Krupskaya, op. cit., p. 175.
10. See above, pp. 258–61.
11. See V. D. Bonch-Bruevich's memoir from 1925, reprinted as 'Smert' i pokhorony Vladimira Il'icha', *Pravda*, 21 January 1990, p. 3.
12. *Pravda*, 25 January 1924.
13. See the account by Tumarkin, *Lenin Lives!*, pp. 136–43.
14. See the extensive collection in M. Rafes *et al.*, *U velikoi mogily* (Moscow, 1924), *passim*.
15. See Tumarkin, op. cit., p. 153.
16. See idem, p. 154.
17. Stalin, *Sochineniya*, vol. 6, pp. 46–51.
18. *U velikoi mogily*, pp. 25–6.
19. L. D. Trotskii, *Moya zhizn'*, vol. 2, p. 483.
20. See Tumarkin, op. cit., p. 161.
21. See idem, pp. 161–2.
22. See idem, p. 162. The note about the placards was given to me by Vladimir Buldakov.
23. V. D. Bonch-Bruevich, *Vospominaniya o Lenine* (Moscow, 1965), p. 435.
24. The precise line-up of votes and the occasion of voting have not been revealed. At the time of writing a veil of secrecy surrounds the embalming policy.
25. See Tumarkin, op. cit., p. 179.
26. See idem, p. 182–3.
27. See N. Valentinov, *Novaya ekonomicheskaya politika*, pp. 46–8.
28. *Pravda*, 25 January 1924.

Index